'Recent centuries have been the theatre of a "war of the gods" pitting religion against religion and also against quasi-religious secular values. In an eirenic spirit, the contributors to this remarkable volume discuss the compromises and accommodations that prevent moral conflict turning into physical violence.'

David d'Avray, Professor of History, University College London

'This is an important and impressive collection. Eschewing simplistic answers, it opens a series of windows into the negotiation of religion in European societies, past and present. It asks how religion has been identified, accommodated, navigated around, or engaged with, how the terms of such interactions have been moulded and remoulded in the process, and how numerous settlements have emerged, persisted, and disintegrated as negotiations have continued. The subject matter is diverse, complex, and contested, but the excellent team of writers assembled here provide a feast of lucid descriptions and compelling analyses.'

Mike Higton, Professor of Theology and Ministry, Durham University

'A deeply impressive interdisciplinary collection which addresses an issue of overwhelming contemporary significance. This book recognises the persistent importance of religion in modern people's lives and uses the insights of political theory, law, urban studies and history to understand the ethical and theoretical issues which emerge from attempts to find a satisfying and creative role for different religions within modern multicultural societies.'

Professor Peter W.D. Mack, University of Warwick

Negotiating Religion

Negotiating religious diversity, as well as negotiating different forms and degrees of commitment to religious belief and identity, constitutes a major challenge for all societies. Recent developments such as the 'de-secularisation' of the world, the transformation and globalization of religion and the attacks of September 11 have made religious claims and religious actors much more visible in the public sphere. This volume provides multiple perspectives on the processes through which religious communities create or defend their place in a given society, both in history and in our world today.

Offering a critical, cross-disciplinary investigation into processes of negotiating religion and religious diversity, the contributors present new insights on the meaning and substance of negotiation itself. This volume draws on diverse historical, sociological, geographic, legal and political theoretical approaches to take a close look at the religious and political agents involved in such processes as well as the political, social and cultural context in which they take place. Its focus on the European experiences that have shaped not only the history of 'negotiating religion' in this region but around the world provide new perspectives for critical inquiries into the way in which contemporary societies engage with religion.

This study will be of interest to academics, lawyers and scholars in law and religion, sociology, politics and religious history.

François Guesnet is Reader in Modern Jewish History in the Department of Hebrew and Jewish Studies at University College London. He specialises in the early modern and nineteenth century history of Polish and eastern European Jewry. Most recently, he co-edited *Antisemitism in an Era of Transition. Continuities and Impact in Post-Communist Poland and Hungary* (2014, with Gwenyth Jones) and *Warsaw. The Jewish Metropolis. Essays in Honor of the 75th Birthday of Professor Antony Polonsky* (2015, with Glenn Dynner).

Cécile Laborde is Professor of Political Theory and the Director of the Religion and Political Theory (RAPT) Centre at University College London. She has published widely on theories of law and the state, global justice, republicanism and secularism. Her last book is *Critical Republicanism: The Hijab Controversy and Political Philosophy*.

Lois Lee is Research Associate at the Institute of Advanced Studies, UCL (University College London). She has published widely on nonreligion, secularism and religion and is the author of *Recognizing the Non-religious: Reimagining the Secular* (2015), co-editor of *Secularity and Non-Religion* (2013) and of special issues for the *Journal of Contemporary Religion* (2012) and *Religion* (2014). She is founding director of the Nonreligion and Secularity Research Network (NSRN), and co-edits the journal *Secularism and Nonreligion* and the book series, *Religion and Its Others: Studies in Religion, Nonreligion and Secularity*.

Negotiating Religion

Cross-disciplinary perspectives

Edited by
François Guesnet,
Cécile Laborde and
Lois Lee

Routledge
Taylor & Francis Group
LONDON AND NEW YORK

First published 2017 by Routledge

2 Park Square, Milton Park, Abingdon, Oxfordshire OX14 4RN
52 Vanderbilt Avenue, New York, NY 10017

Routledge is an imprint of the Taylor & Francis Group, an Informa business

First issued in paperback 2020

British Library Cataloguing in Publication Data
A catalogue record for this book is available from the British Library

Library of Congress Cataloging in Publication Data
A catalog record for this book has been requested

ISBN: 978-1-4724-3729-7 (hbk)
ISBN: 978-0-367-59616-3 (pbk)

Typeset in Baskerville
by Florence Production Ltd, Stoodleigh, Devon, UK

Contents

Illustrations

Figures

Tables

Editors

François Guesnet is Reader in Modern Jewish History in the Department of Hebrew and Jewish Studies at University College London. He specialises in the early modern and nineteenth-century history of Polish and eastern European Jewry. Most recently, he co-edited *Antisemitism in an Era of Transition. Continuities and Impact in Post-Communist Poland and Hungary* (Peter Lang Verlag, 2014, with Gwenyth Jones) and *Warsaw. The Jewish Metropolis: Essays in Honor of the 75th Birthday of Professor Antony Polonsky* (Brill Academic, 2015, with Glenn Dynner).

Cécile Laborde is Professor of Political Theory and the Director of the Religion and Political Theory (RAPT) Centre at University College London. She has published widely on theories of law and the state, global justice, republicanism and secularism. Her last book is *Critical Republicanism: The Hijab Controversy and Political Philosophy* (Oxford University Press, 2008).

Lois Lee is Research Associate at the Institute of Advanced Studies, University College London. She has published widely on nonreligion, secularism and religion and is the author of *Recognizing the Non-religious: Reimagining the Secular* (Oxford University Press, 2015), co-editor of *Secularity and Non-Religion* (Routledge, 2013) and of special issues for the *Journal of Contemporary Religion* (2012) and *Religion* (2014). She is founding director of the Nonreligion and Secularity Research Network (NSRN) and co-editor of the journal *Secularism and Nonreligion* and the book series, *Religion and Its Others: Studies in Religion, Nonreligion and Secularity* (De Gruyter).

Editors

Contributors

Luke Bretherton is Professor of Theological Ethics at Duke University. Before joining Duke he was Reader in Theology and Politics at King's College London. His books include *Christianity & Contemporary Politics: The Conditions and Possibilities of Faithful Witness* (Wiley-Blackwell, 2010), winner of the 2013 Michael Ramsey Prize for Theological Writing; and *Resurrecting Democracy: Faith, Citizenship and the Politics of a Common Life* (Cambridge University Press, 2015), which examines the intersection of grassroots democratic politics, secularity, religious beliefs and practices, and globalisation via a case study of community organising.

Claire Dwyer is a Reader in Social and Cultural Geography at University College London with research interests in the geographies of faith, migration and multiculturalism. She is currently leading an AHRC-funded research project *Making Suburban Faith*. Her publications include *Transnational Spaces* (co-edited with Peter Jackson and Phillip Crang, Routledge, 2004) and *New Geographies of Race and Racism* (co-edited with Caroline Bressey, Ashgate, 2008).

John Eade is Professor of Sociology and Anthropology at the University of Roehampton, member of the UCL Migration Research Unit and Research Fellow at the Dept for the Study of Religion, University of Toronto. His research interests and publications focus on global migration, urban ethnicity and pilgrimage. Relevant publications include the single edited *Living the Global City* (Routledge, 1997) and the co-edited *Accession and Migration: Changing Policy, Society and Culture in an Enlarged Europe* (Ashgate, 2009), *Transnational Ties* (Transaction, 2008) and *Understanding the City* (Blackwells, 2002).

Myriam Hunter-Henin is a Senior Lecturer in Law at University College London, Laws. Her research examines the implications of *laïcité* for comparative law and human rights methodology. It also addresses the interaction and tensions between law and religion in the sphere of education and family law in a comparative perspective. Her latest articles on the topic were published in *Oxford Journal of Law and Religion* (2015, 4(1): 94–118) and *International Comparative Law Quarterly* (2015, July issue). As co-convenor of the 'Negotiation with' series from which this volume is drawn, she convened the fourth workshop on legal perspectives of 12 June 2012 (www.ucl.ac.uk/european-institute/events/

religion) and the final closing event of 1 May 2013 (www.eventbrite.co.uk/e/negotiating-religion-inquiries-into-the-history-and-present-of-religious-accommodation-registration-5597618628).

Benjamin J. Kaplan is Professor of Dutch History at UCL. He received his BA from Yale University (1981) and his MA and PhD from Harvard (1989). Before moving to UCL he taught at Brandeis University and the University of Iowa, while from 2001 to 2011 he held a joint appointment at the University of Amsterdam. He is the recipient of numerous grants and fellowships, including ones from the Guggenheim Foundation and Leverhulme Trust. In addition to Dutch history, he specialises in the religious history of early modern Europe and has written extensively on the history of religious conflict and toleration in particular. Among his publications is the prize-winning book *Divided by Faith: Religious Conflict and the Practice of Toleration in Early Modern Europe* (Harvard University Press, 2007). His latest book is entitled *Cunegonde's Kidnapping: A Story of Religious Conflict in the Age of Enlightenment* (Yale University Press, 2014).

Maleiha Malik is Professor at Law at King's College, London. Her research and teaching interests include Discrimination Law. She has published extensively on discrimination law, feminism and minority protection. Her recent relevant publications include *Minorities and Law: Past and Present* (*Current Legal Problems*, 2014).

Saladin Meckled-Garcia is a Co-Director of the UCL Institute for Human Rights and has published in a range of subjects in political and legal philosophy.

Robert M. Morris has been an Honorary Senior Research Fellow at the Constitution Unit, Department of Political Science, UCL since 1998. He was formerly a career civil servant at the Home Office.

Lucy Vickers is Professor of Law at Oxford Brookes University. Her main research area is the protection of human rights within the workplace and aspects of equality law. She has written extensively on issues relating to religious discrimination and age discrimination at work. She is the author of *Freedom of Speech and Employment* (Oxford University Press, 2002), *Religious Freedom, Religious Discrimination and the Workplace* (Hart, 2008) and a report for the European Commission on *Religion and Belief Discrimination in Employment – The EU Law* (2007), as well as numerous academic articles.

Albert Weale is Emeritus Professor of Political Theory and Public Policy at University College London. His research and publications have been concentrated on issues of political theory and public policy, especially the theory of justice and the theory of democracy, health policy and comparative environmental policy. His principal publications include *Equality and Social Policy* (Routledge & Kegan Paul, 1978), *Political Theory and Social Policy* (Macmillan, 1983), *The New Politics of Pollution* (Manchester University Press, 1992), *Democracy* (Macmillan, 1999 and 2007 revised), *Democratic Citizenship and the European Union* (Manchester University Press, 2005), *Democratic Justice and the*

Social Contract (Oxford University Press, 2013) and, with others, *The Theory of Choice* (Blackwell, 1992) and *Environmental Governance in Europe* (Oxford University Press, 2000) as well as a number of edited books, journal paper and chapters.

Preface

Negotiating religion at the 'godless institution on Gower street'

François Guesnet, Cécile Laborde and Lois Lee

In 2008, two initiatives at UCL (University College London) were launched, simultaneously and independently from one another, but each reflecting on the possible contribution that the 'godless institution on Gower Street' might make to an emerging scholarship on the relationship between religion and society. The 'religion' in mind was recognised as an empirical fact, something that large numbers of people, in London and around the world, experience and understand their lives in relation to – something that shapes both subjective reality, as a way of seeing, understanding and experiencing the world and making sense of the human condition, and objective reality, manifest as one of the most ubiquitous forms of culture and social organisation in human history.

In some respects, these engagements with religion were a new proposition for UCL – an institution founded in 1826 without a Divinity School or a Faculty of Theology and established with a pluralist secularist constitution that made it possible to undertake university level training, teaching and research without stating a commitment to the Church of England.[1] As a result, contemporaneous critics of this pioneering institution in English educational history gave it the epithet of 'godless institution of Gower Street'. What began as a slur, however, has transformed over subsequent generations into a badge worn with pride by many of its members. As non-religious populations have grown and secularist approaches to education and knowledge have developed across the British and other European academies (and elsewhere), UCL's pluralist mode of secularism came to be reimagined as a more comprehensive form of godlessness, with many involved in the institution assuming that UCL had been intended as a quasi-atheist institution.

This, however, was not the case. Among the earliest decisions of the Council of the University of London we find the requirement for persons applying to house University's students to 'produce satisfactory proof of the correctness of their character, as regards religious habits and morals' and to 'require their boarders to be regular in their attendance at a place of public worship'.[2] Thus, while UCL's

1 On the formation of UCL, see Rosemary Ashton, *Victorian Bloomsbury* (New Haven, CT: Yale University Press, 2012), especially pp. 25–57.

2 'Statement by the Council of the University of London, explanatory of its nature and objects', *Hume Tracts* (1827): 15, 27. The editors wish to thank Felicity Griffiths, currently pursuing a research project on *Ethnicity and Minority Groups in the Colleges of London University* at the UCL Department for Hebrew and Jewish Studies for this reference.

Council did not discriminate on the basis of religious affiliation (in contrast to the Cambridge and Oxford universities), it still considered individual religious commitment to be highly desirable and a requirement of some activities.

Moreover, UCL – like so many secular institutions, educational and otherwise – has a far more complicated relationship with religion than the 'godless institution of Gower Street' epithet suggests. For example, a Hebrew Department was established already in the founding period of the College, in 1828: the first Professor of Hebrew, Hyman Hurwitz, taught the Hebrew language and literature in line with the liberal traditions on which UCL had been founded and, although the materials studied were of a religious nature, the academic training was non-dogmatic, critical and free from the confines of any denominational framework from the start. Today, initiatives in the study of religion are found throughout UCL – as many of the contributions of this volume attest, as do the activities of the Religion and Political Theory Centre (discussed below), which has overseen the project as a whole. One also needs to mention the large number of student societies at UCL that are religion-based and an important part of College students' campus experience. Thus, despite its secular identity, UCL has not been insulated from current debates about the potential and the pitfalls that arise in relation to the cohabitation of people with diverse religious, spiritual, non-religious and secular commitments in societies.

Indeed, one objective of the first of UCL's 2008 initiatives was to recognise knowledge of religion already embedded in the university. In relation to an attempt of the then Centre for the Advancement of Learning and Teaching (CALT) to assess the 'internationality' of UCL's curriculum, the Centre identified a need to highlight and consolidate the considerable expertise of the College's academic staff on religion and its role in historical and contemporary societies. Though it occupies a notable position in the history of the secularisation of higher education, UCL is not alone in its 'godless' identity and this initiative reflected what many institutions and academic disciplines are finding as they seek to think more deeply about religion – that, as well as initiating new research, a pressing task for an era of renewed interest in religion is to bring long-standing engagements with religion within secular education to the fore.

A second initiative sought to harness UCL's research capacity to explore a newly pressing set of research questions about religion. Organised through the then recently founded European Institute, this project interrogated the relationship between religion, politics and society. Perhaps unusually, those involved in these two initiatives agreed to merge, combining them to establish a multi-disciplinary workshop series, entitled 'Negotiating Religion: Inquiries into the Past and Present of Religious Accommodation' and conducted in 2010 and 2011. This series reflected on historical, constitutional and philosophical dimensions of religious accommodation, the negotiation of religious diversity in urban space and last but not least the complex relations between education, religion and the law.[3]

3 www.ucl.ac.uk/european-institute/projects/negotiating-religion (accessed 17 November 2015).

These initiatives have, from the outset, combined questions about religion in contemporary European contexts with a deep reflection on how educational institutions and particular disciplines have negotiated and are negotiating religion. In this, the project has been further influenced by a number of one-off events, the most notable among them being a residential workshop held in May 2013 at Cumberland Lodge and a concluding conference in May 2013 bringing together a large group of academics from UCL and Cambridge University, as well as representatives from the two universities' senior management. The residential workshop, funded by the British Academy, was held in close cooperation with colleagues from a Cambridge University research project, 'Religion and the Idea of the Research University', most notably Alison Wood. This productive workshop focused on the role of issues pertaining to religion in various academic disciplines today and on the impact of religious and non-religious commitments and cultures on campus life, including the conduct of research.

The research initiative as a whole concluded with a high-profile conference on 1 May 2013. Sociologist Craig Calhoun (LSE), historian Benjamin Kaplan (UCL), political philosopher Cécile Laborde (UCL) and legal scholar Maleiha Malik (KCL) discussed the past and present of religious accommodation, from the Reformation to the secular age, from Weberian notions of disenchantment to contemporary emphases on pluralisation, from corporate autonomy to individual conscience and from political negotiation to legal exemption. Meanwhile, thanks to a large European Research Council (ERC) grant on the topic, 'Is Religion Special? Secularism and Religion in Contemporary Political Theory', the Religion and Political Theory Centre (RAPTc) was set up by Cécile Laborde in the School of Public Policy. This is the first international centre dedicated to the concept of religion in contemporary liberal political theory from an interdisciplinary perspective (www.ucl.ac.uk/religion-political-theory-centre). Through a series of lectures, workshops and conferences, RAPT has played a key role in positioning UCL as a cutting edge research environment for the academic study of religion in its relationship to politics, philosophy and sociology.

These wide-ranging initiatives have demonstrated that the idea of UCL's 'godlessness' has force as one way of acknowledging its non-denominational constitution, but also as an imagined history that continues to shape activity, not only at UCL but, given its crucial role in the history of British and European education, far beyond that too.

As will be clear, the present volume is the result of an extended series of collaborations. Thus, the Negotiating Religion research initiative soon found a welcoming home in (and crucial funding from) the UCL Grand Challenge of Intercultural Interaction (GCII); we would like to thank the Vice-Provost (Research), David Price and the GCII's principal facilitator, Ian Scott. Uta Staiger was among the first instigators of the project. Beyond offering logistical support via the UCL European Institute, she encouraged us to take seriously the European dimension in thinking about religion. The volume itself has received invaluable support from Myriam Hunter-Henin, in both the planning and development stages, as well as from the European Research Council (ERC) in association with the

'Is Religion Special? Secularism and Religion in Contemporary Political Theory' project (Grant Number 283867) led by Cécile Laborde and situated in the UCL School of Public Policy. Several meetings between members of the UCL initiative and Alison Wood and her colleagues in the University of Cambridge research project, 'Religion and the Idea of the Research University', headed by Professor David Ford, have been an important and continuous source of inspiration.

The editors wish to thank all colleagues who have contributed to the varied and numerous events organised in the framework of the Negotiating Religion research initiative – especially initiative leaders, Claire Dwyer, Myriam Hunter-Henin, Robert M. Morris and Uta Staiger, who worked alongside François Guesnet and Cécile Laborde in organising and delivering the workshops at the core of the initiative. We would like to extend our particular thanks to all speakers and commentators at the various events held at UCL. Based at universities and colleges across the United Kingdom and from several European countries, their diverse perspectives and insights have made an invaluable contribution to the work presented in this volume. More specifically, the editors wish to thank those colleagues who agreed to turn their presentations at one of the research initiative's events into a chapter to this volume.

Finally, two of the editors of this volume, François Guesnet and Cécile Laborde, would like to thank their colleague Lois Lee, without whose energy, expertise and determination this volume would not have been possible.

References

Ashton, Rosemary. *Victorian Bloomsbury*. New Haven, CT: Yale University Press, 2012.

'Statement by the Council of the University of London, explanatory of its nature and objects', *Hume Tracts* (1827): 15, 27.

Introduction

Negotiating religion: a reflexive approach

Lois Lee[1]

Over recent years, societies and scholars have increasingly expressed a need to negotiate religion – that is, to provide better accounts of, ways of engaging with and recommendations regarding the nature and role of religion in contemporary, often culturally diverse societies. These concerns respond to a number of developments that have made religious claims and actors much more visible in the public arenas that they had for a long time been absent from – or, at least, concealed within. For one, religious beliefs, practices and identifications have failed to decline in proportional relation to modernisation processes, as mainstream ideas about secularisation once anticipated and this has reopened questions about what the relationship between religious actors and cultures and contemporary industrialised and hyper-mediated societies really is. Scholars and social commentators have come to recognise the forms of religiosity that not only persist but are created or revitalised in the contexts of these modernities, as well as the role that globalisation and other processes have played in transforming religious experience and agency into distinctly 'modern' phenomena. The need to attend to the ways in which religion can be bound up with political upheaval, social division and violence has also been reasserted, sometimes dramatically and religion has thereby been brought back into debates about conflict, which had for a long time focused on other forces – nationalism, ethnicity, political ideology, economic inequality and so on. In short, whether seen to be enriching to human life and societies, challenging to them, or both, contemporary expressions of religion are increasingly recognised as being precisely that: contemporary; not a remnant or reawakening of a pre-modern past but a legitimate part of the present and the future, too.

It has consequently become necessary to engage more deeply with the ways in which expressions of religion are shaped by their contexts, including new realities like contemporary forms of global migration flow, with its increased speed of movement, or concurrent geopolitical processes and the politicised religious, non-

1 This introduction builds on programmatic materials developed by Claire Dwyer, François Guesnet, Myriam Hunter-Henin and Cécile Laborde in developing the 'Negotiating Religion' event series at UCL, 2011–13, and this publication. I am grateful to them for providing this rich resource, as well as for their comments on drafts of this introduction.

religious and secularist movements that they give rise to.[2] In academic research, these engagements are increasingly undertaken and come from a number of vantage points. They include new work on secularism: having frequently assumed that religion would become confined to the private sphere and increasingly irrelevant to the lives of many, secularist theories of the state and other social institutions are now being reworked to take account of new and persistent forms of religious activity and religious diversity. This leads some contributors to call for or make slight but crucial refinements to classic secularist ways of engaging with religion, while others argue for a much more extensive reconsideration of religion's role in socio-political life. This second approach is often referred to as 'post-secular': the post-secular literature is associated with a number of distinct and sometimes contradictory propositions and interests and involves a contested view of the 'secular',[3] but it centres on claims that religion is not, cannot and/or should not be located entirely outside of public life. Though the post-secular intervention is sometimes presented in comprehensive terms – a 'turn' in the direction of scholarship rather than a new thread within it[4] – it is best understood as part of a much broader project of negotiating, or renegotiating, religion in scholarly and political work.

Alongside new secularist and post-secular accounts, another major thread comes from those focusing on religious pluralism to understand the role of religion in modern societies. The focus here is on the way in which religious actors and institutions negotiate *one another* and the dialectical effects of these negotiations, with some scholars extending their models to include not only religious actors but alternatively spiritual, non-religious and secular actors, too.[5] Finally, another significant area of activity pursues a more theoretically open-ended goal, concerned instead with providing more detailed empirical accounts of religion in contemporary life in opposition to the broad-brush and presumptuous treatments of religion that have predominated in some arenas over past decades and remain

2 I differentiate between 'non-religion' and 'secularity' according to the model developed in Lois Lee, *Recognizing the Non-Religious: Reimagining the Secular* (Oxford: Oxford University Press, 2015). In this, 'non-religion' indicates phenomena that are primarily identified in contradistinction to religion – New Atheist discourses, for example, or the conduct of civil, humanist and other lifecycle ceremonies that are developed as alternatives to religious ones and bear the marks of this non-religious positioning. By contrast, 'secularism' is a theory via which some domains are designated as secular and immanent, while 'secularity' entails the subordination of religious, spiritual and non-religious 'other-worldly' concerns to other, 'this-worldly' matters (though religious, spiritual and non-religious concerns may still play a secondary role). According to this model, secular school curricula – the typical curricula provided by liberal states – can be contrasted with non-religious curricula, examples of which can be found in State Atheist regimes.

3 James A. Beckford, 'SSSR Presidential Address: Public Religions and the Post-Secular: Critical Reflections', *Journal for the Scientific Study of Religion* 51, 1 (2012): 1–19.

4 Gregor McLennan, 'The Post-Secular Turn', *Theory Culture Society* 27, 3 (2010): 3–20.

5 The crucial role of 'unbelief' in Charles Taylor's highly influential pluralist model of secularity is an example of the latter approach: Charles Taylor, *A Secular Age* (Cambridge: Belknap Press, 2007). See Lee, *Recognizing the Non-Religious* for a discussion.

operative in many, particularly in relation to Islam and 'Islamism'. This work calls for close attention to different forms of religious belief and practice and to the different degrees of commitment and immersion that are possible in relation to religious cultures. It highlights the ways in which religious actors are frequently objectified in accounts of religion and society and instead pays close attention to the role that these actors themselves play as active participants in processes of negotiation.

This volume contributes to these emerging attempts to negotiate religion in a number of ways, both constructive and critical. Developed via a series of workshops conducted at UCL between 2011 and 2013, it draws on expertise from a number of disciplinary traditions – from history, politics, political theory, religious studies, geography, sociology and law. This array of perspectives brings different types and aspects of negotiation to the fore and make it possible not only to build a rich and multidimensional account of new engagements with religion, but also to compare different knowledge and perspectives in order to create a reflexive account of what it means to negotiate religion.

This reflexivity entails the following sets of questions regarding the negotiation of religion:

1. What kinds of questions should we be asking about negotiation processes? What kinds of phenomena do we need to attend to in order to understand those processes?
2. What opportunities are there for consolidating knowledge about negotiation processes across disciplines? When are interdisciplinary approaches to negotiation and to religion apposite and fruitful and when is it helpful to recognise and respect disciplinary differences?
3. What kinds of negotiation processes are underway? What are the historic and contemporary contingencies that give them form?

Through these different areas of enquiry, this volume takes seriously empirical experiences of negotiation and the possibility of investigating these, while at the same time reflecting on how those experiences are approached, understood, constructed and performed by a range of actors within the academy as well as outside it.

This introduction sets out these ways of approaching the volume's theme. It introduces the ambiguities and ambivalences that the editors see in relation to attempts to negotiate religion and it outlines a series of questions that we think may profitably be asked about these attempts. It introduces the volume's anthropologically informed approach to its subject, in which disciplinary accounts as well as empirical cases are viewed as constituents of the 'field' of enquiry rather than distanced observers of it. Finally, it introduces and outlines the substantive contributions that volume contributors have made to our understanding of processes of negotiating religion in contemporary society. These contributions focus on European experiences past and present and this introduction explains why this focus is crucial to any serious and reflexive approach to negotiating religion.

Negotiation as a problematic

As outlined above, an interest in negotiating religion is associated with a broad and dynamic set of interventions and the notion is inevitably as problematic and contested as it is productive. It relies, for example, on a disputed and arguably secularist notion of 'religion' as an autonomously meaningful category of identification.[6] Similarly, the idea of recognising and negotiating religion in public life, as 'public religion', may be, to use the words of the anthropologist, Matthew Engelke, seen as a 'testament to the power of a certain kind of Enlightenment thinking'.[7] As Engelke reminds us, 'religion' is a term that many so-called 'religious actors' themselves dislike.[8] In addition, attempts to accommodate, recognise or otherwise negotiate religion are often asymmetrical in their treatment of actors and cultures, so that religious ones are identified in some detail and singled out as requiring very careful negotiation, while non-religious interlocutors in these negotiations are rendered formless and invisible, appearing by implication to lack their own complicated socio-cultural situations and historical perspectives that might also impact upon these encounters. Such asymmetries are seen likewise in often well-meaning political and policy discussions that encourage constructive engagements with 'faith groups' (as they are commonly termed), but do not specify concretely who the partner in these engagements is. This partner is often just indicated with a generalised 'we'. Such discourses appear to pit religious individuals and groups against much more abstract actors – institutions or even publics or societies as a whole – and therefore involve a fundamental disparity in how religious and other actors are conceived of.

Asymmetries like these make an interest in negotiating religion vulnerable to attack from post-structuralist and critical religion scholars who raise concerns about the identification of 'religion' as a singular and exclusive phenomenon and its often-implicit construction of a secular 'other'. In one argument, the failure to provide a concrete account of non-religious interlocutors exposes an understanding of the latter as superior, possessing not a socio-cultural perspective but knowledge of 'the real world seen aright in its self-evident factuality'.[9] On the other hand, the idea of religion as a unique aspect of human life that has no meaningful equivalent is bound up with claims that serve religious interests, too.[10] Religious parties may benefit from the idea of religion as special and requiring special protections or resources, as they may from the idea that it is religion that is natural and interwoven

6 See e.g. Talal Asad, *Formations of the Secular: Christianity, Islam, Modernity* (Stanford, CA: Stanford University Press, 2003); or Russell T. McCutcheon, '"They Licked the Platter Clean": On the Co-Dependency of the Religious and the Secular', *Method and Theory in the Study of Religion* 19 (2007): 173–99.

7 Matthew Engelke, *God's Agents: Biblical Publicity in Contemporary England* (Berkeley, CA: University of California Press, 2013), 36.

8 Ibid., 36.

9 Timothy Fitzgerald, *The Ideology of Religious Studies* (Oxford: Oxford University Press, 2000), 15.

10 Ibid.

through cultural life in ways that justify its presence and power in public domains.[11] In this way, calls for constructive engagement with religion and religious groups may appear to be inclusive and broadly commendable while at the same time being bound up with complicated struggles for power and access to resources: arguments about the unique contributions and/or challenges to psychological and social life that religion is seen to pose allow religious actors to manoeuvre into or be manoeuvred out of central roles in public consultation processes, funding allocations and other practical matters.

Attempts to 'negotiate religion' are, then, deeply ambivalent and we take up this notion as the central problematic of this volume not in spite of but because of this. We propose that this ambivalence makes it a productive starting point for a set of enquiries that resist easy conceptual solutions or opportunistic agenda-setting, but which instead recognise the complexity of the theoretical problems and empirical realities at hand. To this end, the concept of negotiation is itself a helpfully ambiguous one, even paradoxical: we can negotiate *with* actors or we can negotiate *around* actors and around objects – two fundamentally different forms of engagement that imagine religious agency in fundamentally different ways.[12] These two forms can be internally differentiated too. To 'negotiate *with* religion' can, for example, involve dignifying religious actors with recognition and attention, but it can also recognise and delineate religion in particular ways that are imposed upon religious and, indeed, non-religious actors. This is the view taken by critical scholars of religion, who associate contemporaneous notions of 'religion' with modern, Western, colonial and anti-religious ways of thinking.[13] The idea of negotiating *around* religion makes these potential undertones explicit: to negotiate around religion is to engage with it as an objectified form and as an obstacle and it is a process of negotiation in which the religious actor plays little active role. This triumphal sense of negotiation is quite at odds, then, with more tentative, relational and collaborative ideas of negotiation. Finally, these general senses of negotiation can be contrasted with more specific, legal understandings, to do with contractual settlements and the allocation of ownership. These point to further distinctions to be made between formal and informal processes of negotiation, which may be resolved in treaties and other explicit agreements or simply enacted relationally.

Problematic though it is, then, the notion of 'negotiation' is a helpful starting point for considering dynamics surrounding religion precisely because it helps make these ambiguities and ambivalences visible. At the same time, it does not assume simple or unilinear exertions of power in the same way that ideas like 'managing', 'regulating' and even 'accommodating' religion and religious diversity may do. It nevertheless makes issues of power more explicit than in more neutral concepts like 'interaction', 'relations' or 'dialogue' and it is more flexible than the also unilinear and therefore misleadingly neutral-seeming notions of 'approaching' or

11 E.g. Fitzgerald, *The Ideology of Religious Studies*.

12 See also Laborde, this volume.

13 Asad, *Formations of the Secular*; Fitzgerald, *Ideology of Religious Studies*.

'approaches to' religion. Thus, 'negotiation' pushes us to attend to how influence and agency are allocated in relevant discourses and enables us to consider an array of possibilities, and it facilitates investigations of how well such discourses capture complicated and dynamic empirical realities – in which religious phenomena are not only influenced and acted upon but are also able to influence and to act and in which bounded ideas of the 'religious' may crumble before us.

Questions about negotiation

In view of this, this volume works with two broad sets of questions that need to be asked in relation to attempts to negotiate religion – one set concerning the nature of negotiation as a type of relation between parties and one concerning the parties involved (or excluded) in these relations.

On the nature of negotiation, we need to consider: What different processes of negotiation are undertaken in relation to religion in society? What is it that is being negotiated in these cases? What are the political, social and cultural contexts in which these processes take place and how do process and context shape one another? When religious difference and diversity do emerge as problems, are there best, or better, ways of negotiating this, or political frameworks that are particularly conducive to successful negotiation processes: establishment and the formal recognition of religion versus more exclusively or 'radically' secular political and legal regimes,[14] for example, or the liberal regimes of neutrality advocated by many contemporary political philosophers'? When we consider best and better arrangements, what are the evaluative standards with which we make these assessments? Are these the right ones to use? How does the legacy of past forms of intra-religious and non-religious-religious collaboration, tension and warfare inform the way contemporary societies understand pluralism and undertake negotiation? How are 'negotiation' and similar terms used in formal discourses and how does this compare to informal approaches? How are new negotiations with and on behalf of religious actors interpreted in law?

On the parties involved in these negotiations, we need to ask: To what extent do such negotiations rely on the objectification of 'religion', in general or in relation to specific religions, as well as on particular understandings of religion's 'other'? Do fixed understandings of religion inhibit the kind of flexibility and open-endedness that these negotiation processes are often attempting? The idea of 'negotiating religion' makes, or should make, the parties involved conspicuous – and other parties conspicuous in their absence. Any exploration or application of the term needs to engage with this ambiguity: Which actors are included in negotiations – and, equally importantly, which are not? How are these actors described or understood? Are these representations their own or imposed on them by others? Many accounts solely focus on 'religious' actors, while others introduce 'secularist' participants, construed either as non-religious actors, set apart from

14 Tariq Modood, 'Moderate Secularism, Religion as Identity and Respect for Religion', *The Political Quarterly* 81 (2010): 4–14.

and/or in opposition to religious actors or, paradoxically, as any advocate of arrangements by which religious concerns are subordinated to others in one or several domains of social life and *not* therefore at odds with all (or even many) religious perspectives.[15] Anthropological and sociological work draws attention to the fuzziness of these categories, as well as to the people routinely ignored by problematic but pervasive 'religious/secular' binaries, such as the alternatively spiritual, the 'unchurched' and the substantively non-religious, typically described in Western contexts as 'atheist', 'agnostic', 'humanist' and 'rationalist' as well as 'non-religious'. How are *these* groups included and excluded from discourses centred on religion? How is the construction of actors in ways that facilitate and inhibit their ability to act reproduced through processes of negotiation and what new actors are constructed and enabled as a result of them?

How are different actors involved in processes of negotiation and what makes this involvement possible? How do different actors formulate and present their claims to attention and authority, identify potential spokespeople and their addressees, secure their institutions and assert their physical and political presence and integrity when these are challenged? What is at stake for different and differently situated participants in contemporary negotiations with religion? Do these participants speak and act on their own behalf and 'consciences' or do they speak and act on behalf of or with a mandate from others? How do actors defined by their secular roles – as politicians, journalists, academics, or even as contributors to this volume – conceive of and construct 'religion' in their attempts to understand and represent it? To recognise and identify these actors is to make explicit the strong imbalance between, on the one hand, those positioned as speaking *about* religion from some kind of external and in that sense 'neutral' vantage point (whether they attempt to speak 'from' a scientific, a political, or even a religious tradition) and, on the other hand, those who are more strongly and often more narrowly identified as speaking *from* a religious or an explicitly non- or anti-religious position. What are the political and ethical implications of describing some actors according to their religiosity while identifying other actors according to their professions, or of situating religious actors in relation to rich and complicated cultural formations, while non-religious actors are merely identified in relation to these *religious* formations and occupy a position that may be seen either as culturally impoverished or intellectually liberated?[16] Also at stake here are ethical and theoretical questions about the ways in which engagements within and according to pluralist and multiculturalist frameworks reify cultural difference in the process of recognising and protecting those within it.

Understanding negotiation

These are broad questions and they require an analysis that crosses societal dimensions and disciplinary perspectives – many more than can be gathered

15 Lee, *Recognizing the Non-Religious.*
16 Ibid.

together in a single volume. In asking these questions, the volume seeks to draw attention to the way in which the issues at stake all have descriptive, analytical and normative or ethical dimensions. It addresses not only what negotiation processes look like in practice, but also the concepts we use to understand these processes and the ideals – justice, peace, agreement, etcetera – that animate them. In view of this, the volume seeks to explore how different disciplines attend to these dimensions in their distinctive ways, as well as the extent to which the issues at stake cut across these dimensions and disciplinary responses. It attempts to build upon emerging interdisciplinary conversations in the study of religion by, first, presenting new insights from a number of vantage points, and, second, by providing tools for reflecting on multi- and inter-disciplinary engagements. Multi- and inter-disciplinarity have been core features of new engagements with religion, but these approaches have not always been undertaken reflexively. One problem is that multi-disciplinary collections do not always situate work in relation to the languages, interests and assumptions of the disciplines at work. By bringing together disciplinary accounts that are, necessarily and beneficially, parochial to a degree, meaning may be lost, not so much in translation as through the absence of translation. As sociologist James A. Beckford has shown in relation to the concept of the 'post-secular', there can be nothing so mischievous for the production of knowledge as a shared language understood in different ways,[17] and this is a particular risk when contributors from different traditions converge on a topic, as has happened in recent years with religion. Such work may attempt to be inter-disciplinary but the veneer of understanding that a common vocabulary provides can mean a failure to appreciate and capitalise on the theoretically informed and empirically grounded insights that individual traditions have to offer.[18]

In order to draw attention to distinct bodies of academic knowledge about religion and logics of engagement with it, the approach in this volume is therefore cross rather than inter- or multi-disciplinary, though in this the intention is also to provide tools for future inter- and multi-disciplinary methodologies. Contributors speak from their specialist positions and expertise, taking up the key concerns of those specialisms; but, by placing these contributions together and by providing section introductions that locate them in relation to the traditions from which they derive, this book provides an opportunity to draw out the ways in which discrete approaches support others in diverse, sometimes intriguing ways, as well as to interrogate the moments that they talk past one another, in ways that we recognise as productive – reflecting a specialism's deep intentions and effects – as well as counter-productive.

As well as seeking to 'translate' different approaches to one another, constructing the volume in this way allows readers to consider how contributors themselves negotiate religion as an object of study from the perspective of their disciplinary traditions – historical, political, sociological and legal. These are disciplines that

17 Beckford, 'Public Religions'.

18 Thank you to Cécile Laborde for discussion on this topic.

are, like several others, reassessing past engagements with religion (or the lack of such engagements), through their own work and through inter-disciplinary conversations.

In his introduction to the historical perspectives on negotiation offered in this volume, François Guesnet draws attention to the way in which historical approaches have been brought into general discussions of religion in the West, as well as to the ambivalent effects of this kind of inter-disciplinarity. He highlights how the intuitions and outcomes of this engagement can be profitable and commendable, as those seeking to negotiate religion today seek to learn from the 'endless array of failed as well as successful attempts to negotiate religious diversity' found in the historical record. But he highlights, too, how this search for a 'useable past' is sometimes only achieved by simplifying and remodelling that past. In his words, an important tension can exist 'between contemporary commentators' need to establish analogies between present and past situations – to find continuity across constellations of interreligious conflict and cohabitation – and the complexities and hesitations of the scholarly historical argument'.[19]

Similarly, Cécile Laborde is ambivalent about how concepts like negotiation are brought into political engagements with religion. In her introduction to how religion is negotiated in constitutional politics and political philosophy, Laborde argues that, on the one hand, the concept of 'negotiation' helps understand how settlements between religious authorities and the state come into being and therefore the form that they may take. In order to understand state establishment of religion, for example, Laborde highlights the role that majority churches' influence and power has played in securing favourable settlements from governments. Yet, on the other hand, the idea of 'negotiation' idealises the processes through which settlements between religious powers and the state come about, implying that their relationship is an equal or horizontal one, when in fact the state overshadows churches and other religious organisations in matters of constitutional politics. More importantly perhaps, Laborde argues that a focus on negotiation may run at odds with the core objective of political philosophy. This is to interrogate and develop ethical and moral standards in relation to ideals of justice and fairness. From this perspective, the idea of negotiation is problematic because it implies that engagements with religion are undertaken merely as pragmatic 'modus vivendi' solutions – arrangements in which embattled groups established policies of religious toleration, 'not because they believed toleration was right, but because they did not have the power to impose their own views on others'. This is quite different from the principles developed in political philosophy: political philosophers do not seek to account for achievable terms of peace, but to identify relations between religion and politics that are *just*. In fact, Laborde emphasises, political philosophy is precisely situated in opposition to an approach to negotiation in which, 'anything [that] is negotiated or agreed upon is . . ., by that fact alone, just'.[20]

19 François Guesnet, this volume, p. 19.
20 Laborde, this volume, p. 68.

For political philosophers, then, negotiation is not, in itself, an ideal and their work instead addresses multiple possible relations between methods of negotiation and different normative standards. This work therefore draws critical attention to the way in which the use of 'negotiation' often fudges descriptive and normative standards – and may prompt those seeking to conduct scientific analyses to reflect upon the valorisation of negotiation that can sneak into their accounts and to undertake more critical engagements with negotiation, attentive to the ways in which negotiation processes may themselves exclude actors and entrench privileges.

By the same token, political ideals stand and fail in the 'real world': they must succeed in practice as well as theory and it is the texture and messiness of everyday life that give political philosophers the 'hard cases' that challenge and prompt refinements of their theoretical models. It is this everyday practice that is the business of the sociological, spatial and material methodologies explored in the third part of this book. This part considers the ways in which religion is negotiated in everyday life in general and in urban spaces in particular, from a perspective that draws attention to the way that negotiations are always partially physical – embedded in material forms and expressed as media via which humans communicate, be it theoretical models manifest on the page or the incarnation of religious cultures in human bodies, material objects, buildings and the spaces between them.

In her introduction, Claire Dwyer draws attention to the way that these social scientific perspectives situate politics in the everyday, as well as how public policy is developed in response to perceived challenges from everyday settings, in policy 'dialogues' shaped by securitisation and other fears about the presence of religion in society. Curiosity, understanding and fear may each be stoked by the visibility of religion and this visibility is necessarily and intrinsically to do with materiality, as accounts from this perspective highlight. Visibility is also something that religious actors can themselves negotiate and are partially able to determine according to their needs, though they are not always free to do this. Indeed, some negotiations of religion concern massive monuments to religious life that are physically imposing and necessarily influential, such as church buildings or public spaces appropriated for religious practice. Dwyer draws attention to the way that religious actors can commandeer so-called secular environments, sacralising urban space through, for example, religious processions and other ritual practice. From this perspective, negotiation is above all about relationality – about complex forms of 'dialogical and dialectic social relations where religious groups and individuals are key actors' and giving rise to negotiations that may operate independently of state level arrangements, as well as influencing them in subtle, indirect ways. As Dwyer says, attending to 'the ordinary and prosaic ways in which religious differences are accommodated by believers and non-believers alike is also an important theme for understanding how negotiations need not be codified, formalised or enshrined in law but may be pragmatic and contingent'.[21]

21 Dwyer, this volume, p. 147.

The final disciplinary section in this volume considers these codified, formalised negotiations in detail, focusing on legal perspectives in general and debates surrounding religion and education in particular. From this vantage point, Myriam Hunter-Henin argues, the concept of negotiation promises a less confrontational method of dealing with new tensions arising in relation to religion in 'secular' institutions. Again, the picture here is mixed. On the one hand, negotiation in this sense is about compromise and this is at odds with a legal understanding of religion as concerning 'absolute commitments' of religious people to their faith and of human rights legislators to their humanism. From this perspective, the idea of negotiating *with* religion may be 'questioned for its incompatibility with both religious and legal duties'.[22] The focus on education helps draw out these polarities, because this is a sector in which these and related oppositions have been acute. This is not only because debates around religion have so often, especially in European settings, focused on profound and sometimes incompatible claims to knowledge and epistemological legitimacy. How educational institutions negotiate religion may also have been conflictual because these institutions sometimes compete with one another, to instill norms and values in pupils and to provide support and shape young people in forming their identities – their sense of themselves and their place in the world.[23] Education is also a site at which widespread, fundamental and perennial philosophical and political negotiations around the balance and trade-offs between cooperation and cohesion and individual autonomy are particularly significant, given that there is not only the autonomy of adult citizens in play but the distinctive and contested autonomy of children and young people, too. It is, as Hunter-Henin states in her introduction, no coincidence that so many contemporary debates and controversies around religion revolve around educational institutions – both universities and schools.[24] On the other hand, focusing on this sector provides a way of interrogating such polarisations and considering how they might be bridged. From this legal perspective, it is here that negotiation approaches might be helpful and build upon existing legal procedures. The question then becomes one about the form such negotiations should take and how accommodations of religion might be integrated with commitments to other, sometimes conflicting fundamental rights.

These disciplinary sections provide insights into how different disciplines are negotiating religion, the different questions they are asking and the different actors and artefacts that they have in view. Section introductions contextualise these accounts and draw attention to the ways in which they can only be understood in relation to the particular issues that each discipline is trying to negotiate.[25] On the other hand, reading them side-by-side draws out differences of approach that throw

22 Hunter-Henin, 'A legal perspective', this volume, p. 193.

23 Ibid.

24 Ibid.

25 See also Cécile Laborde, 'Three Approaches to the Study of Religion', *The Immanent Frame*, 5 February 2015, http://blogs.ssrc.org/tif/2014/02/05/three-approaches-to-the-study-of-religion/, accessed 27 October 2015.

disciplinary assumptions and points of blindness into relief. To take one important, general example, we see, in these accounts, the optimisms and pessimisms involved in different disciplinary engagements with religion. From a sociological perspective, for example, ideas of negotiation and dialogue are approached hopefully – responding to issues of social segregation, taking on naïve oppositions to multiculturalism and so on – but perhaps unwittingly discouraging the critical reflection on those ideas that emerge in other fields. On the other hand, such approaches may influence legal and political theoretical understandings of negotiation that, though they may be more sensitive to the limitations and failures of negotiation initiatives, may also benefit from attention to the way in which everyday enthusiasms impact upon these outcomes. In these ways, reflective, cross-disciplinary readings help us to interrogate the motivations and methodological limitations that channel our work. Thus, we hope that the cross-disciplinary approach of this volume may aid those working in different disciplines to negotiate *one another* – to work out ways of translating their insights where it is helpful to do so and to recognise that opportunities for and benefits of translation may be limited in important ways.

Situating negotiation

In support of its reflexive approach, the volume focuses on European societies, past and present. Languages used to negotiate religion today are frequently grounded in European history – its particular needs and its imperial past – and European experiences as well as European thought have played a crucial role in the formation of theories about the role of religion in society. For this reason, this volume is particularly focused on Europe but its accounts do not solely affect Europeans. The extent to which past notions of religion, the secular and secularism are Europeanised has provided a fertile line of critique in recent work and this has produced an increasing number of sorely needed accounts looking outside Europe, where religious and secular life and secularist theories and arrangements may look rather different. But understanding religion, secularity and secularism in relation to Europe is also imperative – not only in order to deepen understandings of the historical role Europe has played in developing ways of negotiating religion and, indeed, in thinking about the question in these terms in the first place, but also in order to explore negotiations of religion occurring within Europe today.

Europe has been the site of a number of tensions in relation to religion in recent years and debate about religion is widespread. In this context, it is not clear how well Europeanised conceptions of religion and secularism actually work for Europeans themselves. Certainly, the extensive decline of religious practice and belief in many European societies has resulted in Europeans frequently taking the role of religion for granted and the anxieties it is experiencing today are partly as a result of this: in tense circumstances, the extent to which understandings of religion – and non-religion – are theoretically and empirically under-developed has made itself felt. The widely held view that secularisation and secularity are concepts that work, at the very least, in relation to Europe – whether Europe is treated as an exemplary or exceptional case – in fact feeds into simplistic notions of religion in Europe that fail to account for complicated and changing realities and for regional diversity.

Several contributions to this volume focus on the local, and on London in particular, and this allows the volume to explore kinds of variety that are found not only between but within regions also. Settings like London have populations that are internally variegated, not only in terms of people's cultural backgrounds but also in terms of their socio-economic circumstances, industrial and occupational experiences and so on. In all of these ways, contributions in this volume build upon work which shows that Europe's relationships with religion are multiple and complicated and that its own discourses about religion may mislead as well as articulate its experiences. Undertaken in this way, a focus on Europe can help to 'provincialise' European negotiations of religion and demonstrate the historicity and open-endedness of these encounters.

Historical chapters in Part I illustrate the multiple and shifting nature of negotiation processes taking place in Europe in the early modern period, a period in which contemporary negotiations of religion, both in Europe and elsewhere, are grounded. Benjamin J. Kaplan's, 'Negotiating religious difference in early modern Europe', explores different kinds of religious diversity and their amenability to different methods of negotiation. Foregrounding other contributions to this volume, both he and François Guesnet – in 'Negotiating under duress: the expulsion of Salzburg Protestants (1732) and the Jews of Prague (1744)' – address several of the different kinds of negotiation explored in this volume: negotiations codified in political theories, treaties and law, and negotiations manifest in informal social relations and practice. This work demonstrates also the extent to which negotiation processes can move in different directions from and even work at odds with one another. Guesnet's comparative approach draws into focus how diverse and contingent negotiations of religion and religious diversity have been across Europe. These chapters begin to show what later chapters will confirm – that there is no one European way of negotiating religion – and that in fact, as Guesnet says in his introduction, negotiation processes are themselves open for negotiation.

Kaplan and Guesnet's chapters document the growing influence of state administrations on religious actors over this period,[26] and the nature of and philosophies underlying these new, increasingly secular authorities is explored in Part II. This section covers philosophical and political theoretical issues – Albert Weale's exploration of ethics and reason in, 'Can there be a public reason of the heart?' and Saladin Meckled-Garcia's arguments about liberal neutrality and the justifications (or not) of religious establishment in, 'The ethics of establishment: fairness and human rights as different standards of neutrality' – and these are issues that, by their nature, transcend time and space. Yet they are located, too, in political philosophical and ethical traditions that have their feet in European thought – the

26 Guesnet, 'Historical trajectories', this volume, p. 28.

Europeanness of which is an area of profitable contestation that has helped move philosophical debates forward. Robert M. Morris's chapter explores the relationship between political theory and practice explicitly. The force of Morris's argument in 'Alternative futures for formal church establishment: two case studies from the UK' is not so much that established religion is philosophically problematic as it is that established religion is politically unsustainable in empirical contexts that are profoundly marked by secularisation and related processes that are taking place in a number of domains. As Laborde says in her introduction to the work, Morris's chapter shows how the fate of contemporary arrangements around religion are themselves the product of ongoing principled negotiations and attempts to respect religious and other actors within them – an analysis that echoes contributions throughout this volume.

The focus in Part III is on everyday negotiations that take place in urban spaces. The chapters in this section centre on London, but on London as a city shaped by its different, overlapping identities and experiences as European, Western and global. In 'Providing religious homes in a deeply globalised city: secular and religious place-making across London', John Eade explores the negotiations that take place between various actors – religious and non-religious – around spaces of congregational worship, while Luke Bretherton's chapter on 'Community organising, democratic citizenship and interfaith relations', demonstrates how urban life can itself become an object around which religious and other actors negotiate their roles and one another. These are complicated processes of negotiation, in which multiple social dynamics – intelligible only in their, in this case European, socio-cultural contexts – play a role in the construction of religious and secular places and of those that use them as insiders and outsiders. Echoing Kaplan's historical study, these chapters work against any homogenous notion of 'secular Europe', demonstrating how, within one city even, the divisions drawn between religion and secular are multiple and shifting and, indeed, how the contestation of these divisions can itself be a productive aspect of civil engagement.

Bretherton's chapter explores the ways in which negotiation – situated, dialogical, tentative – may be apposite to the kinds of heavily contingent religious, nonreligious and secular interactions taking place in contemporary societies and the chapters in Part IV explore this possibility in relation to the implementation of the law. Myriam Hunter-Henin ('Believing in negotiation: reflection on law's regulation of religious symbols in state schools') and Lucy Vickers ('New issues for negotiation: schools and religious freedom') address the prospects for negotiation approaches as a way of responding to new debates about accommodating religion in European institutions and explore the extent to which these challenges can and should be met not within formal law but via negotiation processes surrounding the implementation of these laws. By focusing on educational institutions in detail, these contributions are able to take account of institutional and other cultural specificities that show, again, how and why there can be no such thing as a single European solution to questions about the role of religion in society. These chapters explore in detail how a combination of formal and informal approaches may be best suited to the task of negotiating religion, precisely because these approaches have the capacity to understand and engage with complicated social realities in their specificities.

In exploring these issues from the perspective of the law, this section reminds us of the need to respect differences between related but distinct approaches to negotiation: there is, Hunter-Henin says, some significant degree to which legal, constitutional and other approaches are and must be autonomous from one another:

> Just as the spirit of compromise and the negotiations at play at the policy formulation phase can never dismiss the need for a balancing of these solutions with the local and individual factors which are at stake at the implementation phase, a negotiating process at the level of enforcement cannot re-open the compromises reached at broader level.[27]

This need to understand and respect dimensional or otherwise specialised engagements with religion is of course one that this volume reasserts. As this passage from Hunter-Henin also alludes, however, these projects operate not only in relation to their own logics, but also in relation to one another. The final chapter in this volume is firmly situated in the legal discipline but it considers how dialectics between different dimensions offer prospects for understanding and innovation. In 'Regulating religious diversity in liberal societies', Maleiha Malik demonstrates how broad legal approaches may profitably engage with work from other areas. Echoing a distinction made at several points in this volume, Malik's exploration of dynamics between religion and human rights law is also an exploration of the differences between formal techniques (of regulation, in Malik's language) and informal processes (of negotiation). Malik argues the need for liberal societies to design legal systems that are able to regulate issues in relation to religion and religious diversity, while counter-balancing this with a mixture of legal and non-legal techniques to address a broader range of concerns, including those raised by religious actors themselves.

Malik's work encourages practitioners who are situated firmly and unapologetically within disciplines to build channels via which to access knowledge from other perspectives and thus help to avoid the pitfalls of false tolerance. Thus, she points to how historical and social scientific insights act against the language of 'freedom' and 'choice' that lawyers have often relied on in negotiating religiosity – and to the ways in which religion can even be experienced by individuals as a burdensome and unpleasant imposition, yet be nonetheless compelling for that. These insights, she says, help legal scholars to understand their own languages and ways of thinking about the socio-political challenges they are attempting to negotiate through the law. Such work also helps locate knowledge in space, reminding us of the peculiarly European contingencies that are explored throughout this volume and the need to understand the European experience, not as one liberated from

27 Hunter-Henin, 'A legal perspective', this volume, p. 193.

culture in general in its engagements with religion, but as a historical one, shaped and constrained by its own many cultures. In these several ways, this closing chapter also serves as a helpful reminder that scholarship is going through its own period of rapid negotiation of religion across the disciplines, in which it takes up and considers old concepts and new objections, old settlements and new actors within them and the very histories that give rise to the legal and constitutional concepts we think through these questions with today.

The chapters of this volume are organised according to their disciplinary moorings and, as discussed above, are framed by detailed introductions that locate them in disciplinary context. The perspectives charted here are by no means the only relevant ones, nor is the combination of disciplines the only productive one. But the collection as a whole provides at least one way into understanding the independent momentum and unintended consequences that discrete attempts to accommodate and otherwise negotiate religion have had. All of these chapters demonstrate how negotiating religion relies on boundaries, but also how these boundaries are at once several, differently located and mutually constituting and critiquing. Together, they form a collection that attempts to unpick these different senses of negotiating religion and to explore that concept as a construction we can ask questions of.

References

Asad, Talal. *Formations of the Secular: Christianity, Islam, Modernity*. Stanford, CA: Stanford University Press, 2003.

Beckford, James A. 'SSSR Presidential Address: Public Religions and the Post-Secular – Critical Reflections', *Journal for the Scientific Study of Religion* 51, 1 (2012): 1–19.

Engelke, Matthew. *God's Agents: Biblical Publicity in Contemporary England*. Berkeley, CA: University of California Press, 2013.

Fitzgerald, Timothy. *The Ideology of Religious Studies*. Oxford: Oxford University Press, 2000.

Laborde, Cécile. 'Three Approaches to the Study of Religion', *The Immanent Frame*, February 5, 2015, http://blogs.ssrc.org/tif/2014/02/05/three-approaches-to-the-study-of-religion/, accessed 23 March 2016.

Lee, Lois. *Recognizing the Non-Religious: Reimagining the Secular*. Oxford: Oxford University Press, 2015.

McCutcheon, Russell T. 'They Licked the Platter Clean: On the Co-Dependency of the Religious and the Secular', *Method and Theory in the Study of Religion* 19 (2007): 173–99.

McLennan, Gregor. 'The Post-Secular Turn', *Theory Culture Society* 27, 3 (2010): 3–20.

Modood, Tariq. 'Moderate Secularism, Religion as Identity and Respect for Religion', *The Political Quarterly* 81 (2010): 4–14.

Taylor, Charles. *A Secular Age*. Cambridge, MA: Belknap Press, 2007.

Part I

Negotiating religion

Historical trajectories

1 Negotiating religion

Historical trajectories

François Guesnet

Scholarly interpretations today delve deep into history in order to substantiate claims about how religious actors and agencies relate to secular ones and to reflect on the legacies that shape contemporary intercultural encounters and engagements. The main reason for this proclivity for historical argument in non-historical interpretations of current religious issues is the roots of these conflicts in the distant past. Not only is religious diversity a ubiquitous phenomenon in human history in general, but also, in many contemporary cases, the main actors – religious communities and states identifying with certain belief systems – have been on the stage for hundreds if not thousands of years. Thus, negotiating a religious 'other' is as much a new challenge for the present as it is – or seems to be – the continuation of past encounters.

History also provides an endless array of failed as well as successful attempts to negotiate religious diversity. Thus, authors reflecting on present-day issues will always succeed in identifying a 'useable past' and illustrating the validity of an argument by pointing to historical antecedents. This is seen in interpretations of secularisation processes, the rise of religious fundamentalism, the changing relationship of church and state, the continuities and discontinuities of anti-Semitism and other exclusionary visions of society and of intercultural cohabitation in general. There is a tension between contemporary commentators' need to establish analogies between present and past situations – to find continuity across constellations of interreligious conflict and cohabitation – and the complexities and hesitations of the scholarly historical argument. At the same time, though, historians ask their questions and choose their evidence on the basis of their cultural backgrounds and contexts as well as their political persuasions. The search for solutions in the historical record therefore encounters the possibility of finding the present in the past.

The fertile but complicated relationships between contemporary concerns and historical perspectives are well illustrated by an example. The history of the Iberian *convivencia* (cohabitation) in the late Middle Ages provides a good example, with many themes that resonate with current debates about how religion is and should be negotiated by secular actors – as well as the question of whether it requires negotiation at all. After the harsh and oppressive rule of the Berbarian-Muslim Almohads in the twelfth century, the cohabitation of Muslims, Christians and Jews in both Muslim and Christian territories was marked by a considerable degree of tolerance for the religious other.[1] Philosophical, literary and scientific progress had accelerated because of an intensified exchange across religious and cultural boundaries, a phenomenon epitomised by the achievements of the Toledo School of Translations. In it, Christian, Muslim and Jewish scholars would translate from and to Arabic, Hebrew, Latin, Indian and Castilian (the latter experiencing a decisive period of standardisation in the process).[2] This cooperation came to an end with growing religious mobilisation among the Christian population as a military campaign to regain formerly Christian territories advanced. Widespread anti-Jewish violence at the end of 1391 was one of the consequences. The consolidation of Catholic rule after the completion of the *reconquista* in 1492 led to a 4-year-long process of expelling those Iberian Jews who refused to convert to Christianity and to the forced conversion of Iberian Muslims to Christianity (henceforth known as *moriscos*) in the first decades of the sixteenth century.

The era before the expulsion was soon to be idealised in a considerable number of sixteenth-century Jewish chronicles responding to the trauma of expulsion. These chronicles represent a significant departure in Jewish historiography. In their attempts to explain the genealogy of the catastrophe, some of their authors established a 'secular' reading of history, investigating how political and societal factors had led to the expulsion of the Spanish and Portuguese Jewish communities.[3] Likewise, immediately after the fall of Granada in 1492 that marked the end of Muslim rule in the Iberian peninsula, early modern Muslim chroniclers began to glorify the many generations of Muslim rule. The fact that Muslim rule over large numbers of Christians and exceptionally beautiful lands ended in defeat and expulsion contributed to a millennial interpretation of this rule and a sustained nostalgia of *al-Andalus* (that is, Spain under Muslim rule). Thus, 'the return of Spain to the Moors' ranks high among the demands of Islamist radical movements like

1 John Edwards defines *convivencia* as 'co-existence in the sense of tolerance of religious difference and lack of persecution and violence', see his *The Spanish Inquisition* (Stroud: Tempus), 44. In the past few years, both the pre-*reconquista* period and the notion of *convivencia* have inspired scholarly discussions and research, among others applying this term to different sets of historical encounters, like, for example, Barbara Crostini Lappin, ed. *Negotiating Co-Existence: Communities, Cultures, and 'Convivencia' in Byzantine Society* (Trier: WVT Wissenschaftlicher Verlag, 2013).

2 A comprehensive discussion in Charles Burnett, *Arabic into Latin in the Middle Ages: The Translators and their Intellectual and Social Context* (Aldershot: Palgrave Variorum, 2009).

3 Among the most prominent chroniclers are Gedaliah ben Joseph Ibn Yahia (*Shalshelet ha-kabala*), Joseph Ibn-Verga (*Shevet Yehuda*), Joseph Ha-Cohen (*Emek Ha-Bakha*), Samuel Usque (*Consolaçam ás tribulaçoens de Israel*) and Elia Capsali (*Seder Eliahu Zuta*); about this advent of modern historiography as a consequence of trauma and catastrophe see the pioneering essay Yoseph Hayim Yerushalmi, *Zakhor: Jewish History and Jewish Memory* (Seattle, WA: University of Washington Press 1982). A similar phenomenon of glorification of a lost assumed paradise could be observed in Poland-Lithuania after the destruction of many Jewish communities in the Khmelnitsky-Uprising 1648–9, see Edward Fram, 'Creating a Tale of Martyrdom in Tulczyn, 1648', in *Jewish History and Jewish Memory: Essays in Honor of Yosef Hayim Yerushalmi*, eds Elisheva Carlebach, John M. Efron and David N. Myers (Hanover, NH: Brandeis: 1998), 89–112.

Al-Quaida.[4] For Jewish historians of the nineteenth and early twentieth century, the Iberian–Jewish encounter of religious tolerance before the *reconquista* was marked by a number of positive elements: the very prominent position of Jews in state and fiscal administration, their achievements in philosophy, talmudic study, in the sciences and in literature, and, last but not least, a considerable degree of cultural and linguistic integration. The Iberian–Jewish encounter represented a fascinating vision of what Jewish diasporic civilisation could be expected to accomplish.[5] It was only towards the end of the nineteenth century that this mostly positive assessment was challenged. The rise of political anti-Semitism dampened the optimism of Jewish enlighteners and integrationists. In an Orthodox critique of acculturation and religious reform, the Iberian–Jewish encounter now served as a prime example of the negative consequences of a lack in religious observance and, among adherents of the emerging Jewish nationalist movement, the fatal conclusion of the Iberian–Jewish encounter offered powerful evidence of the precariousness of the diasporic condition.[6]

The deterioration in relations between Muslim-majority societies and Western ones, encapsulated in the deeply pessimistic arguments in Samuel Huntington's book outlining the *Clash of Civilizations and the Remaking of World Order*, first published in 1996,[7] and in discourses surrounding the Islamist attack on the World Trade Center on 11 September 2001, had a massive impact on historical perceptions of the Muslim–Christian–Jewish medieval encounter in Western Europe. The impressive achievements of a sustained intercultural exchange in late medieval Spain now seemed to offer a counter-narrative to the hopeless state of contemporary relations between Muslims and non-Muslims in the West. The medieval *convivencia* reappeared as a centrepiece in historical arguments about the possibility of peaceful co-existence being attained. Research programmes included projects about this period, international conferences and workshops were devoted to *convivencia* and

4 Justin Stearn, 'Representing and Remembering al-Andalus: Some Historical Considerations Regarding the End of Time and the Making of Nostalgia', *Medieval Encounters* 15 (2009), 356, 261–3.

5 This is a prominent feature in the pioneering works of German–Jewish historiography: Heinrich Graetz' *Geschichte der Juden* (1853–75) and Abraham Geiger's *Das Judentum und seine Geschichte. In zwölf Vorlesungen* (1864). Of the later revisions, Fritz (later: Yitzhak) Baer's critical appraisal of the Iberian-Jewish encounter would be particularly consequential, as it would impact on the formation of the so-called Jerusalem school of Jewish historiography in Mandatory Palestine and Israel, see his *Die Juden im christlichen Spanien. Urkunden und Regesten. I: Aragonien und Navarra. II: Kastilien/Inquisitionsakten*, Berlin: Schocken Verlag, 1929–36.

6 For a comprehensive review of these permutations of understanding, see the Iberian–Jewish encounter Casten Schapkow, *Vorbild und Gegenbild. Das iberische Judentum in der deutsch-jüdischen Erinnerungskultur, 1779–1939* (Köln, Weimar, Wien: Böhlau, 2011) and 298–304 for (neo-) orthodox criticism of acculturation and also Fred Astren, 'Historiography/Historical Writing', in *Encyclopedia of Jews in the Islamic World*, ed. by Norman A. Stillman (Leiden and Boston, MA: Brill Academic, 2010), 421–7.

7 Samuel Huntington, *The Clash of Civilizations and the Remaking of World Order* (New York: Simon & Schuster, 1996.)

led to collected volumes and special issues of scholarly journals.[8] The University of Castilla-La Mancha hosted a project to virtually re-create the Toledo School of Translation, offering a comprehensive repository of all works translated at this location from and to the above mentioned languages.[9] The fruitful cooperation of a small group of authors and translators in medieval Toledo was comparatively short-lived and had little impact on the realities of Christians, Muslims and Jews cohabitating the Iberian peninsula at the period. It also could not slow down the deterioration and destruction of this cohabitation. Nevertheless, the *convivencia* has come to be seen, today, as the single most prominent marker of urban identity of the city of Toledo, with the homepage of the Spanish national office of tourism's website offering this description:

> Toledo is one of the Spanish cities with the greatest wealth of monuments. Known as the 'city of the three cultures', because Christians, Arabs and Jews lived together there for centuries, behind its walls Toledo preserves an artistic and cultural legacy in the form of churches, palaces, fortresses, mosques and synagogues.[10]

Likewise, being recognised as a Unesco World Cultural Heritage Site in 1986 was also justified by Toledo's history as an arena of peaceful co-existence.[11]

Despite fascination with incidents of successful brokerage between different linguistic and religious heritages in late medieval Spain, historians have offered new and more nuanced appraisals of the *convivencia* in recent years. Thus, the fate of the *moriscos,* Muslims forced to convert to Christianity in their hundreds of

8 In 2007, the research programme on 'Integration and desintegration of European cultures' at Bochum and Nürnberg-Erlangen universities organised a conference on integration, segregation and expulsion on the Iberian peninsula in the medieval and early modern period, documented in Klaus Herbers and Klaus Jaspert, eds *Integration – Segregation – Vertreibung. Religiöse Minderheiten und Randgruppen auf der Iberischen Halbinsel (7–17. Jahrhundert)* (Berlin: LIT Verlag, 2011). A major international conference was organised by the Spanish Consejo Superior de Investigaciones Científicas and the Max Planck Gesellschaft zur Förderung der Wissenschaften in Madrid in in 2009 on 'Convivencia. Representation, Knowlegde, Identities', to name just two prominent examples. Among recent prominent publications one should mention a special issue of *History and Anthropology*, vol. 18 (2007): *Peace and Wars Between Cultures. Between Europe and the Mediterranean* and a comprehensive appraisal of interreligious relations and cohabitation in the festschrift for Mark R. Cohen: Arnold E. Franklin, Roxani Eleni Margariti, Marina Rustow and Uriel Simonsohn, eds *Jews, Christians and Muslims in Medieval and Early Modern Times. A Festschrift in Honor of Mark R. Cohen* (Leiden and Boston, MA: Brill Academic, 2014).

9 This project is funded by the Fundación Ignacio Larramendi and offers open access to all texts in their original language and the various translations, www.larramendi.es/traductores_toledo/en/micrositios/inicio.cmd (accessed December 2014).

10 www.spain.info/en/que-quieres/ciudades-pueblos/otros-destinos/toledo.html (accessed December 2014).

11 Interestingly enough, the description of the Toledo heritage above all describes the legacy of the three religious communities in the built environment, however this does reflect on intercultural exchange in general or Toledo School of Translations in particular; see http://whc.unesco.org/en/list/379 (accessed December 2014).

thousands early in the sixteenth century has recently become a more prominent topic of research.[12] Also, the paramount significance of economic and financial factors in governing decisions on admitting or expelling the religious 'other' has gained relevance in historical interpretations.[13] Another re-reading of the era preceding the forced conversion and expulsion considers the military campaigns leading up to the completion of the *reconquista*, while the widespread unrest and distrust it incited among Christian Iberians in relation to their Muslim rulers and Jewish neighbours have recently been given as a prime example of the religious roots of the modern nation state.[14]

Thus, historical research soon recognised the appeal and the reconciliatory potential of the narrative of productive and respectful multi-religious cohabitation in medieval Spain. This positive narrative resonates in research programmes, conferences and publications, it represents an important element in the recognition of Toledo as a Unesco World Cultural Heritage site and plays a key role in attracting tourists. The significant qualifications and reservations that have been formulated in the course of this renewed and intensified research activity resonates much less and the potential lessons of critical historical research find considerably less interest.

Religious fault lines in the European trajectory

Both the modern, homogenous nation-state as well as the emergence of more fragmented, federated states and Empires in European history are intimately linked to the fault-lines of religious identifications and their altercations, but are also the outcome of modes of negotiation and accommodation of diversity. These various pathways are particularly interesting to follow for those attempting to reconsider and renegotiate religion in contemporary contexts, despite the irrefutable, massive impact of secularisation on state governance and the negotiation of political and societal issues. So, for example, to fully grasp the specifically European experience of the impact of religious transformation on state- and nation-building and societal change, one needs to integrate the developments in those regions where the Protestant Reformation originated, leading to a sort of confessional *convivencia* of small, relatively homogeneous commonwealths in the Holy Roman Empire, as well

12 See William Childers, 'Disappearing Moriscos', in *Cross-Cultural History and the Domestication of Otherness*, eds Michal Jan Rozbicki and George O. Ndege (New York: Palgrave Macmillan, 2012), 51–64.

13 Javier Castaño, '"Flüchtige Schimären der Convivencia": Die Juden in Kastilien und ihre Eliten (1418–1454)', in *Integration – Segregation – Vertreibung*, ed. Jaspert Herbers (Münster, Berlin: LIT-Verlag, 20111), 79–212.

14 Anthony Marx, *Faith in Nation: Exclusionary Origins of Nationalism* (Oxford: Oxford University Press, 2003), 197–200; see also the pertinent critique of the limits of such a focus on Western European cases in Thomas A. Brady Jr., 'Limits of Religious Violence in Early Modern Europe', in *Religion und Gewalt. Konflikte, Rituale, Deutungen (1500–1800)*, eds Kaspar von Greyerz and Kim Siebenhüner (Göttingen: Vandenhoeck & Ruprecht, 2006), 127–9.

as those in eastern and southern-eastern Europe. This formative impact of different regional pathways of negotiating the relationship between state, society and religion in three European 'historical regions' had first been proposed in 1983 in an essay by the Hungarian historian Jeno Szücs. Reflecting on the astonishing durability of the eastern border of the Carolingian Empire (running north-south along the Elbe river and the Leitha river in Hungary), Szücs argued that a region east of this boundary was constituted through the strong impact of both Renaissance and Protestant Reformation and the presence of autonomous urban communities and strong estates, defining a sort of western east including among others Poland, Lithuania and Hungary. Szücs thus offered an alternative to the prevalent historical interpretation continuing to focus on the history of Empires and nations (or of confessions and religious communities, for that matter).[15] This perspective resonated with the emergence of a new historical paradigm in German historiography. As a result of the attempt to contextualise the impact of the Protestant Reformation on European history, Wolfgang Reinhardt and Heinz Schilling simultaneously though independently from each other proposed the new paradigm of 'confessionalisation', weaving together a variety of religious, societal and political transformations of the early modern period, including a sharpening of theological argument in the wake of the religious confrontations after the Reformation, the implementation of new forms of religious discipline, the new role of publishing and religious propaganda, the growing role of educational institutions in achieving religious obedience and homogeneity and a renewed focus on religious ritual.[16] The obvious advantage of this new paradigm was to combine the analysis of the Reformation with an interpretation of its consequences on non-Protestant territories and societies, like the Counter Reformation – it thus has contributed considerably to a more comprehensive understanding of the interdependence between religious and confessional history on the one hand and societal, cultural and political processes on the other.[17]

Among the criticisms of the confessionalisation paradigm was its focus on developments on the state level. On the local level, cultural and religious diversity was, however, negotiated in a different mode than on the level of commonwealths,

15 Jeno Szücs, *Vazlat Europa harom törteneti regiojarol* [*the three historical regions of Europe*] (Budapest: Magveto, 1983). The essay was translated into French (1985, with a preface by the pioneer of the *Annales* school, Fernand Braudel), German (1990) and Polish (1995), but has not been translated into English.

16 Wolfgang Reinhard, 'Zwang zur Konfessionalisierung? Prolegomena zu einer Theorie des konfessionellen Zeitalters', in *Zeitschrift für historische Forschung* 10 (1983): 257–77 and Heinz Schilling, *Konfessionskonflikt und Staatsbildung: Eine Fallstudie über das Verhältnis von religiösem und sozialem Wandel in der Frühneuzeit am Beispiel der Grafschaft Lippe* (Gütersloh: Mohn Verlag, 1981).

17 A review of the intense and protracted debate around this paradigm can be found in English in John M. Headley, Hans J. Hillerbrand and Anthony J. Papalas, eds *Confessionalization in Europe, 1555–1700: Essays in Honor and Memory of Bodo Nischan* (Aldershot: Palgrave, 2004). Some English contributions also in a reflection on the applicability on Eastern Europe in Joachim Bahlcke and Arno Strohmeyer, eds *Konfessionalisierung in Ostmitteleuropa: Wirkungen des religiösen Wandels im 16. und 17. Jahrhundert in Staat, Gesellschaft und Kultur* (Stuttgart: Steiner, 1999).

nations or empires. Through the Protestant Reformation, the number of towns and cities that developed forms of multi-religious cohabitation increased dramatically. Forms and practices of religious cohabitation in these complex urban and regional settings varied greatly and their frequent occurrence constitutes one of the hallmarks of the specifically European framework to negotiate religious difference. Often located in port cities, these communities and metropolises were the locus of intercultural encounters and facilitated processes of far reaching cultural, societal and political transformation. Prominent examples include not only metropolitan cities like Paris or London, but also trading centres like Amsterdam or Livorno.[18] Among the central European examples for early modern and modern forms of *convivencia* that go back to the Protestant Reformation and to an informal practice of religious tolerance in urban space, one may name the Netherlands, but also the early modern Polish-Lithuanian metropolis of Vilnius.[19]

The evolving debate surrounding the cultural impact of spatial separation in the form of the early modern *ghettos* for Jews emerging in the sixteenth century in Italy illustrates the importance of such a research perspective. These walled communities undoubtedly restricted the freedom of movement of the members of Jewish communities, normally during the night and on the occasion of high Christian holidays. Despite this curtailment of freedoms, separation between Jews and non-Jews led to an increased internal cultural and religious tolerance, as the boundaries between communities were perceived as more secure. Thus, among the consequences of this greater freedom was that esoteric interpretations of the Jewish religious tradition met with less resistance from local rabbinical authorities.[20] No less important was the greater ease with which members of the sequestrated Jewish community would be able to negotiate non-Jewish practices, ideas or innovations, not in the least through access to academic education.[21] In contrast, the Jewish community in seventeenth-century Amsterdam, among the least restrictive of all multi-religious European urban centres, banned one of its most original and radical thinkers, Baruch (or Benedict) Spinoza (1632–77), as his writings, inspired by Socinians and Deists, were considered a threat to the spiritual and religious integrity of the Jewish community.

18 The impact of trade and cohabitation on urban communities in port cities has been intensely scrutinised from a variety of perspectives over the past years. See, for example, Alice Mah, *Port Cities and Global Legacies: Urban Identity, Waterfront Work, and Radicalism* (Hampshire: Palgrave Macmillan, 2014) and David Cesarani and Gemma Romain, eds *Jews and Port Cities, 1590–1990: Commerce, Community and Cosmopolitanism* (London: Vallentine Mitchell, 2006).

19 Benjamin Kaplan, *Divided by Faith. Religious Conflict and the Practice of Toleration in Early Modern Europe* (Cambridge, MA and London: Belknap Press of Harvard University Press, 2007); and David Frick, *Kith, Kind, and Neighbors: Communities and Confessions in Seventeenth-Century Wilno* (Ithaca, NY: Cornell University Press, 2013).

20 Robert Bonfil, 'Changes in the Cultural Patterns of a Jewish Society in Crisis: Italian Jewry at the Close of the Sixteenth Century', in *Essential Papers on Jewish Culture in Renaissance and Baroque Italy*, ed. David Ruderman (New York: New York University Press, 1992), 401–25 and David Ruderman, *Early Modern Jewry: A New Cultural History* (Princeton, NJ and Oxford: Princeton University Press, 2010), 59–64.

21 Ruderman, *Early Modern Jewry*, 120–32.

There have been recent shifts in historical accounts of the ways in which religious diversity was negotiated in European history, now seen as attempts to identify how legacies of religious identity and thought have informed political philosophy since the early modern period. This new perspective is the result of growing dissatisfaction with past tendencies to oversimplify transformations from traditional to more secular societies. Thus, David Sorkin argued that Enlightenment thought had a much stronger impact among Protestants, Catholics and Jews theologians of the eighteenth century than previously assumed.[22] Sorkin identifies four characteristics of what he defines as 'religious Enlightenment': a strong commitment to reasonableness; recognition (in principle) of religious diversity and the need to tolerate it; the prominent role of its authors in public debate regarding religion and issues beyond religion; and the nominal support of established authorities. Rather than constituting a movement, Sorkin's 'religious enlighteners' shared moderate views about the relationship between faith, the commonwealth and society. More recently, Eric Nelson has disentangled the biblical roots of a number of central notions – like republicanism, toleration and church–state relations – in English political thought of the seventeenth century.[23] In a perspective comparable to the one proposed by Nelson, the German sociologist and historian Hans Joas has recently proposed 'a new genealogy of human rights', in which their emergence in eighteenth-century Europe is seen as an extension of religious humanist principles rather than a replacement for them.[24]

Historiography has contributed very significantly to a comprehensive understanding of the impact of religion on the formation of European commonwealths and societies. Or, to put it differently, the way religious differences and conflicts were negotiated (or not) in European history has been among the most prominent topics of historical research since its establishment as an academic discipline. In recent years, the role of transnational developments – like confessionalisation – and of the realities on the everyday and local level of these negotiations have been of particular interest, as both perspectives have considerable potential to elucidate the formation of identifications and of cultural and political affiliations. Also, alternative interpretations to an exclusively secular reading of political theory and thought have demonstrated the lasting impact of religious traditions on Western ideas of the state. These new attempts to recalibrate the local, national and international levels in the accommodation of religious diversity, as well as an acknowledgement of the religious and theological input in Western traditions of political thought are undoubtedly also a requirement for other disciplines.

22 David Sorkin, *The Religious Enlightenment: Protestants, Jews, and Catholics from London to Vienna* (Princeton, NJ and Oxford: Princeton University Press, 2008).

23 Eric Nelson, *The Hebrew Republic. Jewish Sources and the Transformation of European Political Thought* (Cambridge, London: Harvard University Press, 2010).

24 Hans Joas, *Die Sakralität der Person. Eine neue Genealogie der Menschenrechte* (Berlin: Suhrkamp 2011). This argument has been rejected by the legal historian Horst Dreier: *Säkularisierung und Sakralität: Zum Selbstverständnis des modernen Verfassungsstaats* (Tübingen: Mohr Siebeck, 2013), who insists that although most elements in contemporary legal philosophy and practice can be traced back to religious antecedents, the concept of human rights constitutes a radical, secularist departure from these.

Negotiating religion: two case studies

The two chapters in this section provide instructive examples of historical perspectives on negotiating religious differences and diversity. Both focus on the early modern period, that is, the period between 1500 and 1800. Benjamin J. Kaplan's chapter sets out by emphasising that, although European societies of this era had not yet undergone any significant process of secularisation and diversification, the religious landscape was far from monolithic. Consequently, processes of negotiating religious practices and affiliation were omnipresent and themselves diverse. These negotiations might be inter-personal, between ecclesiastic and 'worldly' authorities, for example; or they might be inter-institutional, contesting the scope of canonical and common law, for instance. It was, however, the end of the unity of Western Christendom through the Protestant Reformation and subsequent developments, which made the (in-) ability to negotiate religious differences a political issue of the first order. Kaplan specifies different forms of diversity, showing how the period of confessionalisation saw 'a general trend towards greater specificity and rigidity' – a tendency that made the negotiation of confessional differences both more difficult and more necessary. Kaplan differentiates three ideal typical forms of negotiation: an ecclesiastical one, one in the realm of state politics and the negotiation on a local, informal level. First, Kaplan points to the argumentative strategies employed by theologians and church representatives who argued in favour of a spiritual unity of all Christendom and in consequence pleaded for ecumenical toleration. This was, however, not a dominant trend. 'With the failure of clergy to resolve religious differences, secular authorities had the lead negotiating role thrust upon them', writes Kaplan, 'a role they accepted in their capacity as "Christian magistrates" . . . and also because it furthered their aim of amassing power'.[25] The close relationship between religious and civil authority came to the fore in the negotiations for the peace treaties of Augsburg 1555 and Westphalia 1648, shaping a European landscape of religiously defined commonwealths. Kaplan also discusses unilateral sovereign acts like the edict of Nantes (1598) or the English Toleration Act of 1689 – these would be attempts to negotiate a *modus vivendi* between confessions unable to achieve durable peace. Lastly, using the example of the Dutch Republic in the sixteenth century, Kaplan describes what he calls 'social negotiation' of religious cohabitation on the local level, through everyday practices, based on a shared understanding of the fundamental difference between the private and the public sphere.

As François Guesnet shows in his chapter, a similar case of the tacit toleration of religious dissidence – in this case Protestantism – under condition of the strictly private character of the practices involved, came to the end in the Catholic archbishopric of Salzburg at the end of the 1720s with the sovereign, the archbishop, introducing a number of anti-Protestant regulations. The Crypto-Protestants reacted with confessional and political mobilisation, challenging the archbishop in the assumption that the existing legal framework (the peace treaties

25 See Kaplan, 'Negotiating religious difference in Early Modern Europe', Chapter 2, this volume.

of Augsburg 1555 and Westphalia of 1648) was on their side. The Crypto-Protestants underestimated the resolve of the archbishop to end the tacit toleration and not to yield to the massive political campaign that accompanied the Crypto-Protestants mobilisation. The result – the expulsion of 20,000 individuals in extremely difficult circumstances – demonstrates the coming to an end of an era of informal negotiation of religious difference in the age of absolutism. Comparison of the expulsion of the Salzburg Crypto-Protestants with the expulsion of the Jews from Prague in 1744, however, shows how the need for negotiation to be informal could itself be negotiated, more or less successfully, by actors. Whereas attempting to make their plight a public matter had backfired for the Salzburg Protestants, the Prague Jews undertook an international but covert defensive campaign, supported mostly by court Jews and their non-Jewish correspondents. Guesnet argues that, by avoiding the public sphere and by systematically mobilising members of the aristocratic and ecclesiastical elite in the Holy Roman Empire and beyond on their behalf, networks supporting the Jews of Prague successfully negotiated their return: the expulsion was revoked in 1748 in return for a hefty sum, ironically (or cynically) called a 'toleration tax'.

Both chapters illustrate the growing impact of state administrations and political agencies on religious cohabitation in the early modern period. Absolutist sovereigns jealously guarding their prerogatives reduced the space for informal forms of accommodation. The informal negotiating of religious difference on the local level in post-Reformation Netherlands provided the space for relatively peaceful cohabitation for considerable periods of time. Similarly, the fact that those negotiating on behalf of the expelled Jewish community in Prague avoided the public sphere, allowed for a solution that minimised loss and harm for those targeted by an overly zealous Catholic sovereign. Established legal and constitutional frameworks however proved of too limited reach to secure the well-being of the persecuted Crypto-Protestant community in Salzburg. Are there lessons to be drawn from these historical examples for today? The most important seems to be that the negotiation of religious diversity depends on a multiplicity of factors, among which one should name first and foremost the socio-economic weight of the actors involved. Also, the institutions and principles of the nation-state as it emerges in the period of enlightened absolutism could be used both to rational as well as irrational purposes, at times serving the voluntaristic exertion of power alone. And, finally, examples for religious resentment, prejudice and exclusion abound in history, though are not limited to it. On the other side, history also provides insights into the possibilities of successful, informal and small-scale negotiations of religious difference.

References

Astren, Fred. 'Historiography/Historical Writing', in *Encyclopedia of Jews in the Islamic World*, edited by Norman A. Stillman, vol. 2, 421–7. Leiden, Boston, MA: Brill Academic, 2010.

Baer, Fritz. *Die Juden im christlichen Spanien. Urkunden und Regesten. I: Aragonien und Navarra. II: Kastilien/Inquisitionsakten.* Berlin: Schocken Verlag, 1929–36.

Bahlcke, J. and Arno Strohmeyer, eds. *Konfessionalisierung in Ostmitteleuropa: Wirkungen des religiösen Wandels im 16. und 17. Jahrhundert in Staat, Gesellschaft und Kultur.* Stuttgart: Steiner, 1999.

Bonfil, Robert. 'Changes in the Cultural Patterns of a Jewish Society in Crisis: Italian Jewry at the Close of the Sixteenth Century', in *Essential Papers on Jewish Culture in Renaissance and Baroque Italy*, edited by David Ruderman, 401–25. New York: New York University Press, 1992.

Brady, Thomas A. Jr. 'Limits of Religious Violence in Early Modern Europe', in *Religion und Gewalt. Konflikte, Rituale, Deutungen (1500–1800)*, edited by Kaspar von Greyerz and Kim Siebenhüner, 125–54. Göttingen: Vandenhoeck & Ruprecht, 2006.

Burnett, Charles. *Arabic into Latin in the Middle Ages: The Translators and their Intellectual and Social Context.* Aldershot: Palgrave Variorum, 2009.

Castaño, Javier. '"Flüchtige Schimären der Convivencia": Die Juden in Kastilien und ihre Eliten (1418–54)', in *Integration – Segregation – Vertreibung. Religiöse Minderheiten und Randgruppen auf der Iberischen Halbinsel (6–17. Jh.)*, edited by Klaus Herbers, Nikolas Jaspert, 179–212. Münster, Berlin: LIT-Verlag, 2011.

Cesarani, David and Gemma Romain, eds. *Jews and Port Cities, 1590–1990: Commerce, Community and Cosmopolitanism.* London: Vallentine Mitchell, 2006.

Childers, William. 'Disappearing Moriscos', in *Cross-Cultural History and the Domestication of Otherness*, edited by Michal Jan Rozbicki and George O. Ndege, 51–64. New York: Palgrave Macmillan, 2012.

Crostini Lappin, Barbara, ed. *Negotiating Co-Existence: Communities, Cultures, and Convivencia in Byzantine Society.* Trier, WVT Wissenschaftlicher: Verlag, 2013.

Edwards, John. *The Spanish Inquisition.* Stroud: Tempus, 1999.

Fram, Edward. 'Creating a Tale of Martyrdom in Tulczyn, 1648', in *Jewish History and Jewish Memory. Essays in Honor of Yosef Hayim Yerushalmi*, edited by Elisheva Carlebach, John M. Efron and David N. Myers, 89–112. Hanover, NH: Brandeis University Press, 1998.

Franklin, Arnold E., Roxani Eleni Margariti, Marina Rustow and Uriel Simonsohn, eds. *Jews, Christians and Muslims in Medieval and Early Modern Times: A Festschrift in Honor of Mark R. Cohen.* Leiden and Boston, MA: Brill Academic Publishers, 2014.

Frick, David. *Kith, Kind, and Neighbors: Communities and Confessions in Seventeenth-Century Wilno.* Ithaca, NY: Cornell University Press, 2013.

Headley, John M., Hans J. Hillerbrand and Anthony J. Papalas, eds. *Confessionalization in Europe, 1555–1700: Essays in Honor and Memory of Bodo Nischan.* Aldershot: Palgrave, 2004.

Herbers, Klaus and Nikolaus Jaspert, eds. *Integration – Segregation – Vertreibung. Religiöse Minderheiten und Randgruppen auf der Iberischen Halbinsel (7–17 Jahrhundert).* Berlin: LIT Verlag, 2011.

Huntington, Samuel. *The Clash of Civilizations and the Remaking of World Order.* New York: Simon & Schuster, 1996.

Joas, Hans. *Die Sakralität der Person. Eine neue Genealogie der Menschenrechte.* Berlin: Suhrkamp, 2011.

Kaplan, Benjamin J. *Divided by Faith: Religious Conflict and the Practice of Toleration in Early Modern Europe.* Cambridge, MA and London: Belknap Press of Harvard University Press, 2007.

Mah, Alice. *Port Cities and Global Legacies: Urban Identity, Waterfront Work, and Radicalism.* Hampshire, UK, New York: Palgrave Macmillan, 2014.

Marx, Anthony W. *Faith in Nation: Exclusionary Origins of Nationalism.* Oxford: Oxford University Press, 2003.

Nelson, Eric. *The Hebrew Republic. Jewish Sources and the Transformation of European Political Thought.* Cambridge, MA and London: Harvard University Press, 2010.

Reinhard, Wolfgang. 'Zwang zur Konfessionalisierung? Prolegomena zu einer Theorie des konfessionellen Zeitalters', *Zeitschrift für historische Forschung* 10 (1983): 257–77.

Ruderman, David. *Early Modern Jewry: A New Cultural History*. Princeton, NJ and Oxford: Princeton University Press, 2010.

Schapkow, Carsten. *Vorbild und Gegenbild. Das iberische Judentum in der deutsch-jüdischen Erinnerungskultur, 1779–1939*. Köln, Weimar, Wien: Böhlau Verlag, 2011.

Schilling, Heinz. *Konfessionskonflikt und Staatsbildung. Eine Fallstudie über das Verhältnis von religiösem und sozialem Wandel in der Frühneuzeit am Beispiel der Grafschaft Lippe.* (= *Quellen und Forschungen zur Reformationsgeschichte vol. 48*). Gütersloh: Mohn Verlag 1981.

Sorkin, David. *The Religious Enlightenment. Protestants, Jews, and Catholics from London to Vienna.* Princeton, NJ and Oxford: Princeton University Press, 2008.

Stearn, Justin. 'Representing and Remembering al-Andalus: Some Historical Consideratoins Regarding the End of Time and the Making of Nostalgia', *Medieval Encounters* 15 (2009): 355–74.

Yerushalmi, Yoseph Hayim. *Zakhor: Jewish History and Jewish Memory*. Seattle, WA: University of Washington Press 1982.

2 Negotiating religious difference in early modern Europe

Ecclesiastical, political and social processes

Benjamin J. Kaplan

As the introduction to this volume shows, the phrase 'negotiating religion' can have many meanings. Some of them are indeed applicable to the history of Europe before the modern era. It has sometimes been suggested that the very concept of religion is a modern invention and that the religious sphere once overlapped so pervasively and profoundly with the political, social, economic and cultural spheres that there was no meaningful distinction between them. This is an oversimplification. Conceptual and legal distinctions between religion and the state existed already in the Middle Ages and medieval Europe was not caesaropapist: despite the pretensions of some popes, supreme political and religious authority was never vested in the same person, as it was in the Byzantine Empire. Relations between ecclesiastic and 'temporal' authorities were always subject to negotiation and the tensions between the two sometimes took dramatic forms, as in the Investiture Controversy of the eleventh and twelfth centuries. Likewise, there was always a distinction between the canon law of the Roman Catholic Church, on the one hand, and different forms of civil law on the other. Neither is it the case that, before modern times, ordinary lay people had no freedom or agency in religious matters. Not only the intensity but also the forms and terms of people's religious engagement were variable, so there was always a relationship to be negotiated between individuals and the religious institutions to which they belonged. This was especially the case when people were confronted openly with a variety of religious options from which they could choose – most obviously when they could choose between rival faiths, but also when a single faith, like late medieval Catholicism, encompassed a wide range of schools, movements, devotions and models of piety. The experience of spirituality has always had an intimate, personal aspect as well as communal and public ones, and even within rigid orthodoxies there has always been room for the expression of certain preferences.

The purpose of this chapter is to consider the forms of negotiation between people of different faiths in early modern Europe.[1] The early modern period witnessed the formation of a distinctive form of religious plurality, for it was this period that saw Europe divide for the first time into rival Christian churches – Catholic, Calvinist, Lutheran, Mennonite, Anglican and so on – whose relations with one another, and whose places in the socio-political order, had to be negotiated. A product of the Protestant and Catholic Reformations, the sundering of western Christendom was entirely unintentional, as all the reformers of the sixteenth century conceived of the Christian religion as a single faith, church and body of believers. From the outset, they sought to effect not some division of this entity, but its reform and revitalisation. Even as divisions rapidly emerged – not only between Protestants and Catholics, but between different sorts of Protestants as well – reformers maintained that their own version of 'true Christianity' was the only genuine one, that it alone enjoyed divine favour and that it could not but prevail. When this did not happen in their own lifetimes, they projected this victory into the future. As the victory of God over the devil, Christ over Antichrist, good over evil, it remained in their minds an eschatological certainty.

By the seventeenth century, a 'confessionalisation' process had hardened initial divisions, transforming them into bitter rivalries between opposing churches, each with its own orthodoxies, rites and governing institutions.[2] At the same time,

1 For a broader treatment of the history of relations between people of different faiths in early modern Europe, see Benjamin J. Kaplan, *Divided by Faith: Religious Conflict and the Practice of Toleration in Early Modern Europe* (Cambridge, MA: Harvard University Press, 2007), esp. chapters 5–8. Other works that treat more than one country include Thomas Max Safley, ed. *A Companion to Multiconfessionalism in the Early Modern World* (Leiden: Brill, 2011); Howard Louthan, Gary B. Cohen and Franz A.J. Szabo, eds *Diversity and Dissent: Negotiating Religious Difference in Central Europe, 1500–1800* (Oxford: Berghahn, 2011); C. Scott Dixon, Dagmar Freist and Mark Greengrass, eds *Living with Religious Diversity in Early Modern Europe* (Farnham, UK: Ashgate, 2009); John Marshall, *1 John Locke, Toleration and Early Enlightenment Culture* (Cambridge: Cambridge University Press, 2006); Richard Bonney and D.J.B. Trim, eds *Persecution and Pluralism: Calvinists and Religious Minorities in Early Modern Europe, 1550–1700* (Oxford-Bern: Peter Lang, 2006); Thierry Wanegffelen, *1 L'édit de Nantes: Une histoire européenne de la tolérance du XVIe au XXe siècle* (Paris: Librairie générale française, 1998); John Christian Laursen and Cary J. Nederman, eds *Beyond the Persecuting Society: Religious Toleration Before the Enlightenment* (Philadelphia, PA: University of Pennsylvania Press, 1998); Ole Grell and Bob Scribner, eds *Tolerance and Intolerance in the European Reformation* (Cambridge: Cambridge University Press, 1996); Henry Kamen, *The Rise of Toleration* (New York: McGraw-Hill, 1967); and Joseph Lecler, *Toleration and the Reformation*, trans. T.L. Westow, 2 vols (London: Longmans, 1960). For the distinctive zone of east-central Europe, see E. William Monter, 'Toleration and Its Discontents in East-Central Europe', in *Ritual, Myth and Magic in Early Modern Europe*, ed. E. William Monter (Athens, OH: Ohio University Press, 1983), 130–47. Among the most conceptually innovative works on this subject are Alexandra Walsham, *Charitable hatred: Tolerance and Intolerance in England, 1500–1700* (Manchester: Manchester University Press, 2006) and Keith P. Luria, *Sacred Boundaries: Religious Coexistence and Conflict in Early-Modern France* (Washington, DC: Catholic University of American Press, 2005).

2 For an overview of the large body of historiography on confessionalisation, see Ute Lotz-Heumann, 'Confessionalization', in *Reformation and Early Modern Europe: A Guide to Research*, ed. David M. Whitford (Kirksville, MI: Truman State University Press, 2008), 136–57.

a great complex of factors – social, political, economic and cultural, as well as religious – led Europe's peoples to embrace and Europe's rulers to impose, if they could, different churches. Some parts of the continent ended up monoconfessional, with a single, overwhelmingly dominant faith: for Iberia and Italy, that was Roman Catholicism; for Scandinavia, Lutheranism. Loose polities, most notably the Holy Roman Empire and Swiss Confederation, included some territories that were more or less uniformly Protestant, like Saxony and Zurich and others that were Catholic, like Bavaria. But Europe as a whole was now profoundly divided by faith, as were kingdoms like France and Hungary. On a local level, the division replicated itself in tens of thousands of communities, large and small, scattered across lands from the British Isles in the west to the great Commonwealth of Poland-Lithuania in the east. Thus there arose the difficult question of how, if at all, people of different faiths could coexist peacefully. Of course, in the Middle Ages some Europeans had lived alongside Jewish communities or, more rarely, encountered Muslims. But in the early modern era, divisions within a once-united western Christendom gave new meaning and unprecedented urgency to the problem of toleration.[3]

How could a state divided by religion avoid falling into civil war? How could subjects of one faith be loyal to a ruler who championed a different one? And how could neighbours and fellow citizens form a cohesive, harmonious community – how could they practice Christian love and charity towards one another – if they did not worship the same God, together? To most early modern Europeans, the answer to all these questions was that they could not. Religion was considered the *vinculum societatis*, the chain that bound society together and churches were the religious embodiment of communities that were simultaneously secular and spiritual entities. Religious divisions were thus understood to be fundamentally incompatible with political and social unity either on the local level or within kingdoms and other states.

At the same time, the very existence of such divisions were understood to impose on sincere Christians a sacred obligation to reject and oppose those forms of Christianity that differed from their own. To be pious, one had to be intolerant, otherwise one's loyalty to the 'true' faith was deemed questionable, one's zeal for it weak. To tolerate meant to be complicit in allowing heinous forms of sin – heresy, idolatry, blasphemy – to be committed. It was thus no virtue; to the contrary, toleration was regarded as a morally dubious act by which one grudgingly endured a regrettable situation. The only accepted excuse for it was that one simply did not have the means to eradicate the evil. In learned circles, it was debated whether civil war was an even greater evil than heresy and whether one could justifiably tolerate the latter if it meant avoiding the former. In either case, religious toleration suffered from a fundamental illegitimacy in post-Reformation Europe, an

3 This chapter deals only with negotiations between different sorts of Christians, not ones between Christians and either Jews or Muslims, which are large topics in their own right and followed rather different patterns.

illegitimacy that would be challenged and reversed only with the Enlightenment and even then only among certain segments of society. Thus in the wake of the Reformations, negotiating religious differences was a very fraught business.

This chapter identifies three different kinds of negotiating process that were undertaken to address the dilemmas posed by religious diversity: ecclesiastical, political and social. These three kinds of process should be considered ideal types. They had distinct dynamics, distinct groups of actors involved and to some extent different goals as well. But in reality these processes overlapped and flowed into one another in a host of ways.

Ecclesiastical processes

The goal of the first, ecclesiastical kind of negotiating process was to restore, in whole or at least in part, the lost unity of Christendom. This was grounded on the belief that the ultimate solution to religious divisions was to resolve and heal them, bringing Christians who were divided by faith back together as members of a single church.[4] Such efforts were the work primarily of ecclesiastics, for they involved discussing in an informed manner and seeking agreement regarding the points of difference that divided the churches. Ecclesiastics conceived of those points primarily in theological terms, concerning above all the respective roles of faith and grace in salvation and the nature of the eucharist. It was the latter that Martin Luther and Huldrych Zwingli famously disputed in 1529 at the Marburg Colloquy. Their failure to find agreement ended any chance of an alliance between German and Swiss Protestants and laid the foundation for a permanent split between Lutherans and Reformed Protestants. Other points concerned church governance: from the beginning, Protestants repudiated the authority of the pope and indeed it was this point more than any other that defeated the efforts at reconciliation made by Protestant and Catholic moderates at the 1541 Regensburg Colloquy. Within the Protestant camp, some held that particular forms of church governance were matters of convenience that could be adapted to changing circumstances, while others believed those forms to be established by divine law and thus non-negotiable. John Calvin himself showed more flexibility on this point than many of his later followers and as a result fierce disputes erupted in England in the seventeenth century between proponents of episcopal, presbyterian and congregational models. This trend towards greater specificity and rigidity was a general one, part and parcel of the confessionalisation process that affected all the European churches of the age.

As the splits between churches grew deeper, the challenge of restoring unity grew increasingly difficult. The most cherished hope of all parties remained always that

4 See in general Howard P. Louthan and Randall C. Zachman, eds *Conciliation and Confession: The Struggle for Unity in the Age of Reform, 1415–1648* (Notre Dame, IN: University of Notre Dame Press, 2004); Kaplan, *Divided by Faith*, chapter 5.

they could convince and convert their opponents, but when that failed, what then? The ecumenically inclined formulated a fall-back strategy: if the theological and other differences between the parties could not be resolved and eliminated, the importance of those differences could at least be minimised. They way to do this was to distinguish between 'fundamental' points and 'indifferent' ones. The former were points that distinguished a true church of Christ from a false one and that a Christian had to believe in order to achieve salvation. The latter, known in theological terminology as 'adiaphora', were matters upon which churches and Christians could differ without consequence. But while the general trend of the age was toward defining more and more matters as fundamental, ecumenists went in the opposite direction, suggesting that the points that currently divided the churches were adiaphoral. So as early as the 1530s the German theologian Georg Witzel proposed that the warring Christian 'factions', as he called the emerging confessions, take the primitive church of the first centuries CE as their model and restrict their dogmas to those teachings found in the writings of the ancient Church Fathers. This approach was codified in 1561 by the Catholic scholar George Cassander, whose maxim was, 'we should uphold [only] what has been believed everywhere, always, by everyone . . .'. Cassander equated this truly 'catholic' (in the original sense of being universal) teaching with the contents of the fourth-century Nicene Creed, to which Catholics, Lutherans, Reformed and Anglicans (though not Anabaptists or Socinians) subscribed.[5] Over the following century, a line of eminent thinkers followed Cassander's lead, proposing definitions of orthodoxy that stripped it to a bare minimum. The English divine William Chillingworth went further, arguing in *The Religion of Protestants* (1637) that only the Bible was fundamental and that everyone was free to interpret it as they saw fit, guided only 'by the light of private reason'.[6]

By acknowledging the unimportance of their differences, ecclesiastic negotiators hoped, at the very least, to establish friendlier relations between their churches. In Poland, Protestant negotiators went further, agreeing in 1570 the Consensus of Sendomir, by which they recognised the validity each other's churches. The ultimate goal, though, remained to bring Christians of different stripes back into communion with one another – to reunite them as members of a single church. The ecumenical way to achieve this was to permit a diversity of views and practices within the church. This approach had various names: 'comprehension', 'latitude', 'ecclesiastical toleration'. In England, it was pursued vigorously by the so-called Latitudinarians, who in the late seventeenth century fashioned enough scope for variety within the Church of England that the latter could accommodate Protestants of different inclinations, from the Arminian to the Puritan. This was

5 Paul Eisenkopf, *Leibniz und die Einigung der Christenheit. Überlegungen zur Reunion der evangelischen und katholischen Kirche, Beiträge zur ökumenischen Theologie* (Munich: Verlag Ferdinand Schöningh, 1975), 109; Lecler, *Toleration and the Reformation* 1: 273.

6 Kamen, *The Rise of Toleration*, 169.

the origin of the distinction between 'High' and 'Low' Church Anglicans, both comprehended within the established church.

As the case of England suggests, comprehension was never a matter of concern only to churchmen. From Queen Elizabeth's time onward, some rulers found that they had a powerful interest in promoting it. The electors of Brandenburg, for example, who from the 1610s ruled as Reformed Protestants over a largely Lutheran population, sponsored a series of efforts to reconcile these two faiths. Similarly, in 1631, when in the midst of the Thirty Years' War German Protestantism faced the threat of annihilation, Lutheran and Reformed theologians met in Leipzig to seek a theological rapprochement that would facilitate a military alliance between their princes. In 1645 King Ladislas IV of Poland convened a great ecumenical conference in the city of Torun. Later in the century, Holy Roman Emperor Leopold I supported tentative negotiations for an ecclesiastic union of German Catholics and Protestants, with a view towards forming a common front against both the Turks, who threatened the Empire from the east and the aggressions of Louis XIV from the west. It would be a mistake also to exclude ordinary lay people from the picture entirely. Though they could neither conduct nor sponsor ecclesiastic negotiations, they could initiate arrangements that amounted to forms of comprehension. In England, for example, some dissenters made a point of attending some services in the established church, practising what was called 'occasional conformity'. In the Dutch Republic, where religious eclecticism and seeking were not unusual, a group known as the Collegiants was formed, including Mennonites, Remonstrants, Socinians and others in its membership. With no clergy, the Collegiants did not form a separate church, but at their meetings they prayed, discussed the Bible and twice a year celebrated communion together.

If ecclesiastical negotiations had succeeded in resolving the rifts between rival churches, other negotiations would not have been needed. That is not how things transpired.

Political processes

As early as 1529, the Protestant and Catholic cantons of Switzerland mobilised their armies against one another. In 1546 the Schmalkaldic War broke out in the Holy Roman Empire. These clashes were small-scale compared to the great religious wars that would follow: the French Wars of Religion (1562–98), the Revolt of the Netherlands (1566–1648), the English Civil War (1642–51), the Deluge in Poland (1655–60) and, most destructive of all, the Thirty Years War in Germany (1618–48). These were not the only cases in which military force was applied to resolve religious differences: most notoriously, after he revoked in 1685 the Edict of Nantes, Louis XIV used his dragoons to force about three quarters of a million Huguenots to convert to Catholicism, at least nominally. One could classify such military engagements as forms of religious negotiation, in the sense that their outcome could determine the religious complexion of communities and entire countries. But they did not involve the kind of dialogue or compromise usually implied by the term 'negotiation'. What they make graphically clear is the extent to which the outcome of Europe's great schism was determined by those who wielded coercive force.

Already in the fifteenth century Europe's princes and magistrates had increased their involvement and extended their jurisdiction in ecclesiastic affairs. When in 1521 Elector Frederick III of Saxony prevented the arrest of Martin Luther, he set in motion a process that handed to secular rulers like himself the power to choose between rival faiths, not only for themselves but for the peoples of the lands they ruled. The principle of *cuius regio eius religio* became law in the Holy Roman Empire: the ruler of a territory had a right to choose between faiths (Catholic or Lutheran) and to impose his choice on his territories. Elsewhere in western and central Europe, *cuius regio* became the de facto reality. With the failure of clergy to resolve religious differences, secular authorities had the lead negotiating role thrust upon them, a role they accepted in their capacity as 'Christian magistrates', responsible for the spiritual as well as material welfare of their subjects and also because it furthered their aim of amassing power.

Wars end when those who dispose over armies make peace and the treaties of Augsburg in 1555 and Westphalia in 1648 are arguably the two most important religious peace treaties in European history.[7] Less well known, the Protestant and Catholic cantons of Switzerland concluded a series of four treaties, known as *Landfrieden*, in 1529, 1531, 1656 and 1712.[8] These documents are the products of a literal, formal kind of negotiation over religious differences. Of course, religious and political issues intermingled in all these treaties and only one of the two agreements that comprise the Peace of Westphalia, the Treaty of Osnabrück, primarily addressed religious disputes. But the 109 delegations who fashioned this peace engaged (though not all simultaneously) in explicit negotiations for some 5 years.[9] They consisted mostly of ministers of state, diplomats, lawyers and delegates from political entities such as the Dutch States General. In the case of these and other treaties, the terms of coexistence between Christians of different churches were essentially agreed by rulers and their representatives through political and diplomatic processes. However, these terms were always grounded in the realities of relations between people of different faiths, so that the sensibilities and practices of ordinary people always had at least an indirect influence.

Unlike the abovementioned treaties, the famous Edict of Nantes was a unilateral act by a sovereign king, France's Henri IV. In fact, it was the last in a series of 'edicts of pacification' by which the French crown sought to end the French

7 The text of the two treaties can be found in Ernst Walder, ed. *Religionsvergleiche des 16. Jahrhunderts* (Bern: Herbert Lang & Cie, 1974); 'Die Westfälischen Friedensverträge vom 24. Oktober 1648. Texte und Übersetzungen', www.pax-westphalica.de/ipmipo/index.html (accessed 4 December 2014).

8 G.M. von Knonau *et al.*, ed. *Amtliche Sammlung der ältern eidgenössischen Abschiede*, 8 vols. (Lucern: Meyer, 1839–86), 4/1B: 1478–86, 1567–77; 6/1B: 1633–7; 6/2B: 2330–40.

9 Derek Croxton, *Westphalia: The Last Christian Peace* (Basingstoke: Palgrave Macmillan, 2013), 191–328.

religious wars.[10] With Nantes, it finally succeeded, more or less.[11] There were three, not two, warring parties in the realm: Catholic extremists, known as Leaguers; Catholic royalists; and Huguenots. The Edict of Nantes was not the product of formal negotiation between them, but of an assessment by an astute monarch (himself a convert from Protestantism to Catholicism) and his ministers of what might satisfy the parties sufficiently and create the basis for a lasting peace. To be implemented, though, it had to be approved by the supreme courts of France, known as *parlements*, which were bastions of anti-Huguenot sentiment. Knowing that the *parlements* would never approve them, Henri kept certain provisions of the Edict secret; the *parlements* required modification of others. Essentially, though, the Edict of Nantes was a royal decree and as Huguenots eventually learned to their bitter dismay, what one king could grant, another could revoke.

Like the Edict of Nantes, the English Toleration Act of 1689 was a law issued unilaterally, in this case by King-in-Parliament. It was a product not of civil war but of the Glorious Revolution, whereby the Catholic James II was deposed and replaced by the Dutch Protestant William III of Orange. William had promised that there would be such an Act before launching his invasion of England in 1688, so that the Act was in effect one of the terms on which he was accepted as king. Contrary to expectation, though, Parliament refused to issue an accompanying Comprehension Act, which would have allowed many Protestant dissenters to remain within the established church and would have obviated the need for them to be 'tolerated' in the conventional sense, that is, to be allowed to have their own, separate chapels and services.[12]

The acceptance of a ruler on condition that he grant religious dissenters certain rights was a regular event in Poland. The Polish crown was not hereditary but elected, and in 1573, during an interregnum, the nobles who constituted the national assembly, or *Sejm*, agreed a document known as the Warsaw Confederation. It constituted a pledge that they

> who differ with regard to religion will keep the peace with one another, and will not for a different faith or a change of churches shed blood nor punish one another by confiscation of property, infamy, imprisonment or banishment, and will not in any way assist any magistrate or officer in such an act.[13]

10 André Stegmann, ed. *Édits des guerres de religion* (Paris: Vrin, 1979); Richard L. Goodbar, ed. *The Edict of Nantes: Five Essays and A New Translation* (Bloomington, IN: The National Huguenot Society, 1998). For an introduction, see Mack P. Holt, *The French Wars of Religion, 1562–1629* (Cambridge: Cambridge University Press, 1995).

11 The wars revived temporarily in the 1620s.

12 See esp. Ole Peter Grell, Jonathan I. Israel and Nicholas Tyacke, eds *From Persecution to Toleration: The Glorious Revolution and Religion in England* (Oxford: Clarendon Press, 1991). A facsimile of the 1689 Act appears at 411–28.

13 Earl Morse Wilbur, *A History of Unitarianism*, 2 vols (Boston, MA: Beacon Press, 1945), 1: 363–4. For a general history of toleration in Poland, see Janusz Tazbir, *A State Without Stakes: Polish Religious Toleration in the Sixteenth and Seventeenth Centuries*, The Library of Polish studies (New York: Kosciuszko Foundation, 1973).

This was in the first place an agreement among the nobles to maintain peaceful relations with one another despite their religious differences (at the time, about half the members of the Polish Senate were Protestant). Like the English Toleration Act, it did not enunciate any principle of religious toleration or freedom. Rather, it reflected the character of the Polish polity as a 'republic of noblemen', all of whom were formally equal to one another and the nobles' fear of religious unrest from below and oppression from above. The agreement was struck at a moment when public opinion across much of Europe was reeling from the shock of the St. Bartholomew's Day massacres the year before, in which the prospective candidate for the Polish monarchy was suspected of being complicit. At this juncture, the *Sejm* added an oath to the articles that Polish kings-elect had to swear as part of their coronation ceremony. By it, the future monarch promised that he would 'preserve and maintain peace and quiet among those that differ with regard to religion and will not in any way . . . suffer anyone to be influenced or oppressed by reason of his religion . . .'.[14] As Polish nobles in the seventeenth and eighteenth century discovered, however, the lack of an institutional mechanism to enforce the oath meant that in practice, their Catholic kings were able to undermine and suppress Protestantism, as they did increasingly, though never entirely.

The above are just some of the most important treaties, edicts and laws that regulated relations between Christians of different churches in early modern Europe. What they and others had in common was their character as explicit, public commitments that were made with the authority of the state. This character, in and of itself, had enormous consequences for relations between religious groups. In the first place, the very existence of such written, often legal commitments meant that religious divisions were publicly and officially acknowledged. In an age when a separation of church and state in the modern sense was almost inconceivable, acknowledging such divisions meant that rulers were sanctioning and in effect approving the practice of more than one faith. More than that, it meant that the state would protect the faiths in question and, in many cases, lend them support and funding, in effect creating an official religious establishment that consisted of two or more faiths and churches. All subjects of the state were obliged by law to belong to one or another of the established churches and fell under its jurisdiction, while other versions of Christianity were outlawed. Early modern historians call this arrangement bi- or multi-confessionalism, depending on the number of faiths established.[15] Few rulers found such an arrangement easy to accept, given how directly it seemed to conflict with their duty as Christian magistrates to combat false religions. The bi- or multi-confessionalism of a polity did not mean necessarily that local communities were, or became, religiously mixed: in Switzerland, for example, most of the cantons that formed the core of the confederation were entirely Catholic or Reformed Protestant. At the confederal level, though, institutions like the *Tagsatzung* were indeed mixed, while others were divided into

14 Earl Morse Wilbur, *A History of Unitarianism*, 2 vols. (Boston, MA: Beacon Press, 1945), 1: 363–4.
15 Safley, *Companion to Multiconfessionalism*, xx.

Catholic and Reformed sections. Two cantons, Glarus and Appenzell, were bi-confessional, as were subject territories such as Thurgau and Rheintal that fell under the authority of both Protestant and Catholic cantons. On the local level, in bi-confessional villages that had only one church, Catholics and Protestants often had to share its use, a practice known as *Simultaneum*.[16]

This is not to say that the letter of a law or treaty ever translated neatly into lived realities. To the contrary, interpreting such documents, implementing their terms and subsequently enforcing them were all areas open to contestation and negotiation. Indeed, a large part of their point and purpose was to establish a framework for contestation – a set of limits and rules that excluded (or at least minimised) violence and disorder, channelled hostilities into legal and judicial processes and gave secular authorities a decisive say in the outcome. The intention was not to end hostilities and resolve conflict; that seemed, for the time being, beyond anyone's power. It was rather to contain and regulate them.

The Edict of Nantes offers a prime example. Learning from the experience of past edicts, which had all failed within a few years, its authors made the terms of the edict comprehensive and very detailed, encompassing no fewer than 92 public articles and 56 secret ones, plus 2 secret brevets. Few issues were left unregulated, especially not ones that had triggered violent clashes in the past, such as the refusal by Protestants to celebrate Catholic feast days. Even so, the royal government had to send commissions out to the provinces to determine how the Edict's terms could be applied and effectuated in the extremely varied circumstances of local communities, large and small, across France. This created a first opportunity for negotiation, as commissioners heard representations from both sides – from local Protestants and Catholics – regarding, for example, the places of worship Protestants had been using as of 1577 or 1596–97, which Huguenots had a right of 'possession' to retain under one provision of the Edict.[17] In the longer run, jurisdiction over the enforcement of the Edict was put in the hands of a set of courts known as 'chambers of the Edict', which were annexed to the various supreme courts of the kingdom. These chambers consisted of both Protestant and Catholic jurists, whose numbers in the three southern chambers were kept equal ('mi-parti'), an arrangement known at the time as 'parity'. In the north, however, the chambers proved to be far from neutral. Catholics in provinces like Poitou could often count on favourable rulings from their chamber, which encouraged them actually to use the chambers and the law in general as tools of aggression. Similarly, the only appeal from the chambers was to the royal council, which under Louis XIV was reliably anti-Protestant and indeed colluded with the *parlements* in undermining the jurisdiction of the chambers. The contrast to the Holy Roman Empire is sharp, for there, under the Peace of Westphalia, the equivalent institutions and mechanisms were more balanced and impartial. Even in France, though, the Edict and

16 For an overview, see *Handbuch der Schweizer Geschichte*, 2nd edn, 2 vols. (Zurich: Berichthaus, 1980).

17 See e.g. Elisabeth Rabut, *Le roi, l'église et le temple. L'Éxecution de l'Édit de Nantes en Dauphiné* (Grenoble: Editions la pensée sauvage, 1987).

its chambers channelled a significant portion of the religious conflicts that subsequently arose into legal and judicial processes.

What was the alternative to such processes? Were there ways to accommodate religious diversity without making it official and institutionalising it? Indeed there were and in general rulers preferred them to the kind of arrangements discussed above. We turn herewith to the realm of informal, social processes for negotiating religious differences.

Social processes

According to contemporaries, the most tolerant land in early modern Europe was the Dutch Republic.[18] Created as a result of the Revolt of the Netherlands against their Habsburg overlord, Philip II of Spain, the Republic had a wider variety of religious groups than any other land in Europe and from across the continent refugees from persecution fled to it. Cities like Amsterdam, Rotterdam, Haarlem and Utrecht had thoroughly mixed populations, with people of different faiths living cheek by jowl. Yet the Republic was not bi- or multi-confessional. To the contrary, it was officially a Reformed (Calvinist) polity. To serve in almost any governmental office one had to support the Dutch Reformed Church, which had sole use of the old parish churches inherited from the Middle Ages and was the sole recipient of funding from the public purse. The only religious right that non-Calvinists officially enjoyed was freedom of conscience, a right laid down in the Union of Utrecht (1579), which served the Republic as a quasi-constitutional, founding document. Article 13 of the Union stipulated that 'every individual shall remain free in his religion and . . . no one shall be investigated or prosecuted because of his religion'.[19] This meant that no one could be forced to join the Reformed Church or attend its services, nor could anyone be investigated or prosecuted for their beliefs. The Republic, then, was a polity with a single, uniquely privileged, official church and non-Calvinists were by definition dissenters. However, that church was not established in the conventional sense of membership of it being required by law and its power over non-members was extremely limited. As the faith of the Republic's enemy, Spain, Catholicism was subject to special restrictions; celebrating mass, administering Catholic sacraments and assembling for Catholic worship were illegal. But even Catholics, along with other dissenters, were free to believe as they wished.

Apart from these fairly limited legal stipulations, the negotiation of relations between people of different faiths in the Republic was left mostly to informal processes. To begin with, as everyone recognised, no pious dissenter could content him- or herself with believing correctly; early modern Christianity in all its forms

18 On religious toleration in the Dutch Republic, see most recently Christine Kooi, *Calvinists and Catholics During Holland's Golden Age: Heretics and Idolaters* (Cambridge: Cambridge University Press, 2012).

19 S. Groenveld and H.L.Ph. Leeuwenberg, eds *De Unie van Utrecht. Wording en werking van een verbond en een verbondsacte* (The Hague: Nijhoff, 1979), 34.

demanded that faith be translated into correct forms of divine worship and other pious acts. How and where, then, could non-Calvinists practise their faith? The answer lay in a distinction between public and private spheres. For if the Reformed Church alone was allowed to manifest itself publicly, the freedom of conscience that dissenters enjoyed meant in practice that, behind closed doors in the private sphere, they could do as they pleased. Individuals and families could pray and worship at home in accord with their beliefs. This much they had a right to do. Negotiation began when they sought to do more than that, as they invariably did, out of a duty and a need to have congregations, clergy and churches. What dissenters did therefore was refurbish some of their homes – and also, with time, other private structures such as barns and warehouses – for use as places of communal worship. The result was a topography spotted with dissenting churches, all invisible from the outside, at least superficially. These edifices had none of the external markers of churches – no towers or bells, no crosses, statues or stained glass (something that suited some Protestant dissenting groups, such as the Mennonites, well anyway). Everyone – local magistrates, Calvinist clergy and of course neighbours, who could not help but notice crowds of people coming and going – knew where these places of worship were, but so long as dissenters maintained a façade of privacy and respected the monopoly of the Reformed Church over the public sphere, their churches and assemblies were usually left in peace. Corrupt sheriffs, local politics and other actors and events that temporarily raised fears about Catholics in particular were the cause of occasional raids, but these decreased over time, especially after 1648, when the Republic and Spain finally made peace.

Thus, by a tacit, almost purely informal arrangement, dissenting worship was tolerated in the Dutch Republic to a degree unmatched elsewhere in Europe. On the other hand, the combination of a single official church plus dissenting worship conducted in private was in no way restricted to the Netherlands. In England and Scotland likewise, Catholicism was practised in private chapels, many of them located in the manor houses of gentry. Such quasi-clandestine places of worship for dissenters could be found also in Austria, Switzerland and the Holy Roman Empire. They went by a wide variety of names: house churches, prayer houses, meeting houses, mass houses, house chapels, oratories, assembly places. Their location, size and degree of secrecy were all sensitive matters subject to negotiation between dissenters, on the one hand, and magistrates and ordinary conforming members of the local official church on the other, who could choose to look the other way and tolerate the chapels, or not. Negotiations might be verbal and explicit, but more often they were neither, involving consent granted through silence on conditions that were unstated but understood. When these tacit settlements broke down, as when dissenters sought to expand the limits of the private space within which they were tolerated, the result could be violence.[20]

20 On house chapels, see Benjamin J. Kaplan, 'Fictions of Privacy: House Chapels and the Spatial Accommodation of Religious Dissent in Early Modern Europe', *American Historical Review* 107 (2002): 1031–64.

Drawing a new distinction, for religious purposes, between public and private spheres was not the only way that dissenting worship was informally accommodated in early modern Europe. Another mechanism that involved the (re)configuration of space was the practice known in German as *Auslaufen* and involving travel. If dissenters were allowed to reside in a community where dissenting worship was not tolerated, even privately, dissenters could potentially journey to attend services held in another community, one where their form of worship was tolerated or even established. If states with different official religions shared a border with each other, then dissenters who lived within a reasonable distance from that border might travel across it. This was a common practice particularly in those parts of western and central Europe where the territories of states were small and fragmented. Thus, for example, Protestants who lived in the Catholic city of Aachen in the seventeenth and eighteenth centuries were accustomed to travelling to the Dutch village of Vaals, which lay just beyond the border of Aachen's territory. The trip took them less than an hour, but by crossing the border onto Dutch territory they entered a space where the Reformed faith was official and other forms of Protestant worship were tolerated. The case of Aachen and Vaals, though, also points to a major change in the practice of *Auslaufen* in the mid-seventeenth century. What had begun as early as the 1530s in some places as an entirely informal practice, the expression of a tacit compact between dissenters, magistrates and ordinary conforming Christians, gained legal sanction under the Peace of Westphalia, which granted to dissenters a formal right to travel to other states to worship. Here again we see the blurring of distinctions between our three types of negotiation and overlap between the groups of actors participating in them.

How dissenting worship could be accommodated was hardly the only matter that had to be negotiated between people of different faiths in mixed communities. To give just one example, when people entered into religiously mixed marriages, they had to confront thorny questions such as how their children would be baptised and raised – in the husband's faith or the wife's. This was a matter for negotiation in the first place between prospective spouses, but a wide range of other parties – kinfolk, neighbours, magistrates and of course clergy – might well involve themselves. Agreements between prospective spouses might be purely oral or they might be formalised through inclusion in prenuptial contracts. Likewise, subsequent disagreements between spouses might take the form of intramural quarrels or one party might appeal to external authorities to intervene. In any event, church and state authorities were always a presence, at least in the background of such negotiations, as official norms and laws established a framework, sometimes loose, other times highly constraining, within which individuals acted.[21]

21 On interfaith marriage, see Kaplan, 'Intimate Negotiations: Husbands and Wives of Opposing Faiths in Eighteenth-Century Holland', in *Living with Diversity in Early Modern Europe*, eds C. Scott Dixon, Dagmar Freist and Mark Greengrass (Farnham, UK: Ashgate, 2009); Kaplan, *Cunegonde's Kidnapping: A Story of Religious Conflict in the Age of Enlightenment* (New Haven, CT: Yale University Press, 2014); and the forthcoming Dagmar Freist, *Glaube – Liebe – Zwietracht. Konfessionell gemischte Ehen in Deutschland in der Frühen Neuzeit* (Munich: Oldenbourg Verlag, 2016).

Conclusion

Negotiation of religious differences in early modern Europe was not a one-time affair or restricted to a few key historical moments; rather, it was an ongoing process. Negotiation not only involved clergy and rulers, nobles and magistrates, but also rank-and-file religious dissenters and ordinary conforming Christians. The need for it arose from the unexpected, undesired heritage of the sixteenth-century reformations and the confessionalisation process that followed in their wake, leaving Europe permanently divided by faith. In retrospect, one can see a turning point in the conclusion of the Catholic Council of Trent (1545–63), which defined Catholic orthodoxy in contradistinction to Protestant teaching and reasserted the validity of traditional Catholic practices, even as it reformed them. After that, no full reconciliation of Protestants and Catholics was ever really possible. This was not how things were perceived at the time, though and it is remarkable how persistent the desire for ecclesiastic reunification remained through the seventeenth century and beyond.

The starting point for the political negotiations undertaken by ruling elites was an acceptance, if only a provisional one, of Europe's new religious divisions. The goal of such negotiations was usually to divide rights, powers, territories, properties and/or revenues along religious lines and to regulate relations between religious groups. Unsurprisingly, therefore, resulting treaties, edicts and laws usually entailed a formal recognition of the groups and a ratification of the divisions between them. It is thus no wonder that such negotiations were undertaken extremely reluctantly, usually as a last resort to end religious-civil strife. Informal, social negotiations, by contrast, tended not to have these effects. Even when they involved the acknowledgement of religious differences, they did not reify the latter to the same extent. In states with a single official church, religious dissent was often tolerated precisely by not recognising it – by turning a blind eye while dissenters worshiped either privately or across a border. Such 'toleration by connivance' was the modus operandi of the most tolerant regime in early modern Europe, that of the Dutch Republic.

Both the formal – political and ecclesiastical – and the informal – social – forms of negotiation we have examined were practical responses to the dilemmas posed by religious divisions. While both had certain principled foundations, including commitments to the rule of law and freedom of conscience, neither was based on the modern notion of human rights, which only emerged during the Enlightenment of the eighteenth century. Nevertheless, both the formal and informal processes scored some notable successes in maintaining or restoring peace in early modern Europe. Without valorising religious diversity, they produced workable arrangements to accommodate it.

References

Bonney, Richard and D.J.B. Trim, eds *Persecution and Pluralism: Calvinists and Religious Minorities in Early Modern Europe, 1550–1700*. Oxford-Bern: Peter Lang, 2006.

Croxton, Derek. *Westphalia: The Last Christian Peace*. Basingstoke: Palgrave Macmillan, 2013.

Die Westfälischen Friedensverträge Vom 24. Oktober 1648. Texte Und Übersetzungen. www.pax-westphalica.de/ipmipo/index.html, accessed 4 December 2014.

Dixon, C. Scott, Dagmar Freist and Mark Greengrass, eds *Living with Religious Diversity in Early Modern Europe*. Farnham, UK: Ashgate, 2009.

Eisenkopf, Paul. *Leibniz Und Die Einigung Der Christenheit. Überlegungen Zur Reunion Der Evangelischen Und Katholischen Kirche. Beiträge Zur Ökumenischen Theologie*. Munich: Verlag Ferdinand Schöningh, 1975.

Freist, Dagmar. *Glaube – Liebe – Zwietracht. Konfessionell Gemischte Ehen in Deutschland in Der Frühen Neuzeit*. Munich: Oldenbourg Verlag, 2014.

Goodbar, Richard L., ed. *The Edict of Nantes: Five Essays and a New Translation*. Bloomington, MN: The National Huguenot Society, 1998.

Grell, Ole Peter and Bob Scribner, eds *Tolerance and Intolerance in the European Reformation*. Cambridge: Cambridge University Press, 1996.

Grell, Ole Peter, Jonathan I. Israel and Nicholas Tyacke, eds *From Persecution to Toleration: The Glorious Revolution and Religion in England*. Oxford: Clarendon Press, 1991.

Groenveld, S. and H.L.Ph. Leeuwenberg, eds *De Unie Van Utrecht. Wording En Werking Van Een Verbond En Een Verbondsacte*. The Hague: Nijhoff, 1979.

Handbuch Der Schweizer Geschichte. 2nd ed., 2 vols Zurich: Berichthaus, 1980.

Holt, Mack P. *The French Wars of Religion, 1562–1629*. Cambridge: Cambridge University Press, 1995.

Kamen, Henry. *The Rise of Toleration*. New York: McGraw-Hill, 1967.

Kaplan, Benjamin J. 'Fictions of Privacy: House Chapels and the Spatial Accommodation of Religious Dissent in Early Modern Europe', *American Historical Review* 107 (2002): 1031–64.

——. *Divided by Faith: Religious Conflict and the Practice of Toleration in Early Modern Europe*. Cambridge, MA: Harvard University Press, 2007.

——. 'Intimate Negotiations: Husbands and Wives of Opposing Faiths in Eighteenth-Century Holland', in *Living with Diversity in Early Modern Europe*, edited by C. Scott Dixon, Dagmar Freist and Mark Greengrass. 225–48. Farnham, UK: Ashgate, 2009.

——. *Cunegonde's Kidnapping: A Story of Religious Conflict in the Age of Enlightenment*. New Haven, CT: Yale University Press, 2014.

Knonau, G.M. von, J.K. Krütli, A.P. Segesser, D.A. Fechter, J.A. Pupikoter and J. Kaiser, eds *Amtliche Sammlung der ältern eidgenössischen Abschiede*, 8 vols (Lucern: Meyer, 1839–86).

Kooi, Christine. *Calvinists and Catholics During Holland's Golden Age: Heretics and Idolaters*. Cambridge: Cambridge University Press, 2012.

Laursen, John Christian and Cary J. Nederman, eds *Beyond the Persecuting Society: Religious Toleration Before the Enlightenment*. Philadelphia, PA: University of Pennsylvania Press, 1998.

Lecler, Joseph. *Toleration and the Reformation*. Translated by T.L. Westow, 2 vols. London: Longmans, 1960.

Lotz-Heumann, Ute. 'Confessionalization', in *Reformation and Early Modern Europe: A Guide to Research*, edited by David M. Whitford. 136–57. Kirksville, MI: Truman State University Press, 2008.

Louthan, Howard P. and Randall C. Zachman, eds *Conciliation and Confession: The Struggle for Unity in the Age of Reform, 1415–1648*. Notre Dame, IN: University of Notre Dame Press, 2004.

Louthan, Howard, Gary B. Cohen and Franz A.J. Szabo, eds *Diversity and Dissent: Negotiating Religious Difference in Central Europe, 1500–1800*. Oxford: Berghahn, 2011.

Luria, Keith P. *Sacred Boundaries: Religious Coexistence and Conflict in Early-Modern France*. Washington, DC: Catholic University of American Press, 2005.

Marshall, John. *John Locke, Toleration and Early Enlightenment Culture*. Cambridge: Cambridge University Press, 2006.

Monter, E. William. 'Toleration and Its Discontents in East-central Europe', in *Ritual, Myth and Magic in Early Modern Europe*, edited by E. William Monter. 130–47. Athens, OH: Ohio University Press, 1983.

Rabut, Elisabeth. *Le Roi, L'église Et Le Temple. L'éxecution De L'édit De Nantes En Dauphiné*. Grenoble: Editions la pensée sauvage, 1987.

Safley, Thomas Max, ed. A *Companion to Multiconfessionalism in the Early Modern World*. Leiden: Brill, 2011.

Stegmann, André, ed. *Édits Des Guerres De Religion*. Paris: Vrin, 1979.

Tazbir, Janusz. *A State without Stakes: Polish Religious Toleration in the Sixteenth and Seventeenth Centuries. The Library of Polish Studies*. New York: Kosciuszko Foundation, 1973.

Walder, Ernst, ed. *Religionsvergleiche Des 16. Jahrhunderts*. Bern: Herbert Lang & Cie, 1974.

Walsham, Alexandra. *Charitable Hatred: Tolerance and Intolerance in England, 1500–1700*. Manchester: Manchester University Press, 2006.

Wanegffelen, Thierry. *L'édit De Nantes: Une Histoire Européenne De La Tolérance Du Xvie Au Xxe Siècle*. Paris: Librairie générale française, 1998.

Wilbur, Earl Morse. *A History of Unitarianism*, 2 vols, Boston, MA: Beacon Press, 1945.

3 Negotiating under duress

The expulsion of Salzburg Protestants (1732) and the Jews of Prague (1744)

François Guesnet

Around 100 years after the Peace of Westphalia of 1648 concluded 30 years of religious warfare in central Europe and a number of political and legal instruments to regulate and accomodate religious diversity had been agreed upon, two cases of mass expulsions of religious minorities became *causes célèbres* of their time. In 1732, a large number of Crypto-Protestants were expelled from the Catholic archbishopric of Salzburg and, in 1744, the Jews of Prague, then the largest and most prestigious Jewish community in Central Europe, suffered the same fate. In both cases, the number of exiles was very significant: in the case of the Salzburg Protestants, around 20,000 individuals were directly affected; in the case of the Prague Jewish community, around 15,000 were. Both expulsion decrees indiscriminately banned the entire religious community, but neither was justified on the basis of religious reasons. Rather, these communities were declared a threat to the commonwealth and their removal a necessity to maintain public order and security. In both cases, the expulsion had considerable negative economic consequences, depriving the archbishopric of Salzburg of sought-after craftsmen, especially in the salt mining industry and the imperial city of Prague of an indispensible group of merchants, bankers and entrepreneurs. Contemporary observers saw these harsh measures as a relapse into practices of a bygone era of prejudice and cruelty, not becoming of the age of growing rationalism and enlightenment. The expulsion of Protestants from Salzburg in 1732 and of the Jews from Prague in 1744 was closely linked to the growing executive power of the state in general and the tendency of absolutist rulers to assert themselves, even against reasonable objections.

This chapter juxtaposes the events leading to the expulsions and highlights the negotiation strategies implemented by the two affected religious minorities. It will assess how these communities formulated their grievances and requests, how they built alliances with external actors and how defence lines were drawn in order to protect the communities's wellbeing. The most important strategic difference appears to have been that while the Protestants and their supporters built a massive public campaign to further their cause, those Jews and non-Jews who strove to undo the expulsion of the Prague Jewish community would avoid the unnecessary publicising of their rescue efforts. It seems the harsh fate of the Salzburg Protestants provided an example that the Jews of Prague decided to avoid, which is particularly visible in the striking absence of any attempts on the part of the Prague Jews to plead for support in the emerging public sphere. This comparative history illuminates the different ways in which religious minorities are able to negotiate socio-political contexts in which they are regarded as a problem and the historical pathways that affect the strategies they use to defend their interests.

Salzburg 1732: confessional mobilisation and the failure of negotiation

The archbishopric of Salzburg belonged to the Catholic Church, with the archbishop officiating as Primate of the Catholics in the Holy Roman Empire of German Nations.[1] A substantial number of inhabitants had converted to Protestantism after the Reformation, but growing pressure on them during the counter-reformation had led to the emergence of a large community of Crypto-Protestants. Crypto-Protestants were pro forma Catholic subjects who privately belonged to small, clandestine Protestant congregations led by highly committed laymen.[2] This religious practice relied on migrant Protestant workers and individual exiles smuggling edifying literature from nearby Protestant territories or imperial cities into Salzburg. For generations, Catholic authorities had chosen to prosecute only a limited number of particularly restive individuals as well as highly visible demonstrations of religious insubordination. The reason for this cautious approach was the considerable risk for a relatively small commonwealth to provoke reactions from the Protestant estates and commonwealths within the Empire. After the Peace of Westphalia, these had formed a loose association known as *corpus evangelicorum*.[3] A negative reaction could also come from the leading Protestant commonwealths: England, Sweden, Denmark and the General Estates. Political actors outside and inside the Empire had, on several occasions, forcefully taken the side of Catholic authorities in the Salzburg archbishopric to contain Crypto-Protestantism.[4] As early as the seventeenth century, representatives of this underground religious minority had pleaded their cause at the Imperial Diet and demonstrated thorough knowledge of the stipulations of the Peace of Westphalia. Protestant requests included the plea not to be separated from their children in the process of forced emigration, an extremely distressing practice that the archbishopric's authorities

1 The most recent analyses of the expulsion of the Salzburg Protestants are Gabriele Emrich, *Die Emigration der Salzburger Protestanten 1731–1732. Reichsrechtliche und konfessionspolitische Aspekte* (Münster: LIT Verlag, 2002) and the more comprehensive Mack Walker, *The Salzburg Transaction. Expulsion and Redemption in Eighteenth-Century Germany* (Ithaca, NY, London: Cornell University Press, 1992); see also Rudolf Leeb, 'Die große Salzburger Emigration von 1731/32 und ihre Vorgeschichte (Ausweisung der Deferegger 1684)', in *Glaubensflüchtlinge: Ursachen, Formen und Auswirkungen frühneuzeitlicher Konfessionsmigration in Europa*, ed. Joachim Bahlcke (Münster: LIT Verlag, 2008), 277–306.

2 Leeb, *Salzburger Emigration*, 279.

3 Its most prominent members were Prussia, Saxony, Brunswick-Hanover and the imperial cities of Nurnberg, Frankfurt (Main) and Hamburg.

4 Leeb, *Salzburger Emigration*, 284–5.

routinely undertook when Protestant families chose exile over clandestine religious practice. They asked also to be granted the *triennium*, a hiatus of 3 years granted to members of a dissenting religious community in order that they prepare for emigration (a right intensely debated in the context of the expulsion of 1732) and for privately held Protestant services to be admitted through the authorities. The Peace of Westphalia, however, only granted these rights to those religious minorities who had conformed to the laws of the commonwealth they lived in.[5]

The strong political support that the Salzburg Crypto-Protestants received from Protestant commonwealths represented at the Imperial Diet and from European commonwealths outside the Empire constitutes an important factor shaping Salzburg Protestants' assertive strategy to form delegations, to plead a minority's case and to request accommodation from the local Catholic authorities.[6] Both confessional solidarity and the pursuit of particularistic political agendas contributed to the Protestant commonwealths' resolve to rally behind the Salzburg Crypto-Protestant's requests and to transform it into an issue of major imperial relevance. The Protestant Imperial Estates equally justified their right to speak on behalf of the interests of minoritarian Protestants in Catholic commonwealths, the *ius intercedendi*, with the stipulations of the Peace of Westphalia, a claim energetically contested by their Catholic counterparts in the case of the Crypto-Protestants of Salzburg. They agreed with the archbishopric's authorities' position that, despite their professing to belong to Protestant confessions, the Crypto-Protestants were still born Catholics and were beyond the authority of the *corpus evangelicorum*, which, according to the Catholic estates, lacked constitutional standing anyway. One cause of the political impasse that preceded expulsion was the formal rejection by Salzburg's representative at the Imperial Diet of any legitimacy of the *corpus evangelicorum* to speak on behalf of the Crypto-Protestants.[7] This representative maintained that the Emperor was the only legitimate arbiter of appeal, thus placing individual Crypto-Protestant claimants in a significantly weaker position than they might have been were they represented by major imperial power players. From the point of view of imperial law and administrative practice, the position of the Salzburg prince and sovereign was comparatively strong, which both the local Crypto-Protestant population and their spokespeople at the Imperial Diet in Regensburg attempted to balance above all by insisting on the Salzburg authorities' practice of separating children from their emigrating parents on the grounds of the childrens' formal membership in the Catholic church. Thus, conflicts arising from the presence of a considerable Crypto-Protestant community in Salzburg erupted many times. Until the crisis of 1730, these asymmetric confrontations between the Crypto-Protestant populace and the Salzburg authorities had not

5 Ibid., 287.

6 The *corpus evangelicorum* intervened on numerous interventions with the authorities in Salzburg, as documented in Eberhard Christian Wilhelm von Schauroth, *Vollständige Sammlung aller Conclusorum, Schreiben und anderer übriger Verhandlungen des hochpreißlichen Corpus Evangelicorum. Theil 1–3* (Regensburg: Neubauer, 1751–2), here pt. 1, 113–17.

7 Ibid., 414–18.

undermined the ability of the conflicting parties to maintain an uneasy status quo. Why then was the situation in 1730 different from earlier periods? Which factors exacerbated the confrontation between authorities and Crypto-Protestants to a degree that neither the Protestant nor the Catholic side would be able to compromise or agree on an exit strategy? Among the central factors in this development were the negotiation strategies applied by the Salzburg Crypto-Protestants, the archbishop's need to stabilise his reign and, no less important, the attempt of sovereigns and confessional interest groups within and beyond the Holy Roman Empire to take advantage of this crisis to pursue their own interests.

An important trigger for these developments was the precarious position of archbishop Firmian, who took office in 1729 against the wishes of the Emperor and the Holy See. Among the measures taken to prove himself as Catholic Primate were attempts to force Crypto-Protestants to use a Catholic greeting formula, to wear a specific cloth on the shoulders, to pray the rosary and to enforce these steps by police force.[8] Widespread popular resistance was the result. Two Crypto-Protestants who were to be put on trial for possessing and distributing Lutheran literature fled Salzburg territory, went to Regensburg in the early summer of 1731 and turned to members of the *corpus evangelicorum*, the above mentioned assocation of Protestant estates and commonwealths represented in the Imperial Diet in Regensburg. The latter were also the recipients of a *Petition of the 19,000*, written by 'spokespeople of 19,000 people of the Augsburgian confession sighing under a intolerable yoke' and a strong signal of growing organisation of the Crypto-Protestant community.[9] Delegates from Salzburg called on Protestant powers in the Empire to support the suffering minority, one consequence of which was the emergence of a very considerable number of publications, both popular and academic, defending the oppressed Crypto-Protestants in Salzburg.[10] The first history of the expulsion was published in 1732 (and reprinted four times in the next 2 years)[11] and continuing tensions between Protestant and Catholic Estates at the Imperial Diet were documented on an ongoing basis by the young and energetic expert in constitutional law and ardent Protestant, Johann Jacob Moser (1701–85).[12] Catholic representatives to the Imperial Diet would routinely challenge

8 Walker, *Salzburg Transaction*, 39–47.

9 Ibid., 45 and Franz Xaver Huber, *Aktenmäßige Geschichte der berühmten salzburgischen Emigration: Nach dem Manuskript des Johannes Baptist Caspari übersetzt und mit Vorbericht begleitet von Franz Xaver Huber* (Salzburg: Mayer Verlag, 1790), 8–9.

10 A comprehensive bibliography in Artur Ehmer, *Das Schrifttum zur Salzburger Emigration 1731/33* (Hamburg: Verein für Familienforschung in West- und Ostpreußen, 1975).

11 Christoph Sancke, *Ausführliche Historie derer Emigranten Oder Vertriebenen Lutheraner aus dem Erz-Bisthum Salzburg* (Leipzig: Teubner, 1732).

12 About Moser see Reinhard Rürup, *Johann Jacob Moser: Pietismus und Reform* (Wiesbaden: Steiner, 1965). Moser started editing the *Reichs Fama* (Imperial News) in 1730 and by 1732 had published nine volumes; two volumes with documents as *Saltzburgische Emigrations-Acten* (Frankfurt am Main, Leipzig: Roth, 1732, 1733) and an update *Das Neueste von denen Salzburgischen Emigrationsactis* (Frankfurt am Main, Leipzig: Roth) in 1732.

the entitlement of their Protestant counterparts to act on behalf of the Crypto-Protestants in Salzburg, insisting that the Emperor, Charles VI. (1705–40), was the only legitimate instance of appeal in matters of religious minority rights. In contrast with earlier instances when debates at the Imperial Diet about the status of the Salzburg Crypto-Protestants had a limited public echo, the conflict entered a new phase when the requests of the harrassed Protestants as well as their endorsement through members of the *corpus evangelicorum* were published.[13] The Catholic side considered the publishing of these materials as a very serious raising of the stakes, decrying this as a '*desabusirung deß Publici*', that is, a manipulation of the public and demonstrating the degree to which it was concerned with the public nature of the confrontation.[14] The above mentioned 'Petition of the 19,000' requested a recognition as a religious minority, or to receive the right to emigrate under the stipulations of the Peace of Westphalia, allowing for a secure and well-ordered departure from the archbishopric. The Crypto-Protestants now explicitly asked their supporters at the Imperial Diet to petition the archbishop and the Catholic representatives to the Diet with 'august and powerful intercessions'.[15] The growing degree of unrest and of mobilisation started now to worry even the supporters of the Salzburg Crypto-Protestants and delegates were sent from Regensburg to appeal to the latter 'to leave the mediation of the conflict to the representatives to the Diet, to hitherto follow the orders of the Prince and to continue to conceal their religious affiliation', a clear indication that to the outside world, the situation in Salzburg was starting to get out of hand.[16]

As a consequence, archbishop Firmian ordered a systematic investigation about the size and religious attitudes of the Crypto-Protestant population under his authority. The visits of two high-ranking officials to all districts with Crypto-Protestant subjects sometimes became occasions for turbulent manifestation of public discontent. In the course of this investigation, lists of over 20,000 people professing Protestant affiliation were drawn up.[17] Confessional mobilisation in the archbishopric in the summer of 1731 was intense. Because of repeated expressions of support from prominent Protestant leaders and sovereigns, Crypto-Protestants in Salzburg came to believe that this backing would not only be symbolic and political, but that in the case of a failure of negotiations with Salzburg authorities, Protestant forces from the outside of the archbishopric would intervene and even offer military support.[18] In this period of intensified conflict between Crypto-Protestants and state officials, a series of assemblies took place in several of the archbishopric's districts. At the final and largest of these gatherings, on 5 August 1731 in Schwarzach, 150 representatives of the repressed minority joined in a

13 Huber, *Aktenmäßige Geschichte*, 4–5.
14 Walker, *Salzburg Transaction*, 53.
15 Moser, *Emigrations-Acten*, 427.
16 Huber, *Actenmäßige Geschichte*, 22.
17 Walker, *Salzburg Transaction*, 56.
18 Ibid., 55 and Huber, *Actenmäßige Geschichte*, 24–33.

solemn ceremony of confirming their unity, involving the licking of a salt stone, a traditional ceremony equivalent to an oath.[19] Their central request was to be recognised as a religious minority with appropriate, open institutions and Protestant clergy, or to be granted the *ius emigrandi* on the basis of the Westphalian Peace Treaty.

Archbishop Firmian however chose a different course of action. Based on intelligence gathered during the visitation of all districts with Crypto-Protestant populations earlier in the summer, on 26 September 1731 the archbishop ordered the arrest of a group of over 30 leaders of the minority, while an Austrian battalion under the orders of prince Eugene of Savoyen (1663–1736) crossed the borders into the archbishopric to secure public order. Over the next few weeks, a list of all Crypto-Protestants in the archbishopric was prepared and, on 26 October, Firmian signed an order to 'extirpate this unruly, seditious and insurgent population in its entirety to the root'. The authorities published the expulsion order on 11 November 1731, allowing 1 week for unregistered and 3 months for registered Crypto-Protestants to leave the commonwealth.[20] In the next few weeks, thousands of expelled Salzburgians had to give up their homes and were forced to leave the archbishopric. Many of them settled provisionally in Protestant or mixed imperial cities in the German south. Early in 1732, Frederic William I of Prussia personally interrogated two representatives of the expelled group, found them to be of sufficiently righteous faith and virtuous character and, on 2 February 1732, issued his Immigration Patent inviting exiles to settle in Prussian-Lithuanian territories previously devastated by the plague.[21] As a result, around 15,000 Salzburg Protestants in 16 large groups marched from the Alps across German lands to the Empire's eastern border, neighbouring Russia. Exiles experienced significant losses and suffering in the trek and in the first years of settlement: around 4,000 exiles died in the first 2 years after arrival and civic unrest and conflict with the local authorities were frequent occurences. These experiences have often been downplayed in popular accounts and in historiography, favouring a redemptive narrative about the benign and generous Prussian monarch welcoming the exiles and enabling them to openly professing and practising their religious beliefs. This narrative, however, obscures the more complicated motivations of powerful, imperial actors, for whom the fate of the Crypto-Protestants from Salzburg was, as the catastrophic outcome in part indicates, a secondary concern. By supporting the cause of the Crypto-Protestants and taking advantage of the political mistakes of archbishop Firmian, the Protestant commonwealths within and outside the Empire gained political leverage at the expense of the Emperor's court, the Diet and due judicial process. This politicisation of the issue appears clearly in the threat

19 Emrich, *Emigration*, 21–3 and Walker, *Salzburg Transaction*, 53–9.

20 'Registered' referred to a married couple with a fixed and registered place of residence. Thus, a large number of indigenous subjects of the archbishop would not qualify as 'registered' subjects and were given one week to leave the principality.

21 Leeb, *Salzburger Emigration*, 295.

from Denmark to restrict the religious freedoms of her Catholic subjects in retaliation for the expulsion of Salzburg's Crypto-Protestants.[22] Support for their cause from Protestant commonwealths and *corpus evangelicorum* was so unequivocal and sustained that Crypto-Protestant leaders in Salzburg indeed believed that the former planned a military intervention on their behalf. From a strictly legal and constitutional point of view, however, Crypto-Protestants in Salzburg had few arguments on their side. Their confessional sensitivities, which had been respected to a limited degree in an uneasy status quo for many generations, came under attack from a Catholic sovereign aiming to increase his religious credentials, but they did not have any legal claim to be accepted as Protestants. Likewise, archbishop Firmian had put himself in a problematic position as both the 1555 Peace of Augsburg and the Westphalian Peace had recognised the desirability of religious homogeneity in a given commonwealth. Firmian however justified the expulsion of a significant portion of the population not on religious grounds (which would have required the observation of the triennium and other clauses of the Westphalian Peace), but on the grounds of insubordination, unacceptable in both local and imperial law.

Thus, the real achievement of Frederic William I was not that he had demonstrated generosity and tolerance, but rather that he offered a plausible solution to a political impasse: archbishop Firmian could get rid of an unruly religious minority, the *corpus evangelicorum* could claim to have courageously defended it and the emperor avoided a too obvious demonstration of his lack of political skill and impact. Also, the Peace of Westphalia remained largely intact, as the emigration of the Salzburg Crypto-Protestants to Lithuanian Prussia was based on the sovereign decision of the Prussian King to invite them and not on the provisions of the treatise for safeguarding the rights of religious minorities. This, however, had dramatic consequences for the victims of this negotiation process gone wrong: the Salzburg Crypto-Protestants themselves. Whereas the *triennium* would have allowed for a considerable period of time to sell properties and prepare for emigration, the exiles had to leave with nothing. The expulsion process took a massive toll on their livelihoods and in thousands of cases resulted in illness and death.[23]

Prague 1744–5: keeping quiet and mobilising friends in high places

The expulsion of the Jews of Prague, the largest and most prominent Jewish community in central Europe in the early eighteenth century, was ordered on 18 December 1744 by the young and fervently Catholic Maria Theresia (1717–80), archduchess of Austria and queen of Bohemia. The expulsion was a punishment for cooperation between Jewish merchants in the Bohemian capital with the

22 Huber, *Actenmäßige Geschichte*, 163–8 and Walker, *Salzburg Transaction*, 129–32.
23 Walker, *Salzburg Transaction*, 145–86.

enemy Prussian army that had laid siege to Prague during the Austrian Wars of Succession.[24] Close ties between Jewish merchants and the Prussian army had already been forged during the French siege of the Bohemian capital 1 year earlier, provoking the monarch's wrath. In 1743, however, the Jewish community had been able to appease Maria Theresia with a gift of one hundred fifty thousand taler.[25] The elders rightly assumed that the sovereign had been informed about the commercial involvement of the Jewish community and had sent a low-ranking community clerk to Vienna in order to find out whether a comparable gift was required. While still on his way to the imperial capital, this clerk learned that the monarch had ordered the expulsion of the Jewish community of Prague, to be implemented within one month and of the remaining Bohemian Jewish community – tens of thousands of people – after 6 months, by the end of June 1745.[26] A group of senior members of the community was immediately dispatched to Vienna in order to overturn the expulsion decree. At the same time, the office representing the imperial administration (the *Statthalterei*) had independently intervened with Vienna and had achieved a first postponement of the expulsion until the end of February 1745. The *Statthalterei* had argued that an expulsion in January was almost impossible to implement since the Jewish and non-Jewish spheres were too closely connected to be severed that quickly and had also suggested that an expulsion in the middle of winter would inevitably lead to the death of many. A flurry of interventions took place in the period after the expulsion order was issued, trying to negotiate its revocation or its repeal. Before discussing the characteristics of these interventions and the very significant network mobilisation that made them possible, the ensuing course of events should be briefly summarised.

News of a further delay in the expulsion of the entire Jewish population of Prague, now fixed for the end of February 1745, reached the Bohemian capital only one day before this deadline, at which point, between 10 and 14,000 Jews had already left their neighbourhood. Most of them had found temporary shelter in nearby villages and small towns, most notably Brandýs nad Labem.[27] Thus, the expulsion order was simultaneously executed and delayed. Maria Theresia added to the confusion in May 1745 by rescinding the order expelling the Jews from Bohemian territories, but upholding the ban on Jews residing in Prague. In practice, Jews entered the Bohemian capital on a daily basis in order to pursue

24 Surprisingly enough, the expulsion of the Jews from Prague has not been the subject of a monographic study. Undoubtedly one of the most dramatic events of eighteenth-century European-Jewish history, it has been investigated in a number of substantial scholarly articles, among which Baruch Mevorah, 'Intercessory efforts in Europe to prevent the expulsion of the Jews of Bohemia and Moravia [in Hebrew]', *Zion* 3–4, 28 (1963), 125–64, stands out. Further references in François Guesnet, 'Textures of Intercession: Rescue Efforts for the Jews of Prague, 1744/1748', *Simon Dubnow Institute Yearbook* 4 (2005), 355–75.

25 Guesnet, *Rescue Efforts*, 357.

26 Josef Bergl, 'Die Ausweisung der Juden aus Prag im Jahre 1744', in *Die Juden in Prag. Bilder aus ihrer tausendjährigen Geschichte*, edited by Samuel Steinherz (Prag: Die Bücherstube, 1927), 210.

27 Ibid. and Hana Legnerová, 'Das Exil der Prager Juden auf der Herrschaft Rothenhaus (Cerveny Hradek) in den Jahren 1745–1748', *Judaica Bohemiae* 38 (2002): 51.

their trades. As residence remained prohibited, however, buildings and businesses suffered significant deterioration.[28] Another twist in the tale came 1 year later, when the sovereign found that unsatisfactory progress had been made in terms of the dissolution of economic links between Jews and non-Jews in Prague, holding a local agency created for this task, the Expulsion Commission (*Ausweisungscommission*), responsible. Maria Theresia dissolved the Commission and transferred the task of eliminating the Jewish presence in Prague to the military high command in Bohemia. One month later, in May 1746, Maria Theresia (now Empress after her husband Franz I had been elected Emperor of the Holy Roman Empire) ordered not only the Jews of Prague and Bohemia to leave, but extended this order to Moravia.[29] These measures were never implemented: after further delays, Maria Theresia revoked her expulsion decrees in the late summer of 1748 and allowed for a return of the Jews to their homes in Prague. The right of residence was granted to the Jews of Bohemia (including Prague) and Moravia for 10 years in return for an extortionary payment of 300,000 guilders to the treasury in Vienna – the so-called 'tolerance tax'. Jews' right of residence was not put into doubt again during Maria Theresia's long reign.

As with the archbishop of Salzburg's actions a decade before, the community threatened by expulsion attempted to prevent the catastrophe through intense negotiating and interceding. In both cases, the affected communities were faced with a new type of executive order: absolutist, radical measures meant to solve a political problem through mass deportation of a religious community thought to be at the root of this problem.[30] Whereas the Crypto-Protestants from Salzburg had confronted the challenge to their religious practice with an unprecedented confessional and political mobilisation, appeals for support from Protestant powers within and beyond the Empire and a mobilisation of the European Protestant public sphere, those attempting to defend the Jews of Prague chose fundamentally different strategies. Even before the first expulsion order was published, the community board, aware of the monarch's ire, presented her with a letter detailing the long-standing loyalty of the Jews of Prague to the crown.[31] After the order's publication and the dispatching of intercessors from Prague, the very generous offer to pay for all Austrian military expenses in Bohemia for a period of 6 months was submitted through an intermediary – no other than the husband of Maria Theresia,

28 Hugo Lieben, 'Handschriftliches zur Geschichte der Juden in Prag in den Jahren 1744–1754', *Jahrbuch der Jüdisch-Literarischen Gesellschaft* 3 (1905): 259.

29 The Jewish community in Bohemia was around 30,000 people, with more than half of the population residing in Prague in the mid-eighteenth century. At that time, the Jews of Moravia, who had been granted far-reaching autonomy in the late Middle Ages and had established numerous small communities counted around 20,000 people, see Hillel J. Kieval, 'Bohemia and Moravia', in *The Yivo Encyclopedia of Jews in Eastern Europe*, edited by Gershon D. Hundert, vol. 1 (New Haven, CT, London: Yale University Library, 2008), 202–11.

30 Guesnet, *Rescue Efforts*, 359–61.

31 Salomon Hugo Lieben, 'Briefe von 1744–1748 über die Austreibung der Juden aus Prag', *Jahrbuch der Gesellschaft für Geschichte der Juden in der Cechoslovakischen Republik* 4 (1932), here no.1: 363–5.

Franz I.[32] It is noteworthy that one of the strategies applied to overturn the monarch's decision to expel the Jews of Prague was to enrol almost everyone in Maria Theresia's intimate circle to plea to her to reconsider her decision. Within just 2 weeks of the publication of the expulsion decree, Maria Theresia's brother-in-law, her mother, her mother-in-law, her grandmother and her royal tutor had spoken to her on behalf of the Jews of Prague.[33] The spokesmen dispatched from Prague followed traditional forms of intercession: they threw themselves at the feet of the monarch and influential courtiers and pleaded their cause: 'The people from Prague run around all day seeking Count Kinsky and lament, crying bitter tears, to the effect that he sharply rebuked them and replied with words I cannot repeat here', wrote one Jewish observer at the court in Vienna, Samuel Wertheimer, to his father.[34] To contemporaries, these tried and tested procedures not only seemed insufficient, but also out-dated and conducted 'in confused manner', as one courtier observed.[35] Letters between Samuel Wertheimer and his father Wolf Wertheimer (1681–1765), together with letters between Wolf and a large number of correspondents from across the Holy Roman Empire and beyond, illustrate the traditions of Jewish intercession as well as the significant shifts that took place in their lifetimes. Wolf Wertheimer, the son of one of the most influential Jews in the Viennese court, Samson Wertheimer (1658–1724), was well-versed in courtly manners and stratagems and he clearly understood that, even though core elements of intercession – arguing, pleading, bribing – remained indispensable, new strategies for negotiating the readmission of the Jews of Prague to their homes were necessary. His large, Europe-wide network of correspondents illustrates that Wertheimer, himself part of the emerging elite of court Jews, was able to mobilise many powerful people on behalf of the distressed Prague community. One of the noteworthy shifts in the rationale of intercession, which the case of Wertheimer's involvement in the defence of the Jews of Prague illustrates, is the growing disconnection between the community board in Prague and court Jews such as Wertheimer, living at the time neither in Prague nor in Vienna, but in Augsburg. Wertheimer's objective during the weeks and months after the expulsion decree was its repeal. None of the surviving documents demonstrate, however, any coordination between him and the board of the Jewish community in Prague, or with the community's delegates in Vienna. Based on information he received from his son at the imperial court and from his numerous correspondents across Europe, Wolf Wertheimer would make interventions – writing letters, organising petitions – applying great care to formulate a coherent narrative when writing to

32 Ibid., no. 54: 440–1.

33 Guesnet, *Rescue Efforts*, 367–8.

34 Duke Philipp Joseph Kinsky (1700–49), chancellor of Bohemia, was one of the few declared supporters of the expulsion decree. For a discussion of the tradition of intercession in European Jewish history and references to existing scholarly literature, see François Guesnet, 'Politik der "Fürsprache" – Vormoderne jüdische Interessensvertretung', *Synchrone Welten*, edited by Dan Diner (Hamburg: Vandenhoeck & Ruprecht, 2005), 67–92.

35 Lieben, *Briefe*, no. 48: 353–7.

his correspondents. This included suggesting, via his correspondents, the exact wordings for letters to be sent to the court in Vienna from Jewish and non-Jewish advocates, such as the English, Danish and the Polish kings, as well as members of the highest echelons of the Catholic church.

A striking example of this type of intervention was Wertheimer's successful mobilisation of the Holy See to plead on behalf of the Jews of Prague. The rationale for this was that, as Maria Theresia was a devout Catholic, a letter from Rome would be consequential.[36] Thus, Wolf Wertheimer dictated a letter that was then sent by the Jewish regional assembly of Swabia (in southern Germany) to several Italian Jewish communities, including Mantua, Rome, Venice and Turin. This letter contained drafts for two further letters. The first contained a short line of argument that the recipient Italian communities were supposed to pursue when negotiating with the local non-Jews who might possibly gain access to the Holy See. The second draft was to be used by someone inside the Vatican as the template for a letter from the Pope writing to the monarch in Vienna. This intervention shows how a court Jew in Augsburg imagined the highest authority in the Catholic church would admonish a European Catholic sovereign: in very strong wording, the Austrian queen here was exhorted not to pass 'bad, incorrect judgment against tens of thousands of innocents'; the letter asked the monarch, 'what law she is referring to when expelling innocent people without proper inquiry' and warned that she might 'kill the just along with the wrongdoer'.[37] These are words even a high-standing court Jew would never have dared use in negotiating with a monarch. Among the most impressive features of Wertheimer's efforts is the fact that a letter from the Holy See based on Wertheimer's template did indeed reach the court in Vienna, just 3 weeks after the expulsion order had been published. Wertheimer and his correspondents would also send letters containing templates with arguments and demands to the General Estates in the Netherlands, the English King, the Saxonian Elector and many other high standing dignitaries. The care and precision in gathering information about letters sent, people contacted, results obtained and the efficiency in the handling of these missives is highly impressive.[38] The most striking difference between the activities of the Crypto-Protestants in Salzburg and their supporters on the one hand and the handling of the campaign in favour of the Jews from Prague on the other was the strictly confidential character of the latter, in contrast to the massive publicity efforts by the former.[39]

Although it is difficult to assess the impact of the intercessory effort of Wertheimer's correspondents' network, many authors writing on behalf of the exiled Jewish community warned Maria Theresia of the damage her intransigence

36 Guesnet, *Rescue Efforts*, 369.

37 Lieben, *Briefe*, no. 15: 383–8.

38 Guesnet, *Rescue Efforts*, 367.

39 Although at times members of Wertheimer's network would reinforce their arguments by referring to articles in the press (see for example Lieben, *Briefe*, no. 18, 394–5 and no. 21, 397–8), there is no evidence indicating that the press itself was targeted to establish a specific public perception of the fate of the Jews of Prague.

did to her reputation. The Earl of Harrington, British minister of foreign affairs, who intervened in December 1744, very shortly after the publication of the expulsion decree, referred to 'the prejudice the world might conceive against the Queen's actions' and explained in another letter in February 1745 that her 'severe and merciless resolution could not but be esteemed by all mankind as an indelible stain both in point of justice and clemency upon her hitherto moderate and equitable Government'.[40] Indeed the expulsion resonated especially among the Protestants in the Holy Roman Empire, who established a link between the actions of the Catholic archbishop Firmian in 1732 and Maria Theresia in 1744.[41] However, there are few indications that the public in the Holy Roman Empire took sustained interest in the affair and there are no indications that the few expressions of indignation or dismay had been the intended outcome of initiatives taken by Jews intervening on behalf of the Prague community. Court Jews would limit their efforts to governments and sovereigns, the aristocracy and the highest echelons of the Catholic Church and very clearly and deliberately avoided mobilising the public. They would rather focus on complementing written interventions with face-to-face communication, the latter offering opportunities to reinforce specific points, to test the grounds for bribing officials or to pass on information with the intention to maximise impact. Thus, Wertheimer encouraged a court Jew at the Saxonian court in Dresden, 'to tell those noble men to whom one turns that Duke Kinsky, chancellor of Bohemia, is a great enemy of the Jews. He has led the Queen astray and apparantly has lost his mind'.[42] The surviving letters however only rarely explicitly address this difference in approach between a written intervention in contrast to the potential of a personal encounter. Equally rare are references to the use of bribes to instigate actions by influential non-Jews with access to the court or the monarch. Allusions to the appropriate way or moment to offer material incentives leave, however, little doubt that these were an important part of the negotiation process. As Michael Apt, a Polish Jew at the Saxonian court in Dresden and one of Wertheimer's closest allies, put it: 'For this kind of business someone has to stand up in person with a purse full of golden dinars, because a physician that costs no money does no good . . . but so far nobody appeared with this most important cure'.[43]

The monarch remained implacable. As one correspondent reported from an audience with Maria Theresia, the queen was fully aware of the massive injustice her order meant for many: 'She admitted that the Jews are honest, but maintained that she had her reservations and did not wish any Jews in her lands'.[44] In February 1745, Samuel Wertheimer reported from Vienna that, 'the Queen has not budged from her position' and, towards the end of March, explained that

40 Johann Krengel, 'Die englische Intervention zu Gunsten der böhmischen Juden im Jahre 1744', *Monatsschrift für Geschichte und Wissenschaft des Judentums* 44, 5 (1900), 271.

41 Guesnet, *Rescue Efforts*, 373.

42 Lieben, *Briefe*, no. 34: 417–19.

43 Guesnet, *Rescue Efforts*, 372.

44 Ibid., 359.

> in the matter of the community [of Prague] everything has been in vain so far. The King of England has sent another envoy, and Holland has also intervened once more, but it's all to no avail. A cardinal has undertaken another attempt, with no success.[45]

A report by Thomas Robinson, the British envoy to the court in Vienna, sheds light on the remarkable fact that, even in the highest circles of the Austrian government and at the court, officials and ministers distanced themselves from the 'precipitation and severity' of the monarch's measures. Robinson continued that, 'in general, there is not one who does not disclaim all share and part whatever in this rigorous sentence and what is certain, they had all, both separately and jointly, given their advice against it'.[46] This included, as mentioned above, the representative of the Viennese court in Prague, the *Statthalterei*, who sent a detailed report about the massive losses to be expected for the Bohemian economy and the Austrian treasury as a consequence of the expulsion.[47] The Christian merchant guilds in Leipzig, Hamburg, Amsterdam and London also intervened on behalf of the Jewish community in Prague, with Wolf Wertheimer observing in January 1745 that they acted, 'only in their own interest, not in favour of the children of our nation'.[48] After spring 1745, there was a marked reduction in correspondence on behalf the Jews of Prague who, by this point, had resettled in provincial towns near the capital. Despite Maria Theresia's threats in 1746 against the Jews of Moravia, however, no further expulsions were ordered. The situation changed only when, in 1748, the monarch was forced to compromise with the Bohemian Estates. As the crown needed their approval to introduce a new system of centralised taxation to Bohemia and the Estates made their consent dependent on a repeal of the expulsion decree, Maria Theresia relented and graciously accepted the payment of a very substantial 'toleration tax' and the return of Jews to their homes in Prague.[49]

Negotiating religion under duress: Salzburg and Prague in comparison

The most striking difference in the approach of Crypto-Protestants in Salzburg and the Jews of Prague in defence of their interests is the role assigned to the public sphere. Attempts to mobilise other Protestants in support of their cause happened in public: in market places, churches, at large public gatherings in Salzburg proper. In 1731, this public mobilisation was crystallised in public oaths and celebrated in publications, first within Salzburg, with the *Petition of the 19,000* and

45 Lieben, *Briefe*, no. 55, 441.

46 Krengel, Englische Intervention, 276.

47 Gerson Wolf, 'Die Vertreibung der Juden aus Böhmen im Jahre 1744 und deren Wiederaufnahme im Jahre 1748', *Illustrierte Monatshefte für die gesamten Interessen des Judenthums* 2 (1865) 452–9.

48 Lieben, *Briefe*, no. 14, 380–2.

49 Guesnet, *Rescue Efforts*, 374.

then in the larger Protestant public sphere, across the Holy Roman Empire and beyond, through ministers, legal experts and high-ranking officials of Protestant commonwealths and the *corpus evangelicorum*. This confessional mobilisation raised the stakes for all parties involved such that a complicated political solution could only be negotiated after the King of Prussia had agreed to invite and accept thousands of Salzburg Protestants into his territories. Mack Walker has convincingly argued that the difficult economic situation in the archbishopric and, above all, a considerable surplus in the population was a significant motivation for Protestants to push their agenda to the limits.[50] By involving the Protestant commonwealths represented at the Imperial Diet and by avoiding due legal process, they wider Protestant community deliberately politicised the conflict. In a joint effort, representatives of the Salzburg Crypto-Protestants and the *corpus evangelicorum* got the political backing of the Protestant European powers who had guaranteed the Peace of Westphalia: England, the General Estates, Denmark and Saxony. The Crypto-Protestants in Salzburg were wrong, however, about the degree of political commitment of their powerful allies, who never intended to risk a military confrontation and were even unable or unwilling to negotiate the application of the stipulations of the Peace treaties of 1648, the *ius emigrandi* including the *triennium*. The 'precipitation and severity' in the implementation of the expulsion decrees illustrates the growing power of the sovereign in the age of absolutism in both cases. The consequences for the Crypto-Protestants, mostly farmers, salt-mine workers and craftspeople, were catastrophic, as they lost their homes, many of their movable assets, their children, their health and very often their lives.

The different outcome of negotiations leading to the re-admittance of the Jews of Prague in 1748 also has to do with a very significant difference in socio-economic status between them and the Crypto-Protestants of Salzburg. Although the loss of a large group of often highly skilled farmers, miners and craftspeople was detrimental to the economy of the Salzburg archbishopric, few people beyond its borders were materially affected. In contrast, Jewish merchants and bankers in Prague were of central relevance for the economy of the Bohemian capital and the entire kingdom and constituted an important link in international commerce. By defending the Jews of Prague, they were defending their own best interest, as Wolf Wertheimer dryly observed. The court Jews' mobilisation of European sovereigns, courts and church dignitaries certainly contributed to an overwhelmingly negative reception of Maria Theresia's unforgiving resentment. It is noteworthy that Wertheimer and other court Jews targeted the Protestant European powers guaranteeing the Peace of Westphalia to intervene on behalf the Jews of Prague and it is not too far-fetched to assume that they were well aware of their active role in defending the Crypto-Protestants in Salzburg and hoped to mobilise their support in the case of yet another religious minority oppressed by a ruthless Catholic sovereign. The exile of the Salzburg Protestants was often

50 Walker, *Salzburg Transaction*, 22–4.

compared to the diasporic fate of the Jews and would certainly have continued to resonate in the aftermath of the event.[51] The fact that the widespread rejection of Maria-Theresia's course of action did not become part of an open political confrontation allowed the sovereign to relent in the end and accept the bargain proposed by the Bohemian Estates. It may well be that in the case of the Jews of Prague, the absence of a legal framework like the Peace of Westphalia made finding a political solution easier.

Several conclusions emerge from this comparison of two cases of efforts to rescue a religious minority from expulsion. Although a complex legal and constitutional fabric had emerged in the Holy Roman Empire in consequence of the Protestant Reformation and religious (civil) warfare, the Crypto-Protestants in Salzburg were unable to assert themselves as sovereigns of their own fate. Their apparent allies, the Protestant commonwealths within and beyond the Empire, would encourage the minority to pleads its case with the greatest possible publicity, thus contributing to a political situation that rapidly became unmanageable. By branding the Crypto-Protestants as a seditious population, religious affiliation became an issue of state security, providing the Catholic players the opportunity to react with military measures to the religious challenge. It has been argued that the *cause célèbre* of the Salzburg Protestants served as a lesson to those who took up to defend the Jewish community of Prague in 1744. This campaign, sustained above all by the emerging mercantile elite of court Jews, left political or constitutional arguments aside, pleading on behalf of the threatened community almost exclusively on humanitarian grounds. They avoided publicly cornering the Austrian sovereign, despite the almost complete consensus among European elites about the irrational character of her decision. Recognising the overwhelming power of the absolutist monarch, they contributed to creating a setting in which all parties could claim some achievements: the Jews of Prague returned to their homes, the Empress had not been forced to recognise her error and could claim royal magnanimity and Prague continued to thrive as a center of commerce and banking. Despite the differences in outcome, both cases of expulsion asserted and expanded the role of central state authorities to govern affairs that would pertain to religious affiliation and affairs, to the detriment of representatives and spokespeople of religious communities.

References

Bahlcke, Joachim. *Ungarischer Episkopat und österreichische Monarchie: von einer Partnerschaft zur Konfrontation (1686–1790).* Stuttgart: Verlag Steiner, 2005.

Bergl, Josef. 'Die Ausweisung der Juden aus Prag im Jahre 1744', in *Die Juden in Prag. Bilder aus ihrer tausendjährigen Geschichte,* edited by Samuel Steinherz, 187–247. Prag: Die Bücherstube, 1927.

Ehmer, Artur. *Das Schrifttum zur Salzburger Emigration 1731/33.* Hamburg: Verein für Familienforschung in West- und Ostpreußen, 1975.

51 Walker, *Salzburg Transaction*, 102–5, 202.

Emrich, Gabriele. *Die Emigration der Salzburger Protestanten 1731–1732. Reichsrechtliche und konfessionspolitische Aspekte.* Münster: Lit Verlag, 2002.

Guesnet, François. 'Politik der "Fürsprache" – Vormoderne jüdische Interessensvertretung', in *Synchrone Welten*, edited by Dan Diner, 67–92. Hamburg: Vandenhoeck & Ruprecht, 2005.

——. 'Textures of Intercession – Rescue Efforts for the Jews of Prague, 1744/1748', *Simon Dubnow Institute Yearbook* 4 (2005): 355–75.

Huber, Franz Xaver. *Aktenmäßige Geschichte der berühmten salzburgischen Emigration. Nach dem Manuskript des Johannes Baptist Caspari übersetzt und mit Vorbericht begleitet von Franz Xaver Huber.* Salzburg: Mayer Verlag, 1790.

Kieval, Hillel J. 'Bohemia and Moravia', in *The Yivo Encyclopedia of Jews in Eastern Europe*, edited by Gershon D. Hundert, vol. 1. New Haven, CT, London: Yale University Library, 2008.

Krengel, Johann. 'Die englische Intervention zu Gunsten der böhmischen Juden im Jahre 1744', *Monatsschrift für Geschichte und Wissenschaft des Judentums* 44 (1900) 4: 177–85, 5: 259–81.

Leeb, Rudolf. 'Die große Salzburger Emigration von 1731/32 und ihre Vorgeschichte (Ausweisung der Deferegger 1684)', in *Glaubensflüchtlinge. Ursachen, Formen und Auswirkungen frühneuzeitlicher Konfessionsmigration in Europa* edited by Joachim Bahlcke, 277–306. Münster: LIT Verlag, 2008.

Legnerová, Hana. 'Das Exil der Prager Juden auf der Herrschaft Rothenhaus (Cerveny Hradek) in den Jahren 1745–1748', *Judaica Bohemiae* 38 (2002): 48–71.

Lieben, Salomon Hugo. 'Handschriftliches zur Geschichte der Juden in Prag in den Jahren 1744–1754', *Jahrbuch der Jüdisch-Literarischen Gesellschaft* 2 (1904): 267–330 and ibid., 3 (1905): 241–76.

——. 'Briefe von 1744–1748 über die Austreibung der Juden aus Prag', *Jahrbuch der Gesellschaft für Geschichte der Juden in der Cechoslovakischen Republik* 4 (1932): 353–479.

Mevorah, Baruch. 'Intercessory efforts in Europe to prevent the expulsion of the Jews of Bohemia and Moravia [in Hebrew]', *Zion* 3–4 (1963): 28.

Moser, Johann Jacob. *Saltzburgische Emigrations-Acten.* Frankfurt am Main, Leipzig: Roth, 1732.

Rürup, Reinhard. *Johann Jacob Moser. Pietismus und Reform.* Wiesbaden: Verlag Steiner, 1965.

Sancke, Christoph. *Ausführliche Historie derer Emigranten Oder Vertriebenen Lutheraner aus dem Erz-Bisthum Salzburg.* Leipzig: Teubner, 1732.

Schauroth, Eberhard Christian Wilhelm von. *Vollständige Sammlung aller Conclusorum, Schreiben und anderer übriger Verhandlungen des hochpreißlichen Corpus Evangelicorum, Theil 1–3.* Regensburg: Neubauer, 1751–2.

Walker, Mack. *The Salzburg Transaction. Expulsion and Redemption in Eighteenth-Century Germany.* Ithaca, NY, London: Cornell University Press, 1992.

Wolf, Gerson. 'Die Vertreibung der Juden aus Böhmen im Jahre 1744 und deren Wiederaufnahme im Jahre 1748', *Illustrierte Monatshefte für die gesamten Interessen des Judenthums* 2 (1865): 271–80, 358–77, 447–58.

Part II

Negotiating religion in constitutional politics and political philosophy

4 Negotiating religion in constitutional politics and political philosophy

Cécile Laborde

For comparative political scientists and political philosophers, an important starting and focal point for discussions around the empirical and philosophical dimensions of church–state relations is that several European states have established churches. This fact is startling, for many reasons. First, it reminds us that, even in largely secularised societies, particularly in Europe, which is the focus of this volume, there are still formal (and informal) connections between democratic states and religious organisations. Second, in an age of globalisation of modes of religious governance, it suggests that the US model of the 'non-establishment' of religion might be more of an exception than a universalisable model. And third, it raises profound questions about the compatibility of religious establishment with liberal democratic notions of citizenship and equality in diverse societies.

Work in this area explores how controversies about religious establishment are connected to wider constitutional and philosophical discussions about the nature of European secularism and the religious neutrality of the liberal state. How are majority religions enshrined within constitutional and legal settlements and what implications does this have for the secularist attributes of modern European states? And, beyond formal establishment, how do states recognise religious groups? What are we to make of the emergence of plural legal orders – both within Europe as a whole and within individual European countries? Moving to philosophical, normative questions about the moral defensibility of establishment and state recognition of religion, academic discussions connect debates about 'just establishment' to broader, political philosophical concerns about liberal justice and neutrality. What does it mean to say that the state should be neutral towards religion? Is secularism a proper form of neutrality? Is state neutrality compatible with the granting of certain privileges – legal exemptions, for example – to religious believers? Does the requirement of 'public reasoning' unfairly exclude religious believers from democratic debates?

In this introduction, I take stock of scholarly reflections about the philosophical, constitutional and political dimensions of the negotiation of religion – focusing on the contrasting uses of notions of 'negotiation' in political and in philosophical debates. I use the concept of negotiation to frame key discussions on constitutional politics (section 1) and political philosophy (section 2) before introducing the three chapters that make up this section (section 3).

Constitutional politics

Recent academic work analyses how traditional western European state–religion models are changing and/or being challenged, notably influenced by the collapse of communism, increasing religious diversity in Europe, the post-9/11 global context and the impact of human rights-based equality agendas. The 'return of religion', as a multidisciplinary scholarly concern, has made itself felt in the discipline of political science. A rich scholarship has quickly developed on the comparative study of 'state–religion' relations, the treatment of religion in the law and the emergence of transnational models of religious governance, for examples via European Court of Human Rights (ECtHR) jurisprudence.

There is an array of national approaches to state–religion relations around the world and states committed to formal separation themselves exhibit widely divergent modes of state regulation of religion.[1] In Europe (with France as an ambiguous exception) the predominant approach involves establishment of the historically dominant confession twinned with the more or less *de facto* toleration of the principal religious minorities.[2] The role of religion in the European public sphere has been the object of heated debates – from reference to Christian values in the European Constitution[3] to the haphazard and half-hearted elaboration of a 'separationist' and 'neutralist' jurisprudence of state–religion relations by the European Court on Human Rights.[4] Generally, while European populations are more secular than the US, European states have historically been more tolerant of church–state entanglements and of the public presence of (traditional, mostly Christian) religions.[5] Over the last few decades, they have mobilised the rhetoric of secularism to articulate profound anxieties about the immigration and settlement of populations of Muslim origin. Contemporary European secularism is shaped and framed by a perception and construction of Islam as the paradigmatic 'anti-secular' religion.[6] Complex patterns of European state-religion involvement have emerged from the late twentieth century. Although formal church establishment is in retreat, its place has been taken not by regimes of formal separation, but by forms of accommodation that fall well short of the non-establishment criteria of the US constitution.

1 Ahmet T. Kuru, *Secularism and State Policies toward Religion: The United States, France, and Turkey* (Cambridge: Cambridge University Press, 2009).

2 John Madeley, 'Six degrees of separation? Variants of Religious Establishment in Europe', paper presented at the UCL workshop of 12 February 2012. See also his '*Religion and the State*', in *Routledge Handbook of Religion and Politics*, ed. Jeffrey Haynes (New York: Routledge, 2009), 174–91.

3 Joseph H.H. Weiler, 'A Christian Europe? Europe and Christianity: Rules of Commitment', *European View* 6: 1 (2007), 143–50.

4 Caroline Evans, *Freedom of Religion Under the European Convention on Human Rights* (Oxford: Oxford University Press, 2001).

5 Danièle Hervieu-Léger, *La religion en mouvement: le pèlerin et le converti* (Paris: Flammarion, 1999).

6 Jocelyne Cesari, *Muslims in the West After 9/11: Religion, Politics and Law* (London: Routledge, 2009).

The concept of 'negotiation' is to some extent apposite to describe the emergence of these new settlements. Established churches, in particular, have been able to use the influence and power they had accumulated over centuries to secure favourable settlements from governments. For churches, securing a range of new consultative, social, educational and welfare responsibilities helps shore up their authority and power in a context of profound societal secularisation. States, in turn, have cultivated formal and informal links with religious organisations for a variety of – at times incompatible – aims. In an age of financial austerity and welfare retrenchment, many states have opted to delegate welfare and educational functions to churches and 'faith groups'. The security agenda emerging from the so-called 'war on terror' has underlined political interventions to support moderate and repress radical, Islamic groups. The ethical complexity of debates around bioethics, assisted suicide and other 'life' issues has motivated the inclusion of religious groups in public deliberative bodies. And national modes of church–state relations have provided the template from which European states have dealt with new religious diversity. For example, as Robert M. Morris (University College London) shows in his chapter on English (and Scottish) establishment, the UK government continues informally to use the Church of England as an accommodationist conduit for relations with non-Christian religions. All such cases give credence to some notion of 'negotiation', whereby roughly equally situated parties bargain over mutually beneficial terms of agreement.

Yet, in other ways, the concept of negotiation obscures what is at stake in the relationships between the state and religious groups. It overestimates the power and authoritative standing of religious groups and wrongly assumes that churches stand in a 'horizontal' relation to states, as parties to a conflict negotiating a peace settlement may be. Yet this belies two facts. The first is the profound secularisation of European societies; or at least their religious de-institutionalisation. In an age where, if we are to believe Grace Davie, people want to 'believe without belonging'[7], the institutional power of traditional churches is slowly and probably irreversibly eroding. The second factor is the pervasive and growing influence of public norms, notably legal norms of equality, within religious organisations themselves. Ironically, as states lose much of their social and economic power, they have secured (sometimes via supranational agencies) increasing regulatory power. While churches and other religious actors mobilise against norms of gender or sexuality equality in the name of religious and associative freedom, they do so from a defensive position, one in which public authorities (whether national or transnational) are able to impose – not 'negotiate' – norms of anti-discrimination and human rights (imposing norms, of course, is not incompatible with granting exemptions and accommodations).

Nowhere are those tensions more in evidence than in the debate over legal pluralism and the relationship between religious law and civil law, notably around the question of gender equality. We need more informed debate about the actual

7 Grace Davie, *Religion in Britain Since 1945: Believing Without Belonging* (London: Wiley, 1994).

workings of religious tribunals – Muslim, Jewish and Roman Catholic. Empirical studies, for example, about marriage and remarriage within the faith, have shown how such courts are usually very alive to the limits of their consensual jurisdiction in relation to state law.[8]

Political philosophy

Looking now at these issues from an explicitly normative, philosophical perspective, we can slightly change the question we pose. The question is not, how *do* states and religious groups interact: on which terms, with which purposes and to what effect? It rather becomes, how *should* they interact? What are the norms and standards according to which certain patterns of state–religion interaction are to be preferred to others? Political philosophers are typically interested in ethical and moral standards (i.e., not flatly empirical standards such as bureaucratic efficiency, economic growth, or social stability); and their preferred standards tend to be ideals of justice or fairness. Justice, as John Rawls put it in his seminal *Theory of Justice* (1971), is the 'first virtue' of institutions.[9] When political philosophers turn their attention to questions of state–religion relationships, they seek to determine what a just settlement would be. This is not a settlement that comes about simply from the vicissitudes of history or the relative strength of the groups in presence. It is not a settlement that happens to be 'just there'. Rather, it is just if it can be justified by good public reasons, which (to simplify matters slightly) are reasons of justice.

From this perspective, philosophers are reticent about the notion of 'negotiation'. To them, it is reminiscent of what Rawls called the 'modus vivendi' solution to the wars of religion in seventeenth-century Europe. Warring religious factions agreed to a policy of toleration, not because they believe toleration was right, but because they did not have the power to impose their own views on others. Toleration, then, was a prudential second-best solution, one contingent on existing power relationships. By contrast, Rawls argued, a stable, just arrangement must be agreed for reasons of principle, not simply reasons of prudence.[10] This Rawlsian view of principled toleration has many ramifications for thinking about religion and politics.[11] Here I just mean to draw attention to one basic thought about political normativity: this is that anything that is negotiated or agreed upon is not, by that fact alone, just. Instead, Rawls and other liberal philosophers have sought to identify the criteria of just political interaction. Even though Rawls himself avails

8 Gillian Douglas (Cardiff) 'Boundaries of Toleration: Moderating Multiple Religious Jurisdictions', paper presented at the UCL workshop on 10 February 2012. See Douglas, G., Sandberg, R., Doe, N., Gilliat-Ray, S. and Khan, A. 2014. 'Religious Divorce in England and Wales: Religious Tribunals in Action', in Shah, P., Foblets, M. and Rohe, M., eds *Family, Religion and Law: Cultural Encounters in Europe* (Farnham, UK: Ashgate), 195–208.

9 John Rawls, *A Theory of Justice.* (Cambridge, MA: Harvard University Press, 1971).

10 John Rawls, *Political Liberalism* (New York: Columbia University Press, 1993).

11 Rainer Forst, *Toleration in Conflict* (Cambridge: Cambridge University Press, 2012).

himself of the device of a negotiated 'social contract' in his theory of justice, the fairness of a contractual arrangement ultimately hinges on the way that the hypothetical contract is construed. Political agreements and states more generally, are just if they respect the equality of all citizens. One way in which such equality is achieved, for liberal philosophers, is through the ethical neutrality of the state: the state is not to favour any particular conception of the good. Historically, liberals fought against the inequality, oppression and subordination inherent in old-style religious establishments, where the rights of dissidents, non-Christians and atheists were denied. The modern ideal of liberal neutrality, we could say, is a generalisation of the old ideal of toleration and disestablishment, one informed by an ideal of equality between all citizens, regardless of their beliefs and conceptions of the good. But how should liberal egalitarians assess existing 'vestigial' states of establishment in Europe? Which state–religion connections are problematic at the bar of liberal justice? Political philosophers have been engaged in two debates, which we can call the 'equality debate' and the 'neutrality debate', respectively.

The equality debate asks whether it is fair that religious groups or individuals receive special treatment from the state and, in particular, whether religious exemptions from general laws can be justified. This body of research has had two main sources: the political theory of multiculturalism and the US Free Exercise jurisprudence. Theorists of multiculturalism criticised the 'difference-blind' nature of traditional liberalism and suggested that identity-based differences should be recognised by the law. Since the publication of the seminal work of Canadian writer Will Kymlicka, theorists have debated the nature and limits of 'cultural rights', the challenges posed to national model of assimilation by immigration and the conflict between individual rights (in particular women's rights) and the 'right to culture'.[12] Yet the early Canadian, multinational inspiration of multicultural theorising obscured the fact that most difference-related controversies in Western societies concern not so much *culture* as they do *religion*. What is at stake in the now classic 'hard cases' of liberal toleration was the legitimacy of *religious* accommodation in the secular state. The fiercest controversies concern the legitimacy of religious exemptions from general laws (religious dress v. uniform requirements; minority religion worship v. official days of rest; anti-discrimination legislation for women and homosexuals v. internal religious rules of organisation), the conflict between public and religious education (*Wisconsin v. Yoder*) and the moral – if not legal – limits of free speech (controversies over caricature of, and offense against, religion). As multiculturalism morphed into the political theory of religious freedom, new questions were raised about the difference between culture and religion on the one hand, and the grounds and limits of freedom of religion as a distinctive liberal freedom on the other. Why should religious belief be specially accommodated? Should we construe religious belief as a matter of choice, as a special burden, or

12 Will Kymlicka, *Multicultural Citizenship* (Oxford: Oxford University Press, 1995); Brian Barry, *Culture and Equality* (Cambridge: Polity, 2001).

as constitutive of the very identity of persons?[13] How should the 'costs of belief' be distributed fairly?[14] Is it fair to give religion special treatment?

Such questions have dominated US First Amendment jurisprudence since World War II. Over the years, the US Supreme Court developed an interpretation of the religious clauses that assigned religion a special place in the constitution – from *Sherbert v. Verner* (1963) to *Allegheny v. ACLU* (1989). While the Establishment clause subjects religion to a disability that is not imposed on other forms of thought and action (the state should not 'aid' religion), the Free Exercise clause extends a special privilege to religion (the state should not 'hinder' religion). Yet recent developments have seen the erosion both of the Establishment Clause (cf. voucher programmes for faith schools) and of the Free Exercise Clause (*Employment Division v. Smith*, 17 April 1990). US jurisprudence has elaborated a vast and rich body of work about the coherence of the two clauses and the grounds for the special treatment of religion.[15]

First, in relation to the Free Exercise clause of the First Amendment, political philosophers have been asking probing questions about the special nature of religious obligations and the justification of religious exemptions from the law. A variety of rationales for religious exemptions have been put forward: freedom of religious conscience, equal opportunities to express one's deep commitments and the basic need for self-respect. Some have argued that there is a *prima facie* claim for an exemption from laws that would otherwise force individuals to live below their own moral standards. The US Supreme Court's Free Exercise jurisprudence, for its part, holds that an exemption can be given when a law places a substantial burden on the religious life of the group and the law is the least restrictive means of securing a compelling state interest. But how are we to understand the key terms of this proposed balancing test – in particular, 'substantial burden' to religion and 'compelling state interest'? Are such burdens unique to religion and how can we design an equitable exemptions policy?[16]

The 'neutrality debate', for its part, tracks not the Free Exercise but the non-establishment dimension of the US debates. The US experience – with its exceptional combination of constitutional non-establishment and a highly religious civil society – has provided the template for the secular conception of religion implicit in Rawlsian political philosophy. US Supreme Court jurisprudence about

13 Barry, *Culture and Equality*; Brian Barry, *Equality* (New York: Perseus Books, 2008); Bhikhu Parekh, *Rethinking Multiculturalism* (Basingstoke: Macmillan, 2000); Paul Bou-Habib, 'A Theory of Religious Accommodation', *Journal of Applied Philosophy* 23.1 (2006): 109–26.

14 Peter Jones, 'Bearing the Consequences of Belief', *Journal of Political Philosophy* 2 (1994): 24–43.

15 Kent Greenawalt, *Religion and the Constitution*, 2 vols (Princeton, NJ: Princeton University Press, 2007); Martha Nussbaum, *Liberty of Conscience: In Defense of America's Tradition of Religious Equality* (New York: Perseus Books, 2008).

16 See Stuart White, 'Religious Exemptions: An Egalitarian Demand? *Law and Ethics of Human Rights* 6 (1): 97–118 (2012); Jonathan Seglow (Royal Holloway) 'Accommodating Religion: The Case of Legal Exemptions', paper presented at the Negotiating Religion in Politics and Political Theory Workshop, London: UCL, 12 February 2012.

the 'non-establishment' clause of the First Amendment has produced an extensive body of case law about what it means to 'aid', 'promote' or 'endorse' religion and what is wrong with state entanglement with religion. Yet the relationship between First Amendment principles and the public role of religion in the US has been fraught and complex. As recent controversies about the teaching of Darwinism in school, the constitutionality of school vouchers or the display of traditional Christian religious symbols in public spaces have underlined, the meaning of 'non-establishment' remains elusive and contested – notably by those who wish for a greater state recognition of religion.[17] European theorists have also resisted, on egalitarian grounds, the idea of a strict separation between state and religion. British sociologist Tariq Modood, for example, has advocated 'multi-faith establishment'[18] and Dutch political theorist Veit Bader has rejected traditional models of institutional separation in favour of more flexible associational democracy and 'non-constitutional pluralism'.[19]

Two principled questions, however, remain. The first concerns the ethical standard that should be applied when assessing state institutions and practices. While most theorists would agree that the state should not explicitly endorse and promote one religious doctrine or closely support one church at the expense of others, there is disagreement about the legitimacy of state-endorsed religious symbols.[20] One focal point of controversy in Europe has been the two ECtHR *Lautsi* decisions concerning the display of the Christian crucifix in Italian public schools. While '*Lautsi I*' (3 November 2009) declared it 'incompatible with the State's duty to respect neutrality in the exercise of public authority', '*Lautsi II*' (18 March 2011) held that a preference for majority religion reflected the 'history and tradition' of the state and that this was no 'departure from the principles of pluralism and objectivity' as long as it did not amount to 'indoctrination'. Legal theorists have analysed the compatibility of both *Lautsi I* and *Lautsi II* with the notion of liberal neutrality. One argument, put forward by Lorenzo Zucca among others, is that the conclusion reached by the Grand Chamber is not wrong in itself: the place of religious symbols in the public sphere should not be the object of a blanket ban; and it is possible for a secular state to carve out an exemption in relation to the presence of symbols in some educational contexts. However, the decision was poorly reasoned on every important point. It relies on a very dubious notion of 'passive symbols'. It dodges the problem of secularism as if it were a mere ideology. It preaches respect only to go on to grant the state freedom to disrespect

17 Noah Feldman, *Divided* by *God: America's Church–State Problem, and What We Should Do About It* (New York: Farrar, Straus & Giroux, 2005).

18 Tariq Modood, *Multiculturalism, Muslims and the British State* (London: British Association for the Study of Religion, 2003).

19 Veit Bader, *Secularism or Democracy? Associational Governance of Religious Diversity* (Amsterdam: Amsterdam University Press, 2007).

20 Cécile Laborde, 'Political Liberalism and Religion: On Separation and Establishment', *Journal of Political Philosophy* 21: 1 (2013), 67–86.

minorities. The ECtHR, then, can be said to have made a poor use of the justificatory notion of neutrality.[21]

The second application of liberal neutrality concerns the type of *reason* that can permissibly be invoked in public reason. Many European and American political theorists now agree that religions can play a legitimate, positive role in public debates and political life and that secularism should not be seen as a substantive, rationalist, anti-religious doctrine but rather as the framework for democratic deliberation and engagement.[22] Yet a difficult question remains, which concerns the ultimate justification of laws. Can religious convictions, by themselves, be sufficient to justify a coercive law – say, a law on abortion or homosexuality? This philosophical controversy is now the principal way in which the 'theological-political problem' is posed in normative Anglophone political philosophy.[23] Two positions can be identified in the literature. 'Exclusivist' political philosophers[24] argue that the legitimacy of the liberal state cannot be grounded by appeal to religious arguments. While religious citizens can present religious arguments in the background culture[25]or even in the public sphere *lato sensu*,[26] they should not, when advocating a coercive law, present religious arguments that cannot be translated into or complemented by secular reasons. 'Inclusivist' political philosophers[27]disagree. In their view, the differences between religious and secular reasons are not significant enough to justify the special exclusion of the former from public justification. Religious arguments are part and parcel of vibrant democratic debate; and the secular nature of reasoning does not guarantee that it will be less divisive, controversial or inaccessible than religiously inspired arguments. Public debate should not exclude those who seek to lead a 'religiously integrated' existence and who are unable or unwilling to translate or complement their deeply held religious views with secular reasons.[28]

21 Lorenzo Zucca, 'Exploring the Neutrality Dilemma', paper presented at the UCL 12 February 2012 workshop. See his *A Secular Europe: Law and Religion in the European Constitutional Landscape* (Oxford: Oxford University Press 2012).

22 Veit Bader, *Bader, Secularism or Democracy?*; Jürgen Habermas, *Between Naturalism and Religion: Philosophical Essays* (Cambridge: Polity, 2008).

23 Chris Eberle and Terence Cuneo, 'Religion and Political Theory', *The Stanford Encyclopedia of Philosophy. Winter 2008 Edition*, http://plato.stanford.edu/archives/win2008/entries/religion-politics, accessed 23 March 2016.

24 Robert Audi, *Religious Commitment and Secular Reason* (Cambridge: Cambridge University Press, 2000); Rawls, *Political Liberalism.*

25 Audi, *Religious Commitment.*

26 Habermas, *Between Naturalism and Religion*; Cécile Laborde, 'Justificatory Secularism', in *Religion in a Liberal State: Cross-Disciplinary Reflections*, eds Gavin D'Costa, Malcolm Evans, Tariq Modood and Julian Rivers (Cambridge: Cambridge University Press, 2013), 164–86.

27 Christopher Eberle, *Religious Conviction in Liberal Politics* (Cambridge: Cambridge University Press, 2002); Michael Perry, *Under God?* (Cambridge: Cambridge University Press, 2003); Nicholas Wolterstorff, *Justice: Rights and Wrongs* (Princeton, NJ: Princeton University Press, 2008); Jeffrey Stout, *Democracy and Tradition* (Princeton, NJ: Princeton University Press, 2004).

28 Michael Sandel, *Public Philosophy: Essays on Morality in Politics* (Cambridge, MA: Harvard University Press, 2005); Bader, *Secularism or Democracy?*

Chapters in this section

The chapters in this section address the three core issues of the establishment-neutrality debate: (1) religious argument and public reason; (2) neutrality and establishment; and (3) the future of constitutional establishment in a secularising society. They are written by three UCL experts on the topic, all based in the School of Public Policy: Albert Weale, Saladin Meckled-Garcia and Robert M. Morris. Each chapter considerably advances our understanding of key issues left unaddressed in the literature that I have just briefly surveyed and each presents an important contribution to the politics and philosophy of religion in its own right.

In 'Can there be a public reason of the heart?' (Chapter 5), Albert Weale addresses a question that, strangely, has not taken centre stage in the debate between inclusivists and exclusivists, namely, the question of the nature of religious argument and its compatibility with public reason. Weale endorses the ideal of public reason, but notes that, at the heart of our most cherished political ideals, there are 'rock-bottom beliefs or principles, in which we might have intuitive convictions but which it is hard to see as the outcome of a chain of reasoning'. Among these ideals are those of justice, solidarity and the dignity of human life. Those ideals have their roots in religious belief, but they have been demythologised and secularised in order to provide ethical guidance in a non-theistic world. Arguing against those who insist on a strong divide between faith and reason, or between 'reasons of the heart' and 'reasons of the head' (to use Pascal's phrase), Weale draws on Protestant modernist theology to show that the demythologisation of religious ideas reveals the 'grain of truth' inherent in transcendental, metaphorical, comprehensive worldviews.

Yet just as Weale endorses the project of demythologisation, he worries about what may get lost in the process of translation of religious into secular views. He provides three evocative illustrations of the potential and limits of such 'public reasons of the heart'. The first is John Rawls's notion of the moral arbitrariness of personal merit. Rawls's political philosophy was deeply informed by his early theological views and nowhere is this more evident than in his rendering of the idea that one's talents are a 'gift of God' into the secular idea that they are the product of a 'natural lottery'. Yet, as Weale points out, the two ideas point in importantly different directions. The difficulties involved in fully rendering the semantic power of a religious metaphor are also evident in Weale's second example, that of the annulment of Third World debt under the principle of the Jubilee. Can this be expressed as a principle of justice (and, if so, which one?) or does it rely on a broader principle of human solidarity (and on what bases)? The third indeterminacy pointed out by Weale concerns the ethical principles underpinning environmental protection. It is doubtful that these can be reduced to inter-personal, inter-generational principles. But how can we explain our duties to protect an impersonal good such as the natural world? How can we make sense of the 'ethics of stewardship' in a non-theistic, steward-less universe? If Weale is right, our 'rock-bottom beliefs' – about what a person is, how people should relate to one another and how they should relate to nature – have been demythologised but are difficult fully to grasp without the 'residue of metaphor' that they contain.

In 'The ethics of establishment: fairness and human rights as different standards of neutrality' (Chapter 6), Saladin Meckled-Garcia clarifies the relationship between religious establishment, human rights and liberal neutrality. Meckled-Garcia demonstrates that not all forms of religious establishment are illegitimate – they are not necessarily, that is, in violation of human rights – even though they may be in violation of fairness-based neutrality. He distinguishes between two different standards of liberal neutrality. Human rights standards protect the value of 'equal respect' for people's faculty to adopt, develop and pursue their beliefs and commitments. For example, they make it impermissible for states to limit people's basic religious freedoms, in a way that violates human integrity. Fairness-based neutrality, by contrast, is a different, more exacting standard. It requires not only equal respect but 'equal concern' and social fairness. It focuses on relative advantages and disadvantages, not on a basic minimum threshold. In particular, it makes it impermissible for states to favour one conception of the good, or one religious view, over others.

Meckled-Garcia warns against the tendency to confuse the two standards, a tendency he sees at work in recent judgements about religious freedom debates in Europe. Like Zucca, Meckled-Garcia takes the *Lautsi* decision as his test case. Practices of symbolic establishment such as the display of Christian crucifixes in state schools may be in violation of fairness-based neutrality, but they are not necessarily in violation of human-rights neutrality. This is because not every discrimination is a human rights violation: in the *Lautsi* case, the mere display of a crucifix does not amount to indoctrination or violation of basic rights of freedom of conscience. But it may well be the case that this display is incompatible with fairness-based neutrality, in that it publicly endorses and privileges one particular (Christian) culture in ways that fail to show equal concern with non-Christian cultures. If Meckled-Garcia is correct, religious non-establishment cannot be presented as a human rights requirement, which all states have to meet to be minimally legitimate. In turn, disestablishment – including the non-endorsement by the state of particular religious symbols – might be required by fairness-based neutrality within states.

In 'Alternative futures for formal church establishment in two countries' (Chapter 7), Robert M. Morris shows that the constitutional and political realities of establishment are not typically guided by the principles of public reason, neutrality or justice elaborated by philosophers. Historical path-dependency and self-interested pragmatism are more reliable guides for constitutional scholars. Yet while Morris provides a detailed, comprehensive account of the complex and shifting dynamics of church establishment in England and Scotland, he does not recoil from putting forward normative, principled evaluations of their 'alternative futures'. Most of establishment in Britain is vestigial: neither the Anglican nor the Scottish church (the Kirk) receives direct subvention from the state, nor does the state collect any form of tax for the church. Yet the Church of England, in particular, is constitutionally linked to the monarchy and the House of Lords, as well as enjoying long-standing institutional presence in school and prisons. The future of establishment, Morris argues, is now an open (if rarely openly posed) question. This is because both churches are undergoing a 'slow implosion', under the pressure of falling membership, the rapid decline of people seeking to train for the priesthood, financial pressures, religious de-institutionalisation and pluralisation and the pressures of equality and non-discrimination agendas.

Morris suggests that the latter, in particular, make the status quo hardly sustainable in the middle term. The recent discontinuation of the ban on royal Catholic marriages has only made the remaining religious tests (for succession to the Crown) glaringly archaic. And the Executive's withdrawal from church appointment has just made the position of bishops in Parliament more precarious, especially against the background of required Lords reform. This is all the more the case because Episcopal membership is not purely vestigial or symbolic, as evidenced by the bishops' role in rejecting a key amendment to the Equality Bill in 2010. Morris suggests that removing the compulsory link between churches and the British state would not be fatal either to the church or the monarchy and Parliament. Nor is he convinced by the Anglican Church's attempt to 'retrofit' the rationale for its continued institutional presence. He thinks that fears concerning an 'aggressive secularism' are exaggerated and he is not convinced by the church's attempt to paint itself as the leader of a 'multi-faith' coalition, a benevolent conduit for the integration of minority religions. In the end, he argues, even the purely symbolic dimension of establishment might be incompatible with civic equality and pluralism. Morris's chapter, then, provides a nice illustration of a productive dialogue between constitutional scholars and political philosophers on the matter of the principled 'negotiation' between states and religious organisations.

References

Audi, Robert. *Religious Commitment and Secular Reason*. Cambridge: Cambridge University Press, 2000.

Bader, Veit. *Secularism or Democracy? Associational Governance of Religious Diversity*. Amsterdam: Amsterdam University Press, 2007.

Barry, Brian. *Culture and Equality*. Cambridge: Polity, 2001.

Bou-Habib, Paul. 'A Theory of Religious Accommodation', *Journal of Applied Philosophy* 23.1 (2006): 109–26.

Cesari, Jocelyne. *Muslims in the West After 9/11: Religion, Politics and Law*. London: Routledge, 2009.

Davie, Grace. *Religion in Britain Since 1945: Believing without Belonging*. London: Wiley, 1994.

Douglas, G., Russell Sandberg, Norman Doe, Sophie Gilliat-Ray and Asma Khan. 'Religious Divorce in England and Wales: Religious Tribunals in Action', in *Family, Religion and Law: Cultural Encounters in Europe*, eds P. Shah, M. Foblets and M. Rohe. Farnham, UK: Ashgate, 2014, pp. 195–208.

Eberle, Christopher. *Religious Conviction in Liberal Politics*. Cambridge: Cambridge University Press, 2002.

Eberle, Christopher and Cuneo, Terence. 'Religion and Political Theory', *The Stanford Encyclopedia of Philosophy*, Winter 2008 Edition, http://plato.stanford.edu/archives/win2008/entries/religion-politics, accessed 21 March 2016.

Evans, Caroline. *Freedom of Religion under the European Convention on Human Rights*. Oxford: Oxford University Press, 2001.

Feldman, Noah. *Divided* by *God: America's Church–State Problem, and What We Should Do About It.* New York: Farrar, Straus & Giroux, 2005.

Forst, Rainer. *Toleration in Conflict.* Cambridge: Cambridge University Press, 2012.

Greenawalt, Kent. *Religion and the Constitution,* 2 vols. Princeton, NJ: Princeton University Press, 2007.

Habermas, Jürgen. *Between Naturalism and Religion: Philosophical Essays.* Cambridge: Polity, 2008.

Hervieu-Léger, Danièle. *La religion en mouvement: le pèlerin et le converti.* Paris: Flammarion, 1999.

Jones, Peter. 'Bearing the Consequences of Belief', *Journal of Political Philosophy* 2 (1994): 24–43.

Kymlicka, Will. *Multicultural Citizenship.* Oxford: Oxford University Press, 1995.

Kuru, Ahmet T. *Secularism and State Policies toward Religion: The United States, France, and Turkey.* Cambridge: Cambridge University Press, 2009.

Laborde, Cécile. 'Political Liberalism and Religion: On Separation and Establishment', *Journal of Political Philosophy* 21: 1 (2013), 67–86.

——. 'Justificatory Secularism', in *Religion in a Liberal State: Cross-Disciplinary Reflections,* eds Gavin D'Costa, Malcolm Evans, Tariq Modood and Julian Rivers. Cambridge: Cambridge University Press, 2013, 164–86.

Madeley, John. 'Religion and the State', in *Routledge Handbook of Religion and Politics,* ed. Jeffrey Haynes. New York: Routledge, 2009, 174–91.

——. 'Six Degrees of Separation? Variants of Religious Establishment in Europe. Paper presented at the Negotiating Religion in Politics and Political Theory Workshop, London: UCL, 12 February 2012.

Modood, Tariq. *Multiculturalism, Muslims and the British State.* London: British Association for the Study of Religion, 2003.

Nussbaum, Martha. *Liberty of Conscience: In Defense of America's Tradition of Religious Equality.* New York: Perseus Books, 2008.

Parekh, Bhikhu. *Rethinking Multiculturalism.* Basingstoke: Macmillan, 2000.

Perry, Michael. *Under God?* Cambridge: Cambridge University Press, 2003.

Rawls, John. *A Theory of Justice.* Cambridge: Harvard University Press, 1971.

——. *Political Liberalism.* New York: Columbia University Press, 1993.

Sandel, Michael. *Public Philosophy: Essays on Morality in Politics.* Cambridge: Harvard University Press, 2005.

Seglow, Jonathan. 'Accommodating Religion: The Case of Legal Exemptions', paper presented at the Negotiating Religion in Politics and Political Theory Workshop, London: UCL, 12 February 2012.

Stout, Jeffrey. *Democracy and Tradition.* Princeton, NJ: Princeton University Press, 2004.

Swaine, Lucas. *The Liberal Conscience: Politics and Principle in a World of Religious Pluralism.* New York: Columbia University Press, 2006.

Weiler, Joseph H.H. 'A Christian Europe? Europe and Christianity: Rules of Commitment', *European View* 6: 1 (2007), 143–50.

White, Stuart. 'Religious Exemptions: An Egalitarian Demand?' *Law and Ethics of Human Right* 6: 1 (2012), 97–118.

Wolterstorff, Nicholas. *Justice: Rights and Wrongs.* Princeton, NJ: Princeton University Press, 2008.

Zucca, Lorenzo. *A Secular Europe: Law and Religion in the European Constitutional Landscape.* Oxford: Oxford University Press, 2012.

5 Can there be a public reason of the heart?

Albert Weale

Le cœur a ses raisons, que la raison ne connaît point.

(Pascal, *Pensées*, 397)

Pascal famously said that the heart has reasons of which reason does not know. He was of course primarily thinking of reasons for religious belief and the leading of a religious life, contrasting those reasons with the natural reasoning of the wager. Much modern liberal political theory seeks to exclude distinctively religious beliefs from the public sphere arguing that free and equal citizens in a morally pluralist society must reason from a point of view that does not presume comprehensive religious or metaphysical commitments. In this respect, the principles of liberal political theory echo the practice of modern democracies, which, whatever their other variations, are generally committed to principles of religious toleration and pluralism. Even when there is an established religion, as in England, Scotland or the Scandinavian countries, the civil disadvantages associated with not being a member of the established church are either nugatory or, as with restrictions on marrying in a church that one does not support, seem perfectly reasonable. The same principles of toleration and pluralism are also taken to imply that matters of law or public policy should not to be settled by reference to the specific doctrines of a particular religion, but instead by appeal to considerations and interests that all citizens can share and affirm in their capacity as citizens.

In recent years political theorists have spent much time formulating a way of thinking about these principles of toleration and pluralism and what they imply for liberal democratic practice. Following Rawls, political theorists have construed the issue as being one about the scope and limits of 'public reason', where the idea of public reason refers to a mode of deliberation about political values that, in matters of constitutional essentials, can be shared among all citizens, because the considerations on which it relies do not depend upon any specific religious or metaphysical views.[1] Reliance on the *idea* of public reason in this sense is an appeal

1 John Rawls, *Political Liberalism* (New York: Columbia University Press, 1996); John Rawls, 'The Idea of Public Reason Revisited', *University of Chicago Law Review* 64 (1997): 765–807. Reprinted in John Rawls, *Collected Papers* ed. Samuel Freeman (Cambridge, MA: Harvard University Press, 1999), pp. 573–615, from which references are taken.

to a certain political *ideal.*[2] The ideal is that just relations among citizens with different and incompatible moral and religious beliefs require respect for conscience and liberty in a system of mutual toleration. Just relations understood in this way are based upon a principle of reciprocity, according to which no one can expect other citizens to adopt constitutional arrangements on grounds that they cannot accept within their own conception of the good life. Since there are distinct and incompatible conceptions of the good life, the task is to find reasons that all can endorse. The legitimation of a political order requires justice to take the form of reciprocal recognition of the conscientious convictions of others. It follows from these claims, it is alleged, that no one should advance distinctively religious claims as a ground of public action, since in a pluralist society others will not be able conscientiously to accept such claims. Only those claims logically equivalent to secular reasoning, excluding distinctively religious or metaphysical premises, are rightly grounds of public reasoning.

When Pascal said that the heart has its reasons of which reason cannot know, this was part of his larger theoretical claim that understanding is divided between those things that can be shown by the intellect and those things sensed by the heart. Thus, according to Pascal, the heart senses that there are three dimensions, but the intellect demonstrates that there cannot be two squared numbers of which one is the double of the other.[3] The contrast here is between a truth intuitively recognised and a truth that can only be recognised as the result of a chain of explicit reasoning. However, Pascal also holds that only those who are disposed to put themselves in the right frame of mind to be receptive to the word of God will come to true belief. This latter argument suggests that behind the intuition of a truth there lies the need for a certain attitudinal disposition, one that does not always see the intuitively graspable truth that is present to the senses. To acknowledge the force of reasons of the heart, one must be disposed to be receptive to such reasons.

In this chapter I am going to use (perhaps abuse) this notion of reasons of the heart to discuss the role of religious argumentation in a liberal political order. In particular, I am going to generalise Pascal's notion of reasons of the heart to denote those beliefs that we take seriously as guides to life but for which we cannot provide an intellectually satisfactory ground beyond the simple statement of those beliefs. They are important rock-bottom beliefs or principles, in which we might have intuitive conviction but which are hard to see as the outcome of a chain of reasoning. Examples of such beliefs include the belief in the intrinsic dignity of human life or the importance of social solidarity as well as justice in economic relations. I wish to suggest that religious ways of talking, ways that can be understood in a demythologised sense, provide us with devices for expressing these beliefs for which it is hard to find functional substitutes and for which a literal rendition, though sometimes necessary, is not always adequate. The idea of demythologisation, on

2 Compare Charles E. Larmore, *Patterns of Moral Complexity* (Cambridge: Cambridge University Press, 1987), 45.

3 Blaise Pascal, *Pensées*, edition de Michel Le Guern (Paris: Gallimard, 1977), § 101.

which this argument rests, is associated with modernist Protestant theology in the twentieth century. Demythologisation was the principle that, in interpreting Biblical texts, literal meaning was to be replaced by the existential truths implicit in that literal meaning. The programme of demythologisation attracts less interest now than it did at one time, being squeezed between the forces of a vigorous Biblical fundamentalism (particularly in the US), Catholic neo-Thomism (particularly in Europe and the US) and radical orthodoxy (particularly in Anglicanism).

In this chapter I will not argue the abstract merits of taking up once again this programme. Instead I will seek to exhibit its continuing relevance through its approach to the construal of public reason. I leave it an open question as to whether those with firm religious convictions of any sort would find the approach satisfactory.

I begin by setting out the basic line of argument in favour of a secular notion of public reason as it appears in Rawls, noting some other variants of the claim. I then lay out the essentials of the programme of demythologisation in order to illustrate the method on which it relies and the characteristic claims to which it gives rise. To illustrate its force I discuss three examples – merit and justice, the forgiveness of debt and environmental protection – before drawing some general conclusions.

The idea of public reason

The basic idea of public reason as adumbrated in Rawls is quite clear. On matters of constitutional essentials, involving questions of justice, citizens are to advance their preferred view of what should be done solely by reference to the political values that underlie the political constitution:

> [Our] exercise of political power is proper and hence justifiable only when it is exercised in accordance with a constitution the essentials of which all citizens may reasonably be expected to endorse in the light of principles and ideals acceptable to them as reasonable and rational. This is the liberal principle of legitimacy.[4]

The principle of public reason applies to citizens, when they advocate political decisions in respect of constitutional essentials, as well as public officials acting in their official capacity, most notably as judges in constitutional courts.

The basic rationale for the principle of public reason is that the political values that are realised in a well-ordered liberal constitutional regime are very great, and given a duty of civility, it would be wrong for citizens to seek to make political determinations on the basis of the views and doctrines of an association that was not universally shared.[5] Supporting this line of argument is the assumption that

4 Rawls, *Political Liberalism*, 217.
5 Rawls, *Political Liberalism*, 218.

there is a reasonable plurality of views about matters such as religion, a plurality arising from what Rawls calls 'the burdens of judgement', making it intrinsically difficult to come to conclusions on complex matters.

Rawls adopts what he calls an 'inclusive view' with respect to public reasons.[6] That is to say, he allows that people may have religious reasons for advocating a particular law or policy, but, if they can reformulate their view in terms of public reasons, then they have not violated the requirements of public reason. Thus those campaigning for the abolition of slavery in the US or civil rights campaigners like Martin Luther King often phrased their claims in religious terms. For Rawls, such persons did not violate the requirements of public reason because the upshot of their actions was to realise the values of the constitution. Thus, 'the civil rights movement did not go against the ideal of public reason'.[7] Explicating this view, Rawls formulates a proviso, according to which reasons drawn from religious beliefs can be introduced into public political discussion, provided that 'in due course proper political reasons . . . are presented to support whatever the comprehensive doctrines introduced are sufficient to support'.[8]

The proviso is an important element in understanding the liberal position. It is not a violation of the principle of public reason as formulated by Rawls to advance political claims that are extensionally equivalent in practice to policies that can be advocated on grounds that are related to constitutional values. Thus, to take one possible example, the civil rights movement used, as an argument for social and political equality, the claim that all persons were 'children of God'. However, they could have used the principle stated in the Fourteenth Amendment to the US Constitution, which stipulates that no citizen shall be deprived of 'the equal protection of the laws'. Insofar as these are extensionally equivalent in their practical effects, the Rawlsian proviso would allow the religious version of the statement in the public realm as much as the second. It is, of course, an interesting problem in this context as to how a US citizen might appeal to the American Declaration of Independence ('We hold these truths to be self-evident, that all men are created equal, that they are endowed by their Creator with certain inalienable rights, that among these are life, liberty and the pursuit of happiness') as a ground of civil liberties, but presumably the proponent of a strict thesis of public reason could argue that this theistic account of equality had in fact been incorporated in the US Constitution in a suitably public form. What is precluded by the Rawlsian principle of public reason is the advancing of principles for public action that rely upon considerations that are only meaningful within a particular religious or metaphysical set of assumptions. The web of citizens' public belief is not allowed to extend beyond what is inter-subjectively agreeable to citizens with different religious and metaphysical views.

Central to this account of public reason is a conceptual distinction between comprehensive doctrines, on the one hand, and public political reasons, on the

6 Rawls, *Political Liberalism*, 247–54.

7 Rawls, *Political Liberalism*, 251.

8 Rawls, 'The Idea of Public Reason Revisited', 591.

other. Rawls's usual example of comprehensive doctrines is religious belief and it is easy to see why religion should be such an important point of reference. However, at one point, he gives general equilibrium theories in economics as an example of a comprehensive doctrine.[9] Now many people (count me in) are inclined to think that general equilibrium theories and their close cousin the efficient market hypothesis have the status too often in economic discussions of metaphysical commitments rather than empirically supported beliefs. Be that as it may. There is an obvious question as to how we draw the line in respect of complex social scientific theories between what should be allowed in public reason and what should be disallowed. What about partial equilibrium theories? Do we exclude the labour theory of value? Are we allowed to invoke notions of the 'just price' as is done in Catholic social teaching for example? Rawls contrasts comprehensive doctrines with 'plain truths', but this seems to ignore the extent to which what is 'plain' may depend upon the intellectual paradigm within which it is located. In other words, the whole approach rests upon a distinction between 'comprehensive doctrines' and doctrines that can be affirmed from the point of view of citizens with different comprehensive doctrines, but that distinction is fuzzy at best. Between the deliverances of plain truths and the abstractions of highly developed social scientific theories there is much ground to be trod. And if this is so for social scientific theories, it will apply equally to religious beliefs.

Although Rawls's voice has been the dominant one in the advocacy of a liberal principle of public reason, his has not been the only voice. For example, Gutmann and Thompson are clear that the requirement to give public reasons in a deliberative democracy rests on the principle of fair cooperation among citizens and the reciprocity this requires excludes appealing only to the authority of revelation.[10] Larmore argues that the state should not promote any particular conception of the good because it is thought to be intrinsically superior and Audi argues that respect for others means that in matters of law and public policy all should be motivated in their arguments only by adequate secular reasons.[11]

Against this background, Jeremy Waldron has forcefully suggested that members of a democratic society are depriving themselves of the opportunity to understand public issues better if they do not attend to points of view that are expressed in religious terms.[12] As examples he cites the 1986 National Conference of Catholic Bishops' Pastoral Letter on economic justice, in which the final purpose of human life is said to be to share the divine life and in which it is asserted that all property

9 Rawls, *Political Liberalism*, 225.

10 Amy Gutmann and Dennis Thompson, *Why Deliberative Democracy?* (Princeton, NJ and Oxford: Princeton University Press, 2004), 3–4.

11 Larmore, *Patterns of Moral Complexity*, 43; Robert Audi 'The Place of Religious Argument in a Free and Democratic Society', *San Diego Law Review* 30 (1993): 677–702. These and other examples are cited and discussed in Christopher J. Eberle, *Religious Conviction in Liberal Politics* (Cambridge: Cambridge University Press, 2002), chapter 3.

12 Jeremy Waldron, 'Religious Contributions in Public Deliberation', *San Diego Law Review* 30 (1993): 817–48; 'Two-Way Translation: The Ethics of Engaging with Religious Contributions in Public Deliberation', *New York University Public Law and Legal Theory Working Papers*, No. 241 (2010).

is held in trust for others, as well as a 2007 statement by 'Evangelicals for Human Rights' published as an 'Evangelical Declaration against Torture', the basic principle of which is phrased in terms of the sacredness of human life bestowed by the atonement for sin by the suffering of Christ on the cross. Waldron's argument is that, though these arguments will seem strange to non-believers, it is in this difference and strangeness, when approached in a spirit of charitable translation, that their value resides. My own argument resembles Waldron's in a number of ways, but it ultimately rests upon a different basis. I suggest that what is notable about religious arguments is not their being strange but their reminding us of the familiar. In religious language we may see through a glass darkly, but what we see, when rightly understood, is only too familiar in its basic aspects, though it may leave much open to further enquiry. In exploring this possibility I shall rely upon the idea of 'demythologised' religious understanding.

The programme of demythologisation

Alasdair MacIntyre once pointed out that there were two types of atheism.[13] The first was of the Hume–Russell variety in which atheism rests upon the assertion that the purported intellectual grounds for believing in God are fallacious. As an example of the sort of fallacy that such atheists have in mind, consider the 'first-cause' argument for the existence of God. Suppose someone reasons that, since there is a cause for everything, everything must have a cause and so God exists. Such an argument would be fallacious. One cannot validly move from 'everything has a cause' to 'there is a cause for everything', since a property that may hold for the individual terms of a series may not hold collectively for the whole series. (In the series of natural numbers, all numbers are either odd or even, but the series is not odd or even.) Much writing of the Hume–Russell variety consists of pointing out logical errors of this type, perhaps the most famous example being Hume's *Dialogues on Natural Religion.* As MacIntyre notes of this sort of atheism:

> Insofar as it seeks to explain religion it tends to lay stress on the general folly and weakness of human beings; its panacea is usually education, and its grief is that increased education by no means always produces increased skepticism about Christianity.[14]

This form of atheism is widely prevalent and one of its most distinguished contemporary practitioners is Richard Dawkins.[15]

The second sort of atheism MacIntyre identifies is one he attributes to Ludwig Feuerbach, David Strauss and Karl Marx (in my view Friedrich Schleiermacher presented a proto-version). According to this view, although religion may be false,

13 Alasdair MacIntyre, *Against the Self-Images of the Age: Essays on Ideology and Philosophy* (London: Duckworth, 1971), 12–13.

14 MacIntyre, *Against the Self-Images of the Age*, 13.

15 Richard Dawkins, *The God Delusion* (London: Bantam Press, 2006).

it nonetheless states important truths about human and social life. Thus, when Marx said that religion was the opiate of the people, he did not mean that religion was being used by a ruling class for their own ends to dupe the populace into submission. Rather, just as members of the ruling class turned to opium for consolation, so the people turned to religion to satisfy their craving for meaning. Marx's metaphor of the camera-obscura used in relation to his discussion of Hegel is a good one here: in a camera-obscura we see the object truly, but we see it upside down. Within this second tradition of atheism the search is for a form of social life in which authentic human needs are fulfilled. Its humanism is social rather than intellectual. Its method is not the identification of fallacies but the reinterpretation of religious meanings.

By the mid-twentieth century this second tradition of atheism had informed and penetrated biblical criticism and theological interpretation. In its vulgar version its manifesto was John Robinson's *Honest to God.*[16] However, its most sophisticated exponents included Rudolf Bultmann and Paul Tillich, two of the greatest Christian theologians of the twentieth century.[17] Bultmann's programme of demythologisation involved accepting that, in literal terms, much that was to be found within the Bible was false, but when properly interpreted, it stated important existential truths. Thus, the mythology of the Bible expresses a certain understanding of human existence. 'It believes that the world and human life have their ground and their limits in a power which is beyond all that we can calculate or control.' When God is said to reside in heaven, it means that God is beyond the world. The belief in Satan expresses the truth that our own actions are puzzling to ourselves and others and that people often lose control of themselves and so lose possession of their authentic existence. Freedom is not a matter of satisfying momentary desires but of following a law that one can affirm, a truth often expressed in the need to follow the spirit of God. 'History goes on and pulls down all the towers of Babel again and again' so revealing human finitude.[18]

It may be argued that, insofar as the programme of demythologisation is successful, its effect is to bring religious belief into conformity with the requirements of the liberal conception of public reason. If religion is simply a matter of revealing human finitude or talk of Satan is a way of saying that our actions are puzzling to ourselves and others, we can render these ideas in a purely secular idiom – that is after all what Bultmann's own existentialist interpretation does – and in doing so we have met the Rawlsian proviso. The original form of the claims may have been religious, but in being rendered in a demythologised idiom, the claims have been reduced to 'plain truths'. Reasons of the heart have become reasons of the head.

16 John A.T. Robinson, *Honest to God* (London: SCM Press, 1963).

17 Rudolf Bultmann, *Jesus Christ and Mythology* (London: SCM Press, 1960); Paul Tillich, *Systematic Theology: Three Volumes* (Welwyn: James Nisbet, 1968). Dietrich Bonhoeffer is often regarded as the third of this group because of his idea of 'religionless Christianity', but for various reasons I regard his theology as more conventional. As the late Stephen Sykes once pointed out in a series of lectures I attended, when Bonhoeffer spoke about religionless Christianity, he was really criticising the pietistic tradition in German Christianity.

18 For all these claims, see Bultmann, *Jesus Christ and Mythology*.

However, the thesis that demythologised religious language satisfies the conditions of 'plain truths' relies on a tacit theory of translation to the effect that what is said in religious language is *fully* captured in its demythologised equivalent. Yet, this reductionist thesis is untrue if religious language is metaphorical. Metaphor cannot be explicated either by reference to literal equivalents or by the notion of simile. When congregations at evensong pray that we 'have erred and strayed strayed from thy ways like lost sheep', they do not intend the metaphor to establish a similarity in all respects between themselves and lost sheep (for example wondering when they will be sheared), but neither do they think that simply saying that they have sinned captures all that is meant by the metaphor. The metaphor implies a disposition and dependence that is not part of a simple confession of wrong. As Max Black pointed out, when somebody is making a metaphorical statement (his example is 'The Lord is my shepherd'), that person may be taken charitably to be using the words that are most apt to express his or her thoughts and feelings.[19] It is simply a prejudice to suppose that the non-metaphorical use of language is somehow logically prior to the metaphorical use of language. As Black also noted, since the world is necessarily the world under a certain description, the construction of a metaphor changes something about the description of that world, creating a similarity that was not there before.[20]

To interpret in accordance with the requirements of demythologisation does not imply the thesis that the demythologised literal version of the belief is more basic than the mythical version. It is, however, to discard from the mythical version the unnecessary elements that prevent our seeing the truth that the myth metaphorically expresses. Reasons of the heart are typically expressed in metaphors; perhaps to be truly reasons of the heart they can only be expressed in metaphors. This is true in the theory of justice, in the understanding of forgiveness and solidarity and in our understanding of environmental protection, important examples to which I now turn.

Public reason and the rejection of desert

Consider, first, the theory of justice. As is now well known, Rawls's views on justice have an interesting pre-history in his earlier religious views, as expressed in his

19 Max Black, *Perplexities: Rational Choice, the Prisoner's Dilemma, Metaphor, Poetic Ambiguity, and Other Puzzles* (Ithaca, NY and London: Cornell University Press, 1990), 51.

20 Black, *Perplexities*, 70–4. On one occasion when I was privileged to hear Max Black speak on metaphor, he was fond of quoting the lines from Wallace Stevens, a poet whom he admired, from 'The Man with the Blue Guitar':

> They said, 'You have a blue guitar,
> You do not play things as they are'.
> The man replied, 'Things as they are
> Are changed upon the blue guitar'.
>
> Wallace Stevens, *Selected Poems* (London: Faber & Faber, 1965), 52.

undergraduate dissertation *A Brief Inquiry into the Meaning of Sin and Faith.*[21] There are many interesting elements in this work, but one that is particularly striking is Rawls's discussion of the place of merit in a just distribution. In his mature general theory of justice, Rawls rejected the idea of merit as a basis of economic distribution arguing that it permitted the distribution of wealth and income to be determined by the natural distribution of abilities and talents, a natural lottery that was arbitrary from a moral perspective.[22] By contrast, he asserted,

> The difference principle represents, in effect, an agreement to regard the distribution of natural talents as in some respects a common asset and to share in the greater social and economic benefits made possible by the complementarities of this distribution. Those who have been favoured by nature, whoever they are, may gain from their good fortune only on terms that improve the situation of those who have lost out.[23]

Because no one deserves his or her greater natural capacity, no one deserves higher economic reward.

As it stands this seems a curious line of argument. It is hard to see why viewing one's talents as part of a natural lottery should lead to the view that there is a case for regarding the distribution of natural talents as part of a common pool. The standard response most people have to a lottery that they have won is to bank the prize. It may be that one cannot carry over the intuitions from a lottery that all have entered into voluntarily to the lottery of life, but the case is surely not clear-cut one way or the other. Moreover, insisting on the common assets principle has for many people the counter-intuitive implication that, by labouring, instead of distinguishing what is private from what is common (for example by the labour that is involved in harvesting natural resources), one is incurring an obligation to others.[24]

With the publication of the *Brief Inquiry*, however, we now see that the rejection of desert by Rawls was originally based in a theological belief that believers should see their talents and assets as a gift of God.

> The human person, once perceiving that the Revelation of the Word is a condemnation of the self, casts away all thoughts of his own merit. He sees that the givenness of God is everywhere prevenient, and that he possesses nothing that has not been given. He knows that what he has received has been given by some 'other', and that ultimately all good things are gifts of God. There in the face of this givenness of God, in the face of His perfect and righteous mercy, he knows that he has no merit. Never again can he

21 John Rawls, *A Brief Inquiry into the Meaning of Sin and Faith, with 'On My Religion'*, ed. Thomas Nagel (Cambridge, MA: Harvard University Press, 2009).

22 John Rawls, John, *A Theory of Justice* (Oxford: Oxford University Press, 1999, revised edition), 63–4.

23 Rawls, *A Theory of Justice*, 87.

24 Albert Weale, *Democratic Justice and the Social Contract* (Oxford: Oxford University Press, 2013), 86.

> hope to boast of his good deeds, of his skill, of his prowess, for he knows that they are gifts.[25]

In their thoughtful introduction to the *Brief Inquiry*, Cohen and Nagel write, there is 'a particularly striking continuity between the thesis and Rawls's later views' on this point.[26] They also note that this position is linked to the rejection of Pelagian doctrines in other parts of the thesis.[27] They go on to say that these reflections, 'though linked here to revelation, can be given a purely secular significance and they lead directly to the moral sensibility that underlies the difference principle'.[28]

The notion of 'a purely secular significance' needs some interrogation, however. Are the religious and secular formulations are genuinely of equivalent logical effect? Contrast the following two statements:

1 My talents are a gift of God and so should be regarded as part of the stock of common assets.
2 My talents are a result of the natural lottery and so should be regarded as part of the stock of common assets.

These two formulations are very different. The first involves all sorts of ancillary beliefs, including the belief that this is what God requires and faithful obedience to the word of God consists in following that requirement. In this conception the understanding of one's talents as a gift of God provides, as Adams puts it in his discussion, 'a positive motive of gratitude for giving back to God by giving to the community that God is establishing'.[29] By contrast, there is no broader framework of belief in which the understanding of one's talents as given underlying the appeal to the supposed significance of the natural lottery of life.

Adams also points out that Rawls's views about merit are linked to his account of the experience of conversion, which involves recognising that the totality of what a person possesses is a gift of God.[30] It also involves seeing merit as linked to a claim of social superiority. Since the interest in social superiority is egotism, conversion is in a large part turning away from egotism. Comparing the argument in *A Theory of Justice* with the *Brief Inquiry*, Adams observes:

> I doubt, however, that seeing everything as a gift of God is simply superfluous as a support for the rejection of meritorian perfectionism. It is not obvious

25 Rawls, *A Brief Inquiry*, 239–40.
26 Joshua Cohen and Thomas Nagel, 'Introduction', in John Rawls, *A Brief Inquiry into the Meaning of Sin and Faith, with 'On My Religion'* ed. Thomas Nagel (Cambridge, MA: Harvard University Press, 2009), 18.
27 Rawls, *A Brief Inquiry*, 170–4 and 229–30.
28 Cohen and Nagel, 'Introduction', 19.
29 Robert Merrihew Adams, 'The Theological Ethics of the Young Rawls and Its Background', in John Rawls, *A Brief Inquiry into the Meaning of Sin and Faith, with 'On My Religion'* ed. Thomas Nagel (Cambridge, MA: Harvard University Press, 2009), 89.
30 Adams, 'The Theological Ethics of the Young Rawls', 86, citing Rawls, *A Brief Inquiry*, 238–40.

> that the merely negative consideration that one's acquisition of any perfection is never wholly one's own doing gets a strong grip on perfectionist thinking. For the perfectionist claims that Rawls most wishes to oppose are typically seen by perfectionists as grounded in the actual or possible *possession* of perfections, rather than in any *earning* of a reward by the mode of acquisition of the perfections. Seeing everything as a gift of God provides a positive motive of gratitude for giving back to God by giving to the community that God is establishing.[31]

I do not pursue this line of argument simply to make an *ad hominem* point against Rawls. His discussion of merit, both in the dissertation and in his later theory, is deep and thoughtful. However, the contrast that Adams highlights is illuminating. One cannot assume that the views expressed in religious terms are reducible to their later secular formulation. The metaphorical force of being a creature of God's making carries significance over and above the appeal to the idea of a natural lottery. For in a natural lottery there is no constraint on simply taking the prize. In the religious formulation there is – if one takes one's status as the recipient of a gift of God seriously. That broader framework of belief has relevance not only for our understanding of the motive to act justly but also for our understanding of the limits of justice and the role of the idea of social solidarity.

Social solidarity, jubilee and the remission of debt

> And if your brother becomes poor besides you, and sells himself to you, you shall not make him serve as a slave: he shall be with you as a hired servant and a sojourner. He shall serve with you until the year of the jubilee; then he shall go out from you, he and his children with him, and go back to his own family, and return to the possession of his fathers. For they are my servants, whom I brought forth out of the land of Egypt; they shall not be sold as slaves.[32]

In the theology of *Leviticus*, Hebrew cannot own another Hebrew as a slave and may only have Hebrew males as servants, although the purchase of male and female foreigners as slaves is permitted. At the time of jubilee, the male Hebrew servants are to be released and allowed to return to their own families. The general principle of jubilee is a principle of debt forgiveness and restitution. When part of a poor person's property is sold, it may be redeemed (for land cannot be sold in perpetuity) at an appropriate rate, but at jubilee it shall be returned. Money may not be lent at interest to the poor, who are entitled to be maintained. The rationale for these rules is stated in the quotation: 'For they are my servants, whom I brought forth out of the land of Egypt . . .'

31 Adams, 'The Theological Ethics of the Young Rawls', 89.
32 *Leviticus*, 25: 39–42.

The bringing forth from the land of Egypt is made up of a specific series of events, including the plagues, the parting of the Red Sea and the wanderings in the desert and these events lead to the covenant between God and Israel and the associated obligations involved in possession of the promised land. Among these obligations are to be found debt forgiveness and the restitution of property in the practice of jubilee. Although the obligations are upon individuals to release other individuals from their economic obligations, the requirement underlying the obligation arises as a consequence of the relationship between God and His people. It is the people who were brought out of slavery. By virtue of God's having brought the people out of slavery, individual members of the people are required to ensure that no member of the same people is allowed to enter into slavery and even the milder obligations of service are to be remitted at jubilee. Such an account cannot form the basis for a public conception of the scope of justice and legitimacy in a morally and religiously pluralistic society. The rationale of the practice depends upon participation by a people and its descendents in a particular history. Without that shared history, the rationale for the practice is simply irrelevant.

To demythologise is to find the general principle in the particular case, however. The principle at work in the practice of jubilee is that obligations of justice at the individual level must be set aside if the pattern of social relations in which those individual obligations are contained lead to slavery or to debt that cannot be repaid by work. These are obligations beyond justice and they rest upon a principle of solidarity in membership. To see how this is so, note that there is no assumption within the rationale of the practice of jubilee that the master has unjustly acquired the servant, particularly if the servant does not have the status of a slave. If someone is poor and yet finds work, then they have improved their situation over what it would have been had they not been able to find work. And everyone who can has the obligation to work. Moreover, there is presumption that the poor who have faced the hard choice of selling themselves into service have reached that position as a result of an injustice. Perhaps they have been unlucky or the terms of trade in their previous occupation have moved against them, but that is not the same as saying that they have suffered an injustice. Suppose the master is good and treats the servants well. The obligation under the rule of jubilee is still to release them from their service. Although the master has committed no injustice and has acted justly in respect of the servants, there is a more demanding requirement of remission and release.

It may be argued at this point that there is no need to invoke a principle of social solidarity beyond justice because justice is a matter of sustaining a certain pattern of economic outcomes.[33] Such holistic conceptions do not see the repayment of debts as a basic requirement of justice, but instead define a profile of allocations to which the fair shares of the members of society should conform. Scheffler correctly points out that, for all their other differences, utilitarian and Rawlsian accounts of justice are holistic in this sense, making the justice of individual

33 The point has been put to me by Cécile Laborde.

advantages depend upon the definition of a just overall distribution.[34] So, if some persons were to end up at an economic disadvantage as a result of the exchanges into which they entered with others, rectification of the resulting inequalities would itself be a matter of justice. The point obviously raises deep and extensive questions. Here I shall simply assert that any plausible theory of justice must be consistent with the obligations that are implied by a just basic structure of society. Within such a structure exchanges freely entered into will set up obligations and to suppose that justice is conformity to some overall profile is to suppose that a benevolent social planner is capable of wiping the tear from every eye, which is an implausible belief.

Hence, we are still left with the question of whether over-riding the principle of justice for the sake of solidarity make sense outside of the particular history of the relationship between God and Israel. If one's membership of a people carries obligations by virtue of that membership, then of course the obligation of jubilee will make sense. But how can it make sense for those who are not participants in that history? Here I think we need the public reasons of the heart to support the ideal of social solidarity that in religious terms is stated in terms of God's activity in bringing Israel from out of the conditions of slavery. To suppose that justice is sufficient for the good ordering of society and that we can dispense with solidarity beyond justice is to ignore the extent to which any system of just relations is embedded in conditions beyond individual and social control. It is to suppose that as individuals we not only make our own history, but also that as a society we collectively make the conditions for individual action. Yet: 'It is he that hath made us, and not we ourselves' (Psalm 100: 3). Justice is a human convention – a social contract – for the peaceful and mutually beneficial conduct of our business and practical affairs. In economic relations it relies upon the willingness and ability of people to enter into reciprocal arrangements in ways that are credible and reliable. Essential to ensuring these conditions of credibility and reliability are maintained is an enforcement system by which payment of debt is enforced and obligations are fulfilled. If those who sell themselves into service have not been unjustly forced to do so, then they have an obligation in justice to fulfil their part of the bargain. However, this is to ignore the requirements of social solidarity.

At this point it might be argued that a practice like the remission of debt will not abrogate justice, because the rules of remission are known before any economic relations are created and so those employing servants will know that their contractual rights will be limited by the requirements of any such remission. Yet, this only pushes the problem back a stage. Why in a world without the obligation to God should someone not argue that no rule of remission should be established? The only answer that can be given is that there is a human solidarity beyond justice, so that the demands of justice have to be tempered by that solidarity. Such solidarity cannot be rationalised by principles of mutual advantage. It is a reason

34 Samuel Scheffler, 'Distributive Justice and Economic Desert', in *Desert and Justice* ed. Serena Olsaretti (Oxford: Clarendon Press, 2003), 81–2.

of the heart and, to the extent to which it underlies a social order, it is a public reason of the heart.

In its demythologised version, then, the practice of jubilee provides an understanding of how justice may be over-ridden, indeed must be over-ridden, if important values are to be preserved and enhanced. This does not mean that the remission of debt is a morally easy question in any context and particularly in a context like the present when indebtedness is a tangled phenomenon. In an inter-dependent world, one can have more argument as to who is obliged to waive their rights under justice than about anything else. However, that the remission of debt is often a requirement of morality, including a political morality, is the demythologised interpretation of jubilee.

The idea of stewardship and environmental protection

A number of people have pointed out that religiously motivated intervention in public debate on environmental protection has often appealed to distinctive doctrines about the relationship between human beings and the natural world in the light of an understanding of the world as created by God. Wolterstorff, for example, cites the case of the Christian Environmental Council supporting the US Endangered Species Act on the basis of Psalm 24: 1 ('The earth is the LORD's and the fullness thereof . . . ') and Matthew 6: 26 ('Look at the birds of the air; they neither sow nor reap nor gather into barns, and yet your heavenly Father feeds them').[35] Greenawalt has also pointed out that, although the protection of nature in its own right, is not contrary to purely secular reasons, it is hard to ground a principle for the protection of nature solely in such reasons.[36]

The idea that human beings have responsibility for the protection of nature is often stated in terms of the ethics of stewardship, an idea often associated with the work the Brundtland Commission report *Our Common Future*.[37] The idea of stewardship is important in drawing attention to the diffuse responsibilities that attach to all actors in a world in which environmental effects cut across political and jurisdictional boundaries. It suggests responsibilities that go beyond legal and constitutional obligations, to invoke the idea that human beings, individually and collectively, have to use natural resources in a way that recognises their continuing value. However, it goes without saying that the notion of stewardship does not make literal sense outside the context of a theistic conception of the universe. Stewards are charged by the true owners to look after the resources that have been entrusted to them. But, in a non-theistic universe, there is no overall owner. Does

35 Nicholas Wolterstorff, 'Why We Should Reject What Liberalism Tells Us about Speaking and Acting in Public for Religious Reasons', in *Religion and Contemporary Liberalism* ed. Paul J. Weithman (Notre Dame, IN: University of Notre Dame Press; 1997), 180.

36 Kent Greenawalt, *Religious Conviction and Political Choice* (Oxford: Oxford University Press, 1988), 112.

37 The World Commission on Environment and Development, *Our Common Future* (Oxford and New York: Oxford University Press, 1978).

this mean that the idea of stewardship is an idle one? It would be if one were to take it in a literal sense. However, the programme of demythologisation encourages one to interpret the idea charitably as expressing a sense that the human responsibility for nature is not self-assumed – and therefore self-abrogatable – but something that is instead part of the givenness of human/nature relations.

Interestingly, Rawls explicitly rejects invoking the idea of 'stewardship' in relation to the human responsibility for environmental protection, since it is an example of a political argument that goes beyond public political values.[38] He thinks that the exclusion of this idea from public discussion is not a problem, because environmental protection is not 'a constitutional essential or a basic question of justice'.[39] But whether protection of the environment is a constitutional essential or not in part depends upon which constitution one is considering. For example, article 20a of the German Basic Law, on the protection of the natural foundations of life and animals, does give the protection of nature constitutional status in the following formulation:

> Mindful also of its responsibility toward future generations, the state shall protect the natural foundations of life and animals by legislation and, in accordance with law and justice, by executive and judicial action, all within the framework of the constitutional order.[40]

So the case for excluding the language of stewardship must rest not upon the admissibility or not on a denial of the protection of the environment as a matter of constitutional duty, but on the claim that the ground of this duty must be related solely to principles of (inter-generational) justice. Rawls himself seems to acknowledge this in a footnote. Yet, many hold the view that the human responsibility for nature is not simply a by-product of the human responsibility to act justly towards other humans, but rather invokes a wider sense of the need to maintain the integrity of the natural world. Perhaps this sentiment cannot be given a meaningful non-metaphorical interpretation. But perhaps that is also a reason for, on some matters, not seeking to go beyond metaphor.

Conclusions

The examples in terms of which I have sought to express the value of some religious insights, demythologised but always with a residue of metaphor remaining, are all ones in which the concept of the person, and of persons' relationship to each other and to nature, are involved. This is, I conjecture, not an accident. Modern liberal theory rests upon an attempt to construct a free-standing conception of justice and social relationships more generally, in the sense that political principles can

38 Rawls, *Political Liberalism*, 246.

39 Ibid.

40 www.btg-bestellservice.de/pdf/80201000.pdf (accessed 29 March 2016).

be detached from the concept of persons and their social relations. Either that or a rather ill-defined and unjustified notion of individual autonomy is presupposed. However, the continuing resonance of religious language in expressing fundamental values for many citizens of modern liberal democracies is a reminder that important values cannot always be rendered explicit. They remain reasons of the heart.

What does this mean for the idea of negotiating religion? The principle that controversial metaphysical and religious beliefs are ultimately inadmissible as grounds of public action renders in the logic of modern liberal theory the institutional separation of church and state that is so important in some modern democracies. If it could be made to work, there would be no need to *negotiate* religion, because all that was meaningful in a religious discourse could effectively be rendered in non-religious terms. There would be demythologisation without metaphorical remainder. However, it is one thing to make an institutional separation; it is another to separate the constitutional and political standing of different types of argument. Where the presuppositions of justice, the role of forgiveness and the relation of humans to the natural world are concerned, issues of a metaphysical and religious quality are encountered not as hindrances to public judgement but as an element in the determination of that public judgement. Negotiating religion is required because publicly relevant religious reasons themselves need interpretation and interpretation is best conducted in dialogue.

Of course, the mere fact that people express their views in religious terms does not preclude criticism of those views. When, to take a much discussed example, some people assert that homosexual relations between consenting adults should be illegal because, according to *Leviticus*, 'it is an abomination', the person willing to accept religious vocabulary into public discussion has also to allow this view to be put forward. But to permit and weigh the force of a view is not to abjure criticism of that view. The point, however, is that such criticisms have to distinguish some religious propositions from others, rather than seek to establish a categorical distinction between those claims (metaphysical and religious) to be excluded from consideration in the public realm and those claims (secular statements of plain truths) that are admitted to the public realm.

The idea of public reason is an important and valuable one in liberal democracies. It represents the ideal of citizens openly and freely determining the collective conditions of their own existence, while respecting individual freedom of conscience. However, it should be thought of as a practice to be collectively constructed rather than as establishing a precondition for each individual citizen to satisfy. After all, when the practice of free and open public reasoning is finally achieved, who knows what reasons of the heart will be found at its centre?

References

Adams, Robert Merrihew. 'The Theological Ethics of the Young Rawls and Its Background', in John Rawls, *A Brief Inquiry into the Meaning of Sin and Faith, with 'On My Religion'* edited by Thomas Nagel. Cambridge, MA: Harvard University Press, 2009, 24–101.

Audi, Robert. 'The Place of Religious Argument in a Free and Democratic Society', *San Diego Law Review* 30 (1993): 677–702.

Black, Max. *Perplexities: Rational Choice, the Prisoner's Dilemma, Metaphor, Poetic Ambiguity, and Other Puzzles*. Ithaca, NY and London: Cornell University Press, 1990.

Bultmann, Rudolf. *Jesus Christ and Mythology*, London: SCM Press, 1960.

Cohen, Joshua and Nagel, Thomas. 'Introduction', in John Rawls, *A Brief Inquiry into the Meaning of Sin and Faith, with 'On My Religion'*, edited by Thomas Nagel. Cambridge: Harvard University Press, 2009, 1–23.

Dawkins, Richard. *The God Delusion*. London: Bantam Press, 2006.

Eberle, Christopher J. *Religious Conviction in Liberal Politics*. Cambridge: Cambridge University Press, 2002.

Greenawalt, Kent. *Religious Conviction and Political Choice*. Oxford: Oxford University Press, 1988.

Gutmann, Amy and Thompson, Dennis. *Why Deliberative Democracy?* Princeton, NJ and Oxford: Princeton University Press, 2004.

Larmore, Charles E. *Patterns of Moral Complexity*. Cambridge: Cambridge University Press, 1987.

MacIntyre, Alasdair. *Against the Self-Images of the Age: Essays on Ideology and Philosophy*. London: Duckworth, 1971.

Pascal, Blaise. *Pensées*, edition de Michel Le Guern. Paris: Gallimard, 1977.

Rawls, John. *Political Liberalism*. New York: Columbia University Press, 1996.

Rawls, John. 'The Idea of Public Reason Revisited', *University of Chicago Law Review* 64 (1997): 765–807. Reprinted in John Rawls, *Collected Papers*, edited by Samuel Freeman. Cambridge, MA: Harvard University Press, 573–615.

Rawls, John. *A Theory of Justice*. Oxford: Oxford University Press, 1999, revised edition.

Rawls, John. *A Brief Inquiry into the Meaning of Sin and Faith, with 'On My Religion'*, ed. Thomas Nagel. Cambridge, MA: Harvard University Press, 2009.

Robinson, John A.T. *Honest to God*. London: SCM Press, 1963.

Scheffler, Samuel. 'Distributive Justice and Economic Desert', in *Desert and Justice*, edited by Serena Olsaretti. Oxford: Clarendon Press, 2003, 69–91.

Stevens, Wallace. *Selected Poems*. London: Faber & Faber, 1965.

Tillich, Paul. *Systematic Theology: Three Volumes*. Welwyn: James Nisbet, 1968.

Waldron, Jeremy. 'Religious Contributions in Public Deliberation', *San Diego Law Review* 30 (1993): 817–48.

Waldron, Jeremy. 'Two-Way Translation: The Ethics of Engaging with Religious Contributions in Public Deliberation', *New York University Public Law and Legal Theory Working Papers*, no. 241, 2010.

Weale, Albert. *Democratic Justice and the Social Contract*. Oxford: Oxford University Press, 2013.

Wolterstorff, Nicholas. 'Why We Should Reject What Liberalism Tells Us about Speaking and Acting in Public for Religious Reasons', in *Religion and Contemporary Liberalism*, edited by Paul J. Weithman. Notre Dame, IN: University of Notre Dame Press, 1997, 162–81.

The World Commission on Environment and Development. *Our Common Future*. Oxford and New York: Oxford University Press, 1978.

6 The ethics of establishment

Fairness and human rights as different standards of neutrality

Saladin Meckled-Garcia

Is any degree of religious establishment compatible with human rights? A number of theorists have recently claimed that respect for human rights or basic rights, rather than complete church and state separation, can serve as a sufficient threshold for justified state action.[1] Yet the truth of that claim requires that some degree of establishment is compatible with respect for those rights. One way to argue respect for human rights and establishment are not compatible is to argue that human rights necessarily require state neutrality. This, indeed, has formed the basis of recent criticism of judgements of the European Court of Human Rights that allow states some discretion on matters of state–church relations.[2] Those who wish to be more permissive about establishment would need, then, an argument for compatibility.

In this chapter I argue that there are two standards of neutrality to which we might hold states. Each is morally justified but each has a different emphasis. The first, political liberal neutrality, requires that state institutions do not design policies aimed at favouring any one conception of the good (lifestyle choice, moral view, religious or otherwise) for people to follow in their personal lives *because* of a judgement about the content or value of that conception. On that view of neutrality states can legitimately interfere with people's life choices only where that limitation is necessary to prevent them impeding each other in freely pursuing their reasonable life plans or where it is necessary to secure a fair share of resources towards pursuing such plans. A reasonable life plan here means one that avoids using inter-personal coercion or state power to gain advantages for a particular

1 S. Laegaard, 'Religious Neutrality, Toleration, and Recognition in Moderate Secular States: The Case of Denmark', *Les Ateliers de l'ethique/The Ethics Forum* 6, 2 (2011): 85–106; S. Cabulea May, 'Democratic Legitimacy, Legal Expressivism, and Religious Establishment', *Critical Review of International Social and Political Philosophy* 15, 2 (2012): 219–38; C. Laborde, C., 'Political Liberalism and Religion: On Separation and Establishment', *Journal of Political Philosophy* 21, 1 (2013): 67–86.

2 This is discussed and challenged at, for example, D. Kyritsis and S. Tsakyrakis, 'Neutrality in the Classroom', *International Journal of Constitutional Law* 11, 1 (2013): 200–17. I shall address their critique below.

conception of the good life.[3] Public institutions cannot, on that version of neutrality, use their powers with the policy aim of giving advantage to any one conception of the good *because* they value that conception as superior. The key condition is that evaluation of a conception as superior cannot be the basis of policy aimed at giving social advantages to a conception.

Often this idea of liberal neutrality has been confused with the notion of absolute moral neutrality, which is an incoherent ideal. Human rights, however, imply a second and distinct sense of neutrality. This is less stringent, in that it only requires neutrality with regard to a range of issues. So long as the basic requirements of human rights are upheld, some degree of establishment is compatible with this kind of neutrality. This, different threshold of neutrality, is due to the point of human rights standards being different from the point of a fully liberal political morality. Each addresses different moral competences of the state. I conclude, then, that those who wish to argue that the state must avoid any form of establishment will need to argue on the basis of liberal neutrality. Human rights standards can be upheld, and to that extent so can the legitimacy of state institutions, without complete disestablishment.

After addressing some definitional questions below, I set out the key distinction between the two kinds of neutrality and their distinct points. I sharpen the difference between these two standards of neutrality by showing how discrimination, as a type of prohibited behaviour, also means something different in each case. Discrimination in terms of lack of liberal neutrality is different from discrimination in terms of human rights standards and their point.

Defining establishment

Before considering the two standards of neutrality and their consequences for religious establishment it is worth clarifying what the latter means. That a country chooses a flag with a crucifix on it, or that its national anthem mentions a deity might be taken as forms of establishment. However, unless these expressions of national identity can be shown to impinge on citizens' rights, duties and privileges, it will not be the kind of establishment that raises serious questions of justice or legitimacy.

In political controversies, instead, we can take establishment to involve the exercise of public power. This means the powers of institutions to assign rights and duties that are socially recognised in a political community as having community-wide authority. This is a very important point. The distinctive abilities of public institutions lie in their ability to assign rights and duties to people. Often political power has been taken to reside in coercion, but coercion is not distinctive to political institutions and even where institutions do exercise coercive power, in a characteristically monopolistic way, this is through a command hierarchy that

3 From here on I shall use 'conception of the good' as short hand for any way of life, lifestyle that implies evaluation of options, sets of beliefs, or commitments by which people guide their life plans.

assigns socially recognised rights and duties to coerce. The police, acting as a public body, exercise socially recognised rights and duties, such as the duty to enforce standards of public order, granted by socially authorised chains of command that include legislation; officers of the penal system incarcerate persons as a matter of assigned public duty.

It is important that these institutions and their powers *legitimately* assign rights and duties that are to be socially recognised. Without that condition we would not be concerned with public authority, in the sense of legitimate political institutions at all. Instead we would have mere coercion and violence on the part of institutions that claim public authority but have none. I will return to one condition for institutions having public authority in that way. However, it is plausible that there are circumstances when institutions have legitimate authority and circumstances when they do not, but merely claim they do.[4]

This account of public power helps us to define establishment more precisely. We can say establishment exists in a society to the degree that decisions on how socially recognised rights and duties are arranged are based on a religious rationale. This would contrast, for example, with a purely personnel-based definition where establishment depended on whether church officers held public positions. A person with religious convictions, even one employed by a religious organisation, can participate in policy decision-making and not threaten the disestablishment of public institutions. That would require, however, credible guarantees that her role ruled out appeal to a religious justification for those decisions and that the aim of policy was demonstrably non-religious.[5]

Clear examples of establishment, then, include cases where religious organisations have a say in elections or other direct elements of political life.[6] Establishment also exists where judicial processes that impose and enforce decisions are required to make decisions on a religious basis.[7] There are also more subtle forms of establishment such as where religious representatives, in that capacity, are given rights in decision-making on education policy, say on the content of a part of the official syllabus.[8] Consider too, cases where planning permission for certain types

4 I am treating that question distinctly from the question of when citizens have moral obligations to obey their state, also known as the question of 'political obligation'. These two matters are subtly different and worth keeping apart, A.J. Simmons, *Moral Principles and Political Obligations*, Princeton, NJ: Princeton University Press, 1979, pp. 195 ff.

5 If a religious body or organisation were given decision-making powers, given its commitments, it would have to be assumed that the basis for its decision-making was a religious one. It would, then, be a sufficient basis for claiming establishment had taken place.

6 The *Guardian Council of the Constitution* plays this role in Iran for example.

7 For example, the introduction of *Sharia* courts in some states of Nigeria since 1999.

8 *UK Education Reform Act 1988*, section 11, mandates that Community Schools and Voluntary controlled faith schools have their RE syllabus drawn up by local committees (Standing Advisory Councils on Religious Education) made up of teachers, local faith groups, local churches, the Church of England and the local authority. Non-religious, or anti-religious groups have minimal representation and no voting rights (unlike the other groups).

of buildings is subject to religious vetting.[9] In all these cases, we have decisions within public bodies that will extend rights or impose duties and religious perspectives are given a role in defining the content of those rights and duties. By establishment, then, I will mean *any powers or privileges given to persons to decide the content of citizens' publicly recognised rights and duties with the aim of advantaging or disadvantaging a conception of how citizens should live their lives, based on an evaluation of the religious content or lack thereof in that conception.*

Consider a case where people make decisions on the basis of religious views, yet those decisions are consistent with no special advantage being given to, or withheld from, any one conception of the good. This is probably true of most electoral systems where the voters are not vetted. However, given the right to make such decisions is not itself grounded in the evaluation of conceptions of the good, this is not a case of establishment. If the clergy, however, are given decision-making powers permitting appeals to an evaluation of the content of religious views, even if they do not currently act to favour one view, this is nevertheless a case of establishment. That is because there is here a right to configure the distribution of social advantage and disadvantage based on evaluation, in this case religious, of the content of conceptions of the good.[10] The powers allow that advantage and disadvantage can be allocated on that basis, even if they presently result in neutral decisions. Alternatively, if a legislative body decides to accord special privileges to a religious association, for reasons not to do with the content of its views but, say, because it is the only way to preserve certain historical buildings, again we do not have establishment. Establishment requires

9 For example, in Greece until 2006, Greek Orthodox clergy had a say in a number of decision-making processes including planning permission such that to build any religious building and use it as such, an applicant had to have their planning application vetted by an Orthodox Greek Bishop. This law was amended in 2006 to remove these decision-making powers, though conditions still remain (given Art. 13.2 of the Greek constitution) prohibiting proselytising by religious groups.

10 Note that the account of establishment here (and the corresponding account of neutrality below) combine three conditions: evaluation on the basis of the content of a conception of the good life, aiming at advantaging or disadvantaging such a conception on the basis of the evaluation and that this is done in terms of allocating social advantages and disadvantages. This deals with counter-examples like Patten's, who thinks aiming at associating a particular religion with the state, but not for religion-favouring reasons, is non-neutral because it still seems like establishment. The question is what 'associating with' means – as in Patten's example, being associated with the state is deliberately left open-ended, potentially long term and its basis is unclear. If it means a policy might favour a group because this benefits society at some juncture, then it is unclear why that is establishment any more than the fact that a policy that accidentally benefits a religious group is establishment. If, on the other hand, it means giving powers to that group to decide policy on the basis of religious evaluation (as in 'association with the state' seems to imply) then this is establishment on the above definition and non-neutral on the corresponding account below. See A. Patten, 'Liberal Neutrality: A Reinterpretation and Defence', *Journal of Political Philosophy* 20, 3 (2012): 249–72, pp. 255 ff. The view of neutrality I propose below is based in fair treatment, it is to that extent compatible with Patten's approach.

the evaluative component and being empowered to allocate advantage or disadvantage on that evaluative basis.[11]

By contrast, neutrality applies to the correct choice of principles for distributing social benefits and burdens. Neutrality is where such principles are not justified by reference to a particular conception of how citizens should live their lives, whether religious or otherwise, based on an evaluation of the beliefs or values in such a conception. This is importantly different from *secularism*, which is anti-religious rather than neutral in the relevant sense. In its modern political manifestation, secularism is the view that public institutions can impose rights and duties with the aim of defining an aspect of citizens' identity and so an aspect of their lives, as non-religious. This is based on an evaluation of what counts as an acceptable identity or way of life. For example, consider a ban on religious clothing in public places or institutions because the state asserts a non-religious civic identity is a secularist policy. It is non-neutral because some aspect of personal choice is constrained on the basis of a negative evaluation of the expression of religious identity and with the aim of disadvantaging that expression and so that choice in life.

On the other hand, consider a policy that is credibly based on a principle that certain roles should be facilitated and advanced in a society not because they advance a particular conception of the good, but because they facilitate citizens in choosing and pursuing their reasonable conceptions, whatever they might be. The role of medic would fit this description and the principle would justify certain restrictions in how the role is pursued, based on making the role effective. So, if certain religious robes prevent the effective pursuit of the role of medic, as they get in the way of treatment, neutral principles justify public restrictions on the use of that attire for medics. The principle does not evaluate the content of the religious commitments or identity behind wearing such robes in any sphere and acting on the principle does not distribute advantages and disadvantages on that basis.

Below I define neutrality more carefully for each sense I argue it must have, given the application of different standards. However, it is important to avoid a common mistake early on. This is the assumption that neutrality is impossible because no state can be neutral, as making any policy decision will involve

11 So note that I am not exactly working with the distinction between justification of a policy and its aims or the distinction between intention and effect. In the above tri-partite account of establishment non-neutrality involves both a certain type of justification and a certain type of aim: one manifested in terms of allocating social rights and duties. That there is any difference in advantages must be plausibly justified on grounds that do not evaluate the content of conceptions of the good. Cf. C. Laborde, 'Political Liberalism and Religion', pp. 75 ff. For the slightly different distinction between neutrality of intention and neutrality of effect, C. Larmore, *Patterns of Moral Complexity*, Cambridge: Cambridge University Press, 1987, p. 44; J. Waldron, 'Legislation and Moral Neutrality', in his *Liberal Rights: Collected Papers 1981–91*, Cambridge: Cambridge University Press, 1993, pp. 149 ff; J. Rawls, *Political Liberalism*, Columbia, NY: Columbia University Press, 1993, 49 ff.

adopting an evaluative stance. If one were to understand neutrality as being neutral with regard to any value, principle, or moral justification this argument would be right. Such a notion of absolute moral neutrality is incoherent as any policy, even the most pragmatic, will be motivated by some notion of what is valuable, or valuable enough to be pursued pragmatically.

Political neutrality is the idea that, in exercising their powers, public institutions have overriding moral reason to act on principles for the configuration of social benefits and burdens that are not justified by evaluating citizens' commitments, ways of life, or conceptions of the good. Neutrality means evaluating and adopting policies guided by neutral principles such as (plausibly) giving fair opportunity to citizens to pursue their chosen plans of life. Neutral principles can even justify policies designed to disadvantage certain conceptions of the good, say through education policy. This would be where the consequences of people adopting such conceptions are bad for social peace, rather than because of the value for an individual in pursuing such conceptions. This sense of neutrality, then, is explicitly based in a moral evaluative stance about political relations, just not one based in considerations of what is best for individual lives.

Neutralities

Political neutrality

Liberal political neutrality is a feature of principles and their justification. It is the constraint that principles for public institutions avoid guiding policy on the basis of an evaluation of the content of conceptions of the good, within a broad range. Neutral principles will find a way of assigning fair opportunities to pursue reasonable conceptions of the good: ones that do not contain the aim of using private coercion or public power to gain advantage for any one conception over others. A religious view that included the aim of capturing public institutions to use to its advantage, or the aim of intimidation, threats, or coercive restrictions to other religious or non-religious ways of life, would be unreasonable. Public institutions are permitted to thwart, disincentivise and educate against such conceptions. Importantly, on this view of political ethics, policies need not express equal opportunities or freedom in the pursuit of unreasonable views. Reasonable views are those that accept that the only way a conception of the good life should be advanced, or come to be adopted in people's personal lives, is through non-coercive means, like reasoning with others.[12] Neutral principles require that public institutions do not interfere with people's adherence to such conceptions. They do not require that public institutions refrain interfering with people holding unreasonable conceptions.

The value behind such a political ideal of neutral principles is that it describes how we might exercise public authority *fairly* in a society where citizens hold a

12 Rawls, op cit., 58 ff. and 194 ff.

plurality of different conceptions of the good. A principle based on positively evaluating any one conception of the good or negatively evaluating any other would fail to treat people holding such conceptions with equal concern and implies an unfair use of public powers. Even where that conception is not directly imposed on people in their personal lives, advancing it politically implies using state resources derived from imposing social burdens on citizens who do not adhere to this conception. So, for example, republics like France and Turkey use state resources and impose legal burdens in order to promote a secularist public civic identity, or at least hinder non-secularist ones. Costs are imposed on some for the sake of promoting the life choices and values of others. In other words it is based on an evaluation of which life choices are worth promoting and which are not. This is unfair, not only where some have different conceptions of the good to the one they are asked to resource, it is also unfair to people given they might (given the chance) change their conceptions over time. Nevertheless, unfairness of this kind is not in itself a ground for questioning the legitimacy of public institutions, as we shall see. It describes one grade of injustice and illegitimacy describes another.

To reiterate, on this ideal there is no obligation to treat conceptions of the good in the same way, only those conceptions that are reasonable. People are unreasonable if they aim to use private coercion or public power to give advantages to their conception of the good. It is permissible to impose disadvantages on the pursuit of such conceptions and pursue education policies that stigmatise them, because they fail to respect others adopting and pursuing their own commitments and they fail to allow public institutions to show equal concern for people adopting and pursuing their own commitments. So, the common refrain that fairness-based neutrality is not neutral 'all the way down' is correct. While fairness-based neutrality does not *promote* conceptions of the personal good, it is based on moral values such as equal respect and concern. It only allows policies to promote other-regarding reasonableness. Thus, even deeply religious views that ultimately value salvation, yet accept a duty to pursue the advancement of their views by non-coercive discussion, are protected from interference on the grounds of neutral principles for designing policy.

Political neutrality is ultimately grounded in equal concern. Justifying principles on the basis of equal concern requires that we do not judge people by the content of their conception of the good. If the justification of a principle were to show preferences for a way of life on the basis of its content, beliefs, or values it would imply that we should treat people according to whether they adopt that way of life rather than as persons who happen to pursue certain ways of life, who might not have pursued them or might stop pursuing them and adopt another. This implies giving advantages to those who adopt a favoured way of life over those who do not. In turn, it implies that the way of life itself is more important than any person's choices and priorities and so fails to show equal concern for all persons in developing, prioritising and pursuing their commitments, irrespective of the conception of the good they presently prioritise and pursue.

Discrimination in terms of the standard of political neutrality is where state institutions either impose disadvantages or give positive advantages to the pursuit of some conceptions of the good over others, based on an evaluation of those conceptions. It is discrimination against the pursuit of a reasonable conception of the good, not necessarily with regard to the condition of specific individuals. So, a state that gives monetary advantages to a specific religion and not others could be said to be discriminating against those other religions in this sense. That would be even where the advantages to the one religion did not make worship of any other religion impossible or even more difficult. This kind of discrimination is not individual-directed, in that no individual need suffer a personal disadvantage. Neutrality would be threatened even by a state giving additional resources to a group with fewer resources than others in order to give its members equal opportunities for worship. What is problematic from the point of view of neutrality, even in those cases, is state resources and legal power being used for these ends and people bearing the social burdens that make this possible.

Social justice

There is another standard which is part of liberal political morality that might be confused with neutrality and when breached is also potentially described as discrimination. This is the positive standard of social distributive justice. A liberal account of social distributive justice is an account of how advantages and disadvantages should be distributed in a society, through the allocation of social rights and duties.[13] The standard of political neutrality, by contrast, is a constraint: a requirement on accounts of liberal distributive justice with which such accounts should be consistent. Neutrality does not tell us which of the possible candidate forms of neutral distributive justice we should adopt. Consider three options: a welfare maximising conception of distributive justice and equal opportunity conception and a conception that prioritises improving the conditions of the least advantaged.[14] None of these need be justified on the basis of evaluating individual's conceptions of the good on the basis of their content. They are all potentially consistent with political neutrality, yet we must assess each on its merits as to whether it is the right account of distributive justice. If there is a right account, then views can be politically neutral and yet wrong about the complete account of justice. That is, political neutrality is a necessary condition for principles of justice, but it is not sufficient.

If an individual fails to receive her fair share of benefits and/or burdens, as it is set out by whatever the right principle might be, we can say that she has suffered

13 S. Meckled-Garcia, 'Giving up the Goods: Rethinking the Human Rights to Subsistence, Institutional Justice, and Imperfect Duties', *Journal of Applied Philosophy* 30, 1 (2013).

14 A version of the last of these is put forward by J. Rawls, *A Theory of Justice*, Cambridge, MA: Harvard University Press, 1971, Sections 11–17. Others include equality of resources, as put forward by R. Dworkin, *Sovereign Virtue*, Cambridge, MA: Harvard University Press, 2000, pp. 65 ff.; a version of the second is put forward by Richard Arneson, 'Equality and Equal Opportunity for Welfare', *Philosophical Studies* 56 (1989): 77–93 and there are of course many others.

a social injustice. If the cause of this is not a policy but merely some arbitrary decision or personal preference on the part of officials, whether motivated by simple caprice or by group characteristics like gender or race, we might say that she has suffered personal discrimination. If, however, the injustice results from aiming to advance or thwarting a particular conception of the good it would be accurate to say that people had suffered as a result of non-neutrality. So, of these different possible forms of discrimination in such a case, only the last is properly described as discrimination that violates political neutrality.

Human rights neutrality

As if this was not complicated enough, I wish to introduce another kind of neutrality. Political neutrality and accounts of social justice that conform to it, can be distinguished from human rights standards in an important way. To show this, I will first look at how neutrality is used in European Court of Human Rights jurisprudence and then give an account of the moral value of human rights that explains and justifies this use. That distinct role for human rights brings with it a special kind of neutrality, reflected in ECHR practice, but reflecting a different value to political neutrality or fair distribution.

The ECHR (the Court from now on) employs a principle of neutrality in interpreting and applying the rights of the Convention.[15] This involves a subtle rendering of the implications of Convention rights. It would appear, sometimes, to be a principle of neutrality in all dealings and uses of public authority, similar to the political neutrality discussed above. However, it is not. Rather, it is a principle of neutrality in the protection of Convention rights such that public authorities are not permitted to assign social privileges and responsibilities in a way that undermines the enjoyment of these. As I will show, there are some instances where political neutrality would go further than this principle.

The Court interprets freedom of religion as an individual right that can also imply certain collective rights.[16] The right to freedom of religion means the right to pursue one's religion. But, given the collective component of most religious traditions, being denied the ability to pursue one's religious observance in association with others would render the right meaningless. In addition, the right to freedom of association, also explicitly protected by the Convention, protects this ability to pursue religious aims in association with others. The test the court has used, then, in interpreting whether an infringement of religious freedom has wrongly taken place is to ask whether a measure by a public body makes it impossible for citizens, meaningfully, to act collectively in pursuit of their religious views. Any imposition, or omission, that renders that collective right meaningless is taken

15 By the Convention I shall from here mean the *European Convention on Human Rights and Fundamental Freedoms*, Council of Europe, 1950, including all its additional *protocols*.

16 *Religionsgemeinschaft der Zeugen Jehovas and others v Austria*, ECHR no. 40825/98, 2008, para. 62.

to interfere with a citizen's religious freedom rights and only special circumstances could justify that interference.[17]

Legal recognition for an association is, in certain contexts, pivotal to exercising religious freedom rights. Without it an association would not be able to even hold a bank account, retain association property such as temples, land, paraphernalia, or even make collective representations on behalf of those who have chosen to consociate. Without the right kind of legal status, the association cannot meaningfully maintain an identity as the kind of entity that it is. Given that religious worship can require collective, congregational activity and a recognised place of worship, absence of legal recognition for those rights effectively undermines the possibility of meaningful association. It thereby removes a religious freedom right from those who need to form an association in order to meaningfully pursue their convictions.

Importantly, this right to legal recognition is not based in social justice, as it is not about giving all members of such associations equal or fair opportunities. Nor is it focused on making sure that policies that impact on religious observance are not based on the religious (or anti-religious) evaluation of ways of life. So it is not based on political neutrality. The core consideration is rather whether individuals are protected in adopting and pursuing a religious conception.

To use another example, the Court distinguishes between two types of case. First, there are those where state interference with individual aims is serious enough for it to look more closely at the case, assessing whether a correct balance has been reached. Second, there are those where it allows the state in question discretion to get the balance right between collective interests and individual freedoms. In the former the margin of discretion given to states is taken to be 'narrow' (less discretion) and in the latter 'wide' (more discretion). A key test for whether it ought to scrutinise the balance in freedom of religion, especially in education cases, has been whether individuals face indoctrination or pupils face 'undue influence'. If they can be plausibly said to face such interference, the Court will not allow the state discretion in balancing the competing interests in the case.[18] If, on the other hand, it is not plausible or well supported that the individual has faced indoctrination, the Court will give a wide margin of discretion to state authorities to decide how best to balance individual freedoms and collective aims.[19] The test is not based in social justice or political neutrality, given how I have defined those standards above.

In the *Lautsi* case the Court took the question of whether to apply a narrow or wide margin to turn on whether crucifixes on the walls of classrooms in Italian state schools constituted indoctrination of the students. This was irrespective of

17 These are set out in the limitation clauses to a number of Articles of the convention, *European Convention on Human Rights and Fundamental Freedoms*, 1950, Arts 8.2, 9.2, 10.2 and 11.2.

18 *Lautsi and others v Italy*, ECHR [GC] no. 30814/06, 2011, para. 62; *Dahlab v Switzerland*, ECHR no. 42393/98, 2001, section 1; *Følgerø and other v Norway*, ECHR [GC] no. 15472/02, 2007, paras 84(h) and 102.

19 *Lautsi*, ibid.

the justifying source for the state policy and irrespective of its effect on opportunities for people from different religious or non-religious groups. It was found that no adequate evidence had been presented to the Court to show that it did. So, the test for adequate 'neutrality' here concerns the effect of the policy on the ability of individuals to adopt and pursue their chosen religious convictions. Indoctrination would have failed that test. Previously, however, the court had taken the view that a female teacher wearing an Islamic headscarf might thereby indoctrinate students, even though in that case too no adequate evidence had been presented to prove this.[20] So the Court could be said to have been inconsistent with regard to the evidential base that it takes as adequate for the test to be passed. It has not, however, been inconsistent on the test itself – whether the policy challenges something more fundamental than equal opportunities or what the source of the policy might be.

So, where the state imposes certain duties and extends benefits to associations that are necessary to enjoy any meaningful recognition as an association, the right to freedom of religion demands neutrality from public institutions in how these benefits are allocated. Access to such fundamental benefits should not be decided on the basis of evaluating the religious or non-religious stances in question. The only ground for evaluating an association is whether it tangibly threatens the political order that makes human rights possible.[21]

These requirements for *human rights* neutrality by public institutions, however, are not and need not be based in a general commitment to politically neutral policies. A state can extend privileges and rights to religious organisations and lifestyles based on an evaluation of these and with the aim of advancing them, or disadvantaging others, without violating individuals' individual or collective human rights to freedom of religion. It is only where doing so additionally restricts the *core* of a person's right, her ability to adopt or pursue a religious view to any meaningful extent, that human rights neutrality is infringed. A standard approach, however, in the literature has been to think that political neutrality actually explains the content of human rights to religious freedom.

So consider a state that allows religious voices and evaluations to have an input into public institutional decision-making, such as on the curriculum or the allocation of planning permission. So long as public power is not used to prevent individuals adopting a religious view, or to withdraw the kind of public rights, such as legal recognition for associations, that makes it possible for them meaningfully to collectively pursue it, no violation of human rights can be asserted. There is no discrimination in the enjoyment of human rights, even if there is absence of political neutrality.

So what justifies this limited human rights approach to religious rights? Why not apply the more far-reaching test of whether institutions give any advantage to a religious or non-religious way of life over any other, based on an evaluation of such ways of life? To make sense of such restrictions – as opposed to simply

20 *Dahlab*, ibid.
21 See note 14.

accepting them as legal artifice or the arbitrary results of history – one would need to argue that there is a moral value in play with human rights, different from that behind political neutrality or social justice, that justifies this different approach.

Let us call this alternative value, equal respect (to distinguish it from the fairness behind political neutrality and social justice). It is valuable that public institutions respect the capacity of all persons to adopt, develop and pursue commitments and personal attachments. If anything is inherently and minimally valuable about human life it is each of us exercising sovereignty over that capacity in ourselves. Those capable of challenging this sovereignty have a duty not to do so. Political agents that have a claim to act authoritatively on our behalf can over-extend their powers to claim authority over this capacity in us and so over what commitments individuals can and cannot adopt, develop, prioritise, or pursue. They can challenge our sovereignty over this capacity by imposing socially recognised rights and duties on us and on others, such as duties to repress us because of our views, to indoctrinate us, or to purposefully undermine our ability to exercise this sovereignty through social stigma and starvation. Given these special powers, political institutions must then have special duties to respect our sovereignty over this human capacity. Without such respect there could be no genuine sense of political community or society, because individuals could not be guaranteed to authentically accept their legal order and political practices without that guarantee. Without basic protections these might easily be in place through a purely coercive imposition and through interference in people's ability to form commitments, prioritise them, and pursue them.

Note that the value here, in equal respect, is not like the aim of promoting people's access to opportunities to exercise this capacity, as it would be if it were based in promoting autonomy. Rather it is the minimal respect required so as not to challenge a person's sovereignty over her own attachments, commitments, and the way she prioritises and pursues these in her life, individually or in association with others. A commitment to equal respect is a commitment to not targeting or for that matter negligently creating conditions that undermine that sovereignty. So one way to understand the distinctive role of human rights is to see them as setting out the limits of respect for people's human integrity. In this sense, equal respect for citizens and non-citizens sets the limits to political sovereignty, the limits to legitimate political institutional action. Any policy proposal based in aims that imply disrespect for human integrity is, on this view, based on reasons we can discount as illegitimate in inception.

The above helps to distinguish the value of equal respect from social justice. Accounts of social justice aim to describe what counts as a fair allocation of socially recognised rights and duties, together with the distribution of goods and costs these imply. It is possible for states to get it wrong as to the best account of this kind of social distribution. But they can get it wrong and still act legitimately. A political society can democratically uphold laws and policies with a religious basis and that favour a religious conception. In fact, in order for societies to embark on a process of developing the right answers to the social justice question it must be possible for their institutions to act with some legitimacy. This is also true for political neutrality, which is a requirement of liberal accounts of social justice. So there is a difference between institutions acting unfairly and acting illegitimately.

Equal respect, on the other hand, focuses on certain absolutes: does a measure challenge people's sovereignty over their adoption and development of certain commitments? Does it rely on reasoning about collective policies that disallows the making of laws that limit people's ability to pursue such commitments in any meaningful way? It can, as one would expect of human rights standards, be a standard both for how institutions should treat people within a political community and outside it. After all, the justification for avoiding being engaged in torture, slavery, detention without trial, or the suppression of speech on the basis of its content is not that these give unfair advantages to any one reasonable view of the good life over any other. It is rather that such actions inherently fail to respect human integrity. One could appeal to politically neutral reasons to challenge peoples' right to pursue their prioritised commitments, such as that pursuing personal priorities detracts from contributing to the common good. It is a well-known complaint against utilitarianism that it implies this. Equal respect, however, rules out such appealing to neutral grounds for policy that nevertheless challenge human integrity.[22] While equal respect and fairness (equal concern) are of course related in that they focus on the value of individual lives, they nevertheless answer different kinds of questions about how institutions should treat people.

A government can rule legitimately if it fulfils certain conditions such as somehow garnering public consensus (whether democratically of by other forms of public consultation), respecting the rule of law, and treating people with equal respect, which is to say respecting their human rights.[23] It may nevertheless develop unfair and unjust social policies, unfairly disadvantaging the poor, say. But, while this lacks social justice, it would not be a sign that the government was illegitimate, lacking all authority, or that any of its laws were.[24] For so long as governments try in good faith to get it right about social fairness, which is to say about what terms they should extend to partners in social cooperation, they cannot be said to undermine the kind of fundamental respect for individuals that is necessary to underwrite genuine political community. Those human rights that express equal respect are indeed a threshold for whether governments do indeed act in good

22 Indeed, one objection to a utilitarian account of social fairness is that while it is neutral it nevertheless challenges equal respect when it benefits overall social utility to do so, see J. Rawls, *Theory of Justice*, pp. 26–7, see also T. Scanlon, 'Contractualism and Utilitarianism', in B. Williams, ed. *Utilitarianism and Beyond*, Cambridge: Cambridge University Press, 1982, p. 123.

23 S. Meckled-Garcia, S., 'Which Comes First, Democracy or Human Rights?' *Critical Review of International Social and Political Philosophy* 17, 6 (2014): 681–8.

24 J. Cohen, 'Is There a Human Right to Democracy', in J. Cohen and C. Sypnowich, eds *The Egalitarian Conscience: Essays in Honour of G. A. Cohen*, Oxford: Oxford University Press, 2006, 226–50, pp. 234 ff.; S. Cabulea May, 'Democratic Legitimacy, Legal Expressivism, and Religious Establishment', p. 219; S. Meckled-Garcia, 'Which Comes First, Democracy or Human Rights?'

faith, guaranteeing respect for human integrity in people's interactions with public institutions and protection against being outweighed by other social projects.[25]

I should also point out that while the ECHR jurisprudence is principally within the framework of 'negative' rights, the notion of equal respect is not restricted in this way. Rather, the view helps us understand any kind of rights claim. Where public bodies use or threaten people's access to elements of their well-being, such as food, shelter and health provisions, in such a way that implies a right over those people's sovereignty over the attachments they can make, how they prioritise them and whether they pursue them, we have a human rights issue. So, a government adopting a policy that starves a people shows disdain for their ability to form, prioritise and pursue their commitments. Even where people starve through government neglect, this is still a violation because governments' special powers over people given them special stewardship duties. Governments control the conditions in which citizens can operate, through the allocation of socially recognised rights and duties. That means that any choices governments make, whether to act or omit to act, is a way of setting terms of social interaction that affects how those rights and duties are configured. States are, for that reason, responsible if that configuration leads to the undermining of people's capacity for adopting, prioritising and pursuing their commitments, as it is by starvation. Configuring conditions that allow it to be undermined amounts to failure to respect human integrity.

The jurisprudence on discrimination in the human rights sphere has merely focused on differential treatment for which there is no good, or objective, or reasonable justification.[26] However, the different standards of non-neutrality I have set out identify different ways one can fail to have a good reason. Human rights standards rule out any reason that implies a breach of equal respect. So, a policy permitting or imposing racial discrimination uses racial features to decide whether people have a right to adopt, prioritise, or pursue their own commitments, or at least some of their own commitments.[27] Claiming a right to decide people's sovereignty over which commitments they should pursue, whether in private interactions or public relations, is an infringement of equal respect. To this extent this is distinct from the question of whether society gives them fair opportunities. Of course it will also clash with any reasonable account of social fairness to individuals. It will not, however, obviously clash with political neutrality, as it is not about treatment on the basis of competing conceptions of the good.

25 The idea that human rights set the threshold for legitimacy, among other things, is explored in R. Dworkin, *Justice for Hedgehogs*, Cambridge: Belknap Press, 2011, pp. 332–44, although Dworkin does not supply any content for these rights.

26 Viz. in *Savez crkava 'Riječ života' and Others v. Croatia* (no. 7798/08, 2010), para 85. However, the court restricts discrimination to rights and freedoms protected within the Convention and even then only recognises discrimination on the basis of certain 'protected characteristics' (which include a person's religious convictions), *Eweida and others v United Kingdom* (no. 48420/10, 59842/10 and 36516/10, 2013), paras 85 and 86.

27 There are of course many reasons why racism is wrong. However, here I am focusing on discrimination by public institutions as a special wrong.

What is wrong with confusing these standards?

The problem with running together human rights neutrality, political neutrality and social fairness, is that the standards imply different things in our assessment of a society. Applying the wrong standard to a case can lead to the wrong evaluation. If one was testing for whether a state upholds political neutrality one would ask what kind of arrangements its political community has adopted through legitimate political mechanisms. Are these designed to favour or disfavour certain conceptions of the good and is this on the basis of an evaluation of the content of those conceptions? If one were asking about human rights, then the question to ask is whether public bodies adopt policies that fail to accord equal respect to any individual. In the latter case we have a challenge to the legitimacy of a policy, law or action. In the former case, it is a challenge to its fairness or liberal justice, but not necessarily the political community's right to adopt it. Claiming that a state has failed in its human rights obligations because it is not fully politically neutral would be a confusion of the two standards.

Unfortunately some authors do exactly that. They have taken human rights to require disestablishment in public institutions.[28] This is on the assumption that human rights standards require a fully non-religious state, based on the further assumption that human rights require public institutions to be neutral in all respects when developing policy.[29] One way to sharpen that argument is through the claim that establishment inherently implies discrimination in the distribution of privileges and resources. Any kind of discrimination, on this view, is a human rights violation and it seems to then follow that establishment violates human rights standards.

So, criticism of the Court over the *Lautsi* case has centred on the assertion that schools placing crucifixes in a classroom where non-Christian, or non-religious, pupils might attend is an insufficiently neutral policy.[30] This implies an assumption that non-neutral institutions, because they are non-neutral, violate human rights to freedom of religion and conscience. The Court avoided pronouncing on whether the symbols are or are not compatible with neutrality. But for the Court to be able to avoid pronouncing on neutrality, the policy needed to pass an important test. It had to be shown that what is at stake is not the active teaching of a particular religious perspective that might constitute *indoctrination*.[31] The presence of the symbol was not taken to represent a serious imposition of that kind of incursion,

28 Especially D. Kyritsis and S. Tsakyrakis, 'Neutrality in the Classroom', pp. 211 ff; C. Panara, '*Lautsi v Italy*: The Display of Religious Symbols by the State', *European Public Law* 17, 1 (2011): 139–68; L. Zucca, '*Lautsi*: A Commentary on a Decision by the ECtHR Grand Chamber', *International Journal of Constitutional Law* 11, 1: 218–29; S. Mancini, 'The Crucifix Rage: Supranational Constitutionalism Bumps against Counter-Majoritarian Difficulty', *European Constitutional Law Review* 6, 1 (2010): 6–27; M. Evans, '*Lautis v Italy*: An Initial Appraisal', *Religion and Human Rights* 6, 3 (2011): 237–44;.

29 Kyritsis and Tsakyrakis, op cit., p. 205.

30 Kyritsis and Tsakyrakis, op cit.

31 *Lautsi v Italy*, para. 62.

based on religious reasons. And so, whether it represented a neutral, secular, or religious symbol in itself was a matter left to the state to interpret and to decide in terms of its legitimately adopted ends.[32] The same treatment is adopted in giving societies committed to secularism a margin of discretion in their regulation of religion in public institutional contexts.[33]

Establishing non-indoctrination in an educational context means establishing that the practice does not prevent people meaningfully adopting or pursuing their own religious, non-religious, or anti-religious views or the possibility of entering into associations that make pursuing these views possible as an associative activity. *Lautsi* illustrates, then, the distinction between human rights standards and the kind of neutrality they require as opposed to political neutrality. States can legitimately adopt non-neutral laws but not human rights-violating laws. The former renders the state open to criticism as not fully fair or liberal and potentially to movements for social change but does not challenge the legitimacy of its laws, as is implied by the Court judging there has been a violation. If the business of the Court were to enforce fairness-based neutrality in Council of Europe states then it would have to pronounce on decisions of any kind that can be seen to favour one group or disfavour another. As I have said, the court did not even pose that question of relative advantage and disadvantage when addressing religious symbols, or religious attire in public places in secular states. The form of interpretation of the different standards I have presented makes sense of this jurisprudence and provides a justification for it. It also challenges the argument that runs together human rights and political neutrality under the heading of discrimination.

I have so far argued that there are different kinds of neutrality to which one might be committed. One is concerned with how institutions representing members of a political community should be used in order to be fair or exhibit equal concern for all members. Another focuses on how public institutions ought to treat people in order to treat them with equal respect. In some cases treatment in line with equal respect is invariant between persons in or outside a political community, as with a right to freely adopt one's own religious or non-religious commitments. In other cases it will draw in an already existing institutional component, as where, due to the way access to rights is legally structured, religious associations need legal recognition in order to be able to collectively pursue their religious aims in a meaningful way. I have also proposed that states can pursue mistaken conceptions of political neutrality and social distributive justice without that fact rendering their laws illegitimate. Human rights, however, seem to precisely focus on the limits of legitimacy.

One might, at this stage, ask why we should consider one set of concerns to be more than human rights and the other merely human rights. Why not call all of

32 *Lautsi v Italy*, paras 68–72.

33 *Leyla Sahin v Turkey* ECHR [GC] no. 44774/98, 2005, sections 114–16; Dogru v France ECHR no. 27058/05, 2009, sections 65–72.

it 'human rights standards'?[34] In fact, the authors of views I have cited that run together political neutrality and human rights seem to think that it is sufficient for a human rights violation that public institutions are not entirely fair. For them it is enough that a question of moral right is in play for it to be a human rights matter.[35] Labels indeed do not matter. However, if I am right about the different features and focus of these two different types of standards, it matters that they are not confounded. Doing so would lead to incoherence in practice, leading us to challenge the legitimacy of certain laws because they are not neutral. It would lead to claiming that resourcing religious buildings because of a state commitment to a religious outlook is a fundamental violation of human rights that no society is allowed to pursue, at pain of rendering its laws illegitimate. Similarly, the taint of illegitimacy would apply with equal force to societies advancing a secular outlook. Even if these non-neutral conceptions are wrong, confusing the two standards would mean political communities had no right to get these matters wrong or for that matter to find their own winding way towards the correct account of justice.

There is one view, however, that cannot help but run these standards together. That view holds that human rights, and in fact any rights, are justified by reference to the importance of human interests that need protecting – interests the importance of which needs to be weighed in order to decide what must be done about anyone's rights. On that view, what defines these rights is a set of important targets: to maximise the enjoyment or protection of certain interests. How the targets are reached or who is charged with reaching them is a matter of practicability or at best efficiency, it is not a matter of a specific value that can be honoured or disrespected. So, on that view, there is indeed no reason for a state to respect religious freedoms that is not also a reason for that state to give fair advantages to people in accessing the means to pursue their religious aims. Both are about advancing interests, only one advances them through standards of respect that will protect citizens' interests while the other sets out standards for promoting the interests of members of a community.

The problem with this view is that it either adds nothing to the above account of the distinct values of equal respect and political neutrality, or it undermines the valuable point of treating them as distinct standards. The view could say that different values guide us in how to balance people's varying and different interests. Public institutions should show equal respect where they are capable of threatening it. For those over whom they exercise authority to distribute socially allocated rights and duties, they should establish conditions of fairness for people to pursue their different and sometimes competing conceptions of the good. That understanding

34 There are authors who take human rights to be simply a subset of the rights of justice, e.g., J. Tasioulas, 'Taking Rights Out of Human Rights', *Ethics* 120, 4 (2010): 647–78, pp. 650 and 654.

35 Kyritsis and Taskyrakis, op cit. p. 211 ff.

of the view, as I say, adds nothing to an account based on respect and fairness and furthermore it tells us nothing new about the attitude public institutions should adopt towards establishment. All the work is done by the values of respect and fairness and the distinct role played by these values and the standards they justify.

The alternative way to understand this view is as boiling down other values, like respect and fairness, to the single value of protecting interests of high importance to people's wellbeing. However, on that version one loses an important distinction. A value like equal respect disqualifies certain considerations as irrelevant yet one like fairness gives us a way of balancing competing considerations. Sometimes it makes more sense to appeal to one type of value and in other cases the other type. Consider two people that have competing aims or conceptions of the good life in a society, such as a religious and a non-religious conception. That each one has a particular and distinct conception of the good is a consideration that we have to consider against the other. We need a rule or principle that treats the people holding these conceptions fairly. For example, an equal opportunity rule for accessing resources would be fairer than a rule that the strongest or most popular view gets all the resources. The human right not to be enslaved, on the other hand, is different. It does not try to balance considerations such as the importance to a person's well-being of not being enslaved versus competing considerations such as the opportunity costs for another person in refraining from enslaving others. The latter 'consideration' is not a competing consideration at all; it is irrelevant for the purpose of deciding what the right should protect. The relative importance or weight of an interest for people cannot help us make this distinction, as highly important interests are involved in both types of case. Only appeal to different types of standards can uphold the distinction, such as the difference between equal respect (respect for each person's sovereignty over her forming, prioritising and pursuing commitments and attachments) on the one hand and social fairness on the other.

So one either adopts the version of the view that does not challenge the political neutrality *versus* human rights distinction or one adopts the version that gives up what matters in it. If this argument is right, then there is good reason to have these different values and to keep them and the different standards they imply, apart. Certainly, for the purposes of evaluating policies that involve establishment, they imply different things. In one case a standard that if breached attracts the charge of unfairness, but nevertheless may still be legitimately adopted by as society, in the other a standard setting, among other things, the limits of legitimacy for public policy.

Conclusion

In conclusion, I have set out two different kinds of standards for state neutrality, with special reference to neutrality across religious points of view. The standards require different things, for different reasons, from public institutions. This difference is most acute when we ask whether a state is permitted to adopt policies aimed at giving some advantage to certain religious perspectives, i.e., in terms of establishment. This would be compatible with human rights standards, but not with political neutrality. The upshot, I have also proposed, is in terms of laws that can be unfair yet legitimate and those which breach moral conditions for legitimacy itself. Anyone, then, wishing to argue that public institutions should never aim to give advantage to any religious conception of the good is better off deploying arguments for fairness-based neutrality and social justice. But they cannot challenge the legitimacy of public choices on that basis. Human rights standards, on the other hand, are a ground for challenging legitimacy but will not help in pursuing this kind of neutralist aim.

References

Arneson, R. 'Equality and Equal Opportunity for Welfare', *Philosophical Studies* 56 (1989): 77–93

Cabulea May, S. 'Democratic Legitimacy, Legal Expressivism, and Religious Establishment', *Critical Review of International Social and Political Philosophy* 15, 2 (2012): 219–38

Cohen, J. 'Is there a Human Right to Democracy', in *The Egalitarian Conscience: Essays in Honour of G. A. Cohen*, edited by J. Cohen and C. Sypnowich, 226–50 (Oxford: Oxford University Press, 2006).

Dworkin, R. *Sovereign Virtue*. Cambridge, MA: Harvard University Press, 2000.

Dworkin, R. *Justice for Hedgehogs*. Cambridge: Belknap Press, 2011.

Evans, M. 'Lautis v Italy: An Initial Appraisal', *Religion and Human Rights* 6, 3 (2011): 237–44.

Kyritsis, D. and S. Tsakyrakis. 'Neutrality in the Classroom', *International Journal of Constitutional Law* 11, 1 (2013): 200–17.

Laborde, C. 'Political Liberalism and Religion: On Separation and Establishment', *Journal of Political Philosophy* 21, 1 (2013): 67–86.

Laegaard, S. 'Religious Neutrality, Toleration, and Recognition in Moderate Secular States: The Case of Denmark', *Les Ateliers de l'éthique / The Ethics Forum* 6, 2 (2011): 85–106.

Larmore, C. *Patterns of Moral Complexity*. Cambridge: Cambridge University Press, 1987.

Mancini, S., 'The Crucifix Rage: Supranational Constitutionalism Bumps Against Counter-Majoritarian Difficulty', *European Constitutional Law Review* 6, 1 (2010): 6–27.

Meckled-Garcia, S. 'Giving Up the Goods: Rethinking the Human Rights to Subsistence, Institutional Justice, and Imperfect Duties', *Journal of Applied Philosophy* 30, 1 (2013): 73–87.

Meckled-Garcia, S. 'Which Comes First, Democracy or Human Rights?' *Critical Review of International Social and Political Philosophy* 17, 6 (2014): 681–8.

Panara, C. 'Lautsi v Italy: The Display of Religious Symbols by the State', *European Public Law* 17, 1 (2011): 139–68.

Patten, A. 'Liberal Neutrality: A Reinterpretation and Defence', *Journal of Political Philosophy* 20, 3 (2012): 249–72.

Rawls, J. *A Theory of Justice*. Cambridge: Harvard University Press, 1971.

Rawls, J. *Political Liberalism*. Columbia: Columbia University Press, 1993.

Scanlon, T. 'Contractualism and Utilitarianism', in *Utilitarianism and Beyond*, edited by B. Williams, 103–28 (Cambridge: Cambridge University Press, 1982).

Simmons, A. J. *Moral Principles and Political Obligations*. Princeton, NJ: Princeton University Press, 1979.

Tasioulas, J. 'Taking Rights out of Human Rights', *Ethics* 120, 4 (2010): 647–78.

Waldron, J. 'Legislation and Moral Neutrality', in *Liberal Rights: Collected Papers 1981–91* by J. Waldron (Cambridge: Cambridge University Press, 1993).

Zucca, L. 'Lautsi: A Commentary on a Cecision by the ECtHR Grand Chamber', *International Journal of Constitutional Law* 11, 1 (2013): 218–229.

List of European Court of Human Rights cases

Dahlab v Switzerland, ECHR no. 42393/98, 2001.
Dogru v France, ECHR no. 27058/05, 2009.
Eweida and others v United Kingdom ECHR no. 48420/10, 59842/10 and 36516/10, 2013.
Følgerø and other v Norway, ECHR [GC] no. 15472/02, 2007.
Lautsi and others v Italy, ECHR [GC], no. 30814/06, 2011.
Leyla Sahin v Turkey ECHR [GC] no. 44774/98, 2005.
Religionsgemeinschaft der Zeugen Jehovas and others v Austria, ECHR, no. 40825/98, 2008.
Riječ Života' and Others v. Croatia ECHR no. 7798/08, 2010.

7 Alternative futures for formal church establishment

Two case studies from the UK[1]

Robert M. Morris

The UK forms of state–religion relationships reflect cognate arrangements throughout Europe descended from former modes of state confessional preference that developed in the wake of the Protestant Reformation. Traditionally, these arrangements have been seen as falling into three dominant types: state church, separation and cooperation systems. In his review of European systems, however, Norman Doe has challenged whether the implied distinctions are sustainable:

> The studies in this book suggest that beneath the level of constitutional law such distinctions cannot easily be made. At this level, the dominant model of the States of Europe is that of cooperation between the States and religion.[2]

The UK is not alone in having to reassess inherited structures against significant decay of the assumptions upon which they were predicated. Demographic changes, pluralisation of religious belief, decline in religious observance, growth of non-belief and equality pressures from human rights jurisprudence all question existing structures. These challenges have force irrespective of whether they are to be understood as the outcome of 'secularisation', that is a claimed social process rooted in modernity's emphasis on the primacy of individual choice in a transformed and greatly variegated world.

The case for response is not thought pressing at the political level: apart from the position of relatively small pressure groups, for example, the National Secular Society, there is at present no significant political interest in revisiting church establishment. Rather, the threat to the status quo takes the form of a slow, persistent and largely unappreciated sapping of existing institutions. They struggle with the effects of a growing indifference to the Christian religion, which attacks the ability of many traditional Christian denominations to renew themselves.

1 An earlier version of this chapter was given as a paper at the UCL 'Negotiating Religion' seminar on 10 February 2012. I am very grateful for comments from Jim Beckford and Lucian Leustean particularly.

2 Norman Doe, *Law and Religion in Europe* (Oxford: Oxford University Press, 2011), 259.

It is against such a background that this chapter surveys the Scottish and English forms of church establishment, the main current challenges to their continuation and the alternative possible futures that may emerge.

The state of religion in Great Britain

There are two principal sources of data available to assess the state of religion in Great Britain: the decennial census and the British Social Attitudes survey. While their methods are entirely different, their findings are congruent: religious affiliation is declining but becoming more pluralised, principally but not solely as a result of immigration from South Asia.

The censuses

Data from the censuses in 2001 and 2011 show the principal changes in the Tables 7.1 and 7.2 below:

Table 7.1 England and Wales (000s)

	2001	%	*2011*	%
Christian	42,079	71.8	33,243	59.3
Muslim	1,591	2.8	2,706	4.8
Hindu	559	1.0	817	1.5
Sikh	336	0.6	423	0.8
Other religions	498	0.8	751	1.2
No religion	9,104	15.5	14,097	25.1
Not stated	4,289	7.3	4,038	7.2

Source: Office for National Statistics

Table 7.2 Scotland (000s)

	2001	%	*2011*	%
Church of Scotland	2,146	42.4	1,718	32.4
Roman Catholic	804	15.9	841	15.9
Other Christian	347	6.9	291	5.5
Muslim	43	0.8	77	1.4
Hindu	6	0.1	16	0.3
Sikh	7	0.1	9	0.2
Other religions	8	0.2	15	0.3
No religion	1,409	27.8	1,941	36.7
Not stated	279	5.5	368	7.0

Source: National Records of Scotland

Although compiled on a slightly different basis between the countries[3], the main points are the same. These are that Christianity has declined by 10 per cent over the decade 2001–11 and the number stating they have no religion increased by a similar proportion in England and Wales and by what appears to be a larger percentage in Scotland. Indeed, in Scotland the number stating they have no religion exceeds that of those stating they belong to the Church of Scotland. The numbers of non-Christian believers have increased throughout Great Britain if from a much lower base in Scotland compared with England and Wales. In the latter case, Muslims constitute nearly 5 per cent of the population.

British social attitudes survey

This regular survey based on weighted samples of the population has taken place annually virtually without interruption since 1983. *British Social Attitudes 30* reported findings from 2012.[4] Table 7.3 summarises the findings on religious affiliation over the decade of the censuses 2001–11 compared with the survey's first year in 1983.

Table 7.3 Religious affiliation 1983 and 2001–12

Religion	*83*	*01*	*02*	*03*	*04*	*05*	*06*	*07*	*08*	*09*	*10*	*11*	*12*
	%	%	%	%	%	%	%	%	%	%	%	%	%
Church of England/ Anglican	40	29	31	27	29	26	22	21	23	20	20	21	20
Roman Catholic	10	11	9	9	9	9	9	9	9	9	9	9	9
Other Christian	17	14	14	15	15	18	16	18	18	15	15	17	17
Non-Christian	2	4	4	6	3	6	6	6	7	5	6	7	6
No religion	31	41	41	43	43	40	46	46	43	51	50	46	48

Source: *British Social Attitudes* survey

3 For England and Wales the census did not, unlike Scotland, distinguish between Christian denominations. The fact that the Scottish question asked to what religion respondents *belong* is thought largely responsible for the higher proportion of respondents in Scotland who state they have no religion; the census asked 'What religion, religious denomination or body do you belong to?' See www.scotlandscensus.gov.uk/documents/Householdpre-addressed 27_05_10specimen.pdf, accessed 18 August 2014.

4 See http://bsa-30.natcen.ac.uk/read-the-report/key-findings/identities.aspx, accessed 15 April 2013. New data released on 31 May 2015 noted that 2014 figures confirmed that Anglican decline 'appears to have accelerated over the last decade', www.natcen.ac.uk/news-media/press-releases/2015/may/british-social-attitudes-church-of-england-decline-has-accelerated-in-past-decade/, accessed 2 July 2015.

These data show that nearly half of all respondents did not regard themselves as belonging to any particular religion – up from the third in the same category in 1983. (The growth from 31 per cent having no religion in 1983 is almost wholly accounted for by the halving over the same period of those affiliated to the Anglican Church.) Moreover, a generational replacement effect seems destined further to increase the proportion of non-believers. This is because the data show that each generation tends to be slightly less religious than its predecessor and that levels of religiosity do not vary very much over the lifetime of a generation.

Of the respondents, 6 per cent were adherents of non-Christian religions, an important minority drawing attention to the fact that a decline in religious observance has been accompanied by a pluralisation of religious belief.

The reception of these data has led, among other things, to a discussion whether Britain may still be described as a Christian country. Some members of the former coalition government went out of their way to insist that it still was in some meaningful sense. The Communities and Local Government Secretary, Eric Pickles, commenting on 'politically correct intolerance', is reported to have told a Conservative party forum: 'We're a Christian nation. We have an established church. Get over it. And don't impose your politically correct intolerance on others.'[5]

The Prime Minister, David Cameron, endorsed Pickles' comments adding, 'we should be proud of the fact that we are a Christian country'. It is difficult to know what to make of such political assertions though it may be significant that the Prime Minister's remarks were advanced in the context of saying he wished, 'to expand the role of faith and faith organisations in this country. This has been a consistent theme of this government; I'm sure there's more we could do to help make it easier for faith organisations.'[6]

The Prime Minister also wrote in similar vein in the Anglican weekly, *The Church Times*.[7]

Not surprisingly, these assertions by politicians have been both challenged and defended.[8] Challengers have claimed that the assertions are contrary to the facts and divisive in a plural society; defenders have claimed that the English establishment represents the need that every state has for a 'public orthodoxy' and in its present form does no harm. In a radio phone-in programme on 23 April 2014, the then Deputy Prime Minister, Nick Clegg, said it was time the Church of England was disestablished, for reasons that included its own good. A *Times* leader sought to take a pragmatic line: 'Anglicanism may be a typically British fudge, but it is a fudge that works rather well.'[9] Commenting on whether Britain

5 'Eric Pickles: Britain Still a Christian Nation – Get Over It', *Guardian*, 6 April 2014.

6 Downing Street Easter Reception 9 April 2014 – www.gov.uk/government/speeches/easter-reception-at-downing-street-2014, accessed 15 April 2014.

7 'My Faith in the Church of England', www.churchtimes.co.uk/articles/2014/17-april/comment/opinion/my-faith-in-the-church-of-england, accessed 28 April 2014.

8 See, for example, the letters of 20 and 21 April 2014 in the *Daily Telegraph* headed respectively by Professors Al-Khalili and Biggar.

9 *Times*, 24 April 2014.

was a Christian country, the former Archbishop, Rowan Williams, characterd the situation as 'post-Christian', adding 'A Christian nation can sound like a nation of committed believers, and we are not that.'[10]

In practice these exchanges were not the harbingers of a new *kulturkampf* in Britain. Rather, they were reiterations, over a 'low news' holiday, of pre-existing positions. Their real point perhaps is that they are evidence of a general consciousness that the tectonic plates of British cultural life are shifting and there is continuing debate about what the future landscape will look like.[11]

The state of establishment in Britain

Scotland

The Church of Scotland's model is distinctive from England's in proceeding from an explicit separation of church and state. In England, church and state were and remain, though now less intimately, intertwined: the Church of England was the state in its spiritual manifestation and yoked with the state in a joint project of governance and social control exercising moral oversight through its universal parochial coverage and ecclesiastical courts.

By the time of union in 1706–7, the Church of Scotland (the Kirk) was separate from the state but recognised and supported by it. Unlike in England, the monarch was not the head of the Kirk or bound to satisfy any explicit religious tests though monarchs or, more commonly, their representatives, attended the annual General Assembly, which had full legislative and judicial authority over the Kirk's internal affairs. Successive secessions and recombinations within the Kirk were rarely caused by objections to establishment as such but, rather, to objections to state actions thought to encroach on Kirk autonomy. The largest secession of all occurred in 1843 when almost a third of the Kirk left over the government's refusal to discontinue clerical patronage.

Currently, the Kirk's constitutional position is governed by two principal instruments: the 1707 Act of Union's stipulation that the Presbyterian form of Kirk government be 'effectually and inviolably secured', among other things, by monarchical oath on succession; and the Church of Scotland Act 1921. By endorsing a series of appended 'Articles Declaratory of the Constitution of the Church of Scotland' drawn up by the Kirk, the 1921 Act paved the way for the eventual reunion in 1929 of the Kirk with the successors to the seceeders of 1843.

The 'Articles Declaratory' contain fulsome assertions of Kirk independence from the state, the terms suggesting to Vernon Bogdanor that the 1921 Act was 'in effect a treaty between Church and State'.[12] The main contemporaneous purpose of the

10 *Daily Telegraph*, 26 April 2014.

11 See, for example, Damian Thompson, '2067: The End of British Christianity', *Spectator*, 13 June 2015.

12 Vernon Bogdanor, *The Monarchy and the Constitution* (Oxford: Oxford University Press, 1995), 237.

Articles was both to reassure those with whom the Kirk was seeking to reunite and to keep on board those who regarded the Kirk as 'established'. As one MP remarked at the time, the effort to square such circles involved 'exhibitions of casuistry which would have been a credit to the Middle Ages'.[13] Moreover, the 1921 Act did not confer any exclusive status on the Kirk. On the contrary, the 'Articles Declaratory' themselves describe the Kirk only as '*a* national' as opposed to '*the* national' church and s. 2 of the Act provided that nothing in the Act should 'prejudice the recognition of any other church in Scotland as a Christian Church protected by law in the exercise of its spiritual functions'. [14]

Commentators have differed about the extent to which the Kirk can be considered 'established' when compared with England. Some have given weight to the extent to which the state and the courts appear to be excluded from the Kirk's affairs; others have noted the Kirk's commitment to universal parochial coverage, to the language of the Act of Union, to the armed forces' and prisons' chaplaincies, the appointment of Royal chaplains from its ranks and the royal patronage of the General Assembly. For some the Kirk is not established at least on the English model and for others it is seen as 'established but free'. Certainly, its position seems several notches above the 'quasi-establishment' that Noel Cox has sought to confer on the Anglican Church in New Zealand.[15] One instance of the Kirk's degree of autonomy is that it was able to introduce female priests in 1968 without any Parliamentary procedure. The Church of England, on the other hand, had to seek Parliamentary approval for the same change in 1993, as it had also to do to permit female episcopal appointments in October 2014 and in early 2015 by statute to expedite their appearance as Lords Spiritual in the House of Lords.

Whatever the case, the Kirk's position is changing juridically and financially. An employment law equality case led to the House of Lords deciding that the 1921 Act did not render the Kirk proof to the requirements of European Community law.[16] This outcome challenged the long-held view that the 1921 Church of Scotland Act confirmed an inviolable autonomy. It now seems the better view that the autonomy was always in fact contingent on changes in the wider polity and, where public policy grounds justified it, subject to changes to its internal policies and practices.

13 Hansard, Commons, 22 June 1921, col. 1451.

14 In this respect, the *Cabinet Manual*, 1st edn published October 2011, www.gov.uk/government/uploads/system/uploads/attachment_data/file/60641/cabinet-manual.pdf, accessed 24 April 2014, errs when it claims – paragraph 1.21 – that the Church of Scotland 'is the [sic] national Church in Scotland'.

15 Noel Cox, *Church and State in the Post-Colonial Era: The Anglican Church and the Constitution in New Zealand* (Auckland: Polygraphia, 2008).

16 *Percy [AP] [Appellant] v. Church of Scotland National Board of Mission [Respondent] [Scotland]* [2005] UKHL 73. The case involved whether a female Kirk minister dismissed for adultery could pursue a complaint of discriminatory treatment when a male minister who had committed adultery had not been dismissed.

Financially, the Kirk's resources are strained in a number of different but mutually reinforcing ways. The numbers of communicants have declined over the last four decades from 1,133,515 in 1971 to 432,348 in 2011, or by over 60 per cent. In the decade up to 2011, it lost 26 per cent of its 2001 numbers.[17] Moreover, the average age of current worshippers has increased so that relatively more financial support is sought from a declining population who also have to bear heavier costs for the maintenance of local church buildings. While women have been eligible for all offices since 1968 and there have been female moderators, the number of ordinands of both genders has declined. While there has been a similar decline for the entirely male priesthood of the Roman Catholic Church in Scotland provoking a shrinkage of parochial cover, that defence is available more readily only to a church that is not committed to universal parochial provision. Retreat for the Kirk, however, would be incompatible with its commitment in the 'Articles Declaratory' to remaining a national church.

For some years now, the Kirk has been actively considering how to escape from what looks like a downward spiral. Its General Assembly has been exploring not only how parochial giving might be increased – 'Stewardship' schemes – but also what might be the scope for a greater degree of ecumenical partnership as a way of continuing to maintain its offer throughout the whole of Scotland.[18] When it is recalled that the 2011 census has shown that the Kirk's membership is outnumbered in Scotland by those of no religion, the size of the task can be appreciated. In practice, unless current trends are reversed, the Kirk is likely to face being unable to maintain the national coverage to which it is committed.

An added 'constitutional' complication has been the uncertainty felt by the Kirk about its status should the September 2014 referendum on Scottish independence have produced a new Scottish state. While the Scottish National Party (SNP) government in Scotland had asserted that 'We propose no change to the legal status of any religion or of Scotland's churches',[19] it published an interim constitution Bill only in June 2014 (after the Kirk's annual General Assembly meeting). The Bill mentioned religion solely in the context of incorporating European Convention on Human Rights provisions and certain equality rights.[20] The Kirk was concerned

17 Kirk *Year Book 2012–13*, 422. It lost a further 12 per cent including up to 2014, www.churchofscotland.org.uk/__data/assets/pdf_file/0020/27119/2015_Vol_I_Blue_Book.pdf, 38, accessed 2 July 2015.

18 Report of [Kirk] Committee on Ecumenical Relations [2014], Appendix I, paragraph 8:

> It is clear from the survey that there is no quick fix to the question of fulfilling the responsibilities of article 3 [of the 1921 Act 'Articles Declaratory'] to provide the 'ordinances of religion' throughout Scotland, by sharing the responsibility with ecumenical partners.
> www.churchofscotland.org.uk/__data/assets/pdf_file/0011/20063/Committee-On-Ecumenical-Relations-report.pdf, accessed 4 May 2014

19 'Scotland's Future: Your Guide to an Independent Scotland' (November 2013), www.scotreferendum.com/reports/scotlands-future-your-guide-to-an-independent-scotland/, accessed 17 August 2014.

20 'The Scottish Independence Bill' (June 2014), www.scotland.gov.uk/Resource/0045/00452762.pdf, accessed 17 August 2014.

about how far the 1706 settlement, predicated on the continuation of a Protestant monarchy, would survive when the Scottish parliament had in the past taken the view that the ban on Catholics succeeding to the throne should be ended.[21] To try to develop a common front, the Kirk has so far taken the lead in hosting a meeting of the members of what Norman Bonney has described as 'Scotland's new religious establishment'.[22] Although the 2014 referendum failed, the likelihood of its repetition will no doubt keep these anxieties alive.

Meanwhile, there continues to be interest in the Kirk model as a possible exemplar for application to England. All four twentieth-century Anglican Church and State commissions examined the possibility of English establishment moving to the greater independence found in the status of the Kirk. In all cases – most recently in 1970 – the prospect was rejected largely on the grounds of the inapplicability of a very different ecclesiastical model developed in entirely different circumstances. The idea is revived from time to time[23] but without attracting clear support: there is probably waning confidence in the very notion of establishment; and, from an Anglican point of view, the Scottish model could be seen to fall well short of fitting the bill when the degree of *actual* Anglican autonomy as opposed to its formal state dependence is considered.

England

The formal components of Anglican establishment include the requirements that the sovereign is Supreme Governor of the church and must be a communicant member of the church. No one who is a Catholic may succeed to the throne.[24] As Supreme Governor, the sovereign appoints all the senior clergy, summons the Synod legislature, approves the church's Canons and has certain churches – the Royal peculiars – under direct control outside the oversight of the diocesan bishops.

Special statutory arrangements give the Synod a right of legislative initiative in the form of Measures having, subject to final Parliamentary approval, the force of primary legislation. The church's courts are full courts of the land, the most senior judges being appointed by the crown. Twenty-six Archbishops and diocesan bishops sit *ex officio* with full voting powers as Lords Spiritual in the House of Lords. The Archbishop of Canterbury crowns the new sovereign though the

21 Scottish Parliament Official Report, 16 December 1999, cols 1633–80. When a UK MP, the SNP Scottish First Minister, Alex Salmond, sought repeal of the ban – Hansard, Commons, 28 June 2006, col. 259.

22 That is, those Christian denominations and other religions – Muslim, Hindu, Jewish and Sikh – who contribute to the Scottish Parliament chamber's regular slot, 'Time for reflection'. See http://blogs.lse.ac.uk/politicsandpolicy/an-independent-scotland-a-religious-or-a-secular-state/, accessed 4 May 2014.

23 Iain Mclean and Benjamin Linsley, *The Church of England and the State: Reforming Establishment for a Multi-Faith Britain*, (London: New Politics Network, 2004).

24 The former ban on Catholic marriages was removed by the Succession to the Crown Act 2013.

latter office is not dependent on coronation. By law, every English – and, despite disestablishment in Wales, every Welsh – prison has to have an Anglican chaplain.

That is the formal position. The actual position is somewhat different. While the religious tests remain in place, since the Prime Minister in 2007 withdrew from any active involvement in the process, all the senior clergy are now appointed in practice by private, unelected, unaccountable committees of the church itself. This means that such committees now appoint members of the legislature directly. The UK legislature remains the sole sovereign democratic legislature with explicit religious representation and, if now of women as well as men, still from England alone. The church's courts lost the last of their most significant powers in the middle of the nineteenth century and nowadays are restricted to clergy discipline and what may be described as relatively minor, almost wholly internal matters, such as church property, changes to the fabric of buildings and interment in churchyards. Although there is nothing to prevent Parliament legislating for the church, there is an understanding if not an actual convention that it will not do so without the consent of the church. Prison and armed service chaplains nowadays are no longer exclusively Anglican, though an understanding that the post of Chaplain General of the prison service in England and Wales might no longer be an *automatic* Anglican preserve was negatived by the then Justice Secretary, Chris Grayling, in 2013.[25]

As in Scotland, the church receives no direct subvention from the state, nor does the state collect any form of tax for the church, as in a number of North European countries.[26] The state used to stand behind the church's collection of church rates (made voluntary in 1868) and the hypothecated tax – the tithe – abolished from 1936. Although the church has in practice been the main beneficiary of state funds made available for the maintenance of cathedrals,[27] it is not a privileged beneficiary of any other funds made available to religious bodies. The church, if not actually poor, is feeling a financial pinch because, although its capital assets have recently appreciated, current expenditure remains under pressure. It has had to seek Parliamentary sanction to use capital to help defray pension costs. Increasing reliance on congregational giving has coincided with declining congregations. Between 2000 and 2010 average adult attendances declined from 878,000 to 784,000 or over 10 per cent in that period alone[28] after heavy losses in the decades from 1960. The more congregations are expected to pay relatively greater sums to support the church, the more they tend to expect greater influence on policies of interest to them as opposed to the interests of policies directed towards goals of national mission. The more 'congregational' interests predominate, the more the church comes to look like any other voluntary sect.

Successive governments have taken the position that the question of establishment is a matter for the church. That did not stop the Prime Minister unilaterally

25 *Times*, 29 March 2013.

26 See Francis Messner, ed. *Public Funding of Religions in Europe* (Farnham, UK: Ashgate, 2015).

27 A new £20m fund was announced in the 2014 Budget.

28 Anglican *Year Book 2013*, Table L, lvi.

deciding in 2007 to withdraw from personal involvement in the appointment of bishops, the significance of which is insufficiently appreciated: it gave a further push to the church's move to a more voluntary status – a position more akin to that of other religious bodies not bound to the state.

It was in pursuit of an equality agenda that the government in October 2011 took the initiative in proposing the discontinuation of the ban on royal Catholic marriages, which necessitated securing the agreement of the fifteen Commonwealth countries, the realms, which also have the Queen as head of state. The removal of this ban in the Succession to the Crown Act 2013 nonetheless leaves intact the ban on any Catholic succeeding to the throne, as well as anyone else not 'in communion with' the church. This includes all non-Trinitarian Christians as well as all non-Christian religions and non-believers. As argued elsewhere, this removal of the Catholic marriage ban draws attention to the bans that remain and the fact that the religious elements of the constitution are based on discrimination rather than equality.[29]

Objectively considered, it is by no means at all apparent why the sovereign should be subject to any religious tests. It is inconceivable, for example, that tests would be imposed on a president should the UK move to become an actual as opposed to the virtual republic it already is. Whether it would be possible for a Catholic sovereign, or any other sovereign not 'in communion with' the church, to be Supreme Governor is a more open question than is assumed. Even if it were not, it would not necessarily be a fatal blow to the church, now already in practice managing its own affairs. Without perhaps wishing to articulate all the issues, the Prince of Wales has put a tentative toe in the water in his remarks about the royal title Fidei Defensor being interpreted in a sense no longer exclusive to the church or, indeed, Christianity. Removing the compulsory link with the crown would not be fatal to either the church or the monarchy. As time goes on, the desirability of ending the compulsory link may become more apparent to the latter than the former. This is because the monarchy is in the end perhaps more conscious of the implied conditionality of its role to be sure to speak to the whole of the nation's population rather than risk fragile credit on protecting the interests of one particular declining section.

The rise of a more evidently secular society has not been accompanied by any political enthusiasm for secularist policies in the sense pursuing agendas hostile to, or excluding of, religion, or any observable anti-clericalism. In the church itself, on the other hand, nervousness and apprehension about the apparent degree of loss of faith has led to clerical pushback in the form of alleging the existence of 'aggressive secularism' where, in truth, the larger condition seems now one of indifference.[30] Postures of victimhood are sometimes adopted and

29 'Half-Opening Cans of Worms: The Present State of "High" Anglican Establishment', *Law and Justice* 172, 2014, 10–26.

30 See, for example, S. Bagg S. and D. Voas, 'The Triumph of Indifference: Irreligion in British Society', in *Atheism and Secularity – Volume 2: Global Expressions*, ed. P. Zuckerman (Santa Barbara, CA: Praeger, 2009), 91–111.

government indifference has been characterised as 'one-sided reciprocity'. Anxiety about the implications of the incorporation of the European Convention on Human Rights led to the inclusion in the 1998 Act of a declaratory provision urging sensitivity but no more to religious concerns. Russell Sandberg has pointed out that, while most permitted exceptions under discrimination law have been uncontroversial, 'religious exceptions have proved controversial'.[31] Lord Carey, former Archbishop of Canterbury, sought to argue for explicitly Christian judges in relevant religious cases, an argument rejected by the court with some vehemence by a – known Anglican – senior judge:

> The promulgation of law for the protection of a position held purely on religious grounds cannot . . . be justified . . . The precepts of any one religion – any belief system – cannot, by force of their religious origins, sound any louder in the general law than the precepts of any other.[32]

At present, apart from the slow, grinding effects of financial pressure, there are two particular issues that may prompt change. These are the removal of Catholic marriages as a bar to crown succession and the position of bishops in Parliament. As to Catholic marriages, the removal of the ban exposes, as pointed out above, the anti-Catholic and other religious prohibitions that remain, the existence of which becomes increasingly difficult to defend.

While episcopal membership of the House of Lords is not a vital part of establishment, it is a prominent part. There is no modern rationale for their presence: they are simply – with the rump of hereditary peers – one of the last feudal vestiges marooned in a democratic state, the fortuitous beneficiaries of a peculiarly British absence of political discontinuity. The question that should be considered during the interminable discussions about Lords reform is not *how many* bishops should survive in a reformed House but whether *any* corporate *ex officio* representation of a particular interest, religious or otherwise, is justified. It follows that past Government proposals to reduce the number of bishops or vary the religious identity of those appointed on grounds of their membership of religious bodies beg the entire question. As Meg Russell has argued, in approaching possible further reform of the House of Lords, it would seem best to treat episcopal membership as a standalone issue to be resolved before any final, general package is tabled.[33]

This situation has led the bishops to try to retrofit a rationale by constructing a contemporary justification for their continued presence. The bishop of Leicester, the former convenor of the Lords Spiritual, has pointed out that bishops constitute only 4 per cent of the House, as if size/proportion is relevant and asserted that

31 R. Sandberg, *Law and Religion* (Cambridge: Cambridge University Press, 2011), 117.

32 Laws LJ, *McFarlane v Relate Avon Ltd* [2010] EWCA Civ 880; [2010] IRLR 872; 29 BHRC 249.

33 Meg Russell, *The Contemporary House of Lords: Westminster Bicameralism Revived* (Oxford: Oxford University Press, 2013), 272.

this is not, therefore, anything remotely like the clerical dominance in Iran – as if Iran's legislature was for a moment regarded by anyone as an apt comparator.[34]

The bishop then also claimed that diocesan bishops are 'in many ways more in touch with public opinion than the government'. This claim was apparent in the debate in 2012 on a temporarily successful bishops' amendment to exempt child benefit from a proposed cap on benefits. Participating in politics is a two-way process and not everyone appreciated the initiative. An *Evening Standard* commentator pointed out the popularity of the cap and that it, 'helps, too, that the source of the trouble should have been unelected bishops looking otherworldly, clueless and meddlesome in their episcopal purple'.[35] An earlier occasion where the bishops *did* make a difference was on 25 January 2010 when they were instrumental in the rejection of a government amendment to the Equality Bill. The effect was to secure an exemption from treating church employees equally rather than confining the exemption to ministers of religion and others engaged in promoting or explaining doctrine. To put it mildly, this was not well done.[36]

Maintaining that they represent an 'hospitable' establishment, bishops claim to be able to speak for religions as a whole – a claim to authority that cannot be true but which is acquiesced in by a number of religious groups, including the Chief Rabbi, leader of one of the smallest minority groups. In what has become a classic explanation of this position, Tariq Modood explained why this should be so:

> [The] minimal nature of an Anglican establishment, its proven openness to other denominations and faiths seeking public space, and the fact that its very existence is an ongoing acknowledgment of the public character of religion, are all reasons why it may seem less intimidating to the minority faiths than a triumphal secularism.[37]

It seems that minority religions see the bishops both as keeping a foot for religion in politics and as possible conduits into government. In his oral evidence to the joint parliamentary committee considering the former government's draft House of Lords reform Bill, the then archbishop of Canterbury (Rowan Williams) clothed the church's claims in among other things the mantle of civil society and, in effect,

34 'Does Christianity Have a Future?', BBC1 17 April 2011.

35 London *Evening Standard*, Matthew D'Ancona, 25 January 2012.

36 An unusually large number of bishops present – eight – voted against a government amendment intended to implement a European Union Directive to confine employment discrimination on religious grounds to ministers of religion and those involved in promoting or explaining the doctrines of religion. The government was defeated by a majority of five (that is, in effect by the bishops), an outcome permitting unfettered employment discrimination to continue (HL Deb 25 January 2010, cols 1211–48). The then government reluctantly decided not to challenge the outcome at so late a stage in the Parliamentary session. As the *Church Times* noted (29 January 2010), this left the legislation 'at variance with European law, which generally has little room for special pleading'. See also Bob Morris, 'The Future of "High" Establishment', *Ecclesiastical Law Journal* (2011): 271–2.

37 Tariq Modood, 'Establishment, Multiculturalism and Citizenship', *Political Quarterly* 1994: 72–3.

dared Parliamentarians to take religion on. Unless Parliament decides for 100 per cent elections to the Lords when by definition there will be no room for *ex officio* membership, it is unlikely that politicians will challenge religion directly. Nonetheless, retrofitting a rationale for continued membership is equally unlikely to carry conviction, above all in circumstances where the withdrawal of active Prime Ministerial involvement in bishops' selection has removed what tenuous constitutional justification remained. If the bishops hang on – and significant Lords reform is not in sight – then at the very least they could stop voting.

Retrofitting illustrates a problem faced by all bodies that survive from one age into an entirely different one: how are they to remain relevant when their original rationale has faded if it continues to exist at all? Recasting establishment in an entirely benign character has also been supported by the Supreme Governor. Speaking at a Lambeth interfaith event at Lambeth Palace on 15 February 2012 early in her Jubilee year, the Queen said:

> Here at Lambeth Palace we should remind ourselves of the significant position of the Church of England in our nation's life. The concept of our established church is occasionally misunderstood and, I believe, commonly under-appreciated. Its role is *not* to defend Anglicanism to the exclusion of other religions. Instead, the Church has a duty to protect the free practice of all faiths in this country.
>
> It certainly provides an identity and spiritual dimension for its own many adherents. But also, gently and assuredly, the Church of England has created an environment for other faith communities and indeed people of no faith to live freely. Woven into the fabric of this country, the Church has helped to build a better society – more and more in active co-operation for the common good with those of other faiths.[38]

Notable features of this intervention include the synecdoche of using 'England' to constitute the same thing as the nation of the United Kingdom as a whole, the claim that the Church of England has a duty and implied *power* to protect other religions, and that it has had a consistent record of progressive political involvement.

Norman Bonney has described this approach as a multifaith doctrine of the monarchy and the church, which

> marks an important transformation of the religious character of the two institutions – from being agents of an exclusive Protestant state denomination jealous of its distinctiveness and primacy, they are attempting to become leaders of a multifaith coalition of diverse religious interests promoting and

38 See http://rowanwilliams.archbishopofcanterbury.org/articles.php/2358/the-queen-attends-multi-faith-reception-at-lambeth-palace, accessed 1 May 2014. The speech appears to have been a personal initiative by the Supreme Governor.

> protecting the role of religion in the public sphere while not sacrificing their own ritual and doctrinal centrality and dominance in the state.[39]

Bonney goes on to argue that, endorsed by Prime Minister Cameron, what is in effect a new civil religion[40] attempts to create a wider religious sphere still retaining the church as the lynchpin of the system and that it 'is a civil religion because it is constructed in the interests of the state to create as inclusive a sphere of religious belief and collaboration as possible'.[41]

One manifestation of this approach under the 2010 Conservative/Liberal Democrat coalition was the 'Near Neighbours' initiative. This programme begun in 2011 under the Department for Communities and Local Government states that 'Funding is given to communities with significant religious diversity to help them run projects which will bring about lasting benefits to their neighbourhoods.'[42] One of the programme's cardinal features is that it is managed by the Anglican Church Urban Fund, which states the programme's objectives slightly differently:

Near Neighbours has two key objectives:

- *Social interaction* – to develop positive relationships in multi-faith areas i.e. to help people from different faiths get to know and understand each other better.
- *Social action* – to encourage people of different faiths and of no faith to come together for initiatives that improve their local neighbourhood.[43]

The same website makes it clear that all the Fund's 'National Partners' are religious organisations. Moreover, applications for the small grants available within the £3m ceiling of the initiative renewed in 2014 have to be made in practice as before via local Anglican incumbents. A similar scheme under the coalition government's predecessors employed the non-religious Community Development Foundation to manage the grant-giving process for an analogous £7.5 million programme.[44] Given the modest size of the sums available under the current programme, it is relevant to bear in mind that another part of government – the Cabinet Office's Office for Civil Society – sponsored community development programmes totalling £80 million during the coalition and the present government

39 Norman Bonney, *Monarchy, Religion and the State* (Manchester: Manchester University Press, 2013), 133.

40 Civil religion: there is a large literature on this subject inaugurated by a seminal article by the American sociologist Robert Bellah – 'Civil Religion in America', *Daedalus* 1967, 1–21. Bonney's argument is that 'Anglicam multifaithism' is a flawed and doomed attempt to manufacture a civil religion for the UK.

41 Bonney, *Monarchy*, 137.

42 See www.gov.uk/government/news/multi-faith-communities-to-benefit-from-new-3-million-grant, accessed 2 July 2015. (The 800th grant was announced on 23 February 2015.)

43 See www.cuf.org.uk/how-we-help/near-neighbours, accessed 5 May 2014.

44 A list of the beneficiaries is at Hansard, Commons, 2 March 2009, col. 1227W.

announced a £20 million Local Sustainability Fund in June 2015.[45] This difference in scale from Near Neighbours may perhaps be taken to imply that there are limits to the government's dedication to funding Anglican multifaithism.

Finally, before moving on to consider some of the external, longer term forces that bear on the principle of establishment, it will be apt to summarise the chief features of the Church of England's current status. Recently summarising survey and Anglican data, Linda Woodhead has set out the position as follows:

- *Anglicans are dying out* – of the third of the English population who say they are Anglican, almost half are over 60, 83 per cent rarely attend and of those who say they attend, about half attend weekly. For the young, religion as a whole appears to have become a toxic brand.[46]
- *The church, if more slowly than the Roman Catholics, is suffering a priestly haemorrhage* – full-time male stipendiaries continue to fall but the rise in female numbers has not prevented an overall stipendiary decline where the majority are now over 50 and 42 per cent in their fifties. While non-stipendiary priests have been an important source of support, more than half are 60 or over and their numbers – and that of readers – are declining, the readers more swiftly. 'To put it bluntly', Woodhead judges, 'there are no longer enough troopers to keep the show on the road.'[47]
- *Social engagement: a vignette* – between 2000 and 2010 church baptisms fell from 20 to 12 per cent of live births, and funerals fell from 46 to 37 per cent of deaths. Between 2010–11 alone, Anglican churches in England and Wales conducted 7 per cent fewer weddings.[48]

Longer term external factors influencing change

These fall into two broad categories: the effects of a developing jurisprudence on equality and non-discrimination; and a growing attention to whether the claims of religion to be treated specially can be sustained in modern liberal democracies.

The fact has been previously mentioned that the incorporation into UK law of the European Convention on Human Rights in 1998 was received with some Anglican apprehension. Charlotte Smith, for example, has characterised the situation as one where establishment, 'which demands a place in the public sphere, pulls in an opposing direction to that of a human rights framework, the general tendency of which is to remove religion into the private sphere'.[49] Her conclusion

45 www.gov.uk/government/news/charitable-organisations-given-20-million-boost-by-government, accessed 3 July 2015.

46 Michael Doney, ed. *How Healthy is the CofE? – The Church Times Health Check* (London: Canterbury Press, 2014), 14–19.

47 Doney, *How Healthy*, 50–4.

48 Doney, *How Healthy*, 88–91.

49 Charlotte Smith 'A Very English Affair: Establishment and Human Rights in an Organic Constitution', *Law and Religion in Theoretical and Historical Context*, ed. Peter Cane, Carolyn Evans and Zöe Robinson (Cambridge: Cambridge University Press, 2008), 157.

from a review of the then existing jurisprudence, and in particular a chancel repair case that turned on whether the Church of England was a public authority,[50] is that it is 'undeniable that the time is now more than ripe for a fundamental reassessment and remodelling of the relationship between the church and state'.[51]

This has not been a universal view. Earlier, Ian Leigh criticised a Fabian Commission's preference for a secular state on the grounds that it was 'a fallacy to assume . . . that a secular state is somehow more inclusive because of its professed neutrality between religions; rather, it is equally alienating to people of all religions'.[52] Moreover, Rex Ahdar and Ian Leigh have maintained that the form of establishment found in the Church of England and the Church of Scotland is compatible with religious freedom: 'Establishment, in a modern mild form exemplified by the United Kingdom, we believe is consistent with religious freedom.'[53] Indeed, they have maintained that this position is supported by Cécile Laborde, quoting her remark 'a state of modest establishment that takes seriously the principle of equality between citizens [can] meet liberal desiderata'.[54]

This remark, which turns on an explicit prior requirement of equality ignored by Ahdar and Leigh, further concludes that even though modest establishment does not endorse religion in the strict sense, 'it nonetheless undermines the ideal of a political community of equals by privileging certain sections of the citizenry, albeit symbolically, over others'.[55] An approach on this basis asserts that:

> [J]ustice is not simply about the justification of state coercion and the distribution of basic rights and opportunities, but . . . is also about the fair distribution of more intangible forms of social recognition – the Rawlsian 'social bases of self-respect' . . . It helps us understand why . . . the symbolic establishment of religion is wrong even if, as advocates of the Anglo-European view point out, it does not violate religious freedom.[56]

50 *Aston Cantlow v Wallbank*, [2001] EWCA Civ 713 and [2003] UKHL 37.

51 Smith, 'A Very English', 183.

52 Ian Leigh, 'By Law Established? The Crown, Constitutional Reform and the Church of England', *Public Law* (2004): 273. Elsewhere, Leigh has argued also that the case law of the European Court of Human Rights has had the effect of requiring a policy of state secularism – Ian Leigh, 'The European Court of Human Rights and Religious Neutrality', in *Religion in a Liberal State*, eds Gavin D'Costa, Malcolm Evans, Tariq Modood and Julian Rivers (Cambridge: Cambridge University Press, 2013), 38–66.

53 Rex Ahdar and Ian Leigh, *Religious Freedom in the Liberal State* (Oxford: Oxford University Press, 2013), 123.

54 Cécile Laborde, 'Political Liberalism and Religion: On Separation and Establishment', *Journal of Political Philosophy* (2013): 67–86 at p. 76

55 Cécile Laborde, 'Political Liberalism', p. 86.

56 Cécile Laborde, 'Political Liberalism', p. 86. Laborde has also advanced her argument in Justificatory Secularism', in *Religion in a Liberal State*, eds D'Costa *et al.*, 164–86 – more nuanced, conceptually minimalist form of secularism on the basis that it is mistaken to see secularism as the antonym of religion and as an anti-religious position. Her secular state would not require citizens to be secular but require 'only a basic distinction between temporal and spiritual authority and a public commitment to the non-establishment of religion by the state' (183). In her view 'for many

In other words, religious freedom is not the same as religious equality, let alone civic equality. Ahdar and Leigh proceed on the apparent basis that, if there is religious freedom, equality – in so far as it is not co-extensive with religious freedom – does not matter. In the end, their position really turns on their avowedly Christian viewpoint.[57]

Basing his argument on regarding the various international human rights agreements as 'living instruments' and acknowledging that they are silent on exact modes of internal state organisation, Jeroen Temperman nonetheless argues that 'an assessment of religion on the basis of the "equality before the law" principle shows that the legal establishment of religion is problematic if not indeed incompatible with human rights law'.[58] Other writers have entered an increasingly crowded field arguing for new understandings of how the interface between law and religion might be best managed: Lorenzo Zucca from a European perspective has called for an 'inclusive secularism' and Paul Horwitz – writing from the separatist American tradition – for an 'empathic secularism'.[59]

Julian Rivers' take on the interactive processes set in train by human rights jurisprudence in Europe is that it has resulted in a movement from Christian toleration to one of religious pluralism, of 'mini-establishments': 'It remains to be seen how far this process of religious pluralism can continue and whether it will not, in time, topple the symbolic commitment to Christianity still implicit in the UK's constitutional arrangements.'[60] In his view, increasing religious diversity has been recognised at the same time as there has been an inexorable growth in state regulation and its intrusion into areas of law traditionally considered private:

> This poses considerable challenges. Religious diversity makes it harder to transcend religious difference in the public sphere. Matters that appeared neutral become exposed as only impartial between versions of Christianity. It also calls into question the relatively settled domain of the religious/private.[61]

Where is all this going? A Canadian perspective could be helpful. At a time of the hollowing out or decline of mainline Christian churches and a pluralisation of

purposes, religion does not deserve special treatment' (165). See also Anthony Bradney, *Law and Faith in a Sceptical Age* (Abingdon: Routledge, 2009), 74.

57 'Our evaluation of the merits of the models [of religion-state relations] to be examined is undertaken from a non-neutral vantage point. We analyse the models from a Christian perspective'. Ahdar and Leigh, *Religious Freedom*, 88.

58 Jeroen Temperman, *State–Religion Relationships and Human Rights Law: Towards a Right to Religiously Neutral Governance* (Leiden: Nijhoff, 2010), 161.

59 Lorenzo Zucca, *A Secular Europe: Law and Religion in the European Constitutional Landscape* (Oxford: Oxford University Press, 2012); and Paul Horwitz, *The Agnostic Age: Law, Religion and the Constitution* (New York: Oxford University Press, 2011).

60 Julian Rivers, 'From Toleration to Pluralism: Religious Liberty and Religious Establishment under the United Kingdom's Human Rights Act', in *Law and Religion*, ed. Rex Ahdar (Aldershot: Ashgate, 2000), 155.

61 Julian Rivers, *The Law of Organized Religions: Between Establishment and Secularism* (Oxford: Oxford University Press, 2010), 343.

religion to include equality for non-Christian religions, Peter Beyer sees a growth there of an '*a la carte* religiosity', in which authority is with the individual and in which older forms have not disappeared but have become relativised and revalued. Moreover, he argues that 'In the absence of religious foundationalism[62] – a key characteristic of the Westphalian regime – religion as such may lose its privileged status in the eyes of the state in relation to other domains of regulation.'[63] Consequences could include revisiting tax privileges and exemptions from human rights regimes that permit unique forms of religious discrimination. In other words, religion would no longer be regarded as special among associational activities or justify special treatment.

What is likely to happen in Great Britain?

Following are what seem to be the salient features of the present position and the possible directions of change.

- *Both established churches are experiencing slow implosion.* The present rates of decline suggest further – probably unacknowledged – withdrawal from full parochial coverage in both countries and, in England, further amalgamation of dioceses. Political responses will be instinctively cautious, unheroic, loath to take any initiative and piecemeal.
- *In Scotland, the political responsibility will rest with the devolved Scottish government even though the Kirk's status is legislatively a matter for the UK parliament.* If Scotland becomes independent, all bets will be off. The guarantee for the Kirk under the Act of Union could be deemed replaced by Article 9 of the European Convention on Human Rights and repealed.
- *In England, full disestablishment is unlikely and disendowment off the table.* Most likely are discrete changes over time, which move the Church of England further into voluntary status. Timing will depend on unforeseeable precipitating incident and, not necessarily, change of sovereign. Changes could extend to some redefining into honorary patronage of the Supreme Governor role (if it is to survive at all) accompanied by the state's total withdrawal from clerical and judicial appointments; ecclesiastical law privatised but the current legislative method retained; the movement of Royal Peculiars into diocesan oversight or non-royal trust; and the abolition of the religious tests for succession to the crown with concomitant repeal of the Accession Declaration and Coronation Oaths Acts. Depending on the timing of such changes, thought would have to be given to coronation formularies, for example whether there should be coronations and, if so, in what – possibly multifaith

62 Foundational – the belief that religion not only encompasses but is foundational to the cosmic and therefore the human order.

63 Peter Beyer, 'Deprivileging Religion in a Post-Westphalian State: Shadow Establishment, Organization, Spirituality and Freedom in Canada', in *Varieties of Religious Establishment*, eds Winnifred Sullivan and Lori Beaman (Farnham, UK: Ashgate, 2013), 75–91.

– form. The future of bishops in the legislature – if they wish to remain – would fall to be considered prior to launching largescale Lords reform.

- *There will continue to be no state subvention to the running costs of the churches.* However, consideration will have to be given to the right form of state contribution to the capital costs of maintaining listed church buildings in both countries when falling memberships incapacitate the churches' own ability to retain full responsibility.[64] Local government might be given discretion to contribute similarly to selected unlisted churches.

Conclusion

Although the types of formal establishment in the UK discussed here have many unique features, they are entirely relevant to the issues addressed in this volume. What they represent is the working out over nearly five centuries of two distinct forms of church governance in a particular European union state against backgrounds of profound social change. True, the languages of Rawlsian discourse and 'post-secular' anxieties[65] do not trip readily off pragmatic British tongues but the substance of the issues of negotiating with religion remain identifiably similar to everywhere else even if the emphases differ. In Britain the issues coalesce now principally around what should be the place, if any, of public religion in a country both more secular and more religiously plural than ever before.

And lastly, and more parochially, it will be right to offer a final word on where formal establishment has got to in Britain. It is not a question of waiting for a crisis to become manifest: the churches are *already* in crisis. Parliament now needs to prepare the way for orderly and thoughtful negotiated change. One Select Committee chairman has previously noted that the Succession to the Crown Bill raised 'questions about the future role of the Crown in the Church of England. I believe these questions need to be carefully considered.'[66] If the present parliament cannot find time to address the issues before it ends in 2020, the next one should consider appointing a select committee that will.

References

Ahdar, Rex and Ian Leigh. *Religious Freedom in the Liberal State*. Oxford: Oxford University Press, 2013.

Aston Cantlow v Wallbank (2001) EWCA Civ 713 and [2003] UKHL 37.

64 Cannily, Anglicans have anticipated this problem: the 2013 *Year Book* states 'Nearly half of the population (46 per cent) think that central taxation, the National Lottery or English Heritage should be primarily responsible for providing money to maintain churches and chapels', Anglican *Year Book 2013*, xiii.

65 Admirably contextualised by James Beckford in 'Public Religions and the Postsecular: Critical Reflections', *Journal for the Scientific Study of Religion* (2012): 1–19.

66 Graham Allen MP, 9 January 2013, www.parliament.uk/business/committees/committees-a-z/commons-select/political-and-constitutional-reform-committee/news/royal-succession---chairs-comments/, accessed 22 May 2014.

Bagg, Samuel and David Voas. 'The Triumph of Indifference: Irreligion in British Society', *Atheism and Secularity – Volume 2: Global Expressions*, edited by P. Zuckerman. Santa Barbara, CA: Praeger, 2009, 91–111.

Beckford, James. 'Public Religions and the Postsecular: Critical Reflections', *Journal for the Scientific Study of Religion* (2012), 1–19.

Beyer, Peter. 'Deprivileging Religion in a Post-Westphalian State: Shadow Establishment, Organization, Spirituality and Freedom in Canada', in *Varieties of Religious Establishment*, edited by Winnifred Sullivan and Lori Beaman. Farnham, UK: Ashgate, 2013, 75–91.

Bogdanor, Vernon. *The Monarchy and the Constitution*. Oxford: Oxford University Press, 1995.

Bonney, Norman. *Monarchy, Religion and the State*. Manchester: Manchester University Press, 2013.

Bradney, Anthony. *Law and Faith in a Sceptical Age*. Abingdon: Routledge, 2009.

Cameron, David. Downing Street Easter Reception 9 April 2014, www.gov.uk/government/speeches/easter-reception-at-downing-street-2014, accessed 15 April 2014

Cameron, David. 'My Faith in the Church of England', www.churchtimes.co.uk/articles/2014/17-april/comment/opinion/my-faith-in-the-church-of-england, accessed 28 April 2014.

Church of England Year Books. London: Church House Publishing.

Church of Scotland Year Books. Edinbrugh: General Assembly of the Church of Scotland.

Report of the Committee on Ecumenical Relations, www.churchofscotland.org.uk/__data/assets/pdf_file/0011/20063/Committee-On-Ecumenical-Relations-report.pdf, accessed 4 May 2014.

Cox, Noel. *Church and State in the Post-Colonial Era: The Anglican Church and the Constitution in New Zealand*. Auckland: Polygraphia, 2008.

D'Costa, Gavin, Malcolm Evans, Tariq Modood and Julian Rivers, eds *Religion in a Liberal State*. Cambridge: Cambridge University Press, 2013.

Doe, Norman. *Law and Religion in Europe*. Oxford: Oxford University Press, 2011.

Doney, Michael, ed. *How Healthy is the CofE? – The Church Times Health Check*. London: Canterbury Press, 2014.

Elizabeth II: Lambeth Palace Speech 15 February 2014, http://rowanwilliams.archbishopofcanterbury.org/articles.php/2358/the-queen-attends-multi-faith-reception-at-lambeth-palace, accessed 1 May 2014.

'Eric Pickles: Britain Still a Christian Nation – Get Over It', *Guardian*, 6 April 2014.

Horwitz, Paul. *The Agnostic Age: Law, Religion and the Constitution*. New York: Oxford University Press, 2011.

Laborde, Cécile. 'Political Liberalism and Religion: On Separation and Establishment,' *Journal of Political Philosophy* (2011): 1–20.

Laborde, Cécile. 'Justificatory Secularism', in *Religion in a Liberal State*, edited by Gavin D'Costa, Malcolm Evans, Tariq Modood and Julian Rivers, 164–86. Cambridge: Cambridge University Press, 2013.

Leigh, Ian. 'By Law Established? The Crown, Constitutional Reform and the Church of England', *Public Law* (2004): 266–73.

Leigh, Ian. 'The European Court of Human Rights and religious neutrality', in *Religion in a Liberal State*, edited by Gavin D'Costa, Malcolm Evans, Tariq Modood and Julian Rivers, 38–66. Cambridge: Cambridge University Press, 2013.

McFarlane v Relate Avon Ltd [2010] EWCA Civ 880; [2010] IRLR 872; 29 BHRC 249.

Mclean, Iain and Benjamin Linsley. *The Church of England and the State: Reforming Establishment for a Multi-faith Britain*. London: New Politics Network, 2004.

Messner, Francis, ed. *Public Funding of Religions in Europe*. Farnham, UK: Ashgate, 2015.

Modood, Tariq. 'Establishment, Multiculturalism and Citizenship', *Political Quarterly* (1994): 53–73.

Morris, Robert M. 'The Future of "High" Establishment', *Ecclesiastical Law Journal* (2011): 260–73.

Morris, Robert M. 'Half-Opening Cans of Worms: The Present State of "High"Anglican Establishment', *Law and Justice*, 172 (2014): 10–26.

National Centre for Social research, *British Social Attitudes 30* at http://bsa-30.natcen.ac.uk/read-the-report/key-findings/identities.aspx, accessed 15 April 2013; and update 31 May 2015 at www.natcen.ac.uk/news-media/press-releases/2015/may/british-social-attitudes-church-of-england-decline-has-accelerated-in-past-decade/, accessed 2 July 2015.

'Near Neighbours', www.gov.uk/government/news/multi-faith-communities-to-benefit-from-new-3-million-grant, accessed 5 May 2014; www.cuf.org.uk/how-we-help/near-neighbours, accessed 2 July 2015.

Percy [AP] [Appellant] v. Church of Scotland National Board of Mission [Respondent] [Scotland] [2005] UKHL 73.

Rivers, Julian. 'From Toleration to Pluralism: Religious Liberty and Religious Establishment under the United Kingdom's Human Rights Act', in *Law and Religion*, edited by Rex Ahdar, 133–61. Aldershot: Ashgate, 2000.

Rivers, Julian. *The Law of Organized Religions: Between Establishment and Secularism*. Oxford: Oxford University Press, 2010.

Russell, Meg. *The Contemporary House of Lords: Westminster Bicameralism Revived*. Oxford: Oxford University Press, 2013.

Sandberg, Russell. *Law and Religion*. Cambridge: Cambridge University Press, 2011.

Smith, Charlotte. 'A Very English Affair: Establishment and Human Rights in an Organic Constitution', *Law and Religion in Theoretical and Historical Context*, edited by Peter Cane, Carolyn Evans and Zöe Robinson, 157–85. Cambridge: Cambridge University Press, 2008. Temperman, Jeroen. *State–Religion Relationships and Human Rights Law: Towards a Right to Religiously Neutral Governance*. Leiden: Nijhoff, 2010.

Thompson, Damian. '2067: The End of British Christianity', *Spectator*, 13 June 2015.

Zucca, Lorenzo. *A Secular Europe: Law and Religion in the European Constitutional Landscape*. Oxford: Oxford University Press, 2012.

Part III

Everyday negotiations

Religion in urban life

8 Everyday negotiations

Religion in urban life

Claire Dwyer

The focus of this section is on the negotiation of religion in contemporary urban space, with work drawn primarily from a social scientific perspective. Drawing on discussions from the third workshop at UCL this section suggests that negotiations of religion in urban space may take a range of different forms or modalities.[1] One key site of analysis centres on the material presence of religion in the urban environment, particularly through the establishment of religious buildings. However, there are also more transient and temporal expressions of communal religious identity in public urban spaces, which also require both negotiation and accommodation. A third site of contemporary negotiation concerns the role of religious actors and institutions in urban politics, governance and welfare. Alongside these examples of more obvious and formal sites of negotiation of religion might be set the more 'everyday' urban cultures and practices of religion and faith in the city and the ways in which these require quotidian negotiations between urban residents. In this introductory section I draw out examples of these four modalities of negotiating religion in urban space, suggesting an approach to negotiation that is somewhat different from other perspectives in this volume. In this account negotiation is understood as a relational form of dialogical and dialectic social relations where religious groups and individuals are key actors. They are also multiply positioned as actors, sometimes they may be disadvantaged in relation to existing hierarchies, as suggested by Laborde in this volume, but at other times they may be able to mobilise important networks or shape institutional or political decisions.

In this section introduction I expand further, with examples, on the four different modalities of negotiation of religion highlighted above. I begin, however, by reflecting on the specific role of *the urban* in framing the idea of the secular as a means of emphasising the negotiation of religion in urban space. Within such a broad basis for discussion it is worth highlighting at the outset that the focus of this sub-section is primarily on British cities within a framework of postcolonial, multicultural Europe rather than opening up a wider discussion about how religion might be negotiated in other urban contexts.

1 Negotiating Religion in Urban Space, Seminar, UCL, 7 March 2012. This workshop brought together a range of social science perspectives from planners, geographers, architects, sociologists, anthropologists and historians but was also distinctive in inviting artists, including Liz Hingley, a photographer and filmmaker, to participate in discussions.

The secular city?

As the key site of modernity the city is central to narratives of secularisation. Integral to the secularisation thesis is the role of urbanisation in producing social dislocation, increasing individualisation, new forms of sociality and social status based on consumption and dissolution of earlier traditions of authority and ritual. This coupling of modernisation, urbanisation and secularisation is evident in the laments of contemporary social commentators on processes of urbanisation in the nineteenth century. As R.W. Emerson writes: 'In our large cities the population is godless, materialised, no bond, no fellow-feeling, no enthusiasm. They are not men, but hungers, thirsts, fevers and appetites, walking.'[2] Such sentiments were echoed in responses to twentieth-century suburbanisation such as T.S. Eliot's pageant play *The Rock*, which describes: 'Here were decent godless people, their only monument the asphalt road, and a thousand lost golf balls.'[3]

Contemporary critique of the secularisation thesis has challenged the certainty and stability of this framing of the secular city. Casanova questions the notion of a singular modernising process drawing attention to both social differentiation and straightforward notions of religious decline.[4] Others highlight the privileging of a Western, normative discourse of secular modernity arguing that 'the secular' is actively produced and must be continuously reproduced and reasserted.[5] Recently some social scientists have asserted the possibilities of a 'post-secular' city drawing evidence from the increasing role of faith-based organisations in welfare-provision in Western societies and the role of global migration in stimulating faith membership in global cities.[6] Such framings of the relationship between the religious, the secular and the urban may however overemphasise novelty. While it is undoubtedly true that processes of globalisation have provoked new engagements with diverse religious practices in global cities and that urban spaces, practices and politics must be understood as mutually constituted through the local and the global, a more critical historicised perspective suggests that such negotiations have always been at the heart of the urban experience. As Jane Garnett and Alana Harris point out in a recent collection of essays on *Rescripting Religion in the City:*

> Western theorists of modernity in the nineteenth and early twentieth centuries understood the complexities of what they were dealing with . . . they perceived

2 R.W. Emerson *Journals of Ralph Waldo Emerson, Vol. 5* (New York: Houghton Mifflin, 1911), 311.

3 T.S. Eliot, *The Rock* (London: Faber & Faber, 1934), 30.

4 Jose Casanova, *Public Religions in the Modern World* (Chicago, IL: Chicago University Press, 1994).

5 Talal Asad, *Genealogies of Religion: Discipline and Reasons of Power in Christianity and Islam* (Baltimore, MD: John Hopkins University Press, 1993); Saba Mahmood, 'Religious Reason and Secular Affect: An Incommensurable Divide?' *Critical Inquiry* 35, 4 (2009): 836–62.

6 Justin Beaumont and Chris Baker, *Postsecular Cities: Space, Theory and Practice* (London: Continuum, 2011); Paul Cloke and Justin Beaumont, 'Geographies of Postsecular Rapproachment in the City', *Progress in Human Geography* 37 (2013): 27–51.

> acute dilemmas of agency and challenges of building community at a time of intensified mobility and diversity within metropolitan agglomerations.[7]

While there may have been a marked re-engagement with religion by social scientists in recent decades, such comments are a helpful reminder that studying the negotiation of religion in urban space requires recognition that the relationship between urbanisation and secularisation is complex, uneven, always contested and never complete.

Negotiating space for religion in the city

The visible materialisation of religion in the urban landscape through dedicated congregational buildings is one example of how space for religion is negotiated. While the churches of the established Anglican church may be celebrated urban landmarks and buildings of other faiths (including synagogues and mosques) date back to the eighteenth and nineteenth centuries, negotiations around the construction of new religious buildings in British cities is an important measure of how multicultural belonging and religious diversity is accommodated. Such new buildings are dealt with within the existing planning regimes and studies have highlighted the exclusionary ways in which normative aesthetic or cultural values may work against the granting of planning permission for new religious buildings. In some cases, however, distinctive municipal multicultural policies may shape greater possibilities for new religious buildings or intervene to assist in finding a suitable site, as was the case in the building of the landmark Swaminaryan Hindu Temple in Neasden in London. Richard Gale argues that it is the relationships forged by faith communities and local political actors that are key to ensuring that new religious buildings are granted planning permission, highlighting both the proactive role of religious actors and the limits and contradictions of planning regulations.[8] For example, UK planning regulations prevent domestic spaces being used for public worship despite the widespread practice of such activities in both the past and present. Nuanced analysis of how planning regulations are enacted illustrate that negotiations are often pragmatic, contextual and subject to

7 For examples of recent collections focusing on religion in the global city see Jochen Becker, Katrin Klingan, Stephan Lanz and Kathrin Wildner, *Global Prayers* (Berlin: metroZones/Lars Müller Publications, 2013); M. Martijn Oosterbaan, 'Public Religion and Urban Space in Europe', *Social & Cultural Geography* 15, 6 (2014): 591–602. For critical reflections on the postsecular see David Ley, 'Preface' to Beaumont and Baker, op. cit, xii–xiv; and James A. Beckford, 'Public Religions and the Postsecular: Critical Reflections', *Journal of the Scientific Study of Religion* 51, 1 (2012): 1–19; Jane Garnett and Alana Harris, *Rescripting Religion in the City* (London: Ashgate, 2013), 2.

8 Richard Gale, 'Locating Religion in Urban Planning: Beyond "Race" and "Ethnicity"', *Planning, Practice and Research* 23, 1 (2008): 19–39; Richard Gale, 'Representing the City: Mosques and the Planning Process in Birmingham', *Journal of Ethnic and Migration Studies* 31, 6, (2005): 1161–79; Ceri Peach and Richard Gale, 'Muslims, Hindus and Sikhs in the New Religious Landscape of England', *The Geographical Review* 93, 4 (2005): 469–90.

contestation frequently involving the conversion of existing buildings, particularly former Anglican churches as well as industrial premises, offices and disused cinemas to temporary and provisional spaces of religious worship. Different parts of the city may be subject to different planning regimes and suburban sites may attract greater critical opposition from established residents than more marginal or transitional urban spaces.[9]

Mosques in particular are likely to attract the most opposition in respect of wider discourses of Islamophobia. This is well illustrated in the furore around a proposal to build a spectacular new mosque in Abbey Mills in East London or the arguments about New York's so-called 'Ground Zero Mosque', the Islamic Cultural Centre at 51 Park Place in Lower Manhattan.[10] Yet there is also an emerging interest from architect practioners in rethinking vernacular religious architecture and negotiating new forms of distinctive British Islamic architecture such as the innovative new Salaam Centre under construction in the north-west London suburb of Harrow by architects Mangera Yvars or the Somali mosque in East London by Makespace architects, which references the neighbouring Whitechapel Art Gallery in its glass cube extension decorated with Somali designs.[11] This is a form of negotiation that references competing visions of the material form of the city as well as the social and communal purpose of worship spaces. The production of new religious spaces also includes the emergence of a diverse and distinctive range of 'multi-faith' spaces, which provocatively reconfigure boundaries between 'religious' and 'secular' through the daily negotiation of a shared sacred or worship space in a urban public setting such as an airport, hospital or shopping centre.[12] An often neglected but highly significant aspect of the negotiation of space in the city is space for approved religious burial rights, as Nazneen Ahmed's discussion of the historical struggle for Muslim burial space in Britain illustrates.[13]

9 Claire Dwyer, David Gilbert and Bindi Shah, 'Faith and Suburbia: Secularisation, Modernity and the Changing Geographies of Religion in London's Suburbs', *Transactions of the Institute of British Geographers* 38, 3 (2013): 403–19; Bindi Shah, Claire Dwyer and David Gilbert, 'Landscapes of Diasporic Belonging in the Edge-city: The Jain Temple at Potters Bar, Outer London', *South Asian Diaspora* 4, 1 (2012): 77–94.

10 For discussion of the conflicts around the Abbey Mills Mosque see Ali Mangera, 'The Mega Mosque', in *Faith in the City: The Mosque in the Contemporary Urban West*, eds J. Jaeckle and F. Türetken (London: The Architecture Foundation, 2011), 12–14; Daniel Nilsson DeHanas and Zacharias Pieri 'Olympic Proportions: The Expanding Scalar Politics of the London "Olympics Mega-Mosque" Controversy', *Sociology* 45 (2011): 798–814. For discussion of Park 51 Mosque see Kilde, J. 'The Park 51/Ground Zero Controversy and Sacred Sites as Contested Space', *Religion 2* (2011): 297–311.

11 For a discussion of the Harrow centre see Claire Dwyer 'Reinventing Muslim Space in Suburbia: The Salaam Centre in Harrow, North London', in *The Changing World Religion Map: Sacred Places, Identities, Practices and Politics*, ed. Stanley Brunn (New York Springer, 2015): 2399–414. For an architectural history of mosque building in Britain see Shaheed Saleem, *The British Mosque: A Social and Architectural History* (London: English Heritage, 2016).

12 Andrew Crompton, 'The Architecture of Multifaith Spaces: God Leaves the Building', *The Journal of Architecture* 18, 4 (2013): 474–96.

13 Nazneen Ahmed, 'Making a Good Death: Muslim Burial Sites and Practices in Britain from 1800 to the Present', in Garnett and Harris, op. cit., 2013, 103–14.

Established congregational religious spaces are the most visible and material examples of how space for religious practice and the assertion of religious identity are negotiated in the city. However there are other ways in which we might examine the negotiation of religion in urban space. A particularly important theme of contemporary scholarship concerns the question of how what might be termed 'public space' is contested and configured as both 'public' and 'secular' and how the presence of faith communities might contest such spaces. Recent controversies over the location and funding of municipal nativity tableaux have provided a trigger for more assertively secular organisations in the US, for example, to police their understanding of assumed secular public space.[14] In the UK provocative challenges have been raised concerning the erection of an *eruv* in parts of British cities, a physical boundary that extends the religious space of the home to a wider geographical area to allow greater mobility for Orthodox Jewish families on the Sabbath. Such *eruvs* are usually delineated by existing walls and telephone wires in British and American cities and are often hardly visible to non-believers, but they have nonetheless produced some heated debates within and without faith communities about the blurring of the 'religious' and the 'secular' in relation to assumptions about 'private' and 'public' space.[15] Such debates effectively test the basis by which religion can be easily contained as a 'private' activity – in effect rigid spatialised boundaries of 'public' and 'private' are often pragmatically and informally negotiated, as this example demonstrates.

The extension of the sacred beyond the confines of religious buildings and the incorporation of other urban sites into religious practices is also evident in the performance of religious rituals such as processions. Such processions were still evident around Christian churches in British cities and suburbs until the mid-twentieth century and through migration such practices have often been revived, such as the spectacle of the Italian procession in Clerkenwell, now recuperated into touristic narratives of the multicultural city.[16] As new faith communities consolidate their presence in urban space, religious practices that take worship out of the building and into the surrounding streets may be reanimated. A good example is the Terotsava Chariot Festival, when the sacred deities (statues), are taken out of the temple and paraded on specially built chariots celebrated in Sri Lankan Tamil Temples in London such as in suburban Ealing and East Ham. The festival attracts thousands of devotees who follow the chariots through the streets including traditional *kavadi* trance dancers and musicians and women

14 Nicholas Howe, 'Thou Shalt Not Misinterpret: Landscape as Legal Performance', *Annals of the Association of American Geographers* 98 (2008): 435–60.

15 Sophie Watson, 'Symbolic Spaces of Difference: Contesting the Eruv in Barnet, London and Tenafly, New Jersey', *Environment and Planning D: Society and Space* 23 (2005): 597–613.

16 Anne-Marie Fortier, 'Re-membering Places and the Performances of Belonging(s)', *Theory, Culture and Society* 16, 2 (1999): 41–64, see also Robert Orsi, *The Madonna of 115th Street: Faith and Community in Italian Harlem, 1880–1950* (New Haven, CT: Yale University Press, 2010); Chantal Saint-Blancat and Adriano Cancellieri, 'From Invisibility to Visibility? The Appropriation of Public Space through a Religious Ritual: The Filipino Procession of Santacruzan in Padua, Italy', *Social & Cultural Geography* 15, 6 (2014): 645–63.

carrying *paal kudum* (milk pots) offerings. Anthropologist Ann David argues that the growth of these festivals marks a new self-assurance in performing Tamil identity in public space through embodied performances and rituals by which the gaze and influence of the deity is acknowledged beyond the confines of the temple. Through such performances the streets around the temple are also made sacred, expanding the boundaries of religious space beyond the walls of the temple.[17] The performance of religion in processions in assumed secular, public space is also evident in the accounts of a brass band from the Kimbanguists, a prophetic Congelese Church located in an industrial estate in Edmonton, as they participated in the annual Lord Mayor's New Year Parade in Central London in 2010. While the band was selected to add multicultural diversity to this annual secular event, participants in the band understood their participation in deeply symbolic spiritual and spatial terms. As anthropologist David Garbin explains, their performance as they marched down Oxford Street in Central London was a 'visible and aural appropriation of space and symbolic re-moralising of the (profane) urban landscape'.[18] Such religious performances both allow diasporic religious groups to mobilise what Kim Knott and Manuel Vásquez describe as a 'spatial politics of recognition' and are also potentially transformative of the fixed and certain meanings of secular, modern urban space.[19]

Religion and urban politics

A key element in the thesis of those theorists who have identified the emergence of the 'post-secular city' is what has been described as a 'rapprochement'between faith communities and the state by which faith-motivated groups are increasingly involved in providing services to the urban poor and disenfranchised.[20] Whether in the form of temporary shelter and food for the homeless, street pastors for young night-clubbers or more established forms of social welfare such as housing or day care such services are said to involve new forms of partnership between the assumed secular state and faith communities.[21] These partnerships might also be recognised as new iterations of older forms of partnership between the state and

17 Ann David, 'Sacralizing the City: Sound, Space and Performance in Hindu Ritual Practices in London', *Culture and Religion* 13, 4 (2012) 449–67.

18 David Garbin, 'The Visibility and Invisibility of Migrant Faith in the City: Diaspora Religion and the Politics of Emplacement of Afro-Christian Churches', *Journal of Ethnic and Migration Studies* 395, (2013): 690. See also the film *Soldiers of God in the Global City* (Enrico Massi, 2012).

19 Manuel Vásquez and Kim Knott, 'Three Dimensions of Religious Place Making in Diaspora', *Global Networks* 14 (2014): 326–47.

20 Cloke and Beaumont, op. cit.

21 For examples of the work of Faith-based organisations in cities see Paul Cloke, Jon May and Sarah Johnsen, *Swept Uplives: Re-envisioning the Homeless City* (Chichester, UK: Wiley-Blackwell, 2010); Justin Beaumont and Paul Cloke, eds *Faith-Based Organizations and Exclusion in European Cities* (Bristol: Policy Press, 2012); Jennie Middleton and Richard Yarwood '"Christians, Out Here?" Encountering Street-Pastors in the Post-Secular Spaces of the UK's Night-Time Economy', *Urban Studies* 52, 3 (2015): 501–16.

religious organisations, symptomatic of the rolling back of the neoliberal state and an increase in voluntary forms of social assistance and welfare. Critical accounts of the role faith-based organisations play in social welfare highlight the dangers of proselytisation and the contradictions through which state funding is diverted to religious organisations, in contrast to those who argue that new spaces are opening up for 'collaborative local activism and in narratives of mutual ethics'.[22] Predominantly the domain of mainstream Christian organisations, John Zavos highlights the rise in Hindu and Sikh welfare organisations working on humanitarian projects both in the UK and abroad exploring how traditional religious precepts such as *sewa* or service are reworked to chime with dominant multicultural policy terms such as citizenship and community cohesion.[23] Work on the activities of the Seamen's Mission in the East End of London in the nineteenth century showing how this predominantly Christian organisation adapted to meet the religious needs of Muslim lascar seafarers emphasises both that faith-based organisations have a long history in the city and that negotiations around cultural and religious differences were integral to the Victorian welfare regime.[24]

The revitalisation of the activities of faith communities in urban spaces under late modernity may offer challenges to the narratives of secular urbanism of early twentieth-century theorists but they are perhaps best understood not as some reversal of processes of secularism but as evidence that the secular urban project was never as complete or as uncontested as is often assumed. In the British case articulations of public policy in relation to the perceived challenges of managing contemporary urban diversity have been shaped by an explicit engagement with 'faith communities' although this is also a policy dialogue freighted with securitisation fears in relation to global Islamism. One of the most interesting recent developments in urban politics has been the emergence of new forms of political activism involving faith communities drawing on American traditions of community organising, such as London Citizens. As Jane Wills and Luke Bretherton (this volume) suggest, such organisations reconfigure class-based urban politics through different social formations and different political discourses and may offer important progressive spaces for urban social action even if their emergence is unsettling to more traditional secular urban politics.[25]

22 Cloke and Beaumont, op. cit., 20. For a more critical account see Jason Hackworth, *Faith Based: Religious Neoliberalism and the Politics of Welfare in the United States* (Athens, GA: University of Georgia Press, 2012); William Connelly, *Capitalism and Christianity American Style* (Durham, NC: Duke University Press, 2008).

23 John Zavos, 'Small Acts, Big Society: Sewa and Hindu (Nationalist) Identity in Britain', *Ethnic and Racial Studies* 38, 2 (2015): 243–58.

24 Nazneen Ahmed. '*Making Muslim Space on the London Docks: Lascar Seafarers' Faith Practices, 1880–1945*', paper presented at the workshop Negotiating Religion in Urban Space, 7 March 2012, UCL.

25 Lina Jamoul and Jane Wills, 'Faith in Politics', *Urban Studies* 45 (2008): 2035–54; Jane Wills, 'The Geography of Community and Political Organisation in London Today', *Political Geography* 31, 2 (2012): 114–26; Luke Bretherton, *Christianity and Contemporary Politics* (Oxford: Wiley-Blackwell, 2010).

Everyday negotiations of religion in the city

The final modality of negotiation of religion in urban space I want to highlight is the recognition of negotiations that can be characterised or theorised as mundane, prosaic, 'everyday' practice. While negotiations are sometimes conducted through the discourses of politics, the media or the law, as other examples in this volume attest, sociability in diverse, multicultural cities requires the knowledge and resources to interact through practices of 'everyday multiculturalism'. As Sara Neal *et al.* argue, cultural and religious difference 'is competently lived in everyday settings and routine ways'.[26] The salience of the mundane and ordinary nature of cultural and religious diversity in contemporary British urban life are well illustrated in the photographic ethnography of photographer Liz Hingley, whose photo essay and exhibition *Under Gods: Stories from Soho Road, Birmingham* captures in carefully observed detail the ordinary and unremarkable co-existence of diverse religious traditions and practices in inner city Birmingham.[27] As a visual discipline photography is a 'medium of detail', which 'focuses attention, elevates, intensifies'.[28] As such, photography can act as a powerful aid to the traditional methodological approaches of social scientists in their techniques of survey and ethnography in urban space. Creative practioners may open up different ways to explore how negotiations of religion in urban space can be rendered visible (when often invisible) as well as unremarkable. Artistic engagements with religion – or the negotiation of religion – in urban space also offer alternative approaches and practices to access the emotional and affective registers through which negotiations between cultural and religious differences are performed and enacted. Sociologist Anne-Marie Fortier has drawn attention to the affective dimensions of religious identifications and the challenges required to manage co-existence in diverse urban space, particularly when it is often in the most economically deprived areas of the city where the greatest diversity is manifest.[29] Emphasising the challenges of negotiating diversity in ordinary, everyday urban life, Mike Keith suggests that 'the sites of the city that display the most intense forms of intolerance are commonly also those that demonstrate the potential for the most intimate forms of cultural dialogue'.[30]

This section of the book on the negotiation of religion in urban space has sought to demonstrate the diverse ways in which religion is present in urban space. Sometimes highly visible, the outcome of a self-conscious process of representation

26 Sara Neal, Katy Bennett and Alan Cochrane, 'Living Multiculture: Understanding the New Spatial And Social Relations of Ethnicity and Multiculture in England', *Environment and Planning C: Government and Policy* 31 (2013): 308–23. See also Sophie Watson and Amina Saha, 'Suburban Drifts: Mundane Multiculturalism in Outer London', *Ethnic and Racial Studies*, 35 (2012): 1–19; Amanda Wise and Selvaraj Velayutham, *Everyday Multiculturalism* (Palgrave MacMillan, 2009).

27 Elizabeth Hingley, *Under Gods: Stories from Soho Road* (Stockport, UK: Dewi Lewis, 2011)

28 Elizabeth Edwards in Hingley, 2011, p. 71

29 Anne-Marie Fortier, *Multicultural Horizons: Diversity and the Limits of the Civil Nation* (London: Routledge, 2008).

30 Keith Michael, *After the Cosmopolitan? Multicultural Cities and the Future Of Racism* (London: Routledge, 2005).

in the urban landscape through dedicated congregational spaces that may be architecturally spectacular, self-confident materialisations of a religious presence. At other times religious practices may be temporary performances in public spaces or negotiations or re-territorialisations of the urban, which may not necessarily be visible or obvious to non-believers. While political and policy discourses have opened up spaces for religious organisations to be increasingly involved in urban welfare or urban politics such engagements resist straightforward categorisation as either a new form of 'post-secular city' or a challenge to secular governance. Although forms of post-political engagement, such as London Citizens, point to the salience of forms of collective religious belonging, particularly for new migrants to the city, explorations of the ways in which religion is negotiated in urban space raise questions as to what extent faith communities might choose 'visibility' or 'invisibility' either in urban space or in urban politics. The ordinary and prosaic ways in which religious differences are accommodated by believers and non-believers alike is also an important theme for understanding how negotiations need not be codified, formalised or enshrined in law but may be pragmatic and contingent.

The chapters

In his chapter, John Eade offers a wide-ranging reflection on religious place-making in urban space focusing particularly on congregational worship spaces, both those that are purpose-built new additions to the urban landscape and those that involve the re-use and appropriation of existing buildings. Drawing on the specific examples of the construction of the Dawoodi Bohras Mosque in Northolt, contested as an 'alien' and 'foreign' intervention in a suburban idyll and the Universal Kingdom of God's attempt to purchase a disused cinema for worship, contested as the loss of important local, secular public space, Eade's contribution effectively highlights the challenges for new faith communities in carving out space for worship in urban space while also offering new models, such as the Crossway Centre in Southwark, for co-existence. However, his analysis also points to some of the tensions and contradictions between secular and religious imaginations of urban space, including incommensurabilities, which may not always be easily alleviated through negotiation.

Luke Bretherton's chapter in this section of the book explores the activities of the London campaigning group, London Citizens, based on three years of ethnographic work with the organisation. London Citizens is a grass-roots campaigning group that mobilises in relation to urban social issues through a form of community organising borrowed from the US, which involves existing groups and institutions particularly faith groups. Bretherton's chapter traces the ways in which diverse religious traditions find common cause in the challenges of co-existence in urban space, particularly in the experiences of migrant communities. The analysis celebrates the possibilities of inter-faith relations as a form of civic practice and the ways in which urban citizenship is re-conceptualised through religious discourses. Bretherton's analysis shows how different faith communities, non-religious actors and organisations like trade unions and politicians negotiate forms of dialogue and interaction. London Citizens offer an unsettling of secular public political space and Bretherton highlights how religious languages and performances are enabled and sometimes amplified in the struggle for social justice although they are also contingent and alliances can be fragile and provisional. This chapter offers an effective illustration, then, of one of the modalities outlined above in relation to faith and urban politics.

References

Ahmed, Nazneen. 'Making Muslim Space on the London Docks: Lascar Seafarers' Faith Practices, 1880–1945', Paper presented at the workshop Negotiating Religion in Urban Space, 7 March 2012, UCL.

Ahmed, Nazneen. 'Making a Good Death: Muslim Burial Sites and Practices in Britain from 1800 to the Present', in *Rescripting Religion in the City*, edited by Jane Garnett and Alana Harris, 103–14. London: Ashgate, 2013.

Asad, Talal. *Genealogies of Religion: Discipline and Reasons of Power in Christianity and Islam.* Baltimore, MD: John Hopkins University Press, 1993.

Beaumont, Justin and Chris Baker. *Postsecular Cities: Space, Theory and Practice,* London: Continuum, 2011.

Beaumont, Justin and Paul Cloke, eds *Faith-Based Organizations and Exclusion in European Cities.* Bristol: Policy Press, 2012.

Becker, Joachen, Katrin Klingan, Stephan Lanz and Kathrin Wildner. *Global Prayers.* Berlin: metroZones/Lars Müller Publications, 2013.

Beckford, James. 'Public Religions and the Postsecular: Critical Reflections', *Journal of the Scientific Study of Religion* 51, 1 (2012): 1–19.

Bretherton, Luke. *Christianity and Contemporary Politics.* Oxford: Wiley-Blackwell, 2010.

Casanova, Jose. *Public Religions in the Modern World.* Chicago, IL: Chicago University Press, 1994.

Cloke, Paul and Justin Beaumont. 'Geographies of Postsecular Rapproachment in the City', *Progress in Human Geography* 37 (2013): 27–51.

Cloke, Paul, Jon May and Sarah Johnsen. *Swept Up Lives: Re-Envisioning the Homeless City.* Chichester: Wiley-Blackwell, 2010.

Connelly, William. *Capitalism and Christianity American Style.* Durham, NC: Duke University Press, 2008.

Crompton, Andrew. 'The Architecture of Multifaith Spaces: God Leaves the Building', *The Journal of Architecture* 18, 4 (2013): 474–96.

David, Ann. 'Sacralizing the City: Sound, Space and Performance in Hindu Ritual Practices in London', *Culture and Religion* 13, 4 (2012): 449–67.

DeHanas, Daniel Nilsson and Zacharias Pieri. 'Olympic Proportions: The expanding Scalar Politics of the London "Olympics Mega-Mosque" Controversy', *Sociology* 45 (2011): 798–814.

Dwyer, Claire. 'Reinventing Muslim Space in Suburbia: The Salaam centre in Harrow, North London', in *The Changing World Religion Map: Sacred Places, Identities, Practices and Politics*, edited by Stanley Brunn, 2399–414. New York: Springer, 2015.

Dwyer, Claire, David Gilbert and Bindi Shah. 'Faith and Suburbia: Secularisation, Modernity and the Changing Geographies of Religion in London's Suburbs', *Transactions of the Institute of British Geographers* 38, 3 (2013): 403–19.

Edwards, Elizabeth. 'Places of Feeling: Photographs, People and Things', in *Under Gods: Stories from Soho Road*, edited by Elizabeth Hingley, 72–4. Stockport, UK: Dewi Lewis, 2011.

Eliot, T. S. *The Rock*. London: Faber & Faber, 1934.

Emerson, R. W. *Journals of Ralph Waldo Emerson, Vol. 5*. New York: Houghton Mifflin, 1911.

Fortier Anne-Marie. 'Re-Membering Places and the Performances of Belonging(s)', *Theory, Culture and Society* 16, 2, (1999): 41–64

Fortier, Anne-Marie. *Multicultural Horizons: Diversity and the Limits of the Civil Nation*. London, Routledge, 2008.

Gale, Richard. 'Representing the City: Mosques and the Planning Process in Birmingham', *Journal of Ethnic and Migration Studies* 31, 6 (2005): 1161–79.

Gale, Richard. 'Locating Religion in Urban Planning: Beyond "Race" and "Ethnicity"', *Planning, Practice and Research* 23, 1 (2008): 19–39.

Garbin, David. 'The Visibility and Invisibility of Migrant Faith in the City: Diaspora Religion and the Politics of Emplacement of Afro-Christian Churches', *Journal of Ethnic and Migration Studies* 39, 5 (2013): 677–96.

Garnett, Jane and Alana Harris, eds *Rescripting Religion in the City*. London: Ashgate, 2013.

Hackworth, Jason. *Faith Based: Religious Neoliberalism and the Politics of Welfare in the United States*. Athens, GA: University of Georgia Press, 2012.

Hingley, Elizabeth. *Under Gods: Stories from Soho Road*. Stockport, UK: Dewi Lewis, 2011.

Howe, Nicholas. 'Thou Shalt Not Misinterpret: Landscape as Legal Performance', *Annals of the Association of American Geographers* 98 (2008): 435–60.

Jamoul, Lina and Wills, Jane. 'Faith in Politics', *Urban Studies* 45 (2008): 2035–54.

Keith, Michael. *After the Cosmopolitan? Multicultural Cities and the Future of Racism*. London: Routledge, 2005.

Kilde, J. 'The Park 51/Ground Zero Controversy and Sacred Sites as Contested Space', *Religion* 2 (2011): 297–311.

Ley, David. 'Preface: Towards the Postsecular City', in *Postsecular Cities: Space, Theory and Practice* edited by Justin Beaumont and Chris Baker, xii–xiv. London: Continuum, 2011.

Mahmood, Saba. 'Religious Reason and Secular Affect: An Incommensurable Divide?' *Critical Inquiry* 35, 4 (2009): 836–62.

Mangera, Ali. 'The Mega Mosque', in *Faith in the City: The Mosque in the Contemporary Urban West* edited by J. Jaeckle and F. Türetken, 12–14. London: The Architecture Foundation, 2011.

Middleton, Jennie and Richard Yarwood. '"Christians, Out Here?" Encountering Street-Pastors in the Post-Secular Spaces of the UK's Night-Time Economy', *Urban Studies* 52, 3 (2015): 501–16.

Neal, Sara, Katy Bennett and Alan Cochrane. 'Living Multiculture: Understanding the New Spatial and Social Relations of Ethnicity and Multiculture in England', *Environment and Planning C: Government and Policy* 31 (2013): 308–23.

Oosterbaan, Martijn. 'Public Religion and Urban Space in Europe', *Social & Cultural Geography* 15, 6 (2014): 591–602.

Orsi, Robert. *The Madonna of 115th Street: Faith and Community in Italian Harlem, 1880–1950*. New Haven, CT: Yale University Press, 2010.

Peach, Ceri and Gale, Richard. 'Muslims, Hindus and Sikhs in the New Religious Landscape of England', *The Geographical Review* 93, 4 (2005): 469–90.

Saint-Blancat, Chantal and Cancellieri Adriano. 'From Invisibility to Visibility? The Appropriation of Public Space Through a Religious Ritual: The Filipino Procession of Santacruzan in Padua, Italy', *Social & Cultural Geography* 15, 6 (2014): 645–63.

Saleem, Shaheed. *The British Mosque: A Social and Architectural History*. London: English Heritage, 2015.

Shah, Bindi, Claire Dwyer and Gilbert, David. 'Landscapes of Diasporic Belonging in The Edge-City: The Jain Temple at Potters Bar, Outer London', *South Asian Diaspora* 4, 1 (2012): 77–94.

Watson, Sophie. 'Symbolic Spaces of Difference: Contesting the Eruv in Barnet, London and Tenafly, New Jersey', *Environment and Planning D: Society and Space* 23, 5 (2005) 97–613.

Watson, Sophie and Amina Saha. 'Suburban Drifts: Mundane Multiculturalism in Outer London', *Ethnic and Racial Studies* 35 (2012) 1–19.

Wills, Jane. 'The Geography of Community and Political Organisation in London Today', *Political Geography* 31, 2 (2012) 114–26.

Wise, Amanda and Selvaraj Velayutham. *Everyday Multiculturalism*. London: Palgrave MacMillan, 2009.

Vásquez, Manuel and Kim Knott. 'Three Dimensions of Religious Place Making in Diaspora', *Global Networks* 14 (2014) 326–47.

Zavos, John. 'Small Acts, Big Society: Sewa and Hindu (Nationalist) Identity in Britain', *Ethnic and Racial Studies* 38, 2 (2015) 243–58.

9 Creating religious homes in London

Sacralising space in a deeply globalised city

John Eade

Introduction: religious place-making and urban society

As the proportion of people living in urban settlements around the world has exponentially increased since World War II, it has become evident that cities and towns are not just places shaped by secular political and economic interests. They are not in the vanguard of some universal and unilinear process of secular modernity. Instead, a variety of modernities have emerged around the world (see Eisenstadt 2000) where religious institutions and allegiances sometimes continue to play an important role, both publicly and privately. Globalising cities display most vividly both the decline and persistence of religious solidarities. Diverse 'micro geographies' are emerging where some localities display the vigorous and expanding presence of religion in both public and private life.[1]

The important part played by religious institutions in these localities demonstrates the impact of global migration and increasing religious diversity, but established religious institutions have also responded imaginatively to increasing competition in a crowded religious marketplace.[2] These responses can lead to aggressive exclusions of 'outsiders', which have been explored through studies of

1 See John Connell, 'Hillsong: A Megachurch in the Sydney Suburbs', *Australian Geographer* 36 (2005): 315–32; Deborah Stevenson Kevin Dunn, Adam Possamai and Awais Piracha, 'Religious Belief across "Post-Secular" Sydney: The Multiple Trends in (De)Secularisation', *Australian Geographer* 41 (2010): 323–50; John Eade, 'Religious Place-Making and Migration across a Globalising City: Responding to Mobility in London', *Culture and Religion* 13 (2012): 469–83; David Garbin, 'Marching for God in the Global City: Public Space, Religion and Diasporic Identities in a Transnational African Church', *Culture and Religion* 13 (2012): 424–47.

2 See Lily Kong, 'Global Shifts, Theoretical Shifts: Changing Geographies of Religion', *Progress in Human Geography* 34 (2010): 755–76; David Goodhew, ed. *Church Growth in Britain, 1980 to the Present* (Farnham, UK and Burlington, VT: Ashgate, 2012); Linda Woodhead and Rachel Catto, eds *Religion and Change in Modern Britain* (London and New York: Routledge, 2012); and Peter Beyer, *Religion in the Context of Globalization Essays on Concept, Form, and Political Implication* (London and New York: Routledge, 2013).

communal violence and recent discussions of the 'fundamentalist city'.[3] However, as studies of disputes around churches, mosques, temples and gurudwaras have demonstrated, those claiming to represent a specific religious 'community' engage with powerful others, such as politicians, planning officers, protest groups and the media and have learned how to 'play the game' by building alliances with secular leaders. Exclusion or openness to 'outsiders' involves a variety of discourses and practices where religious and secular representatives may work together in some disputes or find themselves on opposite sides elsewhere. Alliances can cut across religious and secular boundaries and both religious and secular organisations may be internally divided by conflicting interests.

Place-making, therefore, involves communities or groups that are not homogeneous entities but contested, heterogeneous social constructions. We must look behind the essentialising rhetoric of group unity generated by religious and secular leaders and analyse the complex and shifting movement of alliances involved in specific disputes over public space. A highly globalised city such as London provides us with rich opportunities for such an analysis and enables us to offset the tendency to focus on economic processes at the expense of cultural and political dynamics in discussions of the city's development.[4]

London and the growth of religious diversity

Although London is a very diverse city in terms of religious affiliation, this diversity is not a recent phenomenon. During the seventeenth and eighteenth centuries, the Church of England encountered a strong challenge from a range of dissenting sects, while the arrival of Catholic and Jewish immigrants increased this religious diversity. The settlement of French Calvinists (Huguenots) from the late seventeenth century strengthened the ranks of those Christians who worshipped outside the established church and the Anglican churches built across London's East End from the 1740s were intended to strengthen the established church's parochial system in an expanding industrial area.[5]

3 See Nezar AlSayyad and Mejgan Massoumi, eds *The Fundamentalist City: Religiosity and the Remaking of Urban Space* (New York: Routledge, 2010).

4 Although I have drawn on the pioneering work on the global city by Saskia Sassen, *The Global City: New York, London, Tokyo* (Princeton, NJ: Princeton University Press, 1991) in various publications (see, for example, John Eade, 'Introduction' in *Living the Global City: Globalisation As Local Process*, ed. John Eade (London and New York: Routledge, 1997), 1–19 and John Eade and Michal Garapich, 'Settling or Surviving in London: The Experience of Poles and Other "A8" Migrants in a Global City Borough', in *Accession and Migration: Changing Policy, Society, and Culture in an Enlarged Europe*, eds John Eade and Yordanka Valkanova (Farnham, UK: Ashgate, 2009), 143–66), I prefer the term 'globalising city' because of its more dynamic and inclusive character (see Peter Marcuse and Ronald van Kempen, eds *Globalizing Cities: A New Spatial Order* (Malden, MA and Oxford: Blackwell, 2000).

5 See Anne Kershen, *Strangers, Aliens and Asians: Huguenots, Jews and Bangladeshis in Spitalfields, 1660–2000* (London and New York: Routledge, 2004).

Religious diversity was not conflict-free and Catholics bore the brunt of hostility. The 'Gordon riots' of 1780, which followed the Papists Act of 1778 designed to relax some of the restrictions imposed on Catholics, showed that tensions over religious difference could erupt into local violence. Typically, chapels, as the institutional manifestations of Catholicism, were the prime targets together with the houses of prominent Catholics. However, the 1778 Act signalled the central government's willingness to weaken the penal laws that had been passed against those outside the Church of England during the sixteenth century. Hence, between 1828 and 1829 the penal laws were finally repealed and calls began to be expressed for the disestablishment of the Church of England. Disestablishment had already occurred in Ireland and Wales so this was not such a radical move. Nonconformists led the charge and the Anglican religious leaders were stunned when the first national Church census in 1851[6] revealed the strength of the Nonconformist challenge in London and elsewhere. In terms of religious attendance Nonconformists appeared to have almost achieved parity, benefitting from strong support across working- and middle-class areas of London and other cities.

The 1851 census strengthened calls for the Church of England's disestablishment and added spice was given to the competition between Anglicans and Nonconformists when state support for primary education increased after the 1870 Education Act. Central government encouraged the hierarchical institutionalisation of religion by insisting on negotiating with 'community leaders', who could be held accountable for the distribution of state funds. The hierarchical structures of the Anglican and Catholic Churches provided organised leadership that the state could recognise. Nonconformist and Jewish communities were much less centralised but they also generated bodies, which could compete with Anglican and Catholic representatives for resources, viz. the Board of Deputies of British Jews founded in 1760.

Outside of this arena of elite competition between religious leaders for secular state funding, the establishment of churches, chapels and synagogues across the expanding suburbs was a largely peaceful process. From the late nineteenth century local conflicts cohered primarily around class and racial differences. Religious tensions sometimes did erupt but these could just as easily be between rival factions within the Anglican Church as between Anglicans and other Christian congregations. Nineteenth-century attacks on Anglo-Catholic churches by those opposed to their 'papist' ritual practices are a case in point. This low level of religious conflict was also in evidence when there was a rapid influx of poor Jews from Tsarist Russia during the 1880s. Although their settlement in the East End was followed by a certain degree of anti-semitic antagonism, there was no organised, large-scale violence. The long established Anglo-Jewish elite encouraged rapid assimilation, even though traditions were preserved through local community institutions established by first generation immigrants including synagogues and Talmudic schools, some of which were targets of random attack and public

6 The church census was undertaken in the same year as the first general national census.

criticism. Jewish settlement added another element to the religious micro-geography of London's East End.[7]

Yet while social relations between East Enders from the late nineteenth century up to World War II were shaped by religious differences between Jews, Catholics, Nonconformist and Anglicans, the very same people were also involved in other social, economic and political affiliations, which linked them together in some contexts and separated them in others. Working-class solidarities were sustained by the local occupational structure and neighbourhood ties as well as the political institutions of the Labour and Communist parties, language (English, Yiddish) and transnational links with Ireland, Russia and Palestine. In other words, a hyphenated, hybrid Englishness had developed, which allowed for the survival of loyalties beyond the national boundary.

Like other dynamic and economically diverse cities (Chicago, New York, Birmingham), London's inhabitants were relatively mobile. During the 1920s and 1930s, slum clearance in such intensely poor neighbourhoods as Stepney and Bethnal Green was accompanied by the development of state-funded suburban estates, such as London County Council's vast Redbridge estate to the east and the LCC'S local borough estates across south London. This process of out-migration was encouraged during World War II and was accelerated after 1945 by the building of 'New Towns' beyond the 'Green Belt'. Towns such as Crawley, Stevenage, Hemel Hempstead, Basildon and Basingstoke rapidly expanded with the influx of skilled and semi-skilled workers from the East End and other working-class redoubts. This process eroded the tightly knit inner city neighbourhoods and the ties that held them together, including religious allegiances.

This outward movement was countered to some extent by immigration from Britain's unravelling empire, symbolised by the arrival of the MS Empire Windrush in 1948, which brought young men from the Caribbean in search of better paid work, if not a warmer climate! This added a fresh layer of racial and ethnic complexity to London society and, while many African-Caribbean settlers expressed their religious identity through local churches or setting up their own chapels, the 'Notting Hill riots' of 1958 showed that the lines of urban conflict were shaped by racialised differences rather than religion. Indeed, from the late 1950s, urban tensions were linked to wider political and economic arguments about Britain's decline, associated in turn with rapid decolonisation, deindustrialisation, immigration and racial discrimination versus toleration. To these debates were added anxieties concerning policing, institutional racism, far-Right political agitation and economic inequality after the Brick Lane riots of 1978 and the much more publicised Brixton riots of 1985.

Since the late 1980s religious place-making has again become the focus of localised tensions across London, but tensions have been largely contained within

7 See Anne Kershen, *Strangers, Aliens and Asians: Huguenots, Jews and Bangladeshis in Spitalfields, 1660–2000* (London and New York: Routledge, 2004); and Anne Kershen and Laura Vaughan, '"There was a Priest, a Rabbi and an Imam . . .": An Analysis of Urban Space and Religious Practice in London's East End, 1685–2010', *Material Religion* 9 (2013): 10–35.

institutional boundaries and hierarchical structures. Among the plethora of religious centres serving the expanding numbers of 'black' Christians, Muslims, Hindus, Sikhs and Buddhists in the suburbs as well as in the inner locales,[8] certain initiatives attracted particularly heated opposition – namely, proposals to develop secular space by religious 'outsiders', particularly Muslims and black Christians.[9] While I have explored this contestation in terms of the interaction between religious representatives and outsiders elsewhere,[10] I want to approach the process from a different angle: the problems of sharing public space between religious and secular groups where boundaries are drawn between acceptable 'insiders' and unworthy 'outsiders'. To develop this approach I will compare disputes involving different ethnic and religious groups: the Dawoodi Bohras, the Universal Church of the Kingdom of God and 'black majority' congregations – and their (predominantly) secular opponents.

Dawoodi Bohras and the Northolt enclave in West London

During the mid-1990s I undertook one of the earliest comparisons between disputes across London, which involved competing religious and secular interests. I contrasted controversies surrounding mosque development in Tower Hamlets where global migration had resulted in the settlement of large Sunni Muslim communities with a dispute in the West London borough of Ealing over an application by a very small sect of Shia Muslims – Dawoodi Bohras – to build a mosque, *jamaat khana* and 22 houses in an industrial estate.[11] Despite local agitation against the Dawoodi Bohra plan, which included the local MP and commercial and residential pressure groups, the Northolt centre opened with considerable fanfare. Local hostility faded away and such luminaries as the Prince of Wales and the Archbishop of Canterbury have made visits to laud the Bohras' contribution to Britain's cultural diversity and economic vitality.[12]

8 See Claire Dwyer, David Gilbert and Bindi Shah, 'Faith and Suburbia: Secularisation, Modernity and the Changing Geographies of Religion in London's Suburbs', *Transactions of the Institute of British Geographers* 38 (2013): 403–19.

9 See Daniel DeHanas and Zacharias Pieri, 'Olympic Proportions: The Expanding Scalar Politics of the London "Olympics Mega-Mosque" Controversy', *Sociology* 45 (2011): 798–814; and David Garbin, 'Marching for God in the Global City: Public Space, Religion and Diasporic Identities in a Transnational African Church', *Culture and Religion* 13 (2012): 424–47.

10 John Eade, 'Nationalism, Community and the Islamization of Space in London' in *Making Muslim Space in North America and Europe*, ed. Barbara Metcalf (Berkeley, CA and Los Angeles, CA: University of California Press, 1997), 217–33 and 'From Race to Religion: Multiculturalism and Contested Urban Space' in *Post-Secular Cities: Space, Theory and Practice*, eds Justin Beaumont and Chris Butler (London and New York: Continuum, 2011), 154–67.

11 Eade, 'Nationalism, Community and the Islamization of Space in London', 1997.

12 See 'A speech by HRH The Prince of Wales at the Dawoodi Bohra Mosque, Northolt, Middlesex', www.princeofwales.gov.uk/media/speeches/speech-hrh-the-prince-of-wales-the-dawoodi-bohra-mosque-northolt-middlesex, accessed 21 February 2014 and 'Archbishop's visit to Dawoodi Bohra Mosque and Jain Temple', http://rowanwilliams.archbishopofcanterbury.org/articles.

The Northolt centre was part of an international network, which had developed over many centuries through the Bohras' involvement in trade and commerce. Globally, Bohras are approximately one million strong, with a firm base in the Indian state of Gujarat, but increasingly involved in professional occupations across India and around the world, i.e. the Middle East, Pakistan, East Africa, Singapore, Hong Kong, North America and Europe, particularly the UK. This far-flung community is tightly organised around its religious leader – the Syedna, based in Mumbai – and his local representatives. The vast majority of the reported 6,000 living in Britain are based in English cities: half in London and the rest in cities such as Leicester, Nottingham, Bradford and Manchester.

Despite their distinctive community features, the Bohras relied on the 'gathered community' tradition, which Nonconformist congregations had developed in Britain during the nineteenth century and that other global migrants adopted after the Second World War – 'black majority' Christian churches, Sunni Muslims, Hindus, Sikhs, Jains, Buddhists and so on. The Bohras illustrated, in the most dramatic form, the restricted choice and heavy commitment involved in travelling long distances to community gatherings. Not for them the freedom of choice provided by the local churches, integral to the parochial structure inherited by the Church of England after the Reformation and developed by the Catholic Church since its re-establishment during the nineteenth century.

Although eminent visitors hailed the Dawoodi Bohras' contribution to wider British society, the sect kept a very low profile and was highly exclusive. The design of the Northolt centre represented this inward-looking character very well. As Mark Crinson notes in his comparison between the Northolt site and the Regents Park and Woking mosques, a 'small Islamic enclave' was carved out where a right angle of terraced houses created a gateway that led into a square dominated by the mosque and jamaatkhana. The houses provided a perimeter wall by 'turning their backs on the industrial estate and nearby park'. The struggle to build the centre is reflected in 'this image of an embattled community turning in on itself'.[13]

There were powerful internal forces encouraging such an inward-looking approach. The sect's dispersal around the world during the nineteenth and twentieth centuries had threatened the tight, hierarchical structure based around the Syedna's leadership and the last two Syednas – Taher Saifuddin and Mohammed Burhanuddin – had responded by regularly visiting centres outside of India, encouraging devotees to attend major celebrations in Mumbai, insisting on the regular payment of tithes and the tradition of endogamous marriages. Outsiders were useful if they provided local validation – hence the invitations to

php/989/archbishops-visit-to-dawoodi-bohra-mosque-and-jain-temple#sthash.ebyRGHKY.dpuf, accessed 21 February 2014.

13 Mark Crinson, 'The Mosque and the Metropolis', in *Orientalism's Interlocutors: Painting, Architecture, Photography*, eds Jill Beaulieu and Mary Roberts, (Durham, NC: Duke University Press), 2012, pp. 79–102.

a wide range of people who might provide useful connections – but outsiders could also present a lethal threat as the communal riots in Gujarat had revealed since the 1980s.[14]

Yet strict control was limited by disputes over the leadership of the sect, as claims by each Sydena to have been nominated by his predecessor were regularly contested. Furthermore, the emergence during the twentieth century of a breakaway group – the Progressive or Reformist Dawoodi Bohras – in England and Canada, for example, expressed dissatisfaction with 'the authoritarian and un-Islamic system the current Bohra priesthood has put in place to control and fleece the Dawoodi Bohra community' (www.dawoodi-bohras.org.uk). Behind the impressive facade of the purpose built centres, which now symbolise the Dawoodi presence in London, Leicester, Manchester and Bradford, lies a more fractured reality where Reformists seek to expose the limitations of a religious hierarchy to the outside world. Despite the articulation of essentialised discourses concerning group solidarity across local, national and transnational levels, the image of a homogeneous Bohra community promulgated by the religious leaders is contested by the continued presence of the Progressive Dawoodi Bohras.

The Northolt mosque was built through strong internal control and alliances with powerful outsiders, particularly leaders of Ealing's Labour borough council. Party political differences, not surprisingly, became embroiled during the planning dispute, with the local Conservative MP, Harry Greenway, playing a central role. During a debate in the House of Commons he sought to block the proposal by arguing that the mosque development would harm the economic prospects of local residents and, thereby, damage race relations:

> [To] build the facility – if I might call it that – and the 22 houses on Northolt's only industrial estate would do serious damage to race relations and public morale in Northolt, where there is already high unemployment. . . . The residents complained that a mosque on the Sadia site would slowly but surely erode the industrial base of Northolt, on which many residents depend for their livelihood.[15]

Harry Greenway's opposition failed to prevent the development proceeding and his dire warnings appear to have been unfounded; however, the link between economic considerations and 'local community' sensitivities, which his speech emphasised, remain present in disputes over religious place-making, as the next, more recent case illustrates.

14 Ali Asghar Engineer 'Kota: Another Case of Planned Violence?' *Economic and Political Weekly* 24 (1989): 2703–5.

15 See Hansard, 'Northolt Industrial Estate', HC Deb 03 July 1992 vol. 210 cc.1139–46, http://hansard.millbanksystems.com/commons/1992/jul/03/northolt-industrial-estate, accessed 27 August 2015.

Sharing space: the Universal Church of the Kingdom of God and the Walthamstow Cinema dispute

The increasing demand for religious accommodation over the last two decades in London has been accompanied by a large number of unsuccessful planning applications. Of the 602 applications made by religious representatives to 22 of London's 33 borough councils between 2000 and 2007, 160 were for a change of use but only 87 or 54 per cent were granted. This was 'well below the national average for all planning applications'.[16] Given local sensitivities about applications by religious newcomers to take over secular space, one way forward was to share these scarce resources. This was easier said than done, however, as the struggle between religious and secular groups over a redundant cinema on the opposite side of the metropolis illustrated.

The Universal Church of the Kingdom of God (UCKG) is a Pentecostal group that was founded in Brazil in 1977. Its first international venture was in New York in 1986 and it has grown an extensive global network, which includes the UK and other European countries such as France, Poland and Romania. The first UCKG church was established in Brixton during 1995, but, a year later, the group bought the disused Rainbow Theatre in Finsbury Park, which became its main centre after an extensive refurbishment. The purchase of a redundant cinema on a main street in Walthamstow during 2004 seemed to provide an opportunity for further expansion into London's north-east suburbs; however, the borough council opposed the planning application for a change of use, since it wanted the building to play a key role in the economic regeneration of the main street and did not see these religious newcomers fitting within their development plans. A rival, secular group – the Waltham Forest Cinema Trust (WFCT) – sought to restore the cinema to its former glory and argued that its plans served the interests of the 'local community' more fully.

For over 9 years the development of the cinema remained unresolved with the UKCG refusing to move away from the main street to what the council saw as a more suitable site elsewhere in the borough. In an attempt to satisfy local objections, the UKCG revised its change of use application so that they could share the building with the WFCT. This application was not accepted by both the council and the WFCT, primarily on economic grounds and so in November 2012, a planning enquiry was held at Walthamstow Town Hall to adjudicate between rival applications submitted by the UCKG and the WFCT. The UCKG application was rejected by the Secretary of State for the Environment and the UCKG was obliged to sell the site and look elsewhere.

Why was sharing so difficult? Although the planning officer's adjudication emphasised the economic dimension in the context of the main street's regeneration, local activists also sought to defend the cultural interests of the 'local

16 Alastair Rogers, *Being Built Together: Interim Report* (London: University of Roehampton, 2012, p. 80).

community'. Claiming that Alfred Hitchcock attended the cinema during the 1920s, the WFCT quoted a more contemporary cultural icon, Sir Mick Jagger:

> It is heartbreaking to hear such a beautiful, important historical building and centre of entertainment is being lost to the local community. I fully support the campaign to keep it open and provide film, music and the arts for generations to come.[17]

The UCKG were portrayed as unfeeling outsiders, who bought the cinema in 2004 and held on to it despite the council's rejection of their planning application. As one local activist declared, the application was 'clearly an act of extreme arrogance and a complete lack of empathy with what local people want'.[18] Furthermore, the UKCG's proposal to share the premises was roundly rejected on the grounds that, in practice, its religious needs would exclude secular uses:

> There are no examples of a hybrid church/cinema operation on this scale working successfully in the UK. UCKG do not operate their sites in this way. The only venue they previously proposed doing so – at Catford – ended without any cinema provision and left Lewisham as the only other London Borough without a cinema.[19]

The WFCT drew on the consultancy report they had commissioned, which again dismissed the suggestion that the space could be harmoniously shared. The Locum report states 'many potential customers of the cinema are likely to feel uncomfortable about sharing the lobby area with the church congregation' – which is a key part of these plans – and that 'the two activities – worship and entertainment – are not a natural complement'.[20]

Other elements of the UCKG plan demonstrated the incompatibility of religious and secular interests – in this particular case at least. Various experts were agreed that

> (the) use of the bulk of the building for church activities may greatly reduce its potential attraction. This includes the conversion of street facing retail units into a Christian bookshop and training centre and the absence of a licensed bar or restaurant. The auditorium's lower circle will be completely unused on a regular basis.[21]

17 See 'Save Walthamstow Cinema', http://savewalthamstowcinema.org/?p=254, accessed 21 February 2014

18 See 'Pickles to Rule on Controversial Church Plans for Walthamstow Cinema', www.selbyalan.com/blog/pickles-to-rule-on-controversial-church-plans-for-walthamstow-cinema/, accessed 6 July 2015.

19 Ibid.

20 Ibid.

21 Ibid.

If the UCKG wished to engage in local community service through its Helpline and other outreach activities, it was suggested that this could be pursued in a more 'appropriate' space, that is, where religious and secular entertainment needs did not collide.

Clearly, the success or failure of planning applications is determined by a wide range of factors. Obviously, careful attention has to be paid to planning regulations and close cooperation with council officials is crucial. However, local political, social and economic elements also play a significant role. Ideally, alliances are established with local politicians, neighbourhood groups and those concerned about the economic development of the area. Other links can be forged or established at metropolitan, national and transnational levels. For example, the UCKG representatives appealed to the Brazilian embassy and political leaders back in Brazil to support their appeal. Yet, in this complex mixture of forces some might prove to be more influential than others. The Northolt change of use application succeeded with the support of the Labour council leadership despite opposition from the local MP, various neighbourhood groups and business interests. In Walthamstow the UKCG representatives failed to get powerful local actors on their side and found themselves confronted by an alliance forged between the local Labour MP, the Labour borough council, artistic and business interests, which proved to be more powerful than their transnational networks.

Success or failure depended, therefore, on a variety of factors. Religious leaders have to know how to play the rules of the planning game and cannot rely solely on the support of powerful local politicians. As the long running saga of the Abbey Mills mosque proposal in neighbouring Newham indicated, the proposal by the Muslim missionary group, the Tabligh Jamaat, to develop a site next to the Olympic Park was stymied not just by resistance from political opponents of the Labour council, but also by rival Muslim groups and Christian representatives.[22] The Tabligh's leaders failed to control their own followers and lacked the professional resources to deal with the complexities of a rapidly evolving situation. Tightly organised groups such as the Dawoodi Bohras could draw on their professional and business expertise, as well as their connections with members of British secular and religious elites, to buttress their local political networks – resources that both the UCKG and the Tabligh appeared to lack. Knowing how to play the game was also vital in the case of the Jains, who drew on their business and professional skills to build a temple in Potters Bar.[23]

22 See John Eade, 'From Race to Religion: Multiculturalism and Contested Urban Space', in *Post-Secular Cities: Space, Theory and Practice*, eds Justin Beaumont and Chris Butler (London and New York: Continuum, 2011), 154–67.

23 Bindi Shah, Claire Dwyer and David Gilbert, 'Landscapes of Diasporic Religious Belonging in the Edge-City: The Jain Temple at Potters Bar, Outer London', *South Asian Diaspora* 4 (2012): 77–94.

Religious groups sharing space: 'black majority churches' in Southwark

Given the hurdles to be jumped when applying for planning permission and the intense competition for public space between religious and secular interest groups, one obvious tactic is for similar religious groups to share the same building. Yet again a variety of ideological and practical difficulties have to be resolved. Declining Anglican congregations may not be eager to share their church with non-Christians as opposed to their adjoining meeting rooms and halls. Tensions can even arise between Christian congregations, which follow different theological traditions, while many dynamic, proselytising churches wanted to redeem public space for their exclusive use.[24]

To explore the issue of sharing between religious organisations further and to put the Northolt and Walthamstow cases into a wider London perspective, I want to draw on a recent study undertaken by colleagues at the University of Roehampton. Between 2011 and 2012 the project focussed on new black majority churches (nBMCs) in the borough of Southwark and was stimulated by 'the pressing issue of finding suitable premises for churches . . . and the attendant problems surrounding change of use planning permission'.[25] Forty-four per cent of 'non-white churchgoers' lived in the metropolis – the highest proportion across the country. Southwark contained the highest proportion of black Africans (16.4 per cent) in London – the second largest ethnic group after White British – and approximately 240 nBMCs, many of which were clustered in three areas on or near the Old Kent Road.[26] Many of these churches occupied premises without council approval and many applications for a change of use had been unsuccessful. Between 2000 and 2011 47 per cent of the 90 change of use applications made by nBMCs had been refused – only 24 per cent had been successful while 18 per cent had been withdrawn and 10 per cent had been invalid.[27]

The council's view of the social and economic problems involved was reflected in the Head of Planning's review of the situation during 2010:

> There have been many instances of religious groups occupying what are seen by the local planning authority as unsuitable premises such as in residential areas where the noise of their activities and large numbers of people arriving by car causes harm to residential amenity or in industrial areas where their

24 David Garbin, 'Symbolic Geographies of the Sacred: Diasporic Territorialization and Charismatic Power in a Transnational Congolese Prophetic Church', in Gertrud Hüwelmeier and Kristine Krause, eds *Traveling Spirits: Migrants, Markets and Mobilities*, (London and New York: Routledge, 2011), 145–64 and 'Marching for God in the Global City: Public Space, Religion and Diasporic Identities in a Transnational African Church', *Culture and Religion* 13 (2012): 424–47.

25 Alastair Rogers, *Being Built Together: Interim Report* (London: University of Roehampton, 2012), 3.

26 Ibid., 5.

27 *Being Built Together: Final Report* (London: University of Roehampton, 2013), 81.

> occupation of factory and warehouse buildings often contravenes the council's policies to protect these areas for appropriate employment generating uses.[28]

Four years earlier the council had reported that unauthorised use of industrial sites by religious groups was worse than in any other London borough and mostly involved Pentecostal churches supported by BME congregations.

While steps were being made to tackle these problems through dialogue between the religious groups and planning officers in particular, sharing premises offered a way forward. Tensions could still arise, however. One contributor to the Roehampton study sensed 'some bad feeling from the host church' in that 'we had become a threat to them by virtues of our large congregation'.[29] Sometimes arrangements were changed arbitrarily:

> Every day as the church was getting established the man would come and [he] said 'oh no this time you don't have to come to church in the afternoon, come in the night', and so we start at 7 and finish at 9 and people go to work, and when that was almost settled, then they came and said 'can you start early morning', and then 'can you start in the afternoon', so it was challenging.[30]

A more collaborative approach to sharing appeared to be provided by the Crossway United Reformed Church (URC) centre near Elephant and Castle. Eight churches (mostly black majority) used the premises as well as the URC and the relationship between these churches and the URC was gradually changing from landlord/tenant to 'sister church', according to the study. The business element was formalised by agreeing letting arrangements and exchanging constitutions. Yet the URC minister drew attention to the moral dimensions involved, such as

> the inevitable frictions that arise when multiple congregations share a building, largely relating to practical matters such as tidying up. Teaching on 'love thy neighbour' has been part of the response.[31]

Rather than approach the issue of sharing resources in a legalistic, contractual way, he suggested an arrangement whereby congregations could work together to meet their mutual needs. Being good stewards of these resources entailed using them 'wisely', that is, 'neither giving them away too freely, nor hiding them away so that they decay and degrade'.[32]

With the council's decision to redevelop the Elephant and Castle area, the Crossway centre had to prepare to relocate. In 2012 Southwark published its plans to build a large number of new homes and 'also meet the London plan target of 5,000 new jobs by encouraging more offices, hotels, small businesses and developing

27 Ibid., 79.
29 Ibid., 90.
30 Ibid.
31 Ibid., 91.
32 Ibid.

the evening economy and cultural activities'.[33] As in Walthamstow, the service sector was seen as the foundation of the locality's economic regeneration where 'cultural activities' generated a lively evening scene. The religious life of the area was briefly acknowledged:

> There are a range of faith communities in the opportunity area. The current and future needs of these groups need to be taken into account as development takes place over the plan period.[34]

Fortunately for the Crossway centre, the council was eager to maintain its presence in the area and agreed to rebuild 'the church as the Crossway Christian Centre', that is, 'a centre for welfare and wellbeing'.[35] One of the local councillors explained the decision as follows:

> I am delighted that rather than simply buying out the Church, we have instead taken the decision to relocate this important community facility to a new purpose built church at the heart of the Elephant and Castle. . . . Crossway not only provide[s] space for their own congregation to worship, but seeks to maximise the use of their premises by other local community organisations, including other faith groups.[36]

Although the future of the Crossway centre appears to be secure, the fate of the wide range of churches in the area will be shaped by council decision-making and the social composition of those moving into the new housing. Local activists were quick to raise the issue of gentrification and the replacement of poor residents by wealthy newcomers, which would affect the ethnic balance of those local churches that survived the redevelopment. A well supported website, 'Southwark Notes – whose regeneration? Regeneration and Gentrification in Southwark, South London', argued forcefully that:

> Essentially, what is planned for The Elephant then is to change the local character of the area from one of poor people and the type of shops and services poor people use and rely on to a landscape and culture of more well-off people and the mega shops and service industries they require.[37]

33 Elephant and Castle Supplementary Planning Document (SPD) and Opportunity Area Planning Framework (OAPF), 25 March 2012, www.roehampton.ac.uk/uploadedFiles/Page_Content/Courses/Humanities/Being_Built_Together/Being%20Built%20Together(SB)%20web%20(D).pdf, accessed 21 February 2014.

34 Ibid.

35 Elephant Amenity Network 2011, quoted in *Being Built Together: Final Report* (London: University of Roehampton, 2013), 91.

36 *Being Built Together: Final Report* (London: University of Roehampton, 2013), 91.

37 'The Bloody Great Big Elephant Rip-Off! July 2010: Southwark Council/Lendlease Deal Signed!', https://southwarknotes.wordpress.com/our-longer-writings/big-elephant-rip-off-1/, accessed 28 August 2015.

According to the activists maintaining this website at least, the economic imperatives of globalising London threatened to transform the locality, while Loretta Lees, Professor in Geography at Kings College London, argued that Southwark and other London councils 'have a moral obligation to protect the less well-off in society. Refurbishment is cheaper than moving people off estates and rebuilding them and is socially, economically and environmentally sustainable.'[38] It would appear that even if some newcomers might be attracted to Crossway and the other religious centres that survived the redevelopment, many nBMC congregations would probably have to relocate to non-gentrified neighbourhoods, thereby increasing the competition for space in the borough.

Conclusion

This chapter has explored the diverse strategies adopted by religious groups towards establishing a home across London. The strategies were examined through three strikingly different case studies. The first considered a transnational Shia Muslim sect, which established its exclusive space in a western suburb with support from local politicians and members of national elites. The second focussed on a transnational Christian Pentecostal organisation, whose attempt to gain planning permission to develop its property by sharing with a secular cultural group in the north-eastern suburbs was resisted by this cultural group and local politicians. The third case study discussed a mainstream Christian church, which shared its premises just south of the Thames with local Black Majority Christian congregations and enjoyed the support of secular politicians and planners.

What do we learn from these three case studies about religious and secular place-making in the highly globalised context of London? London is a very secular city where the impact of global economic forces are reflected in the dominance of the service sector, especially business and finance institutions, media and the cultural industry, professional services and tourism, as well as high technology enterprise. At the same time, global migration has encouraged the sacralisation of localities through the building of new churches, temples, mosques and gurudwaras on prominent sites. In other words, the dominance of secular institutions in some areas of the globalised city is countered by a process of sacralisation, which reflects the growing religious pluralism of London and other highly globalised cities, e.g. New York, Paris and Sydney and is evident not just across inner areas but also in the outer suburbs.

Urban competition over scarce material resources such as property and land can bring secular and religious groups into conflict – the processes of secularisation and sacralisation can collide as well as co-exist. In these three different areas of London, this conflict involved religious leaders, representatives of secular interest

38 Lees, Loretta. 'Regeneration in London has Pushed Poor Families Out', 29 August 2013, www.theguardian.com/local-government-network/2013/aug/29/mixed-communities-plan-government-regeneration, accessed 18 October 2014.

groups, politicians and planners. While the conflict involved the use of local space, it was shaped by more global interests and actors, e.g. politicians and planners at metropolitan and central government levels, members of national elites and transnational networks.

The Dawoodi Bohras showed how alliances across local and national levels could be harnessed to support a tightly knit network of Bohra communities around the world where power was concentrated in the hands of the Syedna and his inner circle. The Universal Church of the Kingdom of God (UCKG) was another tightly knit transnational religious organisation but it did not enjoy the same success in building local alliances with secular political leaders and interest groups, i.e. the Waltham Forest Cinema Trust (WFCT). A key difference between the Dawoodi and UCKG cases appears to have been location, since the Dawoodis chose a peripheral industrial site while the UKCG bought a cinema in a central location where the borough council and the WFCT had a shared interest in secular redevelopment. If the UCKG wanted to maintain a local presence in the borough, it would have to move to a more peripheral location.

The Walthamstow dispute showed that sharing space between religious and secular groups was fraught with difficulties, which reflected their different moral visions. Religious leaders were engaged in establishing space where their followers could celebrate their distinctive quests for the 'good life' beyond human society. Their secular opponents also advanced a vision of the 'good life' where other considerations were paramount, such as the economic future of the locality in the case of the Northolt dispute or the preservation of the Walthamstow cinema and the development of a prime location. In such a context mutual trust was hard – perhaps impossible – to achieve. Where groups pursued similar moral visions, the building of trust might be easier. The Crossway case study appeared to support this notion: here a declining mainstream congregation collaborated with the new churches, generated by global migration. This example of shared religious space found favour among secular political leaders as the locality was redeveloped – a change with important implications for the socio-economic character of the neighbourhood and, by extension, this religious centre.

Although the Crossway example appeared to demonstrate the advantages of sharing space between groups with similar moral visions, the vast majority of religious organisations sought to carve out their own space in pursuit of their particular mission. In other words, the independent occupation of premises, however humble and cramped, was far more attractive than the Crossway option. UKCG, for example, wanted not only to minister to its growing minority ethnic congregation but also reach out to the majority population and redeem London's secular, globalised space.

During the process of sacralisation religious leaders joined others in representing 'their community' as a unified group. However, behind the essentialising rhetoric of group unity there lay what Brubaker refers to as 'groupness'. This 'contextually fluctuating conceptual variable' is revealed in the complex and shifting movement of alliances, which have been analysed in this chapter. Behind the imposing façade of London's diverse religious buildings, which appeared to represent unitary and highly territorialised groups, there lay the more dynamic reality of competing interests shaped by local, national, transnational and global allegiances.

References

'A speech by HRH The Prince of Wales at the Dawoodi Bohra Mosque, Northolt, Middlesex', www.princeofwales.gov.uk/media/speeches/speech-hrh-the-prince-of-wales-the-dawoodi-bohra-mosque-northolt-middlesex and 'Archbishop's visit to Dawoodi Bohra Mosque and Jain Temple', http://rowanwilliams.archbishopofcanterbury.org/articles.php/989/archbishops-visit-to-dawoodi-bohra-mosque-and-jain-temple#sthash.ebyRGHKY.dpuf, accessed 21 February 2014.

AlSayyad, Nezar and Mejgan Massoumi, eds *The Fundamentalist City: Religiosity and the Remaking of Urban Space* (New York: Routledge, 2010).

Being Built Together: Final Report (London: University of Roehampton, 2013), 81.

Beyer, Peter. *Religion in the Context of Globalization Essays on Concept, Form, and Political Implication* (London and New York: Routledge, 2013).

Connell, John. 'Hillsong: A Megachurch in the Sydney Suburbs', *Australian Geographer* 36 (2005): 315–32.

Crinson, Mark. 'The Mosque and the Metropolis', in *Orientalism's Interlocutors: Painting, Architecture, Photography*, eds Jill Beaulieu and Mary Roberts (Durham, NC: Duke University Press, 2012), pp. 79–102.

DeHanas, Daniel and Zacharias Pieri, 'Olympic Proportions: The Expanding Scalar Politics of the London 'Olympics Mega-Mosque' Controversy,' *Sociology* 45 (2011): 798–814.

Dwyer, Claire, David Gilbert and Bindi Shah. 'Faith and Suburbia: Secularisation, Modernity and the Changing Geographies of Religion in London's Suburbs', *Transactions of the Institute of British Geographers* 38 (2013): 403–19.

Eade, John. 'Introduction', in *Living the Global City: Globalisation as Local Process*, ed. John Eade (London and New York: Routledge, 1997), pp. 1–19.

——, 'Nationalism, Community and the Islamization of Space in London', in *Making Muslim Space in North America and Europe*, ed. Barbara Metcalf (Berkeley, CA and Los Angeles, CA: University of California Press, 1997), pp. 217–33.

——. 'From Race to Religion: Multiculturalism and Contested Urban Space', in *Post-Secular Cities: Space, Theory and Practice*, eds Justin Beaumont and Chris Butler (London and New York: Continuum, 2011), pp. 154–67.

——. 'Religious Place-Making and Migration across a Globalising City: Responding to Mobility in London', *Culture and Religion* 13 (2012): 469–83.

——, and Michal Garapich. 'Settling or Surviving in London: The Experience of Poles and Other "A8" Migrants in a Global City Borough', in *Accession and Migration: Changing Policy, Society, and Culture, in an Enlarged Europe*, eds John Eade and Yordanka Valkanova (Farnham, UK: Ashgate, 2009), pp. 143–66.

Elephant and Castle Supplementary Planning Document (SPD) and Opportunity Area Planning Framework (OAPF), March 2012, www.roehampton.ac.uk/uploadedFiles/Page_Content/Courses/Humanities/Being_Built_Together/Being%20Built%20Together(SB)%20web%20(D).pdf, accessed 21 February 2014.

Engineer, Asghar Ali. 'Kota: Another Case of Planned Violence?' *Economic and Political Weekly* 24 (1989): 2703–5.

Garbin, David. 'Symbolic Geographies of the Sacred: Diasporic Territorialization and Charismatic Power in a Transnational Congolese Prophetic Church', in *Traveling Spirits:*

Migrants, Markets and Mobilities, eds Gertrud Hüwelmeier and Kristine Krause (London and New York: Routledge, 2010), pp. 145–64.

——. 'Marching for God in the Global City: Public Space, Religion and Diasporic Identities in a Transnational African Church', *Culture and Religion* 13 (2012): 424–47.

Goodhew, David, ed. *Church Growth in Britain, 1980 to the Present* (Farnham, UK and Burlington, VT: Ashgate, 2012).

Hansard. 'Northolt Industrial Estate', HC Deb 03 July 1992 vol. 210 cc.1139–46, http://hansard.millbanksystems.com/commons/1992/jul/03/northolt-industrial-estate, accessed 27 August 2015.

Kershen, Anne. *Strangers, Aliens and Asians: Huguenots, Jews and Bangladeshis in Spitalfields, 1660–2000* (London and New York: Routledge, 2004).

—— and Laura Vaughan. '"There was a Priest, a Rabbi and an Imam . . .": An Analysis of Urban Space and Religious Practice in London's East End, 1685–2010', *Material Religion* 9 (2013): 10–35.

Kong, Lily. 'Global Shifts, Theoretical Shifts: Changing Geographies of Religion', *Progress in Human Geography* 34 (2010): 755–76.

Lees, Loretta. 'Regeneration in London has Pushed Poor Families Out', 29 August 2013, www.theguardian.com/local-government-network/2013/aug/29/mixed-communities-plan-government-regeneration, accessed 18 October 2014.

Marcuse, Peter and Ronald van Kempen, eds *Globalizing Cities: A New Spatial Order* (Malden, MA and Oxford, UK: Blackwell, 2000).

Peach Ceri and Richard Gale. 'Muslims, Hindus and Sikhs in the New Religious Landscape of England', *Geographical Review* 93 (2003): 469–90.

'Pickles to Rule on Controversial Church Plans for Walthamstow Cinema', www.selbyalan.com/blog/pickles-to-rule-on-controversial-church-plans-for-walthamstow-cinema/, accessed 6 July 2015.

Rogers, Alastair. *Being Built Together: Interim Report* (London: University of Roehampton, 2012).

Sassen, Saskia. *The Global City: New York, London, Tokyo* (Princeton, NJ: Princeton University Press, 1991).

'Save Walthamstow Cinema', http://savewalthamstowcinema.org/?p=254, accessed 21 February 2014.

Shah, Bindi, Claire Dwyer and David Gilbert. 'Landscapes of Diasporic Religious Belonging in the Edge-City: The Jain Temple at Potters Bar, Outer London', *South Asian Diaspora* 4 (2012): 77–94.

Stevenson, Deborah, Kevin Dunn, Adam Possamai and Awais Piracha. 'Religious Belief across "Post-Secular" Sydney: The Multiple Trends in (De)Secularisation', *Australian Geographer* 41 (2010): 323–50.

Woodhead, Linda and Rachel Catto, eds. *Religion and Change in Modern Britain* (London and New York: Routledge, 2012).

10 Community organising, democratic citizenship and interfaith relations

Luke Bretherton

This chapter looks at how community organising as a practice mediates the relationship between religious groups and democratic citizenship and how democratic politics enables different religious traditions to forge a common life. The chapter draws on ethnographic research from a 4-year study of London Citizens, a broad-based community organising coalition affiliated to the Industrial Areas Foundation, the oldest community organising network in the US, founded by Saul Alinsky in 1940. Community organising is a form of grassroots democratic politics that draws together different groups and institutions in an area to work together on issues of common concern such as safer streets, decent pay for low-wage workers or improved housing. Understanding the relationship between 'faith' and democratic politics is central to understanding broad-based community organising (BBCO) itself, as religious institutions are a key component of this kind of work, both in the UK and the US contexts that this chapter focuses on. This chapter assesses the ways in which the practices of community organising enable the mediation of a common life between diverse religious traditions in a highly contested and religiously pluralistic urban context. In doing so it develops a constructive proposal for conceptualising inter-faith relations as a civic practice.

To comprehend how London Citizens worked with and drew on religious groups the discussion needs locating within a broader historical context. Despite engagement with Alinsky's writings in Britain since the 1950s, it was not until the founding of the Citizens Organising Foundation (which was renamed Citizens UK in 2009) that a fully-fledged broad-based community organisation was developed. So, while its history in the US goes back to the 1940s, it is a relatively recent phenomenon in the UK. Yet leaders and organisers within Citizens UK claim they are reviving traditions that have roots in British history. While the anti-slavery movement and Chartism are sometimes cited as part of the pre-history of community organising in Britain, it is the 1889 London Dock Strike, which had a catalytic effect in the emergence of the Labour movement, that is most frequently held up as a key antecedent.

What is notable about both the framing of this imagined tradition and the actual history of Citizens UK is the role of the churches. This is illustrated in the following representations of the membership institutions by type and affiliation from

2008–12 and how they changed over that period (see Figures 10.1–4).[1] As is clear from the figures, Christianity is the most significant religious constituency involved and the most internally differentiated, while local congregations (whether Christian, Islamic, or Jewish) are the core type of membership institution.

The relationship between the religious groups and the innovative forms of democratic citizenship that Citizens UK represents is not new. In the American and British contexts, forms of popular, local self-organisation and common action emerge within such movements as the anti-slavery and abolitionist movements, the suffragists and the temperance movement. These were aligned and had a symbiotic relationship with popular religion. In the British context, whether it was Methodism, working-class Catholicism or Judaism, popular forms of religiosity were a key social force generating the practices and common values vital for grassroots activism.

The relationship between popular piety and the realisation of democratic citizenship runs counter to many of the dominant interpretations of the relationship between religion and politics in contemporary Western contexts. Many sociologists of religion no longer accept the secularisation thesis that processes of modernisation lead to an inevitable decline in the public significance of religion. Rather, modernisation leads to a process whereby different configurations of belief and unbelief combine to form particular and entirely contingent constructions of secularity. There is, however, still a widespread assumption that the continuing public significance of religion is determined by a defensive reaction against processes of modernisation (and globalisation) rather than a critical appropriation of modern processes such as urbanisation, industrialisation and bureaucratisation. In addition, popular religion is often identified with the phenomenon of 'fundamentalism', which tends to be seen as anti-democratic and authoritarian.[2] Against such an assumption I contend that the involvement in broad-based community organising of religious groups, many of which are seen as very conservative, suggests that popular religion can and often does, co-construct and critically engage with processes of modernisation and that this co-construction can take the form of engagement in and renewal of democratic politics.

The story unfolded here concerns an instance of a contemporary form of the relationship between popular piety and democratic citizenship. In telling it, I do not claim that the relationship between religious traditions and democratic politics is a necessary or inevitable relationship. But it is a historically and conceptually rich relationship and one that is too often ignored both in debates about the relationship between religions and politics and in debates about the future prospects and proper shape of democratic citizenship.

1 All figures based on data derived from the financial and membership records of Citizens UK.

2 Many scholarly identifications of fundamentalism see it as a negative or defensive reaction *against* modernity and as a religiously defined form of political mobilisation. For example, Manuel Castells sees the political role of 'fundamentalist' religious expressions as a form of what he calls 'resistance identities' that build 'trenches of resistance and survival on the basis of principles different from, or opposed to, those permeating the institutions of society'. Manuel Castells, *The Power of Identity* (Malden, MA: Blackwell, 1997), 8.

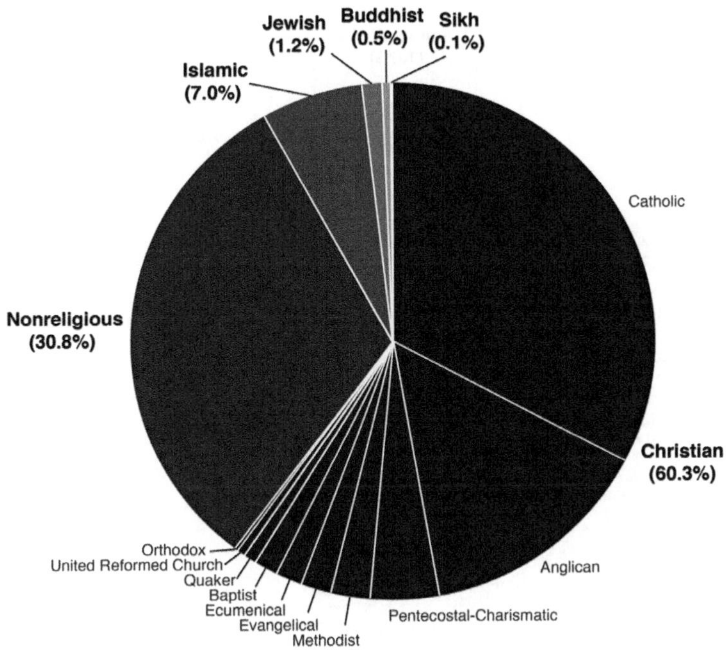

Figure 10.1 Religious affiliation of member institutions (2008–12)

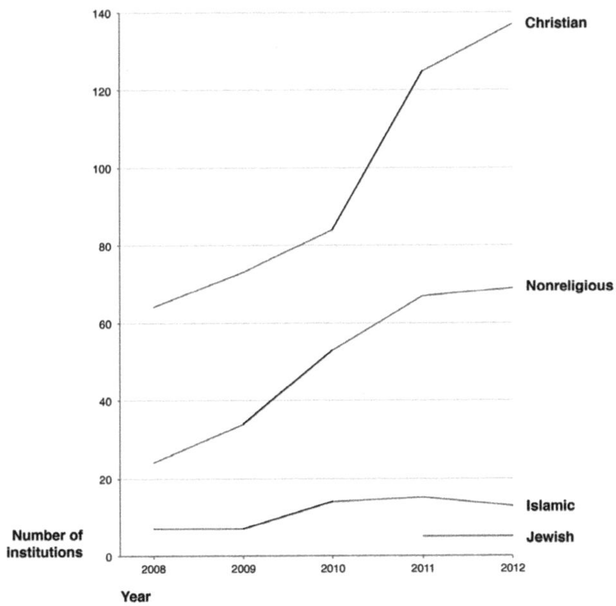

Figure 10.2 Religious affiliation of member institutions

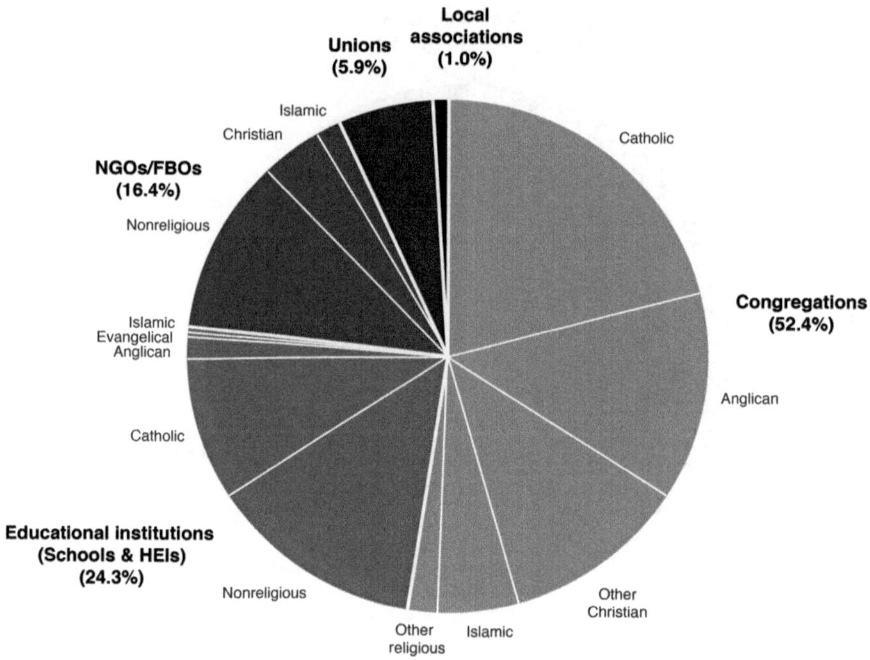

Figure 10.3 Type of member institutions (2008–12)

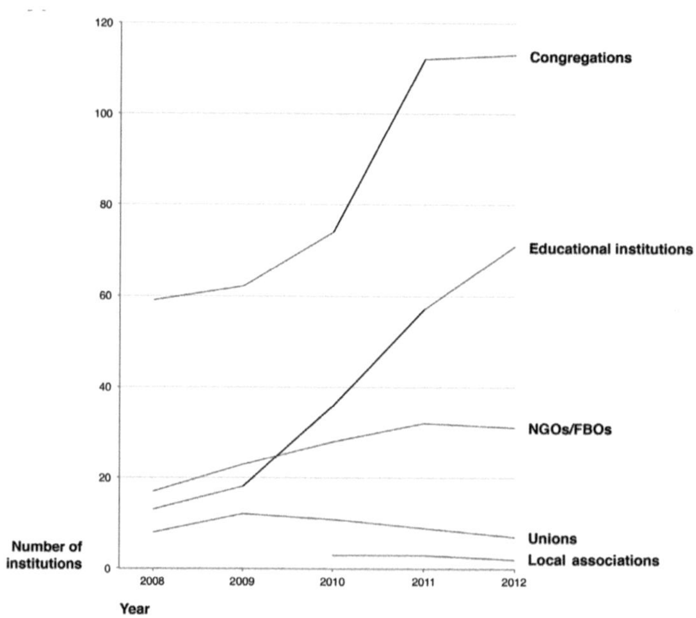

Figure 10.4 Type of member institutions

Interfaith relations and the resignification of secularity

Key to identifying the dynamics through which broad-based community organising mediates the relationship between religious beliefs and practices and the performance of democratic citizenship, as well as how religions may construct processes of modernisation, are the linguistic practices and discursive themes used to frame political engagement. In London Citizens there is no translation between 'public reasons' in the Rawlsian sense and religious languages, nor is there a process of hybridisation whereby different discourses are merged with each other.[3] Rather, different language worlds stand side by side, sometimes collide and sometimes overlap. This differs from John Rawls' advocacy of an overlapping consensus: Rawls demands the exclusion of religious and other 'comprehensive doctrines' when justifying a common policy – an exclusion that London Citizens rejects as *religious* language and beliefs are present alongside and feeding into *secular* public reason. This overlapping and, at times, colliding set of language worlds is best illustrated by an event held at the East London Mosque.

The event was a lecture by the secular Jewish political philosopher from Harvard University Michael Sandel, jointly sponsored by the *Guardian* newspaper, London Citizens and a foundation called the Citizens Ethics Network in 2010.[4] The broader context of the event was the scandal over Members of Parliaments' expenses and the disregard for probity and due diligence exhibited by bankers that contributed to the financial crises. Concern about 'low morals in high places' led to a widespread public debate about the role of ethics in political and economic life. The work of London Citizens came to prominence within this context as it was viewed as a means to combine active citizenship with a moral framework and pursue the common good.

To enter the building for the event, we had to make our way through crowds of men, many in *salwar kameez*, gathered for Friday prayers. Also attending were Rabbis wearing a *yarmulke* and Anglican and Roman Catholic clergy wearing clerical dress. Along with religious leaders and lay people were a clutch of journalists, a number of senior policy advisors from the Conservative Party and the head economist from the Trade Unions Congress. As is customary with London Citizens events, the proceeding began with a reflection. That day the reflection was drawn from the Qur'an and from the Roman Catholic encyclical *Caritas in Veritate*. The Qur'anic reflection came first, with the following Suras being first sung by a cantor and then read out in translation: Sura 5.8, 'Be just, justice is next to piety. Allah knows all you do'; Sura 4.135, 'Stand out for justice, even against the King'; and Sura 16.19, 'Render back trust. Judge with justice'. Then the Anglican Canon theologian of Westminster Abbey read a reflection from

3 See also Albert Weale's chapter in this volume.

4 The event took place on Friday 26 February 2010. It was somewhat atypical of London Citizens public gatherings as it was not an assembly or contentious action. It was framed as an internal 'action' by organisers – the action being in the education of leaders and in the recognition and thereby credentialising of the work of London Citizens by a leading philosopher.

Benedict XVI's *Caritas in Veritate* on the 'common good'. After this Sandel gave an address based on his book *Justice: What's the Right Thing To Do?* and reflected on the work of London Citizens, giving a strong endorsement of its work. During the question and answer session with Sandel, the muezzin began to recite the *adhan*, so against the backdrop of the call to prayer, the discussion ranged over topics such as community land trusts, living wage and a cap on interest rates. No attempt was made to unify these discursive framings into a single framework or metanarrative. But neither did the event represent a form of postmodern *bricolage*. There was an over-arching point of reference and set of common commitments within which different discursive frameworks were collated. The common point of reference was the question of what it means to pursue justice (however conceived) where you live and alongside those who live beside you. What the event represented was a genuinely plural construction of secular space in which faithful speech, along with other kinds of language, was part of the formation of the *sensus communis* of London Citizens.

While representing one of a number of acts of generous hospitality by the East London Mosque, the event raises the question of the nature of the relationship between Islam and broad-based community organising. This question is posed by the struggle, identified by Muslim leaders and organisers, to recruit other mosques.[5] The question is also posed by the contentious nature of views related to patriarchy, apostasy laws and anti-Semitism that non-Muslim participants struggle with in relation to the Islamic institutions in membership. These questions were pressed in an acute way from 2011 onwards as synagogues came into membership of London Citizens for the first time. Tensions came to a head in June 2011 when a series of articles was published in the *Jewish Chronicle* drawing attention to support for the Palestinian political party Hamas and its military wing by Junaid Ahmed, deputy chair of London Citizens board of trustees and a member of the East London Mosque (the UK Government designates Hamas as a whole a terrorist organisation).[6]

Beyond the specificities of Jewish–Islamic relations, the conflicts and tensions touched on here are instances of more generic dynamics relating to the negotiation of a common life between diverse institutions. For example, many trade union

5 There are a range of explanations that can be given for this. While I focus on issues of belief and practice that might or might not inhibit greater participation, a number of material factors are also present. These are identified and summarised by Muslim leaders themselves in the following statement from a document they produced in 2011: see Ali, Ruhana, Lina Jamoul and Yusufi Vali, 'A New Covenant of Virtue: Islam and Community Organising', Citizens UK and IAF, www.citizensuk.org/wp-content/uploads/2012/08/Islam-and-Community-Organising-V3-singles.pdf (accessed December 13, 2012).

6 Ahmed was cited as paying tribute to Hamas founder Sheikh Ahmed Yassin, its present leadership and Sheikh al-Qassam, after whom the military wing of Hamas was named in a speech shown on YouTube and recorded in January 2009 (Martin Bright, 'Rabbi "in pain" over London Citizens link', *Jewish Chronicle*, 2 June 2011). The first article highlighting Ahmed's views in the video and his links with London Citizens was Martin Bright, 'London Citizens stand by Islamist hardliner', *Jewish Chronicle*, 26 May 2011.

participants have grave reservations about Roman Catholic attitudes towards women, abortion and homosexuality; conversely, many Roman Catholic participants struggle with the overly permissive views of trade union members on these same matters. The specific question in relation to Islam is whether, on the one hand, Muslims have good reasons for seeking a more mutual relationship with other religions and those of no religion; and on the other, whether Christians, Jews and non-religious groups have any choice but to engage and try to build a collaborative relationship with institutions like the East London Mosque with whom there are serious points of tension, conflict and disagreement.

One way to frame this question, particularly as it pertains to religious groups involved in broad-based community organising, is as a tension between the duties and responsibilities of being a member of a *community of faith* and those that come with membership of a *community of fate*. What I mean by this is that in a world city you do not choose either who you live next door to or who lives in the next neighbourhood. You find yourself living in relative proximity with people from whom you may be very different, whether individually or collectively. They may speak a different language, have different eating habits, or look at the world very differently. But whether one likes it or not, one shares the same fate as them. If the electricity is cut off, everyone loses power. If gangs rule the streets, everyone is under threat. Living in a world city shaped by global population flows and diverse patterns of life confronts religious and non-religious constituencies with an intense sense of disjuncture between the common life they build as a 'congregation' or collectivity to sustain their beliefs and practices and the common life they inherently share with everyone in their neighbourhood or city. Gated communities, the phenomenon of 'white flight' in the US and *de facto* socio-economic and racial segregation are one, prevalent kind of response to living with others. Community organising and other ways of building a common life are another kind. Practically, the community of fate (law, roads, electricity, etc.) is necessary to make the community of faith possible; however, for some, patterns of belief and practice can locate the community of faith as prior to and the basis of the community of fate. The question to be confronted for all groups is: How are the two to be related?

For many Muslims, building a common life to sustain the community of fate conceptualised in terms of interfaith relations would seem to be problematic: how can Muslims have a mutual relationship with Christians and Jews given that fundamental to Islamic belief is that Islam supersedes both?[7] On questions of belief and practice, a dominant position within Islam is that Christians and Jews are to

7 As Ataullah Siddiqui notes, when it comes to other religious traditions: 'The fulfilment of revelations to the Prophet Muhammed it seems sealed all opportunities to look even with curiosity at "the otherness of the other"', *Christian-Muslim Dialogue in the Twentieth Century* (Basingstoke: Macmillan, 1997), 196. There are attempts within Islam to construct a distinctively Islamic rationale for engagement with religious others. A notable example of such a move emerged within the South African context of the struggle against Apartheid when Muslims worked alongside people of other faiths. See for example Farid Esack, *Qur'an, Liberation and Pluralism: An Islamic Perspective on Interreligious Solidarity Against Oppression* (Oxford: Oneworld, 1997).

be tolerated rather than afforded equal respect.[8] The mainstream of the tradition would seem to rule out approaching other religions as possible bearers of divine disclosure. The same problem affects Christian and Jewish relations, although a non-supercessionist view has become more widespread in the twentieth century.[9] Here we meet the incommensurable ways in which Islam and Christianity understand each other theologically and how this affects their posture towards each other. This incommensurability of understanding by each of the other (and thence the difference of posture each takes towards the other) reflects a broader issue: the status afforded other constellations of belief and practice within different religious traditions and how this orientates members of a particular tradition towards mission to, and dialogue and/or civic cooperation with 'outsiders'. However, it does seem more possible from a Muslim perspective to build a common life with other religious traditions within the context of participation in the kind of democratic politics London Citizens represents.[10] Such participation can be understood as part of a broader collaborative pursuit of the common good, a category familiar within Islamic jurisprudence.[11]

The East London Mosque, among a variety of approaches it takes to political life, includes engagement with London Citizens, giving it a clear endorsement as a primary vehicle through which Muslims may participate faithfully in British politics. While involvement in London Citizens is not the only option favoured, it is available and officially endorsed and encouraged at the most senior levels. At a practical level a number of Muslim leaders recognise that London Citizens helps Muslims negotiate the very difficult line between, on the one hand, not appearing to be 'radical Islamists' in the eyes of political, bureaucratic and intellectual elites and, on the other, not being seen by their own constituency to collude with governments perceived as hostile to Islam because of the international and security policies the British government pursues.

Citizens UK and the Industrial Areas Foundation have self-consciously sought to deepen the involvement of Muslims. This builds on long-term relationships with Muslim leaders in the US and UK and a self-conscious engagement with the

8 On this see Yohanan Friedmann, *Tolerance and Coercion in Islam: Interfaith Relations in the Muslim Tradition* (Cambridge: Cambridge University Press, 2003).

9 Key in this shift were responses to the Holocaust. An important milestone was Pope Paul VI's *Nostra Aetate* (1965) coupled with the expansion at a popular level of Christian Zionism among Evangelical and Pentecostal Christians driven in large part by a particular form of premillennial eschatology. This same development among Protestants problematises Christian–Islamic relations, as it tends to frame the conflict in the Middle East in terms of a cosmic battle between good and evil, with Muslims seen as on the side of evil.

10 Dilwar Hussain, 'Muslim Political Participation in Britain and the "Europeanisation" of *Fiqh*', *Die Welt des Islams* 44.3 (2004): 376–401.

11 In Islamic jurisprudence the notion of the common good is equated with *maslaha* or *maslaha 'amma*. On this see Muhammad Qasim Zaman, 'The "Ulama" of Contemporary Islam and Their Conceptions of the Common Good', in *Public Islam and the Common Good*, eds Armando Salvatore and Dale Eickelman (Leiden: Brill, 2004), 129–55; and Armando Salvatore, *The Public Sphere: Liberal Modernity, Catholicism, Islam* (New York: Palgrave Macmillan, 2007), 156–71.

more explicit tensions between Muslim and non-Muslim communities since 2001. For example, senior community organiser Edward Chambers details how, in direct response to the 9/11 attacks, Chicago United for Power organised an assembly of 4,000 Chicagoans drawn from institutions already in membership. The assembly was put together within only 2 months of the attacks and was held on 18 November 2001. It was designed to depolarise Muslim/non-Muslim tensions and its centerpiece was a 25-minute one-to-one session that paired Muslims and non-Muslims in face-to-face dialogue.[12] It would have been impossible to organise such an event at such short notice and generate the turnout, without the prior trust and long-term relationship building that pre-dated the 9/11 attacks. As a result of this kind of work, the primary vehicle for the attempt to deepen and extend Muslim involvement in the IAF was two events for Muslim members, including those from the East London Mosque, to discuss the relationship between Islam and organising and to identify points of tension and connection. Held in Chicago (August 2008) and Berlin (September 2010), these meetings drew together Muslim leaders from across the IAF's international network and resulted in a statement entitled 'A New Covenant of Virtue: Islam and Community Organising', setting out an Islamic rationale for broad-based community organising. The statement was written collaboratively between organisers with an Islamic faith or background and Islamic leaders and then endorsed by all the leaders involved in the process. The paper as a whole draws on a number of analogies between Islamic practice and belief and community organising, but it is the example of the *Hilf al-Fuḍul* or 'Covenant of Virtue' that informs the key narrative used to frame Islamic involvement in BBCO.[13]

In the context of London Citizens' work, the intensification of efforts by Muslim leaders and organisers with a Muslim background and/or faith from 2010 onwards ran parallel to the uptake of community organising by the Masorti synagogues.[14] Matt Plen, Director of the Masorti Synagogues and a member of the New North London Synagogue, met Neil Jameson and Matthew Bolton in 2009, when they were actively exploring setting up a North London chapter of London Citizens. Plen was persuaded to go on the London Citizens' 5-day training that year with a colleague from Noam, the Masorti youth movement. He saw its potential as a way of training leaders and renewing the organisational culture of the Masorti Synagogues. This led him to approach my research colleague Maurice Glasman (who is a fellow member of the Masorti movement) to develop a Jewish version of the leadership training – something Plen felt was appropriate as he identified a strong resonance between some of the approaches of organising and Jewish

12 Edward T. Chambers and Michael A. Cowan, *Roots for Radicals: Organizing for Power, Action, and Justice* (New York: Continuum, 2003), 121–3.

13 It is significant that while the paper draws on many different periods of the Prophet's life, it is the Meccan/Makkahn period, when Muslims were in the minority, rather than the Medinan period that is used as the best analogy for Islamic involvement in broad-based community organising. It could be argued that this is a departure from the mainstream tradition of interpretation.

14 Since 2012 Liberal and Reformed synagogues have begun joining London Citizens.

practices. As he put it in interview with me, community organising 'doesn't come straight from the tradition, but it goes together very well'.[15] After piloting the training and receiving feedback it is now run regularly.

No explicit link is made between the Masorti version of the London Citizens leadership training and the need to be involved in London Citizens. However, a number of those who have attended the training do become involved in London Citizens. Something of the fruit of this process can be heard in the following statement from an interview with a participant who had attended both the London Citizens training and the Masorti training, published in the *Jewish Chronicle* in anticipation of the founding of North London Citizens on 30 March 2011:

> The principles relate closely to Jewish values. So organising emphasises the importance of the one-to-one (chevruta), why turnout and a strong sense of self-identity are crucial (minyan), how to manage creative conflict and debate (mahloket), and how, through a shared agenda, we can fulfill our obligations to society (mitzvah). But it's not really surprising because the movement was created and in many cases continued by Jews. Despite that, organising has yet to be adopted on a significant scale within Anglo-Jewry. I hope the founding of the north London branch of Citizens UK means that will change. It's Jews, Muslims, Christians, students, trade unionists and many others working together for the common good. It's inspiring.[16]

If we look further back historically, we can see that developments in the relationship between Islamic institutions, the Masorti and Citizens UK form part of a pattern in the relationship between the IAF and the religious traditions that constitute its primary membership. Saul Alinsky, the founder of the IAF, engaged in a theological conversation with Roman Catholicism and in particular with the Roman Catholic philosopher Jacques Maritain that at the same time enriched and informed yet also challenged both the practice of organising and the practices and beliefs of the Roman Catholics involved.[17] In the Southwest IAF, where a number of leaders and organisers had experience working in Latin America, the engagement included discussions about liberation theology.[18] This mutually critical dialogue between community organisers and religious authority figures, which was and is often rambunctious, continues to this day. In the UK a parallel process has

15 Interview, 31 March 2011, London.

16 Jessica Elgot, 'I can do more as an organiser than as a politician', *The Jewish Chronicle Online*, 17 March 2011, www.thejc.com/46695/i-can-do-more-organiser-a-politician (accessed March 18, 2011).

17 See especially Jacques Maritain and Saul Alinsky, *The Philosopher and the Provocateur: The Correspondence of Jacques Maritain and Saul Alinsky*, ed. Bernard E. Doering (Notre Dame, IN: University of Notre Dame Press, 1994).

18 Paul Osterman, *Gathering Power: The Future of Progressive Politics in America* (Boston, MA: Beacon, 2002), 96–100.

resulted in the publication of a formal study of the links between Catholic social teaching and community organising.[19]

As more religious traditions became increasingly involved in organising, a similar pattern of engagement took shape. Interactive dialogue with liberal Protestantism developed from the late 1960s onwards as more mainline Protestant clergy participated, a particular point of reference being the work of the then leading Protestant theologian Reinhold Niebuhr.[20] Although they had long been a bulwark of the IAF, it was not until the late 1970s and 1980s that there was intentional engagement with the Black majority churches and this resulted in the formulation of the statement entitled 'The Tent of the Presence: Black Church Power in the 1980s.[21] Again, like the engagement with Catholicism, the formulation of the 'Tent of the Presence' document inspired a parallel process in the UK with the formation of a Black clergy caucus in 2011 and an edited, Anglicised version of the 'Tent of the Presence' statement being issued to the caucus for discussion. In collaboration with former IAF organiser Mike Miller, Christian leaders and theologians involved in the network Christians Supporting Community Organising have done much to frame community organising in terms directly related to evangelical and Pentecostal congregations in North America.[22] An independent, but parallel process is emerging in Citizens UK with organisers and leaders trying to develop a strategy of theological engagement with evangelical and charismatic congregations. The engagements with Islam and the Masorti are thus but one iteration of this broader pattern.

The motivations for engaging in this kind of dialogue are multiple and range from an instrumental desire to mobilise a particular set of institutions as campaign fodder to a quest to align organising with deeply held values and theological beliefs. What can be said for certain is that the need to negotiate a common life with diverse traditions in an ambiguous and sometimes hostile political and economic environment necessarily provokes questions within religious traditions. It is my contention that broad-based community organising is a form of democratic politics through which these questions can be explored internally and constitutes a means through which to negotiate these questions externally in collaboration with others outside one's own tradition. The questions provoked will be specific to each tradition, while the environment and the practices of organising are shared across multiple traditions. A necessary condition for this kind of exploration within each tradition is that the practices of community organising are not themselves ideologically over-determined and that both organisers and religious leaders have demonstrated loyalty and trustworthiness to each other through a process of common action.

19 See Austen Ivereigh, *Faithful Citizens: A Practical Guide to Catholic Social Teaching and Community Organising* (London: Darton, Longman & Todd, 2010).

20 Sanford D. Horwitt, *Let Them Call Me Rebel: Saul Alinsky, His Life and Legacy* (New York: Knopf, 1989), 531.

21 *Tent of the Presence: Black Church Power in the 1980s* (New York: Industrial Areas Foundation, 1981).

22 See www.cscoweb.org/(accessed April 4, 2011).

Democratic politics as the mediation of a common life

The East London Mosque is but one institution among many that London Citizens works with as part of 're-weaving civil society'.[23] Common work between Christians, Muslims, Jews and many others besides is mediated through affiliation with London Citizens. This does not entail collusion with what are seen as unsavory or even 'evil' views ascribed to other communities since each institution remains independent of others and is involved for very different reasons. London Citizens is clear that it does not necessarily endorse the views of its membership institutions. Rather, organisers hold the view that, in the world as it is, all those who live in a place need to be drawn into building up the common life of that place via politics rather than violence, whether that violence is inter-communal or monopolised by the state.[24]

The political vision of organising encapsulates the idea that if a group is directly contributing to the common work of defending, tending and creating the commonwealth then it deserves recognition as a vital part of and co-labourer within the broader body politic. The emphasis on participation and contribution to the building up of a common life allows for a greater plurality and affirmation of distinct identities and traditions, as each is able to play a part in this common work. Obviously there are those institutions that do not want to contribute to a shared endeavour and are suspicious of building relationships with others not like them, yet which engage in various forms of unilateral philanthropic activity. These kinds of groups are to be distinguished from anti-political and politically antagonistic forms of association that actively undermine the formation of a common life. However, the task of BBCO is to enable all groups – whether they are unilaterally philanthropic, or political or anti-political in orientation – to identify their convivial and place-based interest in building a common life with their neighbours.

The kind of common life politics BBCO represents is distinct from an identity politics and from multicultural approaches because recognition and respect is not given simply by dint of having a different culture or identity: recognition is conditional upon contributing to and participating in shared, reciprocal and public work. Evidence of this approach in London Citizens is that those groups – often union branches – who paid their subscription but never turned up for meetings, were either asked to leave or the renewal of their annual membership was not pursued or encouraged. The long-term hope of organisers is that involvement in politics through community organising creates space for the emergence of a shared story – not a 'religious' story but a civic one – and a context for real relationship where all participants, however distasteful their views to others, can begin to touch on difficult issues in a place of trust.

23 This term is a common strapline on the banners and posters of Citizens UK.

24 This was taught explicitly in the 5-day leadership training programme.

It can be argued that democracy is not necessarily tethered to liberalism, but is a tradition in itself.[25] It is, however, perhaps more accurate to say that democracy is a constellation of practices that mediate between a wide variety of traditions. Through democratic practices a common life can be forged and some kind of mutual identification crafted between individuals and groups dispersed by class, sexual orientation, religion, ethnicity and legal status. Neither should democracy be preceded by a proper noun: we should not talk of Christian democracy or Islamic democracy and so on, but rather pay attention to the kinds of interactions that allow for a common life to be fashioned in contexts where a plurality of interests and multiple loyalties have to be represented and negotiated.

Politics as practised by London Citizens represents a way of paying attention to others and so stepping out of one's own limited perspective and thereby enabling new understanding to emerge. Community organising can be conceptualised as a form of tent making where a place is created in which hospitality is given and received between multiple traditions.[26] There are some issues heard in the tent that can be collectively acted upon and some that cannot, but the encounter with others and their stories informs the sense of what it is like to live on this mutual ground, to dwell together in a given and shared urban space. The hearing of others' interests and concerns in the context of ongoing relationship and the recognition that everyone in the tent occupies mutual (not neutral) ground fosters the sense that in each others' welfare we find our own. Such tent-making involves listening to others and ensuring that all groups have a clear and reasonably safe means of articulating their interests.

Part of what constitutes BBCO as a practice of building a common life is the centrality it gives to questions of power, structure and changing policy. But it is also profoundly concerned with moral character and the cherished values and beliefs of those who participate. Indeed, against those who identify the political with the juridical and bureaucratic, the nature of BBCO suggests that the definition of politics itself needs expanding to be understood as the negotiation of a common life that takes seriously not just the need for material goods and power but also the moral and social dimensions of that life. One of the paradoxes of BBCO as a performance of democratic citizenship is that it seeks to protect the relative autonomy of the civil sphere from being either co-opted by the state, commodified by the market or rendered overly politicised and competitive by identity politics through, on the one hand, inserting consideration of the social, moral and religious dimensions of life into the making of political judgments and, on the other hand, inserting political consideration into the making of social, moral and religious judgements. In doing so, BBCO reasserts the limits of politics and economics and

25 See, for example, Jeffrey Stout, *Democracy and Tradition* (Princeton, NJ: Princeton University Press, 2004).

26 Luke Bretherton, *Christianity and Contemporary Politics: The Conditions and Possibilities of Faithful Witness* (Malden, MA: Wiley-Blackwell, 2010), 86–8.

the boundaries between the civil sphere and state, market, religious and social processes and thereby repairs the conditions and possibilities of a common life.

Beyond dialogue to a place-based politics

The kind of interfaith relations London Citizens embodies contrasts sharply with that which informs public policy, both in the UK and the US. In the policy arena the tendency has been to conceptualise relations between different faiths in terms of either interreligious dialogue (characterised as 'interfaith relations') or in terms of joint humanitarian endeavors. This call for and resourcing of dialogue is driven by state concerns about the need for 'social cohesion' in response to ongoing questions about how to promote the integration of new migrant communities with strong religious identities and the real and perceived links between terrorist activities and some Islamic groups. In response to the latter, the promotion of interreligious dialogue as a strategy for generating social cohesion and greater political stability is an alternative to the parallel securitisation of religion: the rhetorical construction of religious beliefs and practices as a direct security threat to the state that needs to be dealt with outside the normal legal and political processes within which religion is ordinarily dealt with.[27] The end result of both the promotion of dialogue and securitisation is a deeper level of engagement between state agencies and many religious groups as the government seeks to understand and address internal dynamics within these groups, Islamic ones in particular, that might exacerbate or diminish any resort to violence.[28]

Neither an emphasis on dialogue nor humanitarian service leaves scope for politics. In occluding the need for politics the inherent conflicts that arise in the process of negotiating a common life and the pursuit of shared goods are thereby submerged, as is the need for power in order to achieve change. Policies that emphasise the importance of social cohesion more often than not lack any account of how the kind of relationships valorised are increasingly subordinated to and undermined by the needs of the market and the state. An emphasis on dialogue and volunteerism ignores questions of political economy and the way in which the kind of globalised market pressures and processes of commodification already outlined serve to undermine the very possibility of acting together. Yet if you have to follow the money in order to find work then you have to leave behind people and place, as well as the kind of time-intensive social ties that form the basis of sustaining long-term associative power that can challenge the priorities of either

27 Bretherton, *Christianity and Contemporary Politics*, 32–45.

28 The promotion of dialogue and joint humanitarian endeavours is encapsulated in the 2008 White Paper entitled *Face to Face and Side by Side: A Framework for Partnership in our Multi Faith Society* published by the Department for Communities and Local Government. At a global level, the central idea of this White Paper received a direct echo in President Barack Obama's 2009 Cairo speech in which he called for both greater dialogue between Jews, Christians and Muslims and what he named 'interfaith service'. The term 'interfaith relations' is used in place of 'inter-religious relations' for no other reason than it is the more common term.

the state or the market and thereby defend the interests of citizens, whether they have an explicitly religious faith or not.

There is a place for straightforward dialogue, although this seems more appropriate and sustainable at a more specialist rather than at a 'street level'.[29] But the experience of London Citizens would suggest that real encounters, dialogue and understanding are, at the popular level, best generated as by-products of shared political action. In such shared political action the focus is neither on merely meeting face-to-face nor even on working side by side as volunteers. Rather, it is on the pursuit and protection of goods in common. Instead of trying to generate a relationship either for the sake of the relationship as an end itself, for theological reasons or to comply with state directives, the external point of reference – fighting for a living wage or a cap on interest rates – provides the basis of mutual collaboration out of which dialogue emerges as a by-product.

In addition to shared commitment to concrete issues of mutual concern, a shared commitment to a particular place provides further grounds for common action. Different faith traditions will have different overarching visions of the good life and often very different beliefs and practices; but simply by sharing the same mutual ground, they necessarily have a shared investment in the good of that place. If the council sells off the school playing fields none of their children will have anywhere to play. These are the interests they have in common: they are not selfish interests but mutual interests. And, while each may give different accounts of why law and order or public spaces are good, a common commitment to place can foster a common commitment to the people who live there, despite their differences. Added to the mutual material interests that emerge within particular places there is also what we might call a convivial interest: if we are going to be sharing space with people, we have an interest in maintaining friendly relations with them.

Through a common commitment to shared places (a place-based interest) and local people (a convivial interest), a shared story of belonging and a shared social and political life can emerge, one into which any immigrant tradition may be enfolded. Such a common commitment to place and people can foster a shared identity narrative by connecting each faith story to the story of the ongoing civic life in a particular place and develop a sense of mutual responsibility and commitment for the world around them. Or, in the words of one participant in

29 Examples of the kinds of elite academic and institutional processes include colloquia organised by the World Council of Churches Office on Interreligious Relations in 1992 and 1993; the day of prayer for world peace at Assisi in 1986 and 2002 hosted by Pope John Paul II; the emergence of Scriptural Reasoning as a practice of Jews, Christians and Muslims reading their scriptures together; and the C-1 Dialogue process that has emerged in response to the 2007 statement by 138 Muslim scholars, clerics and intellectuals, *A Common Word Between Us and You*. For a copy of this statement see: www.acommonword.com. For an account of contemporary Christian–Muslim dialogue initiatives, see Hugh Goddard, *A History of Christian-Muslim Relations* (Edinburgh: Edinburgh University Press, 2000), 177–98. For an overview of developments in Britain specifically, see Ataullah Siddiqui, 'Inter-Faith Relations in Britain Since 1970—An Assessment', *Exchange* 39.3 (2010): 236–50.

London Citizens, it involves being more concerned about the drug-pushers on your doorstep than the politics of Israel and Palestine. Yet generating concern for the concrete and the local is hard work as the question 'who is my neighbour?' is often constructed in ways that prioritise the needs of fellow believers (in which case the politics of Israel and Palestine looms large) or 'the poor' in distant lands with whom there is no connection other than those mediated via charitable donations to humanitarian agencies. The challenge for organisers is to help participants put people before programme, whether these programmes are ideological, theological or philanthropic. This involves connecting them relationally to those they live in proximity to so they can see and hear the world around them as it is, not refract it through a lens focused thousands of miles away or on abstractions, distorting their perception and experience of those they actually live near.

Secularity and the contradiction of the modern compact

London Citizens comes across as religious to many external observers. Media reports frequently cited London Citizens as a faith-based organisation or alliance. Many participants reported that others they worked with viewed London Citizens as 'religious'. For example, Hugh O'Shea, branch secretary of the Central London branch of the Union of London Hotel Workers, commented that, when he was considering whether to take his branch into membership of West London Citizens, he spoke to another union organiser,

> and I always remember what he said, he said, 'Hughie, a lot of people in the union think that if you join London Citizens you'll be there at the communion rail with your tongue hanging out every Sunday receiving Communion'. [laughs] As if it was compulsory![30]

O'Shea noted the hostility of many of the senior union officials towards London Citizens, which he said they viewed as a rival union and as too religious. He took a different view:

> I don't regard London Citizens as a religious organisation. I regard its ideals as based quite largely on faith-based ideals. But that doesn't mean to say it's religious. It's religious backed perhaps . . . but the ideas are of social justice.[31]

Partly London Citizens appears 'religious' to non-religiously affiliated non-members because of the large numbers of religious institutions in membership (see figures 10.1–4). This is not, however, necessarily determinative. Many faith-based organisations are directly affiliated to churches or other faiths but do not feel

30 Interview, 8 September 2009, London.
31 Ibid.

religious in manner and style. Something more is going on. To understand this, we can draw a parallel between the linguistic practices of London Citizens and those of Jerry Falwell (1933–2007), the prominent Evangelical Christian leader and key figure in the emergence of the Moral Majority in the US. The anthropologist Susan Friend Harding, in her study of Falwell's political work, notes how religious language functioned to draw in and consolidate insiders through a familiar set of narratives, motifs and linguistic styles while simultaneously alienating and excluding those who were critical such as 'liberals' and mainline Christians, playing to and reinforcing the negative perceptions of those outside the organisation.[32] Broad-based community organising can provoke a similarly hostile or suspicious reaction from outsiders through the discursive practices by which it generates a sense of unity among those in membership. A particularly acute example of this hostile reaction framed wholly in anti-religious terms comes from Berlin. Leo Penta, the lead organiser of DICO, the German Institute for Community Organising, reported that he and his co-workers were accused of being Scientologists and a religious cult when they began trying to establish a broad-based community organisation. In the UK, the hostility it generates mostly splits along ideological lines: the left tend to view Citizens UK as 'too religious' while the right tend to focus on its policies and tactics. For example the neoliberal TaxPayers' Alliance branded London Citizens a 'radical left-wing group'.[33] Within the churches the issue that repeatedly provokes a negative response is that of the confrontational tactics used.

Meetings and assemblies are not monopolised by religious language: a wide variety of discursive frames of reference are invoked at them. Yet the style and language of organising feels familiar to religiously-affiliated members and often alien to the non-religious. Religious institutions meet regularly in assemblies, tithe, demand an intensity of their commitment, are comfortable with an affective dimension to public gatherings and have a strong set of moral commitments. Organisers themselves frequently note the parallels between the demands of democratic politics and those of religious affiliation and see the skills and practices of organising as directly relevant to the institutional renewal of congregations.[34] It is not surprising then that non-religious observers see organising as somehow 'religious' in some unspecified way. What broad-based community organising involves are ways and styles of gathering and association not encountered much outside of religious congregations within the contemporary European political context. By contrast, due to a higher degree of religious affiliation in the US, this form of organising feels more familiar and thence less overtly 'religious' to external observers.

32 Susan Friend Harding, *The Book of Jerry Falwell: Fundamentalist Language and Politics* (Princeton, NJ: Princeton University Press, 2000), 166.

33 TaxPayers' Alliance website article March 31, 2010.

34 This is made explicit in Michael Gecan, *Effective Organizing for Congregational Renewal* (Skokie: ACTA, 2008).

What broad-based community organising does not do as a form of political action is reinforce a secularist demarcation of politics as a non-religious sphere by claiming only 'public' reasons can be used or by claiming that religious ones cannot be used because of they are highly particularistic and idiosyncratic. It thereby contests the construction of religion as private and set apart from politics, resignifying both religion and politics through the performances of what it means to be religious and political.[35] Broad-based community organising as it evolved in the UK simply does not recognise the terms and conditions of an ideologically secularist modernity. Instead, it overtly mixes piety and politics, secular and religious styles and cultures. It is thus post-secularist, or rather a plural and complex instantiation of a religious and secular space, not observing the rules and regimes of public secularity and refusing to let religious groups marginalise themselves by adopting a narrative of exclusion and victimisation.

It is my contention that broad-based community organising is symptomatic of a broader rupture of notions of public secularity in the UK context. In its alignment of religious institutions and democratic citizenship, it represents a different co-construction of secularity between belief and unbelief, one in which the church qua church may play a part. The ways in which community organising called on religious actors to behave politically contradicted self-marginalising dynamics adopted by evangelical and charismatic Christians as well as mainline Christian denominations in the UK in their political engagements from 1945 to the 1990s. Where the churches in the UK were active in public life they self-censored rhetoric that they perceived to be supernaturalist. Community organising as a practice is able to break with and contradict such a stance because it is not derived from a British (and mostly white) Christian sub-culture and so is not constrained by a folk/faux-memory of the exclusion of religion from the public sphere or the very real history of the Establishment's exclusion of both Dissenters and Roman Catholics from holding public office. BBCO was introduced as a set of political and associational practices in the 1990s at the point of the post-secularist turn and the consolidation and coming into public life of religious minorities, notably Muslims, who were also mostly people of colour. Yet these populations refused to be labelled as 'ethnic minorities' and demanded access to state resources on terms of religious affiliation not ethnic or racial identity. These groups become visible politically through religious speech and action and are not constrained by the self-policing compact between Christianity and a simplistically secularist modernity whereby Christians along with liberal and neoliberal elites adopted the secularisation thesis as a self-fulfilling prophecy.[36]

35 Talal Asad, 'The Construction of Religion as an Anthropological Category', in *Genealogies of Religion: Discipline and Reasons of Power in Christianity and Islam* (Baltimore, MD: John Hopkins University Press, 1993), 27–54.

36 On this see José Casanova, 'Immigration and the New Religious Pluralism: A European Union/United States Comparison', in *Democracy and the New Religious Pluralism*, ed. Thomas F. Banchoff (Oxford: Oxford University Press, 2007), 63.

Broad-based community organising emerged in the 1990s at the point where the supposedly teleological process of secularisation was seen to be unfulfilled. The world began to appear as religious as ever and philosophers started to discuss what it meant to be 'post-secular'.[37] While many conservative Christians in the UK remain bound and obsessed by the old compact, broad-based community organising has taught churches in membership to relax and occupy a genuinely plural space in which religious rhetorics and styles are as legitimate contributions to political life as any other, while at the same time demanding that religious voices cannot be the dominant or exclusive voice. This is evidenced in interviews with religious leaders who note that community organising allows them to be explicitly religious in public in a way they did not feel able to be prior to involvement. Contributing to this sense is the call by organisers for religious leaders to look as religious as possible in assemblies and actions and the use of religious speech alongside other discursive forms to narrate and frame issues. This plural and complex secular space is represented well by the London Citizens logo in which people in 'religious' garb hold hands with others of non-descript and ethnic dress around a common space defined by their relations and nothing else (see Figure 10.5).

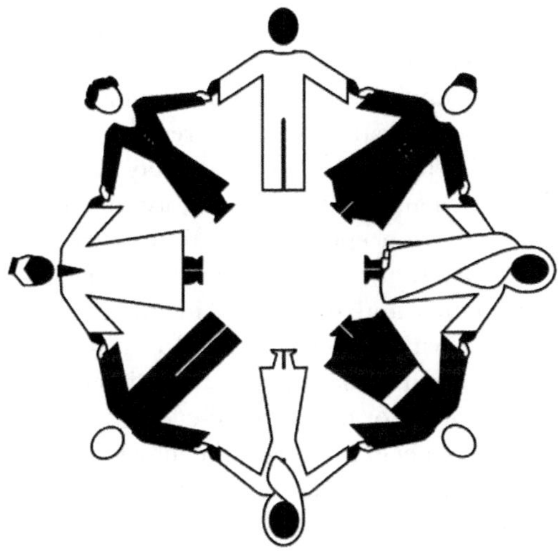

Figure 10.5 The logo of London Citizens

37 Arguably the same applies in the US as well, where there was a distinct increase in the number and variety of broad-based community organisations from the 1990s onwards; see Mark R. Warren and Richard L. Wood, *Faith-Based Community Organizing* (Jericho, NY: Interfaith Funders, 2001). This also mirrors developments among Evangelicals, for whom, as Jon Shields' analysis reveals, the real engagement in political life did not begin and end with the rise and fall of the Moral Majority in the 1980s (which on Shields's account was little more than a form of check book activism that failed to build a broad base). Rather, widespread conservative evangelical involvement only really rose from 1992 onwards. See Jon Shields, *Democratic Virtues of the Christian Right* (Princeton, NJ: Princeton University Press, 2009), 117–46.

Conclusion

This chapter examined how community organising as a constellation of democratic practices mediates the relationship between different religious traditions and politics itself. Religious identities and discourses were seen to be a core component in the ongoing development of Citizens UK. Community organising as a practice of democratic politics was then contrasted with and seen to contradict portrayals of the relationship between 'fundamentalism' and democracy. Building on a view of the democratic possibilities of religious beliefs and practices, an account was developed of how Citizens UK's work constitutes a form of interfaith relations understood as a civic practice. Within this framework consideration was given to how community organising mediates relations between Jews, Christians and Muslims and some of the tensions and issues pertaining to this process of mediation. The final section assessed the way in which broad-based community organising re-configures dominant notions of secularity and the relationship between moral and theological frames of reference and conceptions of political order.

Some broader conclusions can be drawn from what has been said. We live in a time of economic and political turmoil when the efficacy of democracy in bringing accountability to financial markets and ruling elites is being tested. It is simultaneously a time when the relationship between different religions and political life is under intense negotiation at a local, national and international level throughout the world. As outlined here, community organising seems to provide a lens through which to constructively address these concerns and better understand the relationship between religious diversity, democratic citizenship and economic and political accountability. Community organising addresses a core paradox that confronts the conceptualisation of democracy in modern political thought: that is, how democratic citizenship is seen as an expression of individual liberty but its performance and defence is in great measure dependent on participation in a group. Without being embedded in some form of association, the individual citizen is naked before the power of either the market or the state and lacks a vital means for his or her own self-cultivation. Yet at the same time, the market and the state can help to liberate the individual from communal over-determination. The relationship between different religious traditions and democracy encapsulates the triadic tension between market, state and community within which the individual is located. State and market processes limit, challenge and provide alternatives to those derived from religious obligations and identities, yet in an increasingly de-institutionalised and atomised society religions provide one of the few corporate forms of life available for mobilising and sustaining the ability of individuals to act together in defense of their shared interests. Yet political thinking at both the popular and academic levels tends to perceive the vibrant religious groups operating in the contemporary context as anti-democratic and reactionary. In contrast to this kind of view I have tried to suggest in this chapter that community organising represents a paradoxical politics that draws on religious associations to renew democracy, democracy to strengthen religious associations and religious beliefs and practices and democratic politics together to limit the power of market, state and community over the individual. In doing so it represents one way of resolving a problem that ancient and modern political thought has wrestled with: that is, how to coordinate the at times conflicting obligations demanded by faithfulness to the polity and one's fellow citizens with faithfulness to God and one's fellow believers.

References

Ali, Ruhana, Lina Jamoul and Yusufi Vali. 'A New Covenant of Virtue; Islam and Community Organising', Citizens UK and IAF, 2012. www.citizensuk.org/wp-content/uploads/2012/08/Islam-and-Community-Organising-V3-singles.pdf, accessed 13 December 2012.

Asad, Talal. 'The Construction of Religion as an Anthropological Category', in *Genealogies of Religion: Discipline and Reasons of Power in Christianity and Islam*. Baltimore, MD: John Hopkins University Press, 1993, 27–54.

Bretherton, Luke. *Christianity and Contemporary Politics: The Conditions and Possibilities of Faithful Witness*. Oxford: Wiley–Blackwell, 2010.

Casanova, José. 'Immigration and the New Religious Pluralism: A European Union/United States Comparison', in *Democracy and the New Religious Pluralism*, edited by Thomas F. Banchoff. Oxford: Oxford University Press, 2007, 59–83.

Castells, Manuel. *The Power of Identity*. Malden, MA: Blackwell, 1997.

Chambers, Edward T. and Michael A. Cowan. *Roots for Radicals: Organizing for Power, Action and Justice*. New York: Continuum, 2004.

Department for Communities and Local Government. *Face to Face and Side by Side: A Framework for Partnership in our Multi Faith Society*. White Paper. London: Department for Communities and Local Government, 2008.

Esack, Farid. *Qur'an, Liberation and Pluralism: An Islamic Perspective on Interreligious Solidarity Against Oppression*. Oxford: Oneworld, 1997.

Friedmann, Yohanan. *Tolerance and Coercion in Islam: Interfaith Relations in the Muslim Tradition*. Cambridge: Cambridge University Press, 2003.

Gecan, Michael. *Effective Organizing for Congregational Renewal*. Skokie, IL: ACTA Publications, 2008.

Goddard, Hugh. *A History of Christian–Muslim Relations*. Edinburgh: Edinburgh University Press, 2000.

Harding, Susan Friend. *The Book of Jerry Falwell: Fundamentalist Language and Politics*. Princeton, NJ: Princeton University Press, 2000.

Horwitt, Sanford D. *Let Them Call Me Rebel: Saul Alinsky, His Life and Legacy*. New York: Knopf, 1989.

Hussain, Dilwar. 'Muslim Political Participation in Britain and the "Europeanisation" of *Fiqh*', *Die Welt des Islams* 44.3 (2004): 376–401.

Industrial Areas Foundation. *Tent of the Presence: Black Church Power in the 1980s*. New York: Industrial Areas Foundation, 1981.

Ivereigh, Austen. *Faithful Citizens: A Practical Guide to Catholic Social Teaching and Community Organising*. London: Darton, Longman & Todd, 2010.

MABDA. *A Common Word Between Us and You*. Amman, Jordan: The Royal Aal Al-Bayt Institute for Islamic Thought, 2012.

Maritain, Jacques and Saul Alinsky. *The Philosopher and the Provocateur: The Correspondence of Jacques Maritain and Saul Alinsky*, edited by Bernard E. Doering. Notre Dame, IN: University of Notre Dame Press, 1994.

Osterman, Paul. *Gathering Power: The Future of Progressive Politics in America.* Boston, MA: Beacon Press, 2002.

Salvatore, Armando. *The Public Sphere: Liberal Modernity, Catholicism, Islam.* New York: Palgrave–Macmillan, 2007.

Shields, Jon A. *The Democratic Virtues of the Christian Right.* Princeton, NJ: Princeton University Press, 2009.

Siddiqui, Ataullah. *Christian–Muslim Dialogue in the Twentieth Century.* Basingstoke: Macmillan, 1997.

——. 'Inter-Faith Relations in Britain Since 1970—An Assessment', *Exchange* 39.3 (2010): 236–50.

Stout, Jeffrey. *Blessed are the Organized: Grassroots Democracy in America.* Princeton, NJ: Princeton University Press, 2010.

Warren, Mark R. and Richard Wood. *Faith Based Community Organizing: The State of the Field.* Jericho: NY Interfaith Funders, 2001.

Zaman, Muhammad Qasim. 'The "Ulama" of Contemporary Islam and Their Conceptions of the Common Good', in *Public Islam and the Common Good*, edited by Armando Salvatore and Dale Eickelman. Leiden: Brill, 2004, 129–55.

Part IV

Negotiating with religion from a legal perspective

11 Negotiating with religion from a legal perspective

Myriam Hunter-Henin

In a human rights era, European States are increasingly under pressure to give due regard to individual claims to religious expression and manifestation. Simultaneously, States struggle to formulate a coherent approach to religion that is both faithful to their national traditions and constitutional national frameworks and respectful of the growing diversity in religious practices and attitudes towards religion within their societies. Recent trends reveal a tightening of the legal discourse in relation to religion. On the one hand, religion often appears to be incompatible with common duties and is now consequently invoked as a basis for positive rights to derogation/exemption and accommodation in the workplace[1] or in educational settings.[2] On the other hand, responses by national authorities have become more ideologically laden: national identities and fundamental constitutional values are often opposed to religious claims.

Historical constitutional compromises negotiated between 'the' Church and 'the' State are increasingly being put to the test by new religions. In our religiously diverse societies, state endorsement of majority religion is often seen as problematic. It has thus been questioned whether the constitutional privileged position conferred to the Church of England in the established church system practised in Britain is compatible with equality requirements.[3] Some have indeed wondered whether an Established Church might not use its close association with the state apparatus

1 See for example, ECtHR 15 January 2013 *Eweida and others v the United Kingdom*, App. nos. 48420/10, 59842/10, 51671/10 and 36516/10. See also, Maleiha Malik, this volume.

2 See for example, the request by a Canadian student in York to be exempted from contact with female co-students: James Bradshaw, 'Religious Accommodation or "Accessory to Sexism"? York Student's Case Stirs Debate', *The Globe and Mail*, 8 January 2014, www.theglobeandmail.com/news/national/education/religious-accommodation-or-accessory-to-sexism-york-students-case-stirs-debate/article16246401/, accessed 25 April 2014,

3 For the terms of the debate on 'separation' or 'Establishment' in political theory, see Cécile Laborde, 'Political Liberalism and Religion: On Separation and Establishment', *Journal of Political Philosophy* 21(1): 67–86, March 2013; for a human rights argument in favour of non-establishment, see Jeroen Temperman, *State–Religion Relationships and Human Rights Law. Towards a Right to Religiously-Neutral Governance*, Leiden, Boston, MA: Martinus Nijhoff, 2010. For arguments in support of Church Establishment, see Tariq Modood, *Multiculturalism, A Civic Idea*. Cambridge: Polity, 2007.

to implement existing policies to its own advantage.[4] Even assuming that the privileged position of the Established Church is simply symbolic, could this symbolic superiority not generate an 'expressive harm' to non-believers and members of other religions?[5] By contrast, others have praised church establishment as a welcome sign of compromise between secular and religious views. Tariq Modood's normative claim is that such institutional compromises are legitimate and should be further pluralised by being extended and appropriately modified to cover Muslims in addition to Jews and various Christian churches.[6]

Beyond the issue of the constitutional standing of religion, the question has also been raised as to whether law should not be more accommodating of religious norms. The former Archbishop of Canterbury, Dr Rowan Williams, thus suggested, in a 2008 lecture, delivered at the Royal Courts of Justice, that British State courts should engage more constructively with religious courts and, on family law issues,[7] take more seriously the freedom of minority religious groups to live according to their religious norms.[8] Debate about the recognition of religious legal orders has since been vigorous. On the one hand, greater collaboration would seem to flow from our postmodern liberal commitment to cultural diversity and pluralism.[9] To avoid alienating individuals with multiple identities, one should give up on monolithic conceptions of law.[10] The application of inflexible and overtly traditional constructions of religious norms or the imposition of a universalist Enlightenment system, likely to marginalise minority group members, should both be resisted. A system of 'transformative accommodation' where both sides are willing to contemplate internal change as a result of mutual influence has therefore been suggested.[11] To counter the risk of increased vulnerability for 'minorities within minorities'[12] (namely children, women, lesbian and gay members

4 See James A. Beckford, 'The Tensions between an Established Church and Equal Opportunities in Religion: the Use of Prison Chaplaincy', in Paula D. Nesbitt, ed. *Religion and Social Policy*, Walnut Creek, CA, Lanham, MD, New York and Oxford: Rowman & Littlefield: 2001, 39–53.

5 See, for example, the claim that the opening of Council meetings by prayers in Bideford Town Council could make members from other religion or without any religion less worthy. *National Secular Society and Bone v Bideford Town Council* [2012] EWHC 275. The High Court ruled against the Council but on a point of technicality: the inclusion of prayers on the agenda of the meeting was beyond the Council's powers.

6 For an analysis of Tariq Modood's position, see Sune Lægaard, 'Moderate Secularism and Multicultural Equality', *Politics*, 28(3): 160–8, October 2008.

7 For an explanation of the focus on Family law, see Andrea Büchler, *Islamic Law in Europe? Legal Pluralism and its Limits in European Family Laws*. Farnham, UK: Ashgate 2011.

8 Rowan Williams, 'Civil and Religious Law in England: A Religious Perspective', 7 February 2008, reprinted in *Ecclesiastical Law Journal* 10 (2008): 262.

9 Jeremy Waldron, 'Questions about the Reasonable Accommodation of Minorities', in Rex Adhar and Nicholas Aroney, eds *Shari'a in the West*, Oxford: Oxford University Press, 2010, 112.

10 See Prakash Shah, *Legal Pluralism in Conflict: Coping with Cultural Diversity in Law*, London: Routledge, Cavendish, 2005.

11 See Bernard Jackson, 'Transformative Accommodation and Religious Law', *Ecclesiastical Law Journal* May 2009, 131–53, esp. 133.

12 On these vulnerabilities, see, for example, Ayelet Sachar *Multicultural Jurisdictions: Cultural Differences and Women's Rights*. Cambridge: Cambridge University Press, 2008.

of minority religious groups), another model, 'Cultural Voluntarism', has since been put forward by John Eekelaar[13] and Maleiha Malik.[14] Based on the same premise as the model of 'Transformative Accommodation', it confers to state courts the discretion to select, among the substantive issues decided by religious courts, those that conform to human rights and liberal public policy and can therefore receive the stamp of state approval.[15] On the other side of the spectrum, it has been argued that legal recognition of religious courts reflects a disintegrative conception of law, which undermines social cohesion.[16]

Such tensions between common values and religious diversity are particularly acute in the educational sector. Because state schools and religion both compete to instil (common) values and a sense of identity in pupils, the articulation of education and religion is to be found at the heart of political theory reflections upon the relationships between the secular, common values and religion.[17] With the rise of religious diversity and of a Muslim minority in European societies, these longstanding debates have tended to focus on Islam. Recent events in England (the so-called 'Trojan plot' in Birmingham schools) have thus revealed the tensions between a national curriculum (purporting to assert national common values) and an Islamist agenda (in which religious identity would be prevalent). Torn between the goal of ensuring social cohesion and respecting the autonomy of parents and (religious) schools, European States struggle to devise a fair and coherent school framework. The educational sector is moreover emblematic of the tensions between human rights and national constitutional frameworks. As religion has entered the era of Human Rights,[18] schools have become key fora for testing the limits of the religious freedoms of parents, of children and of school staff against school and state policies.

With a focus on education, this section will analyse whether a less confrontational approach can and should be adopted in religious freedom cases. It will address the ambiguities, tensions and assumptions behind negotiation processes in relation to religion at school. Negotiation carries different connotations: often associated with a search for compromise, it may seem at odds with the absolute commitments made by believers towards their faith. Construed as justification for accommodating religious requests against general legal norms, it points to conflicting tensions between the neutrality of the State and its legal system on the one hand and respect

13 John Eekelaar, 'From Multiculturalism to Cultural Voluntarism: A Family-based Approach', *The Political Quarterly* 81(3): 344–55, July–September 2010.

14 Maleiha Malik, *Minority Legal Order in the UK: Minorities, Pluralism and the Law*, London: British Academy 2012.

15 Maleiha Malik, 'Minority and the Law: Past and Present', *Current Legal Problems* 67 (2014): 67–98.

16 Ronan McCrea, 'Why the Role of Religious Tribunals in the Legal System Should not be Expanded', to be published in *Public Law*, April 2016.

17 William A. Galston, *Liberal Pluralism. The Implications of Value Pluralism for Political Theory and Practice.* (Cambridge: Cambridge University Press, 2002); Amy Gutmann, *Democratic Education* (Princeton, NJ: Princeton University Press, 1999 (1st edn, 1987)); Meira Levinson, *The Demands of Liberal Education* (Oxford and New York: Oxford University Press, 1999); Stephen Macedo, 'Liberal Civic Education and Religious Fundamentalism: The Case of God v. John Rawls', *Ethics* 105(3) 1995, 468–93.

18 Russell Sandberg, *Law and Religion*. Cambridge: Cambridge University Press, 2011.

for individual religious freedoms on the other. As a matter of principle, 'negotiation with religion' may therefore be questioned for its incompatibility with both religious and legal duties. Should negotiation with religion – as we will demonstrate – be justified in principle, questions remain as to the shape it should take, particularly when it conflicts with other fundamental rights.

Limits to what can be negotiated

For children, the school 'is the place where they learn about the world, about the place they will occupy in it, about powers and inequality'.[19] In an open society,[20] schools should thus both respect pupils' individual convictions and enable them to develop an understanding and tolerance of others. This sense of sharing hardly seems compatible with requests to opt out from courses or situations on the basis that they might expose pupils to beliefs other than their own. In that sense, 'negotiating with religion' in a school context cannot be about managing fragmented identities. Integralist parents[21] – whether of religious or secular obedience – will by definition object to a pluralistic environment in which either the secular approach to life or a religious outlook is implicitly presented as merely one possible perspective on the world. But if parents were allowed to object to classes on those grounds, it would be tantamount to entitling them to refuse that their children be exposed to any other views but theirs. Allegedly parental rights under article 2 Protocol I[22] of the European Convention on Human Rights would then trump all the other interests at stake, namely children's rights to an open future[23] and the State's interest in making sure that public education provides a tolerant environment where children of all creeds learn to interact.[24] Negotiating with religion should not therefore be equated to granting rights of exemption.

19 Michael D.A. Freeman, 'The Human Rights of Children', in *Current Legal Problems*, eds Colm O'Cinneide and George Letsas, volume 63 (Oxford: Oxford University Press, 2010), 6.

20 See John Eekelaar, *Family law and Personal Life* (Oxford: Oxford University Press, 2006), who draws on Karl Popper's notion of 'open society' in order to offer a grounding for the legal regulation of our personal lives and their religious dimensions.

21 Integralist citizens have been defined as citizens who

> regard their obligation to obey God as totalizing: that is, they will take the scope of their obligation to obey God to extend to whatever they do, wherever they are, and in whatever institutional setting they find themselves. A fortiori, they'll take their obligation to obey God to extend to the political realm.
>
> Christopher Eberle, *Religious Conviction in Liberal Politics* (New York: Cambridge University Press, 2002), 145

22 Article 2 protocol I of the European Convention on Human Rights entitles parents to have their children educated in accordance with their religious beliefs or philosophical convictions.

23 Joel Feinberg, 'The Child's Right to an Open Future', in *Whose Child? Children's Rights, Parental Authority and State Power*, eds William Aiken and Hugh La Follette (Totowa, NJ: Littlefield, Adams, 1980), 124.

24 Myriam Hunter-Henin, 'Law, Religion and the School', in *Handbook of Law and Religion*, ed. Silvio Ferrari (Oxford: Routledge, 2015), 259–70.

But what could then be satisfactory alternatives to allowing individual derogations and exemptions? In relation to religious education (RE) courses, one may wonder whether the exemption mechanism provided by the right to opt out of RE classes could not be replaced by a different approach to RE itself, which would ensure that the content and delivery of the syllabus is more inclusive of minority religions. This crucial question has been raised by Ian Leigh,[25] who rejects the temptation to dispense with the above-mentioned dilemma by removing religion from school altogether. According to civic liberalism thinkers,[26] the common good should take priority over the accommodation of diversity. Leigh argues that even from a liberal perspective, RE courses should be retained: 'Arguably, some minimum of religious education is necessary to fulfil one commonly-stated liberal goal for education – training for citizenship – since religion has played an important historical part in shaping present-day culture and is an important aspect of contemporary society.'[27] If RE classes are to be retained, the question as to their content cannot be avoided. Drawing on the *Toledo Guiding Principles on Teaching about Religion and Beliefs in Public Schools*[28] and on case law from Canada and North America and the jurisprudence of the European Court Human Rights (ECtHR), Leigh contends that RE classes should never amount to religious indoctrination. Their aim should be to distil knowledge and not to instil a particular religious belief. The prospect of a more neutral and academic RE syllabus leads us back to our initial question: would a more inclusive RE syllabus not be a more suitable way to accommodate diversity than individual rights to opt out? More fundamentally, is there not a contradiction between these two mechanisms? As Leigh puts it:

> If the purpose of educating pupils about a number of religions is so that they are aware about key beliefs that different groups within their society hold and are able to assess their cultural and historical importance, it is questionable whether parents or pupils should be able, by opting out, to avoid learning about religions other than their own.[29]

25 Ian Leigh, 'Law's Negotiation with Religious Education in European Human Rights' (paper presented at the Fourth Negotiating with Religion Workshop convened by Myriam Hunter-Henin, *Legal Frameworks: Schools and Religious Freedom*, UCL, Laws, 12 June, 2012); this paper draws on his chapter, Ian Leigh, 'Objective, Critical and Pluralistic? Religious Education and Human Rights in the European Public Sphere', in *Law, State and Religion in the New Europe: Debates and Dilemmas*, eds Camil Ungureanu and Lorenzo Zucca (Cambridge: Cambridge University Press, 2012), 192.

26 E.g., Meira Levinson, *The Demands of Liberal Education* (Oxford: Oxford University Press, 1999), esp. chapter 5; Stephen Macedo, *Diversity and Distrust; Civic Education in a Multicultural Democracy*. (Cambridge, MA: Harvard University Press 2000).

27 Ian Leigh, 'Objective, Critical and Pluralistic?' 199.

28 Office of Democratic Institutions and Human Rights (OSCE), *Toledo Guiding Principles on Teaching about Religion and Beliefs in Public Schools*, (Warsaw 2007), www.osce.org/odhir/29154 (accessed 25 April 2014).

29 Ian Leigh, 'Law's Negotiation with Religious Education in European Human Rights' (paper presented at the Fourth Negotiating with Religion Workshop convened by Myriam Hunter-Henin, *Legal Frameworks: Schools and Religious Freedom*, UCL, Laws, June 12, 2012).

The European Court of Human Rights case law does not offer a straightforward answer to this question. Although the issue has been raised in Strasbourg, the Court has never had to answer the question directly, having found that the relevant RE courses were insufficiently objective and neutral not to warrant an opt-out mechanism.[30] How is one to assess the inclusive nature of the school environment? The challenge of devising courses inclusive for all has been underlined.[31] Difficulties might also be raised in relation to the teaching environment. Should the content of the courses be unproblematic, pupils may nevertheless object to the modes of delivery of classes. The obligatory presence of the crucifix in Italian state school classrooms was thus challenged by two atheist pupils and their mother in the *Lautsi* case.[32] The applicants claimed that this endorsement of the majority religion by the State violated their right to freedom from religion protected under article 9 of the European Convention on Human rights and the mother's right to have her children educated in accordance with her own convictions, under article 2 Protocol I of the European Convention respectively. In Canada, a fundamentalist student from York University requested an exemption from classroom teaching because the mixed gender composition of the class seminars allegedly offended his religious beliefs.[33] Is it for the State to prove that the symbol displayed is neutral; that the seating arrangement in the classroom is respectful of every student's particular beliefs or is it up to the claimant to prove that the alleged offending practice stops him/her from meaningful participation in class? Should exclusion/inclusion be negotiated for each contested school practice or should it be construed more broadly against the general school environment? Should certain requests be dismissed without any negotiation because they are raised against non-negotiable values such as that of equality?

If negotiating with religion in a school context will rarely square with crude rights to opt out, neither will it easily accept shared principles and beliefs at face value. Negotiating with religion at school will thus encourage enquiries about the scope and meanings of deeply felt national values or school ethos. The search for a common good does not preclude all investigation, analysis or negotiation with these broader values. In fact, without such analysis, there is a risk that these national values be turned into empty political slogans. In France, for example, a renewed reflection on the concept of *laïcité* would be called for.[34] At school, it is more the fear of ongoing tensions locally and of pressures on young girls to adopt certain religious practices (namely the wearing of the headscarf)[35] than the attachment to the concept of *laïcité*

30 See ECtHR 29 June 2007 *Folgerø and others v. Norway*, Appl. no. 15472/02.

31 Peter Cumper, 'Religious Education in Europe in the Twenty-First Century', in *Law, Religious Freedoms and Education in Europe*, ed. Myriam Hunter-Henin (Farnham, UK: Ashgate, 2011), 219.

32 ECtHR 18 March 2011 *Lautsi and others v. Italy*, App. no. 30814/06 [Grand Chamber]. On *Lautsi*, see, in this volume, Cécile Laborde, Saladin Meckled-Garcia and Myriam Hunter-Henin (Chapter 12).

33 See fn 2.

34 See also, Cécile Laborde, *Critical Republicanism. The Hijab Controversy and Political Philosophy* (Oxford: Oxford University Press, 2008).

35 See below Chapter 12.

that led to the banning of all ostentatious religious signs in French state primary and secondary schools.[36] In the *Lautsi* case,[37] the challenge to the mandatory presence of crucifixes in Italian state schools led to a vigorous and interesting debate on the meaning of secularism in Italy and its relationships with the dominant religion. However, this does not mean than negotiating with religion is a tool designed to systematically deconstruct common values.[38] It is best conceived as a balancing exercise between individual claims and those common values.

Negotiation with religion appears at different levels: rule formulation (through legislation and regulations) and rule enforcement (through judicial decisions and interpretations by school authorities). Whereas judges will be called upon in the context of litigation to question the proportionate enforcement of rules and policies, legislators or local authorities will be in charge of weighing competing values and interests at the earlier stage of policy and law making. The compromise reached by the latter does not take away the need for careful balancing on the ground. Too often judges – of national courts or the European Court of Human Rights – have arguably been too cautious. But this need for a proper balancing exercise at the enforcement stage should not be an invitation for judges to reassess the general equilibrium reached at broader level. Each level of negotiation should arguably be kept in its own separate remit.

Levels of negotiation

Whatever the position established by the applicable legal framework, negotiation could (and should) take place at the stage of enforcement. A more stringent test of proportionality than the one currently imposed by the European Court of Human Rights[39] could thus at the very least be carried out. Negotiation in the sense of a balancing exercise between competing claims should not therefore be avoided. The outcome of this form of negotiation would not depend on any assessment of the validity of the belief itself but would rely on the evaluation of the concrete interferences caused to the individual pupil or teacher claimant in the case. Individual choices would thus be taken into account in a more fluid way and not be ascribed fixed meanings. In *Begum*,[40] a secondary school pupil unsuccessfully challenged her school uniform policy, which had been drawn up in consultation with religious local communities. As Maleiha Malik puts it regarding the House of Lords decision in *Begum*:

36 Loi n. 2004–228 of 15 March 2004 encadrant, en application du principe de laïcité, le port de signes ou de tenues manifestant une appartenance religieuse dans les écoles, collèges, lycées publics, *JO* 17 March 2004, 5190. (Act regulating, by virtue of the principle of 'laïcité', the wearing of religious symbols or clothing in state primary and secondary schools) (our translation).

37 See fn 16.

38 See Chapter 12.

39 E.g., ECtHR 30 June 2009 *Aktas; Bayrak. Gamaleddyn; Ghazal; J. Singh; R. Singh v. France*, App. nos. 43563/08; 14308/08; 18527/08; 29134/08; 25463/08 and 27651/08. for a more detailed analysis, see Chapter 12 below.

40 *R (Begum) v Governors of Denbigh High School* [2006] *UKHL 15*.

> The House of Lords' decision gives greater weight to the group aspect of religious freedom rather than treating Shabina Begum's choice of the '*jilbab*' as a more fluid individual choice that is open to change and transformation. This approach narrows rather than expands the public space available for individual women such as *Shabina Begum* to negotiate between a range of choices.[41]

Lucy Vickers'[42] analysis also reveals that the compromise reached in the legislative framework applicable in England and Wales is not enough to protect individual teachers' rights. A spirit of compromise, for example, can be seen in the relative moderation of the existing school framework in England and Wales – the School Standards and Framework Act 1998 (SSFA) – although faith schools can discriminate against their staff, the extent to which they can do this depends on their funding and governance structure. Voluntary aided schools can discriminate, although voluntary controlled and foundation schools can only do so for up to one fifth of their teaching staff. However the current system is not one of equilibrium because the balance was tilted in favour of religious voices, who are backed by government support. Moreover, the protection of teachers' religious freedom is lower than that of other workers because of the lack of a proportionality test under the SSFA. Lucy Vickers suggests that a criterion of proportionality

> would enable each case to be considered rather than determining in advance that discrimination against the teacher is always acceptable . . . it would entail considering the facts and the circumstances of the individual case, such as whether there are other options available to teach or look for promotion elsewhere.[43]

It would also guarantee that the legal solutions under the SSFA comply with the EU Employment Equality directive 2000/78.

A spirit of compromise when devising legal solutions and policies may be a valuable tool for strengthening local harmony. However, it does not necessarily guarantee fair outcomes for the individuals concerned. Negotiation techniques cannot of themselves ensure that all interests at stake will genuinely be taken into account. Unless the process of negotiation is reopened at the enforcement stage, the legal solutions will derive from compromises reached at a more general level, independently of a meaningful enquiry into the consequences of legal solutions for

41 Maleiha Malik, 'Religious Freedom and Multiculturalism: *R (Shabina Begum) v. Denbigh High School*', 19(2) *King's Law Journal* (2008): 377.

42 See Chapter 13 below.

43 Lucy Vickers, 'Negotiating Religious Freedom for Staff in Faith Schools, (paper presented at the Fourth Negotiating with Religion Workshop convened by Myriam Hunter-Henin*)*, *Series on Negotiating Religion: Inquiries into the History and Present of Religious Accommodation*, accessed 25 April 2014, www.ucl.ac.uk/european-nstitute/events/religion; www.ucl.ac.uk/laws/events/docs/2012_religion_workshop_programme_v02.pdf

the individual in question. Judges should not therefore shy away from vigorous proportionality tests. In the *Bayrak* case[44] against France, the ECtHR could arguably have been much more attentive to individual needs. In *Bayrak*, the 2004 French law banning the display of ostentatious religious symbols in state primary and secondary schools had been enforced particularly harshly. After a meeting between the school authorities, the student and her family, the student had agreed to unveil if she could wear a black cap instead. The school authorities considered that the wearing of the cap was still religiously motivated and could not be allowed. Following the pupil's refusal to remove the cap, she was finally expelled. The decision to expel the pupil despite the substitution of a cap was said by the ECtHR to fall within the State's margin of appreciation.[45] The French State's argument whereby the legislative ban on religious symbols could otherwise be easily avoided was held to be reasonable.[46] Finally the rather heavy sanction of expulsion was considered to be proportionate since the girl could enrol for distance learning.[47] The ECtHR is not to decide for a particular form of church/State arrangement across Europe[48] but it is expected to defend violations of minority rights. Whereas restraint to engage in the proper contours of the concept of *laïcité* was therefore arguably welcome in *Bayrak*, a more vigorous proportionality test would have been required to ensure an effective protection of pupils' individual rights.

Negotiation is of limited use if it is restricted to the level of policy formulation. Geared towards an ideal of moderation, negotiation at this policy level is bound to miss out on the richness and diversity of individual beliefs. In his work, Julian Rivers has explored how the Government's intervention in the debate on faith schools has pushed forward a tamed expression of religious diversity and encouraged increased regulation and juridification.[49] On the one hand, observes Rivers, this general framework has constrained the options for negotiation, 'confining religions to a pre-determined relevance and an unwillingness to trust lower-level and informal of processes of negotiating the complex tensions at play'.[50] On the other hand, the increased regulation and juridification that it has created is starting to have a life on its own: 'there is an interplay between the regulatory aims of the State, which uses law as one tool and the relatively autonomous logic of a legal system imbued with commitments to equality and human rights'.[51]

The first two chapters of this section examine whether this autonomous logic of law is gradually conducive to opening up more meaningful negotiation at the

44 See note 23.

45 Para. 2(10).

46 Ibid.

47 Para. 2(11).

48 See Rex Adhar and Ian Leigh, 'Post-Secularism and the European Court of Human Rights: Or How God Never Really Went Away', *Modern Law Review* 75, 6 (2012): 1064.

49 Julian Rivers, 'Not Much Faith in the System' (paper presented at the Fourth Negotiating with Religion Workshop convened by Myriam Hunter-Henin).

50 Ibid.

51 Partha Dasgupta, 'The Economics of the Environment', *90 Proceedings of the British Academy* (1996): 165.

enforcement stage. A related issue is the scope that this negotiation should take and the voices that should be heard. Just as the spirit of compromise and the negotiations at play during the policy formulation phase can never dismiss the need for a balancing of these solutions with the local and individual factors that are at stake in the implementation phase, a negotiating process at the level of enforcement cannot reopen the compromises reached at broader level. The scope and the actors of each level of negotiation are and should remain separate.

Actors of negotiation

At the enforcement stage, negotiation will occur before the courts. Actors of negotiation will therefore be the individual claimants and the local school authorities. If genuine negotiation presupposes the opportunity for both parties to fully assess each other's needs and obtain mutually advantageous courses of action as a result, how can genuine negotiation ever take place between these actors? On the one hand, local school authorities will be ill-equipped to appreciate the meaning for the individual of a particular religious practice and the intensity of the individual commitment to it. On the other hand, the individual concerned may have but little power to appreciate and alleviate the constraints under which the negotiation processes take place. In order that someone is able to negotiate, they need to know the extent to which they are empowered to negotiate and the extent to which the other parties are empowered to negotiate; they need to know what they can negotiate with as well as what the other parties can negotiate with.[52] In its full sense of open-ended discussion of each side's beliefs and ideas, the negotiation that can take place at this stage is limited and should in any case be resisted. The attempts by the judiciary to venture into these ambitious forms of negotiation have not been convincing. Courts are ill-equipped to fully assess the meaning of religious commitments. Nor are they the best placed to revisit compromises democratically reached at policy level. Courts have at times tried to ascertain what beliefs and practices qualify as 'religious' in order to restrict the protection to those beliefs and practices that were truly religious. In *Playfoot*,[53] the High Court thus held that the practice of wearing a purity ring (as testimony to the claimant's commitment to chastity before marriage) was not intimately linked to the belief because the claimant was under no obligation by reason of her faith to wear it. Rather than providing for a denser exchange, this negotiation with religious concepts led to a unilateral assessment by the courts of individual actions and beliefs. Unsurprisingly, the so-called negotiation then became the projection of the judiciary's own system of beliefs onto the individual practice. Consequently, most of the individual religious practices that do not conform to the norm will be dismissed. Recent case law reassuringly indicates that judges will no longer question the religious dimension of the practice at stake, as long as it is

52 *High Court 22 June 2007 Lydia Playfoot (a minor) v. Governing Body of Millais School*, [2007] EWHC 1698 (Admin).

53 Julian Rivers, 'Not Much Faith in the System'.

genuinely and cogently felt by the individual as conveying a religious significance.[54] Keeping discussions of religious scholastics outside of the courtroom and Parliament does not however imply that all negotiations should be resisted in respect of religious freedom at school, nor that the meaning, importance and implications of a particular religious practice for the individual concerned should not be explored. However, it should be limited to the assessment of the impact of the alleged infringement for the individual concerned.

Conclusion

Several of the contributions discussed here welcome some negotiation in the legal frameworks and solutions surrounding issues of religion at school. They also emphasise, however, that core features need to be included for that negotiation to lead to fair outcomes. Two aspects are identified as essential components: one relates to the voices that are allowed to have their say in the negotiation process; the other relates to the attention given to the circumstances of individual cases in the implementation of legal solutions. These two questions refer to the form that the negotiations should take, in particular they consider who should take part and at what level. Underlying these issues and intertwined with them are more theoretical issues as to what is being negotiated and why negotiation in law and religion issues at school should be promoted at all. In light of recent developments, the two chapters in this discussion specifically address all these layers of questions and thus further our understanding of the concept of negotiation in the context of the relationship of religion, law and society.

References

Adhar, R. and Leigh, I. 2012. 'Post-Secularism and the European Court of Human Rights: Or How God Never Really Went Away', *Modern Law Review* 75(6), 1064–98.

Beckford, J.A. 2001. 'The Tensions between an Established Church and Equal Opportunities in Religion: the Use of Prison Chaplaincy', in Paula D. Nesbitt, ed. *Religion and Social Policy*. Walnut Creek, CA, Lanham, MD, New York and Oxford: Rowman & Littlefield, 39–53.

Büchler, A. 2011. *Islamic Law in Europe? Legal Pluralism and its Limits in European Family Laws*. Farnham, UK: Ashgate.

Cranmer, F. 2011. 'Beating People is Wrong: Campbell and Cosans, Williamson and their Aftermath', in *Law, Religious Freedoms and Education in Europe*, edited by M. Hunter-Henin. Farnham, UK: Ashgate, 283–304.

Cumper, P. 2011. 'Religious Education in Europe in the Twenty-First Century', in *Law, Religious Freedoms and Education in Europe*, edited by M. Hunter-Henin. Farnham, UK: Ashgate, 207–227.

54 E.g. *R. Secretary of State for Education and Employment and Others ex parte Williamson* [2005] UKHL 15. For an analysis of the decision, see Frank Cranmer, 'Beating People is Wrong: *Campbell and Cosans, Williamson* and their Aftermath', in *Law, Religious Freedoms and Education in Europe*, ed. Myriam Hunter-Henin, 283.

Dasgupta, P. 1996. 'The Economics of the Environment', *Proceedings of the British Academy 90*, 165–221.

Eberle. C. 2002. *Religious Conviction in Liberal Politics*. New York: Cambridge University Press.

Eekelaar, J. 2006. *Family Law and Personal Life*. Oxford: Oxford University Press.

——. 2010. 'From Multiculturalism to Cultural Voluntarism: A Family-based Approach', *The Political Quarterly* 81(3): 344–55, July–September.

Feinberg, J. 1980. 'The Child's Right to an Open Future', in *Whose Child? Children's Rights, Parental Authority and State Power*, edited by W. Aiken and H. La Follette. Totowa, NJ: Littlefield, Adams, 124–53.

Freeman, M.D.A. 2010. 'The Human Rights of Children', in *Current Legal Problems*, vol. 63, edited by C. O'Cinneide and G. Letsas. Oxford: Oxford University Press, 1–44.

Galston, W.A. 2002. *Liberal Pluralism. The Implications of Value Pluralism for Political Theory and Practice*. Cambridge: Cambridge University Press.

Hunter-Henin, M. 2015. 'Law, Religion and the School', in *Handbook of Law and Religion*, edited by S. Ferrari. Oxford: Routledge, 259–70.

Jackson, B. 2009. 'Transformative Accommodation and Religious Law', *Ecclesiastical Law Journal* 131–53.

Laborde, C. 2008. *Critical Republicanism. The Hijab Controversy and Political Philosophy*. Oxford: Oxford University Press.

——. 2013. 'Political Liberalism and Religion: On Separation and Establishment', *Journal of Political Philosophy* 21(1): 67–86.

Lægaard, S. 2008. 'Moderate Secularism and Multicultural Equality', *Politics*, 28(3): 160–8.

Leigh, I. 2012. 'Law's Negotiation with Religious Education in European Human Rights', Paper presented at the Fourth Negotiating with Religion Workshop, 'Legal Frameworks: Schools and Religious Freedom', UCL, Laws, 12 June.

Leigh, I. 2012. 'Objective, Critical and Pluralistic? Religious Education and Human Rights in the European Public Sphere', in *Law, State and Religion in the New Europe: Debates and Dilemmas*, edited by C. Ungureanu and L. Zucca. Cambridge: Cambridge University Press, 192–214.

Levinson, M. 1999. *The Demands of Liberal Education*. Oxford: Oxford University Press.

Macedo, S. 1995. 'Liberal Civic Education and Religious Fundamentalism. The Case of God v. John Rawls', *Ethics* 105(3), 468–93.

——. 2000. *Diversity and Distrust: Civic Education in a Multicultural Democracy*. Cambridge, MA: Harvard University Press.

McCrea, R. 2016. 'Why the Role of Religious Tribunals in the Legal System Should not be Expanded', to be published in *Public Law*, April 2016.

Malik, M. 2008. 'Religious Freedom and Multiculturalism: *R (Shabina Begum) v. Denbigh High School*', *King's Law Journal* 19(2), 377–90.

——. 2012. *Minority Legal Order in the UK: Minorities, Pluralism and the Law*. London: British Academy.

——. 2014. 'Minority and the Law: Past and Present', *Current Legal Problems* 67 (2014): 67–98.

Modood, T. 2007. *Multiculturalism, A Civic Idea*. Cambridge: Polity.

Office of Democratic Institutions and Human Rights (OSCE). 2007. *Toledo Guiding Principles on Teaching about Religion and Beliefs in Public Schools*, www.osce.org/odhir/29154, accessed 25 April 2014.

Rivers, Julian. 2012. 'Not Much Faith in the System', Paper presented at the Fourth Negotiating with Religion Workshop, 'Legal Frameworks: Schools and Religious Freedom', UCL, Laws, 12 June.

Sachar, A. 2008. *Multicultural Jurisdictions: Cultural Differences and Women's Rights*. Cambridge: Cambridge University Press.

Sandberg, R. 2011. *Law and Religion*. Cambridge: Cambridge University Press.

Shah, P. 2005. *Legal Pluralism in Conflict: Coping with Cultural Diversity in Law*. London: Routledge, Cavendish.

Temperman, J. 2010. *State–Religion Relationships and Human Rights Law. Towards a Right to Religiously-Neutral Governance*. Leiden, Boston, MA: Martinus Nijhoff.

Vickers, Lucy. 2014. 'Negotiating Religious Freedom for for Staff in Faith Schools', Paper presented at the Fourth Negotiating with Religion Workshop, *Series on Negotiating Religion: Inquiries into the History and Present of Religious Accommodation*, www.ucl.ac.uk/european-nstitute/events/religion; www.ucl.ac.uk/laws/events/docs/2012_religion_workshop_programme_v02.pdf, accessed 25 April 2014.

Waldron, J. 2010. 'Questions about the Reasonable Accommodation of Minorities', in Rex Adhar and Nicholas Aroney, eds *Shari'a in the West*. Oxford: Oxford University Press, 112.

Williams, R. 2008. 'Civil and Religious Law in England: A Religious Perspective', 7 February 2008, reprinted in *Ecclesiastical Law Journal* 10 (2008): 262.

12 Believing in negotiation

Reflection on law's regulation of religious symbols in state schools

Myriam Hunter-Henin[1]

From a legal perspective, 'negotiating with religion' may refer to the constitutional arrangements that European States have negotiated with their established or majority churches. In consequence of immigration, these historical compromises are being put to the test by the presence of religious communities that were not party to the initial arrangements and judges and legislators are struggling to handle religious claims. Attempts at renegotiating constitutional compromises punctually, through case law or legislation, have produced diverging results ranging from the exclusion of religious views (recent bans on the *burqa*) to the accommodation of 'moderate' forms of religious manifestation (reasoning in the *Begum* House of Lords case). While religious minority claims have prompted a review of the concepts of law, democracy and pluralism and raised the fundamental question as to the limits that law (as opposed to other norms) should impose on individual freedom in the name of social cohesion, legal responses have in turn highlighted the blurred distinction and inner tensions between the religious and the secular[2] and created new subcategories between 'moderate' and 'radical' forms of religion. Focusing on recent developments relating to religious symbols in Western European state schools, this chapter will argue that re-negotiation of historical compromises is possible (and welcome) within existing national frameworks of state–religion relationships. The attention will be on the reasoning adopted at legislative and judicial level. It will be submitted that if courts and parliament more greatly engaged with religious claims, many of the current tensions and contradictions between secularism and religion would dissolve. But how exactly is this new form of negotiating with religion to be undertaken by legislators and judges? To explore this delicate question, the chapter will concentrate on the education sector.

State schools are a particularly opportune field for testing new forms of negotiation between the law and religious claims. From an historical and constitutional perspective, state schools are emblematic of the chosen national model of

1 I am grateful to Dr Lois Lee and Professor Cécile Laborde for their insightful comments on earlier drafts. Any errors remain mine.

2 See the discussion of the cultural/religious dimension of crucifixes in Italian state schools in the two European Court of Human Rights' *Lautsi* cases, infra n 11 and n 18.

church/state relationships.[3] Education is also a network of potentially conflicting rights and interests.[4] Educational systems committed to children's rights will need to respect pupils' convictions (which may coincide or diverge from their parents' beliefs), while maintaining children's right to 'an open future'.[5] How is negotiating with religion likely to take place in this context? In a school context, negotiation with religion usually addresses the equilibrium to be struck between majority and minority religions. Negotiation with religion can thus be construed, first of all, as involving special consideration by lawmakers towards religious views. Furthermore, among those religious views, minority voices would seem to call for particular attention. In this approach, negotiated legal solutions would entitle a greater diversity of actors to intervene in legal regulation of religion than normal majoritarian parliamentary law-making.[6] *In fine*, negotiating with religion could thus be interpreted as a tool to redress the imbalance between majority and minority religious views. As an instrument designed to heighten the role of religion in law-making, negotiating with religion at school may seem to conflict with the requirements of state neutrality. This 'special nature' of religion would certainly warrant justification. Conceptually one may be attracted to one of two sides of the concept of neutrality.[7] Under an inclusive version of neutrality, all local religious beliefs would need to be represented in the local school. Religious education courses would thus have to make room for even time of study for each religion and worldview and classroom walls would be adorned by symbols of each faith. Conversely, an exclusive version of neutrality would be illustrated by blank classroom walls and religion-free syllabi.

This chapter will argue against these two opposite and radical solutions. Not only are they artificial. The illusion that it is possible to strike a fair balance between all forms of belief at school or that a space free of beliefs can be created informs both solutions. Besides, neither of these solutions is necessary to fulfil human rights

3 Myriam Hunter-Henin, 'Religious Freedoms in European Schools: Contrasts and Convergence', Introduction in *Law, Religious Freedoms and Education in Europe*, ed. Myriam Hunter-Henin (Farnham, UK: Ashgate, 2011), 9.

4 Myriam Hunter-Henin, 'Law, Religion and the School', in *Handbook of Law and Religion*, ed. Silvio Ferrari (Oxford: Routledge, 2015).

5 Joel Feinberg, 'The Child's Right to an Open Future', in *Whose Child? Children's Rights, Parental Authority and State Power*, eds William Aiken and Hugh La Follette (Totowa, NJ: Rowman & Littlefield, 1980), 124.

6 For a study of how negotiating techniques have given a voice to politically and economically marginalised indigenous communities, see Christa Scholtz, *Negotiating Claims: The Emergence of Indigenous Land Claim Negotiation Policies. Australia, Canada, New Zealand and the United States* (Oxford: Routledge, 2006).

7 See Roland Pierik and Wibren van der Burg, 'What is Neutrality?' *Ratio Juris* 27, 4 (2014): 496–515. On-line version, *Amsterdam Law School Legal Studies*, Research Paper No. 2011–20, http://papers.ssrn.com/sol3/papers.cfm?abstract_id=1917392, accessed 25 April 2014. Roland Pierik and Wibren van der Burg argue for inclusive neutrality as the default position. However they add that attention to the societal context and the specificities of the issues under debate should guide towards the preferred option, thus suggesting a complex and more fluid interpretation of neutrality. On neutrality, see also Saladin Meckled-Garcia's chapter in this volume.

requirements. Prominence of one particular religion – be it that of the majority – may still comply with state neutrality if its display pursues a legitimate aim and does not stifle the manifestation of other beliefs. As this chapter will argue, imbalance in favour of majority views need not entail a violation of human rights. Furthermore, there is no reason why this conclusion should vary depending on whether the majority views are secular or religious. Negotiating with religion will not therefore be understood in this chapter as an instrument to foster religious views over secular outlooks nor will it necessarily entail systematically injecting more power to minority views. Negotiating with religion is not designed to achieve particular outcomes. It is mainly a process under which each interested party should be given the opportunity to put their view forward and have their interests considered. In fact, tying the negotiating process to particular outcomes (be they the eradication of religion altogether or the exact same standing for all beliefs) would be antagonistic to true negotiating. Negotiating must mean that the end result remains open and that positions of compromise can be entertained.

But this emphasis on the open-endedness of negotiating should not be a vehicle for stronger parties to impose their views. Careful scrutiny will therefore be needed to ensure that the same opportunities are afforded to every participant. The search for a compromise between majority and minority views may not always be sufficient to ensure respect for individual rights to freedom of/from religion. Unless attention is given to the circumstances of individual cases in the implementation of legal solutions, there is a danger that negotiation with religion will muffle the voices of those most concerned: in our setting, usually the students wishing to manifest their beliefs at school. This chapter will in turn address the conceptual and practical hurdles to negotiating with religion in state schools. Conceptually, negotiating with religion implies that radical solutions are not the only possible means to satisfying fairness and neutrality.[8] Welcoming all expressions of religion at school on an equal standing or banning all religious signs altogether may theoretically and constitutionally amount to sound decisions. The purpose of the chapter is to demonstrate that a third option – which gives a greater weight to one or a few religion(s) over others – may *also* be acceptable. Under the prism of negotiation, positions of compromises are not problematic per se. All depends on whether the prominence afforded to a particular religion relies on legitimate grounds in the given circumstances. In this chapter, I will argue that this more subtle apprehension of religion at school is compatible with requirements of state neutrality and human rights prescriptions.

Having overcome the theoretical objections to engaging in open-ended negotiations with religious actors, the chapter will go on to address the practical hurdles involved in these negotiations at school. The infinite possibilities afforded

8 For a study of the articulation of human rights requirements under the European Convention on Human Rights and the concept of neutrality, Ian Leigh, 'The European Court of Human Rights and Religious Neutrality' in *Religion in a Liberal State: Cross-Disciplinary Reflections*, ed. Gavin D'Costa *et al.* (Cambridge: Cambridge University Press, 2013), 38.

by negotiating techniques may in fact prove to be very limited. Depending on who is allowed to have their say and be truly heard, negotiating with religion may or may not be compliant with human rights requirements. If negotiating with religion at a regulatory level is often used to push forward a tamed version of religion, commitments to equality and human rights should encourage a more demanding version of negotiation. As this chapter will argue, negotiation with religion should therefore also be carried out at the enforcement stage. Thus construed and applied, it is submitted that negotiation with religion can achieve a more fluid approach to regulation, which reconciles requirements stemming from constitutional national frameworks, individual human rights and local factors.

Conceptual hurdles to negotiating with religion at school

This part will address objections in principle to negotiating with religion. Interestingly concerns about negotiating legal solutions come from opposite ends of legal theory. For tenants of a strict parliamentary sovereignty, negotiated legal regulation would jeopardise the privileged position of majority views, which are the usual outcome of democratic decision-making. Do claims raised by religious parents or children really require the tweaking of democratic solutions, they would ask? Similarly, but for opposite reasons, most multiculturalists would no doubt see negotiating with religion as an inherently flawed technique.[9] If the stronger position of the majority religion is structurally ingrained,[10] how can negotiations not be tainted and the balance then tilted towards the majority religion? For the former group, the solution lies in legislative uniform intervention, which embodies common values par excellence. Negotiation techniques would simply have no place in law-making except for the realm of contracts. Less radically, this conception of law may accommodate varied solutions at local level, provided powers to regulate have been devolved to local authorities. Social cohesion and the unifying power of law are thus emphasised. From a strong multiculturalist perspective on the other hand, negotiating with religion is not satisfactory because it does not ensure systematic redress of minority positions. On the contrary, the privileged social position enjoyed by majority views gives them a head start in the negotiation process. Negotiation with religion may therefore just be a subtle and deceiving way to reinforce the status quo. Instead – they claim– all instances whereby the majority

9 For a brief but clear overview of the various trends among multiculturalists, see Roland Pierik, 'Multiculturalism', in *International Encyclopaedia of Ethics*, ed. Hugh LaFollette (Oxford: Wiley-Blackwell, 2013), 3470.

10 See for example, denouncing the structural majority bias, Veit Bader, *Secularism or Democracy? Associational Governance of Religious Diversity* (Amsterdam: Amsterdam University Press, 2007); Veit Bader, 'Religious Diversity and Democratic Institutional Pluralism', *Political Theory* 31, 2 (2003): 265; Samuel Scheffler, 'Immigration and the Significance of Culture', *Philosophy and Public Affairs* 35, 2 (2007): 94.

religion is given greater weight or visibility should be challenged. This part will respond to this last claim.[11]

Is the greater prominence given in state schools to the majority religion problematic per se? Does it necessarily contradict state neutrality and/or violate individual human rights to freedom of religion? These crucial questions were addressed by the European Court of Human Rights in the *Lautsi* case.[12] In this case, the Grand Chamber of the European Court of Human Rights confirmed that the prominence given to the country's majority religion need not violate convention rights.[13] The obligatory display of crucifixes in Italian state school classrooms was therefore upheld despite the impressionable age of the audience (young pupils), the enclosed nature of school settings and compulsory school attendance.[14] The fact that the crucifix was mandated by state authorities and that Catholicism was thus endorsed by the State was also set aside. All of these factors may be problematic for a constitutional court. Certainly the endorsement of a particular religion by the State as well as the impossibility for pupils to escape the image of the crucifix has been held to be unconstitutional for the German constitutional court.[15] But the European Court of Human Rights is not a constitutional court.[16] It is up to Member States to choose their own conception of neutrality as long as it is enforced in a manner respectful of religious freedom under article 9 of the Convention. States will thus be free to decide under their own constitutional and legal frameworks whether negotiating with religion at school should be resisted or welcome and if it is, whether it may extend to state endorsed measures, affect civil servants or only concern pupils. There are as many right answers to these questions as they are possible versions of neutrality and forms of church/state arrangements. In that sense, the reference to the concept of margin of appreciation by the Court in the *Lautsi* decision is understandable.[17]

11 The first claim is considered in Part III below.

12 ECtHR 18 Match 2011 *Lautsi and Others v Italy* [Grand Chamber], App. no. 30814/06.

13 For an analysis of the implications of the *Lautsi* case for church–state arrangements, see Saladin Meckled-Garcia, 'Just Establishment? Two Kinds of Neutrality and the Human Right to Freedom of Religion', this volume.

14 By contrast, arguing that because of the special vulnerable position of its viewers, the crucifix had an indoctrinating effect, Alison Mawhinney, 'Crucifixes, Classrooms and Children: a Semiotic Cocktail', in *The Lautsi Papers: Multidisciplinary Reflections on Religious Symbols in the Public School Classroom*, ed. Jeroen Temperman (Leiden: Brill/Martinus Nijhoff, 2012), 93.

15 32 BVerfGE (1995). More generally, see Tobias Lock, 'Religious Symbols in Germany', in *Law, Religious Freedoms and Education in Europe*, ed. Myriam Hunter-Henin (Farnham, UK: Ashgate, 2011), 347.

16 Cf. Applauding for this reason judicial restraint on the part of the ECtHR, Joseph HH Weiler, 'Lautsi: A Reply', *International Journal of Constitutional Law* 10, 4 (2012): 230; Jean-Marc Piret, 'Limitations of Supranational Jurisdiction, Judicial Restraint and the Nature of Treaty Law', in *The Lautsi Papers: Multidisciplinary Reflections on Religious Symbols in the Public School Classroom*, ed. Jeroen Temperman, 59.

17 See Dominic McGoldrick, 'Religion in the European Public Square and in European Public Life: Crucifixes in the Classroom', *Human Rights Law Review* 11, 3 (2011): 451. But the over-reliance by the Court on the concept may be criticised, see *infra*.

The alternative would be to consider that the mandatory display of a symbol of the majority religion in state schools inevitably stands in contradiction with the concept of state neutrality, however construed. It may indeed be argued that by endorsing a particular religious symbol and *a fortiori* by making its display mandatory, state authorities are siding with the majority religion.[18] This can be criticised at two levels: on a theoretical level, it may be seen as incompatible with neutrality; at an individual level, this attitude may be accused of generating an expressive harm to students and staff holding different religious beliefs or none.[19] As a result of the official display of the crucifix, staff and students holding different beliefs may feel that they cannot participate as meaningfully as their peers who belong to the majority Catholic religion. This can however be contested: rather, the prominence given to the majority religion *may* be acceptable at both theoretical and individual levels. The counter-position was taken by the Chamber decision. Let us therefore examine its reasoning.

In the Chamber decision first rendered in the *Lautsi* case,[20] the crucifix was described as carrying, among the plurality of its potential meanings, a predominantly religious – Catholic – meaning. This was then held to be inescapably incompatible with the convictions of non-believers as well as with the beliefs of pupils of other religions. On 3 November 2009, the Chamber of the Second Section of the Court therefore went on to declare that there had been a violation of the European Convention on Human Rights. Such reasoning – with a narrow focus on the symbol of the crucifix itself – is, I would argue, misplaced. Taken to its logical limits, it would imply the removal of all religious symbols from the public sphere because religious symbols will necessarily have an exclusionary effect. This is because the deeper religious meaning of the symbol will be lost on those who do not belong to the faith associated with that symbol. After all, the essence of religious symbols is to denote a particular affiliation and in so doing to differentiate those who belong to a particular faith and those who do not. But must it follow that as such religious symbols run counter to the requirements of pluralism and state neutrality – at least when symbols are exhibited in institutional settings? It need not. Respect for pluralism and state neutrality does not entail the absence of religion in the institutional sphere.[21] As Ooijen says,

> [i]n the end, neutrality is something which can hardly be seen separate from individuals who perceive it. Letting this perception centre on the significance

18 Supporting this position, see Jeroen Temperman, *State–Religion Relationships and Human Rights Law: Towards a Right to Religiously Neutral Governance* (Leiden and Boston, MA: Martinus Nijhoff, 2010).

19 See such reasoning in *Freitag v Penitanguishine* [1997] 47 OR 301. Adde, Christopher L Eisgruber and Lawrence G. Sager, *Religious Freedom and the Constitution* (Cambridge, MA: Harvard University Press, 2007). On the relationships between Harm and religious freedom cases, see Ashleigh Keall, PhD diss., forthcoming.

20 ECtHR 3 November 2009 *Lautsi and Others v Italy* [Second Section Chamber], App. no. 30814/06.

21 Malcolm D. Evans, '*Lautsi v. Italy*: An Initial Appraisal', *Religion and Human Rights* 6 (2011): 237.

and effect of a symbol in fact testifies to the limits of a legal approach in raising theological and empirical questions.[22]

Malcolm Evans has argued, very convincingly, that the European Convention on Human Rights does not require that an *appearance* of strict neutrality be enforced, but more meaningfully demands that the educational experience is – in its *substance* – compliant with the plurality of convictions. Religion may therefore *appear* in institutional settings as long as its display does not have an effect of indoctrination. Put differently, this effect of indoctrination cannot be equated to the mere presence of the crucifix. If it did, it would be tantamount to imposing a separatist model as the only possible 'church–state' model across Europe. The European Court of Human Rights on the contrary has recognised the legitimacy of a diversity of 'church–state' relationships across Europe.[23] The presence of a religious symbol in an institutional setting as such does not necessarily deviate from the requirements of state neutrality and pluralism. When it does, this deviation does not in itself entail a violation of human rights. Second, must it follow from observing the differing impact of religious symbols on members and non-members of the relevant faith that symbols will inevitably give rise to a clash of individual rights? It need not. The decision to display religious symbols – if made by an individual or a group – may amount to a manifestation of religious faith protected under article 9 of the European Convention on Human Rights, but the desire to have these religious symbols removed cannot find justification in any counter individual right. There is no right to be spared from the sight of symbols.[24] The tension therefore remains. A pragmatic approach, however, of negotiating with religious actors, may provide a more satisfying solution.

Negotiating the display of majority religious symbols

The meaning of negotiating with religion at school needs to be clarified. It does not suggest that the issue as to whether crucifixes should remain on or be removed from state school classroom walls be subject to local deliberation, through a vote by parents, pupils and staff members. This is not what I advocate for under the

22 Hana MAE van Ooijen, 'Neutrality and Displaying Religious Symbols', in *The Lautsi Papers* (2012), 219.

23 See for a recent assertion, ECtHR 9 July 2013, *Sindicatul 'Păstorul cel bun' v. Romania*, App. no. *2330/09*, Grand Chamber, para. 38:

> where questions concerning the relationship between the State and religions are at stake, on which opinion in a democratic society may reasonably differ widely, the role of the national decision-making body must be given special importance. This will be the case in particular where practice in European States is characterised by a wide variety of constitutional models governing relations between the State and religious denominations.

24 Grand Chamber judgment, *Lautsi*, at para. 66. For a discussion, see Adhar and Leigh (2012).

concept of 'negotiating with religion'. This prolongation of democratic decision-making at the school level would not ensure satisfactory representation of minority voices. Conversely, one objection to the display of religious symbols should not necessarily override other parents' and pupils' wishes either.[25] The wishes of the majority cannot be discredited simply because they are those of the majority.[26] The negotiating process I advocate is best characterised as a balancing exercise. In the context of the *Lautsi* case, it would have led to weighing up the impact of the crucifix against the overall attitude towards religion in the Italian school in question. In light of the openness of the Italian school to other religions, as illustrated by the possibility for pupils of all faiths to wear religious symbols or the accommodation for attendance to religious festivals of all creeds,[27] one might have concluded that the emphasis given to Catholicism and Christianity through the display of crucifixes in the classroom was balanced by the overall benevolent attitude towards all religions at school.

A 'negotiating with religion' approach would also be more in line with the rights at stake. The presence of the crucifix allegedly violated the atheist claimants' (and other pupils') rights to freedom from religion, which is protected under article 9 of the European Convention on Human Rights. It also potentially contravened their mother's right to have her children educated in accordance with her (atheist) convictions, which is protected under article 2 of the First Protocol to the European Convention on Human Rights. I would argue that article 2 of the First Protocol postulates 'negotiating with religion'. Article 2 of the First Protocol does not entitle parents to protection from all traces of religion or equivalent philosophies different from their own;[28] neither does it allow parents to request that all aspects of the school environment comply with their own beliefs. This provision, however, enables parents to complain should schools aim at or introduce measures that have an effect of indoctrination of students.[29] In other words, article 2 of the First Protocol forbids radical postures that are intolerant of other beliefs, whether they come at the request of parents or are decided by school authorities. In order to assess whether a parent's claim is legitimate, it is therefore essential to verify that both parties (parents and school authorities) are not acting out of pure intolerance. On the part of the school, this entails that the presence of a crucifix does not serve an aim of indoctrination; on the part of the claimant parent, this implies that the infringement suffered hinges on more than distaste for the display of differing beliefs. Neither of these verifications can convincingly be carried out without considering the overall environment surrounding the display of the crucifix and

25 For such a system in some autonomous communities in Spain, decisions of the Administrative Court of Justice of Castile-Leon 20 September 2007, n. 1617/2007, RJCA/2008/109 and of 14 December 2009, *Aranzadi Repertory of Jurisprudence*, available at www.tirantonline.com, TOL 1.724.360, accessed 24 April 2014.

26 Grand Chamber judgment, *Lautsi*, Concurring Opinion of Judge Bonello at para. 3.5 to 3.16.

27 Cf. Grand Chamber judgment, *Lautsi*, at para. 74 and para. 39.

28 ECtHR 20 October 2009 *Appel-Irrgang v. Germany*, App. no. 45216/07.

29 ECtHR 7 December 1976 *Kjeldsen Busk Madsen and Pedersen v Denmark*, App. nos. 5095/71; 5920/72; 5926/72 and 1 EHRR 711.

more broadly, without examining the school context as a whole. It therefore logically follows that a balancing exercise is inherent in the application of article 2 of Protocol I.

It is in the evaluation of the possible powers of indoctrination associated with the crucifix present in state classrooms that the Chamber and Grand Chamber most diverged. The Chamber judgment referred to factors that contributed to reinforcing the message of the crucifix to the point of making it 'compelling'.[30] By contrast, the Grand Chamber downplayed the influence that the crucifix may have had on pupils.[31] If, as decided in the Chamber judgment, the message of the crucifix combined with the vulnerability of its observers amounts to indoctrination, nothing more needs to be said: a violation of article 2 of Protocol 1 must follow. Another educational purpose, however, can also be arguably associated with the crucifix: the presence of the crucifix in European state schools could help familiarise children with the cultural heritage of the nation. The European Court has recognised in the past that emphasis given to the dominant religion for historical reasons is compatible with article 2 Protocol 1.[32] However the emphasis must be carried out in a pluralistic, objective and critical manner.[33] In the absence of an opportunity to opt-out, the verification of these qualities should have led to an examination of the overall school environment, as advocated in the 'negotiating with religion' approach. The Grand Chamber overruled the Chamber decision but did not follow the approach herein recommended. In order to downplay the impact of the crucifix, the Grand Chamber characterised it as a passive symbol[34] and underlined the wide margin of appreciation granted to Member States in those areas.[35] Neither of these justifications is convincing. Not only – for reasons that fall outside the scope of this chapter – is the notion of passive symbol rather puzzling, it also fails to take into account the overall environment and does not balance the impact of the crucifix against surrounding factors. As for the repeated recourse to the concept of margin of appreciation,[36] one might think that it is a

30 Second Chamber judgment, *Lautsi*, para. 55.

31 Grand Chamber judgment, *Lautsi*, para. 66.

32 ECtHR 29 June 2007 *Folgerø and others v. Norway* [Grand chamber], App. no. 15472/02, para. 89:

> the fact that knowledge about Christianity represented a greater part of the Curriculum for primary and lower secondary schools than knowledge about other religions and philosophies cannot of its own be viewed as a departure from the principles of pluralism and objectivity amounting to indoctrination.

But see, pointing to the ambiguities of this assertion, my chapter, 'Law, Religion and the School', in *Handbook of Law and Religion*, ed. Silvio Ferrari (Oxford: Routledge, 2015).

33 ECtHR 7 December 1976 *Kjeldsen, Busk Madsen and Pedersen v. Denmnark*, App. nos. 5095/71; 5920/72 and 5926/72.

34 Grand Chamber judgment, *Lautsi*, para. 72.

35 Grand Chamber judgment, *Lautsi*, para. 64–70.

36 Lorenzo Zucca, '*Lautsi:* A Commentary on a Decision by the ECtHR Grand Chamber', *International Journal of Constitutional Law* 11, 1 (2013): 218. According to Lorenzo Zucca, the concept of margin of appreciation was indeed mentioned 27 times in the whole decision and 8 times in the 20 paragraphs summarising the Court's assessment.

sign of reverence for the national context in which the case emerged. The concept of margin of appreciation[37] affords States some leeway on particularly sensitive issues on which there is no consensus across countries of the Council of Europe. It therefore often enables States to assert their own national distinctiveness on certain delicate issues.[38] If, however, the way that religion is represented in state schools as a whole falls under the margin of appreciation afforded to Member States, the protection granted under article 9 of the Convention and article 2 of the First Protocol may seriously be undermined. The insistence on the margin of appreciation in *Lautsi* is therefore unsatisfactory.[39] Rather than underlining a pertinent reverence to context, it seems instead to signal a reluctance by the Court to carry out a thorough assessment of the circumstances of the case. 'Negotiating with religion' would, on the other hand, necessarily ensure that a vigorous balancing exercise could not be avoided. Does this conclusion preclude any legislative uniform regulation of religion at schools? The concept of negotiation with religion does not demand that all regulations rely on local consultation. It will, however, always require a balancing exercise at the enforcement stage. This requirement should alleviate concerns about the practical implementation of negotiations with religion, notably the fear that the voices of those most concerned would be muffled by compromises reached at higher level between more powerful actors.

Practical hurdles to negotiating with religion at school

Having overcome objections raised in principle against negotiating with religion in state schools and demonstrated that this process, understood as an open-ended balancing exercise between competing interests, can be compatible both with the requirements of state neutrality and human rights, this final part will address more practical concerns. The concept of negotiation – at first associated with contract law – has spread well beyond this field, carried by assumptions about its inherent fairness.[40] This assumption of fairness has long been disputed in contract law and in echo to Fouillée's famous quote,[41] Lacordaire points out that freedom of

37 On the concept see Michael R. Hutchinson, 'The Margin of Appreciation Doctrine in the European Court of Human Rights', *ICLQ* 48 (1999): 638; James A. Sweeney, 'Margins of Appreciation. Cultural Relativity and the European Court of Human Rights in the Post Cold War Era', *ICLQ* 54, 2 (2005): 459; George Letsas, 'Two Concepts of the Margin of Appreciation', *Oxford Journal of Legal Studies* 4 (2006): 705.

38 For an example in relation to abortion, ECtHR 16 December 2010 *A, B and C v. Ireland*, App. no. 25579/05.

39 Besides, the concept of margin of appreciation should not technically come into the reasoning unless the right at stake is subject to limitations and restrictions as is the case under article 9 of the European Convention of Human Rights for example but is not under article 2 of the First Protocol.

40 Alfred Fouillée, *La Science sociale contemporaine* (Paris: Hachette, 1880), 47: 'Qui dit contractuel dit juste', ('What is contractual is fairness' (our translation)).

41 See fn 40.

contracts will benefit the stronger party.[42] Negotiating with religion at school may generate similar fears. Is there not a risk that the negotiating process will benefit the stronger party? The purpose of this final part is therefore to consider the various safeguards that need to be put in place in order to prevent such concerns from materialising. Let us therefore consider the various levels at which negotiating with religion may take place and examine in each instance how to ensure that the weaker parties also have their say in the process.

At a preliminary stage, one may discern that judges will engage with concepts of religion for the sake of defining what beliefs and practices qualify as 'religious' under article 9 of the European Convention on Human Rights. At this preliminary stage, negotiation will take place in the loose sense of stretching the boundaries of concepts in order to welcome (or reject) a given practice within protected categories. In the past, the European Commission on Human Rights seemed to have put claims based on religious freedom to a test of necessity: the applicant, it was suggested in some cases,[43] had to show that a particular practice was necessary to his/her religion in order for it to be protected. According to this test, the wearing of religious dress will often be controversial as in most cases it will be seen at most as being encouraged by a religious institution but will rarely be imposed as being mandatory. The test would thus restrict the protection to practices that are non-negotiable for the believers because they are truly compulsory in the eye of their religious community. English Courts have at times seemed to apply a similar reasoning. In *Playfoot*,[44] the High Court held that the practice of wearing a purity ring was not intimately linked to the claimant's Christian beliefs because the claimant was under no religious obligation to wear it. Such an approach is dismissive of many if not most religious practices. It is now accepted that any manifestation or conduct that gives expression to religion or belief will fall under the ambit of article 9(1) of the European Convention on Human Rights, which protects freedom of religion and belief.[45] In recent cases, the subjective conviction by the applicant that the symbol or attire in question expresses a religious duty has been sufficient to trigger the application of article 9(1) of the European Convention on Human Rights, consequently shifting onto the State the onus to demonstrate that the interference caused to that practice could be justified under the subsequent paragraph. Whether in its first restrictive approach or in the more open model, the European Court does not, it seems, 'negotiate' the concept of religion as such. On the contrary, the early test of necessity was a technique

42 For an analysis of Fouillée's quote and the myths it carries, see Louise Rolland, 'En trois petits bonds, à reculons', *McGill Law Journal* 51 (2006): 765.

43 See European Commission of Human Rights 5 December 1978 *Arrowsmith v. UK*, App. no. 7050/75 8. Comments by Caroline Evans, *Freedom of Religion under the European Convention on Human Rights* (Oxford: Oxford University Press, 2001), 115.

44 High Court 22 June 2007 *Lydia Playfoot (a minor) v. Governing Body of Millais School*, [2007] EWHC 1698 (Admin). See Mark Hill, 'Bracelets, Rings and Veils: The Accommodation of Religious Symbols in the Uniform Policies of English Schools', in *Law, Religious Freedoms and Education in Europe*, ed. Myriam Hunter-Henin, 307.

45 See Ian Leigh, 'Recent Developments in Religious Liberty', *Ecclesiastical Law Journal* (2009): 65.

designed to avoid any confrontation with religion by restricting the protection to unproblematic cases, which obviously had a religious dimension. Similarly, the present approach makes negotiation with religion at this conceptual level unnecessary. By adopting what is essentially a subjective test of what constitutes religion, the European Court (and indeed English courts if we are to follow the precedent of *Williamson*)[46] avoids the issue of definition. Such a delicate enterprise of definition seems indeed unnecessary given that the protection afforded by article 9(1) extends to non-religious beliefs and manifestations anyway. One may also wonder whether judges would be the best placed to discuss matters of religious doctrine. From the angle of negotiation, such attempts may be criticised as conferring too much power on the State (through its judges) to frame the discussion and its outcome. They do not provide for negotiation in the sense of dialogue or exchange of arguments between different sides since definitions and meanings are exclusively derived from a state perspective. Delegating the matter to expert testimony on the correct interpretation of a particular religious requirement may absolve judges from the accusation of mingling with religious affairs; however, even presuming that the identification of the relevant expert does not prove controversial, passing the problem onto religious scholars will not enable a better representation of the minority position. The success of the individual claim will still be dependent on the individual practice conforming to orthodox teaching and rites. The practical hurdles to negotiating with religion at this preliminary stage therefore prove to be too problematic to be overcome. More promising is negotiation with religion at ground level, between local actors.

Negotiation at ground level is carried out between school authorities, governors and representatives of religious communities. This process is often seen as the ideal tool to reach legal solutions that will be acceptable to all at local level. Section 149(1) of the Equality Act 2010 that came into force in April 2011 provides that in the exercise of its functions public authorities such as schools must have due regard to the need to inter alia: foster good relations between persons who share a religion or belief and persons who do not share it.

In England and Wales, school uniform policies in state schools will thus usually be the outcome of consultation with representatives of major religious communities. In the case of *Begum*,[47] it was noted with satisfaction by the Law Lords that the school had gone to great lengths to devise a uniform policy that all representatives

46 In the case of *Williamson*, Lord Nicholls of Birkenhead stressed that,

> it is not for the court to embark on an inquiry into the asserted belief and judge its 'validity' by some objective standard such as the source of the material upon which the claimant founds his belief or the orthodox teaching of the religion in question or the extent to which the claimant's belief conforms to or differs from the views of others professing the same religion. Freedom of religion protects the subjective belief of an individual.
>
> *R. v. Secretary of State for Education and Employment and others, ex parte Williamson* [2005] UKHL 15, para 22.

47 *R (Begum) v Governors of Denbigh High School* [2006] *UKHL 15*. See also Lucy Vickers' chapter in this volume.

of the local religious communities thought appropriate.[48] The governing body of the school contained a balanced representation of different sections of school community; 4 out of 6 parent governors were Muslim and the consultation process had been extensive.[49] At this level, negotiation takes place in a fuller sense as it involves the exchange of arguments and does lead to a solution that is not predetermined but open to the compromises that may emerge as a result of the dialogue. However, the openness of the process is not complete. Undoubtedly moderate solutions of compromise will be favoured. Indeed it is the option on which the majority of the religious groups consulted – generally of mainstream moderate schools – are most likely to concur. Moreover the main addressees of the negotiation outcomes – the pupils in this context – will have no direct influence in the exchange of views. If religious freedom is an individual human right, how can one justify devising solutions that fail to take into account individual views?

The answer, I would submit, lies in the distinction between two normative levels: if the individual or minority views may not legitimately bear a lot of weight in devising the rules and policies relating to religion at school, their voice should be heard at the enforcement stage. How did the House of Lords (now Supreme Court) tackle these two levels in the authoritative case of *Begum*? The House of Lords ruled that individual beliefs should be protected even if, on the facts of the case, it rejected the individual claim. One conclusion to draw therefore is that negotiating with representatives of majority religions may not be extensive enough for schools to comply with legal requirements. In practice it is, however, unlikely that individual claims will be successful if they are raised against well-balanced solutions, which are well accepted by the local community and the majority of students. If schools are under a duty to negotiate in order to promote good relations, so are individuals under an implicit duty to respect the overall harmony and refrain from adopting positions that would potentially jeopardise the overall equilibrium. This equilibrium may conflict with the recognition of individual autonomy and the idea that public recognition of the core features of a person's identity is important to their sense of self-worth.[50] I suggest that a stronger proportionality test should be carried out at the enforcement stage. The pitfall of unduly representing stronger parties will be avoided if a meaningful balancing exercise is carried out at the enforcement stage. The impact of a particular restriction on an individual's right to freedom of religion should thus be assessed against the aim that the measure is pursuing. The *Begum* case may be criticised not because of its unreasonable conclusion but because the point of view of the student concerned was largely ignored.[51] Miss Shabina Begum's desire to wear a less revealing uniform than the attires allowed under her school's policy was assumed to be fickle and coerced. The fact that she

48 Ibid., para. 7.

49 Ibid., para. 4.

50 Charles Taylor, *Multiculturalism and the Politics of Recognition* (Princeton, NJ: Princeton University Press, 1992); Maleiha Malik, 'Progressive Multiculturalism: Minority Women and Cultural Diversity', *International Journal of Minority and Group Rights* 17 (2010): 447.

51 See, however, Baroness Hale's judgment, notably, para. 96.

had worn the permissible uniform for 2 years without complaint was held to suggest that her change of mind was somewhat capricious.[52] The influence of her brother who had joined a fundamentalist Islamist group also shed doubts on the genuineness of Miss Begum's wish.[53] Finally, it was feared that allowing her to wear the *jilhab* might pressurise her peers to adopt a stricter form of dress.[54] It could also have been argued, however, that Miss Begum's change of mind about the proper form of dress to wear coincided with her reaching puberty. The influence that her brother possibly exercised upon her was a valid concern, as was the influence that she herself may have exercised on other female pupils; but we cannot simply assume that the request to change her uniform reveals influence upon her by her brother or that granting her request would inevitably exercise pressure on her school friends. A more vigorous proportionality test, as advocated under the concept of negotiating with religion, would require tangible elements attesting to the reality of those undue influences.

Naturally, if the proportionality test becomes too vigorous, it will be tantamount to granting individuals positive rights of derogations from general applicable laws and policies.[55] Eventually any sense of common values will be lost. But negotiation at the enforcement stage need not be taken this far. What I propose here is not to dilute the overarching values that bind school communities. Negotiating with religion at the enforcement stage would simply ensure that restrictions to individual religious freedoms do not rely on broad assumptions about the meaning and dangers of a particular religious symbol. In that sense, negotiating with religion would not dismiss legal systems that regulate religious symbols in state schools through legislation. In France, the 2004 law[56] is the pertinent legal basis on the matter. Under that law, pupils attending state primary and secondary schools are banned from wearing conspicuous religious symbols. The 2004 law pursues several aims: promoting the core and common French value of *laïcité*[57] (which has always had a special salience in state schools);[58] protecting heads of schools from the media

52 Ibid., para 45.

53 Ibid., para 80.

54 Ibid., para. 65.

55 This position is advocated by Erica Howard, according to whom the proportionality test in religious claims should always include consideration of whether the educational institution could have dealt with the request in a less stringent way and could have accommodated the request (fully or at least partially) without suffering an undue burden. See Erica Howard, *Law and the Wearing of Religious Symbols: European bans on the Wearing of Religious Symbols in Education* (Oxford: Routledge, 2012). Comments by Myriam Hunter-Henin, 4, 12 *International Journal of Discrimination and the Law* 2012: 243.

56 Loi n. 2004–228 of 15 March 2004 encadrant, en application du principe de laïcité, le port de signes ou de tenues manifestant une appartenance religieuse dans les écoles, collèges, lycées publics, *JO* 17 March 2004, 5190 (Act regulating by virtue of the principle of 'laïcité', the wearing of religious symbols or clothing in state primary and secondary schools).

57 Jean Rivero, 'La notion juridique de laïcité', *Revue Dalloz* (1949): 137.

58 Since the reforms of Jules Ferry in the late nineteenth century, schools through free, compulsory, public education for all have become the symbol of integration for all into the Republican State, See Jean-Claude Milner, *De l'Ecole*. (Paris: Le Seuil, 1984).

attention and the difficulties they would face if they were left the responsibility of devising negotiated solutions at local level; and affording a free neutral space where young girls could escape the pressure[59] they experienced in their communities to wear the veil. The purpose of this chapter is not to evaluate the legitimacy of those aims. Reflection on these aims and on the proper contours of *laïcité* would be very valuable;[60] but such enterprise falls outside the scope of the precepts of negotiating with religion. Indeed, in the approach I defend, negotiating with religion at school should not be interpreted as a tool to systematically challenge general values but as a technique designed to ensure that these are fairly enforced in individual cases.[61]

Negotiation with religion at school does not take place in a vacuum. It is carried out against a broader background of national frameworks and international human rights. In that sense, the local negotiation that may (as in Britain) or may no longer (as in France, since the 2004 law) take place at local level is itself constrained by these broader requirements. These constraints themselves need not be challenged. There is value in negotiating legal solutions on the ground: negotiation between local actors encourages trust between people as they co-operate, plan common projects, try to avoid friction and recognise their interdependence. But there is also value in devising legal solutions in Parliament: the legislative route creates a sense of being *part of a larger whole* – a cohesive, unified, integrated society.[62] Negotiating with religion does not postulate that the former is superior to the latter. Whatever the chosen form of law-making, however, negotiating with religion prescribes that negotiation operates at the enforcement stage. It will then take the shape of a balancing exercise between competing claims. Proportionality in concrete cases will be key to determining the acceptable compromise to be reached in each case. The European Court of Human Rights could be more attentive to the proportionality test. In the *Bayrak* case,[63] where a young Muslim girl had been expelled from a French state secondary school after refusing to remove her veil, the European Court showed extreme reverence towards Member States' positions. In effect, the only element that seemed to have been decisive in this case was the legitimate goal pursued by the contested legislative measure. Once the Court

59 See the Stasi Report prior to the 2004 French loi, *Rapport de la Commission présidée par M. Bernard Stasi de réflexion sur l'application du principe de laïcité dans la République submitted on 11 December 2003* (Paris: La Documentation française, 2004).

60 See in relation to the 2010 French ban on the full-face veil in the whole of the public space (Loi no. 2010–1192 interdisant la dissimulation du visage dans l'espace public of 11 October 2010, *JO* 12 October 2010), Myriam Hunter-Henin, 'Why the French Don't Like the *Burqa*: *Laïcité*, National Identity and Religious Freedom', *ICLQ* 61, 8 (2012): 1.

61 There is therefore no inherent tension between *Laïcité* and negotiation. *Laïcité* could be enforced in a manner compatible with the negotiation requirements I have set out. For an illustration of this nuanced application of *laic* principles, see Conseil d'Etat 27 November 1989 (avis), n 346893, *EDCE* 1990, 239.

62 See Roger Cotterrell, 'Justice, Dignity, Torture, Headscarves: Can Durkheim's Sociology Clarify Social values?' *Social & Legal Studies* 20, 1 (2011): 3.

63 ECtHR 30 June 2009 *Aktas; Bayrak. Gamaleddyn; Ghazal; J. Singh; R. Singh v. France* App. nos. 43563/08; 14308/08; 18527/08; 29134/08; 25463/08 and 27651/08.

was satisfied that the relevant legal basis was pursuing a legitimate goal (here, prospectively, the 2004 French law defending the constitutional value of *laïcité*), it paid no attention as to how the law had been applied in the individual case. It thus entirely dispelled Miss Bayrak's willingness to wear a black cap in lieu of her veil. In comparison to the young girl's flexibility and accommodating attitude, the decision by French school authorities to nevertheless expel the student seemed extreme; but it passed the proportionality test before the European Court with no problems. The fact that the pupil could enrol for distance learning seemed sufficient to justify the expulsion. By contrast, I would argue that the possibility – also underlined in the English case of *Begum*[64] – for the pupil to change school or enrol for distance learning cannot make the restriction proportionate. If it did, the onus of reconciling freedom of religion and education would then rest exclusively on the individual. Fortunately this contracting-out approach seems to have been abandoned in more recent ECtHR cases.[65] However it is unlikely to benefit individual claimants who wish to wear religious symbols against national values or school policies. In its recent *SAS* decision,[66] the European Court of Human Rights held the French *burqa* ban[67] to be a proportionate interference with religious freedom rights even though the prohibition extended to the whole of the public sphere. Two considerations were decisive in the Court's reasoning: the extremely concealing nature of the garments prohibited (full-face covering clothing)[68] and the strong national consensus underlying the ban.[69] As a result, the Court was content to grant France a wide margin of appreciation and upheld the ban. To what extent is the reasoning adopted in *SAS* transferrable to religious symbol cases in an educational context? The 2004 French ban on religious symbols at school does not only target full-face covering garments but applies to all ostentatious religious symbols. However, underlying common national values feature more strongly in an educational context than in the general public sphere. State schools have always been at the epicentre of *laïcité* and at the core of the French national identity. It is therefore unlikely that the European Court of Human Rights will, for the near future at least, strengthen its proportionality requirements in cases relating to religious symbols at school.

Conclusion

This chapter has demonstrated that negotiating religion at school is of value for law-makers. Conceived as a balancing exercise between competing interests, it

64 See note 41.

65 ECtHR 15 January 2013 *Eweida and others v the United Kingdom*, App. nos. 48420/10, 59842/10, 51671/10 and 36516/10.

66 ECHR 1 July 2014 *SAS v France*, App no 43835/112014. For a critical analysis of the case, see Myriam Hunter-Henin, 'Living Together in an Age of Religious Diversity: Lessons from *Baby Loup* and *SAS*', *Oxford Journal of Law and Religion* 4, 1 (2015): 94–118.

67 See fn 60.

68 ECHR 1 July 2014, fn 66, para. 146.

69 Ibid, para. 153.

ensures better representation of minority views in legal regulation. In fact, any legal system committed to human rights cannot do away with negotiating with religion – at least at the enforcement stage. A proportionality test that balances the goal pursued by the restrictive school measure against the impact it causes to a particular pupil is necessary if individual religious freedom rights are to have any meaning; but the test need not slide into systematic rights of accommodation for individuals. If it did, negotiating with religion would become the seed for an inclusive version of neutrality under which all religions (gradually) achieve equal standing. This chapter has argued for a more complex and more context-sensitive approach to negotiating with religion. In our approach, neither versions of neutrality is favoured a priori. Outcomes depend entirely on the issues at stake and the relevant circumstances. This seemingly complex balancing exercise is actually already practised to varying degrees and with more or less success.

Several layers and forms of negotiation have thus been identified in this chapter. A first stage of negotiation – at conceptual level, in the courtroom – implies pushing the boundaries of concepts in order to welcome more individual practices within the protected categories. A second stage of negotiation – on the ground, in the classroom – relies on consultation with local religious communities, the result of which are then to be reflected in the local school's policy. Finally, a third stage of negotiation consists of balancing competing claims to individual and group religious identities with claims to national identities and social cohesion. The first stage has been largely rejected and for good reasons: despite the well-intentioned aim of stretching categories in order to allow for greater diversity of manifestations of individual beliefs, this negotiation with concepts by judges is to be resisted. Indeed, it would lead judges into discussions of religious scholastics for which they are ill-equipped. Besides, as judges would retain the control of definitions, this process of negotiation would remain largely unilateral and therefore would fail to meet the requirements of a fair negotiation process.

By contrast, negotiation on the ground is a two-way process, which involves both school authorities and religious actors (via the main religious communities in the vicinity). However, the point of view of the most interested parties – individual pupils – still remains absent and the dynamic of the whole process is therefore skewed in favour of majority mainstream views. If negotiation with religion is to be welcome in education, it cannot therefore be in the restricted sense of consultation and deliberation at local level but has to imply a broader balancing of conflicting values, which leaves room both for individual expression and common national values. Despite the practical difficulties, negotiating with religion is not therefore a far-fetched ideal. A few recent developments, however, push lawyers into the opposite direction: the relaxed application of the proportionality test by the European Court of Human Rights as illustrated in the *Bayrak* case or the attraction for the contracting out approach, for example, go against the advocated approach because they do not allow for a weighing of competing claims but shift all the onus of adapting (for the latter) or all the burden of proof (for the former) onto the individual.

Conceptually, the proposed approach of 'negotiating with religion' may be accused of clouding the concept of state neutrality. It is true that the opposition between inclusive and exclusive neutrality gives a clearer picture. Under an inclusive version, all religions are treated on an equal footing by the State. By contrast, under an exclusive version of the concept, public institutions must keep safely away from religion altogether. My proposed approach does not give such predetermined answers as to the general relationships between the Sate and religion. But far from being a flaw, this chapter has argued that this 'pragmatic plural approach provides more fruitful solutions than a narrow-minded, either/or choice for any one of these neutrality interpretations'.[70]

References

Bader, V. 'Religious Diversity and Democratic Institutional Pluralism', *Political Theory* 31, 2 (2003): 265–94.

Bader, V. *Secularism or Democracy? Associational Governance of Religious Diversity*. Amsterdam: Amsterdam University Press, 2007.

Cotterrell, R. 'Justice, Dignity, Torture, Headscarves: Can Durkheim's Sociology Clarify Social values?' *Social and Legal Studies* 20, 1 (2011): 3–20.

Eisgruber C.L. and L. G. Sager. *Religious Freedom and the Constitution*. Cambridge, MA: Harvard University Press, 2007.

Evans, C. *Freedom of Religion under the European Convention on Human Rights*. Oxford: Oxford University Press, 2001.

Evans, M.D. '*Lautsi v. Italy*: An Initial Appraisal', *Religion and Human Rights* 6 (2001): 237–44.

Feinberg, J. 'The Child's Right to an Open Future', in *Whose Child? Children's Rights, Parental Authority and State Power*, edited by W. Aiken and H. La Follette, 124–53. Totowa, NJ: Littlefield, Adams, 1980.

Fouillée, A. *La Science sociale contemporaine*. Paris: Hachette, 1880.

Hill, M. 'Bracelets, Rings and Veils: The Accommodation of Religious Symbols in the Uniform Policies of English Schools', in *Law, Religious Freedoms and Education in Europe*, edited by M. Hunter-Henin, 307–26. Farnham, UK: Ashgate, 2011.

Howard, E. *Law and the Wearing of Religious Symbols: European Bans on the Wearing of Religious Symbols in Education*. Oxford: Routledge, 2012.

Hunter-Henin, M. 'Religious Freedoms in European Schools: Contrasts and convergence', in *Law, Religious Freedoms and Education in Europe* edited by M. Hunter-Henin, 1–33. Farnham, UK: Ashgate, 2011.

Hunter-Henin, M. 'Why the French Don't Like the Burqa: Laïcité, National Identity and Religious Freedom', *International Comparative Law Quarterly* 61, 3 (2012): 613–39.

Hunter-Henin, M. 'Law, Religion and the School', in *Handbook of Law and Religion* edited by S. Ferrari, 259–70. Oxford: Routledge, 2015.

Hunter-Henin, M. 'Living Together in an Age of Religious Diversity: Lessons from Baby Loup and SAS', *Oxford Journal of Law and Religion* 4, 1 (2015): 94–118.

Hutchinson, M.R. 'The Margin of Appreciation Doctrine in the European Court of Human Rights', *International Comparative Law Quarterly* (1999): 638–50.

70 Pierik and Van der Burg (2014): 21.

Leigh, I. 'Recent Developments in Religious Liberty', *Ecclesiastical Law Journal* 11, 1 (2009): 65–72.

Leigh, I. 'The European Court of Human Rights and Religious Neutrality', in *Religion in a Liberal State: Cross-Disciplinary Reflections*, edited by G. D'Costa, Tariq Modood, Malcolm Evans and Julian Rivers, 38–66. Cambridge: Cambridge University Press, 2013.

Letsas, G. 'Two Concepts of the Margin of Appreciation', *Oxford Journal of Legal Studies* 26, 4 (2006): 705–32.

Lock, T. 'Religious Symbols in Germany', in *Law, Religious Freedoms and Education in Europe* edited by M. Hunter-Henin, 347–69. Farnham, UK: Ashgate, 2011.

McGoldrick, D. 'Religion in the European Public Square and in European Public Life – Crucifixes in the Classroom', *Human Rights Law Review* 11, 3 (2011): 451–502.

Malik, M. 'Progressive Multiculturalism: Minority Women and Cultural Diversity', *International Journal of Minority and Group Rights* 17 (2010): 447–67.

Mawhinney, A. 'Crucifixes, Classrooms and Children: A Semiotic Cocktail', in *The Lautsi Papers: Multidisciplinary Reflections on Religious Symbols in the Public School Classroom* edited by J. Temperman, 93–112. Leiden: Martinus Nijhoff, 2012.

Milner, J.-C. *De l'Ecole*. Paris: Le Seuil, 1984.

Pierik, R. 'Multiculturalism', in *International Encyclopaedia of Ethics* edited by H. LaFollette, 3470–80. Oxford: Wiley-Blackwell, 2013.

Pierik, R. and W. Van der Burg. 'What is Neutrality?' *Ratio Juris* 27, 4 (2014): 496–515.

Piret, J.-M. 'Limitations of Supranational Jurisdiction, Judicial Restraint and the Nature of Treaty Law', in *The Lautsi Papers: Multidisciplinary Reflections on Religious Symbols in the Public School Classroom* edited by J. Temperman, 59–89. Leiden: BRILL/Martinus Nijhoff, 2012.

Rivero, J. 'La notion juridique de laïcité', *Revue Dalloz* 31 (1949): 137–40.

Rolland, L. 'En trois petits bonds, à reculons', *McGill Law Journal* 51 (2006): 765–80.

Scheffler, S. 'Immigration and the Significance of Culture', *Philosophy and Public Affairs* 35, 2 (2007): 93–125.

Scholtz, C. *Negotiating Claims: The Emergence of Indigenous Land Claim Negotiation Policies. Australia, Canada, New Zealand and the United States*. Oxford: Routledge, 2006.

Sweeney, J.A. 'Margins of Appreciation: Cultural Relativity and the European Court of Human Rights in the Post Cold War Era', *International Comparative Law Quarterly* 54, 2 (2005): 459–74.

Taylor, C. *Multiculturalism and the Politics of Recognition*. Princeton, NJ: Princeton University Press, 1992.

Temperman, J. *State–Religion Relationships and Human Rights Law: Towards a Right to Religiously Neutral Governance*. Leiden/Boston, MA: Martinus Nijhoff, 2010.

Van Ooijen, H.M.A.E. 'Neutrality and Displaying Religious Symbols', in *The Lautsi Papers: Multidisciplinary Reflections on Religious Symbols in the Public School Classroom* edited by J. Temperman, 219–38. Leiden: Martinus Nijhoff, 2012.

Weiler, J.H.H. 'Lautsi: A Reply', *International Journal of Constitutional Law* 10, 4 (2012): 230–3.

Zucca, L. 'Lautsi: A Commentary on a Decision by the ECtHR Grand Chamber', *International Journal of Constitutional Law* 11, 1 (2013): 218–29.

13 New issues for negotiation

Schools and religious freedom

Lucy Vickers

The English education system has always contained large numbers of schools with a religious ethos, providing an important space for negotiation between religion, education and the secular. The focus here is on the freedom of teachers in English schools and the ways in which this has been negotiated as part of a system of protection for religious freedom for schools more generally. The various voices in the negotiation of the current settlement, including religious organisations, schools, teachers, unions and teachers themselves, are considered. Although the focus is on English schools,[1] the issues are of broader significance; they speak to other legal settlements with relation to religion and education, as well as raising issues of more general concern relating to the accommodation of religion in contemporary secular law. Thus, the particular concerns in the context of English schools serve as important illustration of more general concerns regarding the ongoing negotiation of religion in modern society.

Turning to the particular position of state schooling in England, the English state school system has long contained large numbers of schools with a religious ethos, due to the historical involvement of churches in the development of universal education in the country.[2] Today, over 30 per cent of maintained schools in England have a religious character.[3] Although these are not all Christian in affiliation, the vast majority are. The very existence of what are, in England, usually termed 'faith schools' within the maintained sector of education is testament to the history of negotiation and compromise between the church and state with regards to education. Faith schools can be different kinds of schools but are associated with a particular religion.[4] They are run like other state schools in that

1 The rules differ from those that operate in Scotland, Wales and Northern Ireland, although the background issues may of course be the same.

2 For a history of religious schooling in the context see J. Rivers. *The Law of Organized Religions: Between Establishment and Secularism* (Oxford: Oxford University Press, 2010).

3 Around 7,000 of the 22,000 maintained schools in the England have a religious character. See www.gov.uk/government/publications/maintained-faith-schools/maintained-faith-schools (accessed 20 August 2014).

4 See UK Government definition: www.gov.uk/types-of-school/faith-schools (accessed 20 August 2014).

they have to follow the national curriculum, where it applies, except that they are free to teach only about their own religion in religious studies.

As explored by Hunter-Henin elsewhere in this volume,[5] negotiation with religion in schools can be seen at a number of levels. It is seen in the organisation of schools, rules pertaining to property ownership, religious education, school uniforms and processes relating to admissions. It is also seen in the regulation of the employment relationship between teachers and schools. It is this relationship that is the focus of this chapter.

In order to set some context to this discussion, the chapter begins by exploring the ways in which the organisational structure of faith schools within the state education sector reflects a broad compromise between religion and education.

A product of negotiation: religion and education in England

At a time when the relationship between education and religion are open for negotiation, it is important to recognise that existing arrangements are themselves a product of a long history of negotiation. In England, education was historically provided as part of a voluntary system. Many schools had religious foundations and were closely linked to the church. Over time, various negotiations have occurred within religious groups and between them, as well as with secular agencies and non-religious groups, regarding the proper parameters of religious education and the correct balance between reflecting religious consensus on the one hand and providing non-denominational schooling on the other. The outcome has always been, however, that the church has remained involved in providing significant levels of public education. When the state introduced public provision of education in 1870, it supplemented that offered by the church, in effect beginning a process of shared provision of public education between the state and religious bodies. By the turn of the twentieth century and the Education Act of 1902, the main elements of the current settlement were in place, with voluntary schools brought within the state system. In relation to church-funded voluntary schools, a compromise was reached to reflect both the interests of the churches that owned the property in which the school was located and the interests of the state in providing universal education without incurring the capital costs of building new schools. The settlement involved bringing existing church schools within the state system by providing the maintenance costs;[6] and, in return for providing school premises,[7] the churches were allowed to control religious instruction within those maintained schools, as well as retaining some controls over staffing. While

5 See Hunter-Henin's chapter, 'Negotiating with religion from a legal perspective', this volume.

6 Faith schools receive grants (of up to 90 per cent of the total cost) towards capital costs of the buildings and 100 per cent of running costs (including teachers' salaries) from the State, www.atl.org.uk/atl_en/education/postition_statements/faith_schools.asp (accessed 17 January 2008).

7 The school site and buildings will be owned by the church.

a number of structural changes have taken place over the twentieth century, this significant compromise between religion and schools has largely survived.[8]

Structural changes include the distinction introduced by the 1944 Education Act between voluntary aided schools and voluntary controlled schools. Again, the variations in the structure make clear the element of compromise that has been reached. Schools were able to opt to become either 'voluntary controlled' (with land and buildings owned by the church, but the local education authority funding the school, employing staff and controlling admissions) or 'voluntary aided' (with land and buildings owned by the church, the governing body employing staff and controlling admissions, but the school funded largely by the local education authority). The Education Act 1944 also required all schools, whether or not they retained a religious foundation, to have a daily act of collective worship and to teach religious education. Under this system, voluntary aided schools enjoy greater independence in terms of admissions and religious education syllabus; in return they provide more financial support as the school governors maintain the school buildings. In voluntary controlled schools the compromise falls differently: in return for greater central government funding for the buildings, the school has less control over its staffing (detailed below).

The twenty-first century legal framework for state funded schools sees the continued existence of faith-based schools. While many of these schools date back to the early days of universal education, the system is now being developed and renewed. First, since 1997, there has been an increase in the creation of faith schools that are not Christian.[9] This development can be viewed as the outcome of negotiation between other faith groups and the state regarding faith schooling. With the increase in religious diversity in England came a pressure to revisit the preferential treatment of Christian denominations in terms of education. In order to address the inequality of treatment, the state was faced with a choice: to scale back the faith element in schools, which are maintained by the state, or allow other faith groups to provide state-maintained education. The government chose the latter option, although the numbers of faith schools that are not Christian remain very small.

Second, the more recent creation of 'free' schools with a religious character,[10] and the significant level of involvement of faith-based organisations in the

8 See J. Rivers. *The Law of Organized Religions: Between Establishment and Secularism* (Oxford: Oxford University Press, 2010); J.C.D. Harte, 'The Development of the Law of Employment and Education', in *Religious Liberty and Human Rights*, ed. M. Hill (Cardiff: University of Wales Press, 2002), 159–94; and P. Petchey, 'Legal Issues for Faith Schools in England and Wales', *Ecclesiastical Law Journal* (2008), 174.

9 For a review of the trend towards greater involvement of religious schools, see L. Vickers, 'Religion and Belief Discrimination and the Employment of Teachers in Faith Schools', *Religion and Human Rights* 4 (2009): 1–20.

10 www.guardian.co.uk/education/2012/jul/13/third-new-free-schools-religious, 13 July 2012 (accessed 29 July 2013).

sponsorship of academy schools,[11] means that numbers of faith schools remain high. Moreover the freedom of free schools from traditional controls over curriculum and local authority regulation has led to a number of schools with a very explicit and strong religious ethos.[12] The existence of faith schools can no longer be viewed merely as the continuation of a historic compromise reached between religion and the state at a time of financial necessity. Nor can it be seen as a relic, which is of academic interest only or the outcome of a nominal religious affiliation. The expansion of faith schools in the early part of the twenty-first century means that the negotiation between religious groups and schools is ongoing. Moreover, the compromise reached, which allows other faiths to run state-funded schools means that the settlement between religion and education can now be developed further, free from any claims of systemic and legally entrenched inequality between religions.

A full discussion of the reasons for the increased governmental support for faith schools is beyond the scope of this chapter, but suffice to say that such schools are said to deliver high-quality education, achieve good academic results and are popular with parents.[13] Of course the reason for the success of faith schools is highly contentious; some would claim that it is the religious ethos itself that is the cause of success. Others, such as the Fair Admissions Campaign, point to the lower percentages of pupils eligible for free school meals in faith schools as evidence that there is a degree of segregation on socio-economic grounds.[14] Moreover, even without such evidence, a causal link between religious ethos per se and success would probably be impossible to prove. Nonetheless, the schools remain very popular, with indications that many parents attend church in order to get children into faith schools, even in the absence of any personal faith.[15] Moreover, there is clear evidence that faith groups themselves are keen to continue their formal links with education, as they see this as a key part of their future growth strategy.[16]

The most high-profile and contentious issue relating to the interaction of religion with schools involves the question of parental choice of school and the admission of pupils. Other issues that have received publicity and have generated case law

11 The Church of England is the biggest sponsor of academy schools under the original academy programme www.churchofengland.org/education/national-society/academies-(1).aspx (accessed 10 May 2014).

12 See https://humanism.org.uk/2012/09/12/news-1111/(accessed 7 May 2014).

13 See *Building on Success*, (London: DFES, 2001).

14 See http://fairadmissions.org.uk/groundbreaking-new-research-maps-the-segregating-impact-of-faith-school-admissions/(accessed 7 May 2014).

15 D. Voas and L. Watt, 'The Church Growth Research Programme Report on Strands 1 and 2 Numerical Change in Church Attendance: National, Local And Individual Factors', Institute for Social and Economic Research (2014) www.churchgrowthresearch.org.uk/progress_findings_reports (accessed 7 May 2014).

16 Evidence for this can be seen in the Church of England document, *The Way Ahead* (London: Church House Publishing, 2001) and the supplementary strategic document setting out strategy for 2007–11.

relate to the adaptation of school policy in order to accommodate religious dress.[17] The legal framework governing the employment terms of teachers at faith schools is, however, an additional site of negotiation between religion and education, albeit one that has received less public attention. The legal framework is set out below.

Legal framework governing teachers in faith schools

As outlined above, the English state school system is made up of schools that have very different governance structures. Apart from community schools, which will not have a religious character, any of the other types of school – voluntary aided, voluntary controlled, foundation schools, free schools or academies – could have a religious character and so be termed 'faith schools'. The level of religiosity of faith schools varies hugely, however, with some merely nominally Christian, designated a faith school due to historical funding arrangements and others infused with a Christian ethos, with an explicitly evangelical agenda. It should be noted, however, that there is no formal link between the legal status of the school and its level of religiosity. A voluntary aided Church of England school or Church-sponsored academy could be very multicultural on the ground with, for example, multicultural assemblies, minority religious dress codes and the accommodation of religious holidays; a voluntary controlled school could have a stronger Christian ethos, with prayers said every day and religious symbols displayed prominently in school. Yet, despite the variation in terms of the strength of religious ethos, the legal regulation of faith schools depends on the legal and governance structure of the school, rather than reflecting the religious character of the school in its day-to-day running.

When it comes to considering the employment rights of staff employed in faith schools, there is a clear tension between the interests of these schools as faith-based entities and the interests of teachers to enjoy employment free from discrimination. Faith schools may well have a desire to uphold their religious ethos by ensuring that staff share the school's religious culture and agree to promote its values. Moreover, it is arguable that faith schools have a right to impose such requirements, given that religious freedom encompasses a right to collective manifestation of religion.[18] Equally, however, teaching staff members have a right to be free from religious discrimination in employment, a right introduced in 2003 under the Employment Equality (Religion and Belief) Regulations and now included in the Equality Act 2010. The legislation covering employment rights for staff in faith schools has long involved a compromise between these two competing interests, even prior to 2003 when religious discrimination was not generally prohibited. A general rule prohibiting discrimination on grounds of religion was introduced for teaching staff in the Education Act 1944,[19] with limited exceptions for religious

17 *Azmi v. Kirklees Met. Borough Council* [2007] I.C.R. 1154, *R (on the application of Begum) v. Headteacher & Governors of Denbigh High School* [2006] UKHL 15, [2007] 1 A.C. 100.

18 Article 9(2) ECHR.

19 s 30 Education Act 1944.

schools. Thus, the compromise negotiated at the time when church schools were incorporated into the state sector was to protect staff from discrimination in community schools but allow some discrimination in voluntary aided and voluntary controlled faith schools.

This compromise is still reflected in the legislation relating to religious discrimination against teachers in state schools, the School Standards and Framework Act 1998 (SSFA). The SSFA protects teachers in non-faith schools from religious discrimination,[20] a provision now replicated by the general rules of the Equality Act 2010. The SSFA, however, provides more detailed provisions governing faith schools, reflecting a compromise that is much more favourable to faith school employers than is allowed to religious employers outside the education sector.

Under the SSFA, voluntary controlled and foundation faith schools can apply religious requirements on up to a fifth of their teachers, thus allowing schools to ensure that they have sufficient staff members sharing the religious ethos of the school to provide religious education and pastoral care. Voluntary aided faith schools, in contrast, can impose religious requirements on all teaching staff, whatever their duties. The different rules reflect the parties' different positions when the compromise was reached: greater funding offered by the churches for voluntary aided schools has led to greater autonomy over appointment of staff, including more freedom to require religious adherence. In the case of voluntary controlled schools, where more state funding is provided, the number of staff members who are required to share the faith of the school is more limited. The overall effect is that the finance and governance structures of the school determine the legal treatment of teachers, rather than the practised religious ethos.

Beyond the appointment of staff, the School Standards and Framework Act (SSFA) goes further in the case of voluntary aided schools and some faith-based academies.[21] Schools in this category can not only take account of religion in deciding who to employ but can also consider religious practice in deciding on promotion, remuneration or dismissal and, in other staffing decisions, whether staff attend religious worship and are willing to give religious education at the school. Further, voluntary aided faith schools can take account of any conduct that is 'incompatible with the precepts, or with the upholding of the tenets, of the religion' in deciding to terminate employment.[22]

The rules governing the employment practices of state faith schools can be contrasted with provisions governing other employers, including those with a religious ethos. In non-education contexts, religious employers are allowed a degree of freedom to reflect their religious ethos in their employment practices, but not an unfettered freedom. Under the Equality Act 2010 and in accordance

20 SSFA, s.59.

21 These schools are governed by similar rules to those governing voluntary aided faith schools, s 62 Education Act 2011.

22 S60(5)(b) School Standards and Framework Act 1998.

with the EU Equality Directive,[23] religious organisations are prohibited from discriminating against staff on grounds of religion unless belonging to a specific faith is an occupational requirement for a role. Thus, for example, a chaplain can be employed by a secular employer such as a prison or hospital and a requirement that he or she be Christian would be justified as a genuine occupational requirement of the job. Where the employer has a religious ethos, a slightly broader exception is allowed, in that the court can take the religious ethos into account in deciding whether the requirement is necessary. How this might work in the schools context can be illustrated by use of the case of *Glasgow City Council v McNab*,[24] in which a faith school imposed a religious requirement on staff. As the case arose in Scotland, the legal position was governed by the standard provisions covering religious discrimination in employment rather than by the SSFA;[25] it therefore serves as a useful example of how teachers might be protected in the absence of the SSFA. The case involved an atheist teacher in a voluntary controlled Catholic school who applied for a post as a pastoral care teacher but was not offered an interview. The legal question essentially was whether the post of pastoral care teacher was covered by the genuine occupational requirement exception to direct discrimination. The Tribunal found that, as the school was voluntary controlled, the employer was the local council, which does not have a religious ethos. It therefore applied the standard genuine occupational requirement provisions, which allow for discrimination on grounds of religion where religion is genuinely needed for the role. The Tribunal found that it was not essential that the holder of the post be Catholic as the responsibilities of the job involved giving advice on a large number of pastoral issues, only a few of which required knowledge of Catholic doctrine; moreover, those that did could be assigned to a different teacher. The case illustrates that, were the employment of school staff to be governed by the general rules in the Equality Act, the extent to which schools could impose religious requirements on staff would be significantly restricted as it might be difficult to convince a tribunal that being of a particular religion or belief is a genuine occupational requirement for teaching, it being rare for religion to be a defining element of the teacher's role, apart from where religious instruction is given.

McNab was decided on the basis that the employer (the local council, as the school was voluntary controlled) was not a religious ethos employer. Where the employer has a religious ethos, the rules allow for greater freedom to employers to require religious adherence: the occupational requirement must still be justified, but the religious ethos of organisations can be taken into account in making this judgment. In order to assess whether the requirement is justified, the employer will need to identify a legitimate aim for the religious requirement and the means for achieving

23 Directive 2000/78.

24 UKEAT/0037/06.

25 At the time the Employment Equality (Religion and Belief) Regulations 2003, now covered by the Equality Act 2010 Schedule 9.

that aim will need to be proportionate, taking into account its religious ethos. This will involve an assessment not only of the type of employment but also its religious context, such as the extent to which organisation is permeated by the particular religious ethos. So, for example, in the case of *Muhammed v The Leprosy Mission International*,[26] the Leprosy Mission (a Christian charity) was allowed to refuse applications from non-Christians because Christianity permeated the organisation, with, for example, prayers at the start of each day. Moreover, in assessing the proportionality of a religious requirement, the court balanced the fact that employing a non-Christian would have had a significant impact on the ability of the organisation to maintain its ethos, whereas, in contrast, a finance administrator who was refused a job would have the chance to work elsewhere: his job prospects were not significantly harmed in practice. One might expect that, had the facts been different, a different outcome would have been reached; for example, if the workplace had not been permeated by religion and the member of staff was going to face difficulty in finding other work, the court might not have been willing to find the religious requirement proportionate.

Applying this approach to the education context and in the light of the *McNab* decision, one might expect that a court would find the imposition of a religious requirement to be disproportionate in the case of most voluntary controlled schools. Even for voluntary aided schools, if the capacity of the school to reflect its ethos is not under threat or if the member of staff might find it difficult to find other work, religious requirements could be found to be disproportionate. Under the provisions of the SSFA, however, such questions are not considered. Instead, the legal regime governing employment in faith schools allows much greater latitude and discretion to the employer as there is no requirement that religious requirements be proportionate. This remains the case whether the employer has a religious ethos (that is, whether the school is voluntary aided or controlled), whether or not the school itself has a very strong religious culture in its day-to-day running and regardless of the impact of the requirement on the job prospects of teachers.

In effect, decisions to impose religious requirements on teaching staff are not fettered by any requirements of proportionality as long as the governance structure and land holdings mean that the school takes the legal form of a religious organisation. The rules governing the employment practices of state faith schools are thus significantly more restrictive to the freedom of religion of teachers than the rules governing employment in religious-ethos charities or other such organisations. Moreover, they apply to a sector that is almost entirely state-funded and covers up to a third of primary schools and an increasing number of secondary schools. Thus, the negotiation between religion and employment in faith schools has been concluded very differently from that between religion and faith-based employment more generally.

Restrictions on the employment of teaching staff have the capacity to significantly affect the career prospects of large numbers of staff members who are unable to

26 (16 Dec 2009, ET/2303459/09).

teach across the full range of state schools. Admittedly, although these rules are highly restrictive in legal terms, in practice they pose a lesser threat to the employment prospects of staff because schools often do not use the powers they are given under the legislation. Many voluntary aided and voluntary controlled schools are in practice extensively multicultural and many such schools do not require their teaching staff to be Christian. Several reasons for concern remain, however, regarding the outcome of the negotiation between religion and schools in this context. First, the number of faith schools is increasing, making rare cases more common overall. Second, while many schools employ large numbers of non-Christian teachers, the rules can cause particular difficulties when it comes to applying for headships, as faith schools tend to be particularly careful in ensuring their head teachers share the faith of the school. Third, the assumption that the rules are often not utilised may be incorrect: there is growing evidence that employment prospects of staff are more affected than has been recognised. The Accord Coalition has collated a range of testimonials from teaching staff demonstrating the impact that these rules can have on individual careers.[27] For example, one head teacher recounts having to resign from a Catholic school because he wished to remarry, contrary to the teaching of the Catholic Church. Another teacher recounts not being considered for posts in faith schools, despite a willingness to support the ethos of the school.

Furthermore, there is evidence that faith groups are increasingly willing to rely on these restrictions as the role of the Anglican Church in the provision of education continues its shift from one of service to one of mission.[28] Current strategies of the Church of England, the biggest provider of faith schooling, are to use church schools as a vehicle for outreach to the local communities in which the schools are situated, in order to provide an experience of Christianity and teach the Christian faith in an era when church attendance is falling.[29] This means that many within the church support the current legal position, despite the fact that it has the potential significantly to affect teachers' freedom of religion within the workplace as well as having an impact on career progression.

The role of 'negotiation'

It has been argued above that staff members who do not share the religion of faith schools may suffer some disadvantage in their careers. Of course, staff interests are not the only ones involved in the equation. Set against the non-discrimination interests of staff members are a number of other interests, not least those of parents

27 http://accordcoalition.org.uk/wp-content/uploads/2011/12/Personal-testimonies-2011-FINAL 1.pdf (accessed 29 July 2013).

28 See L. Vickers, 'Freedom of Religion and Belief and Employment in Faith Schools', *Religion and Human Rights* 4 (2009): 1–20.

29 See *The Way Ahead* (London: Church House Publishing, 2001); and *The Church School of the Future Review*, March 2012, Church of England Archbishop's Council Education Division and the National Society, (www.churchofengland.org/media/1418393/the%20church%20school%20of %20the%20future%20review%20-%20march%202012[1].pdf (accessed 29 July 2013).

to have choice as regards the education of children, religious freedom by religious bodies to provide education and the legally protected interest of parents to educate their children according to their religious beliefs.[30] It should be noted, however, that these competing rights are not absolute in nature and that the right to educate one's children in one's faith, or to offer faith-based education, does not comprise a right that such education be funded by the state nor that it be at the expense of the religious freedom of staff. It would seem then that there are no absolute rights in play when it comes to determining how much protection should be provided to the religious freedom of parents, religious organisations and teachers. Instead, to the extent that they conflict, these interests clearly need to be dealt with via some form of compromise or negotiation.

An element of negotiation regarding the role of religion in public life is reflected in the fact that, in international and European law, the right to religious freedom is a qualified one, which often requires balancing with other rights including the right to freedom from religion. In the context of the ECHR, article 9 provides an absolute right to freedom of religious belief, but the right to manifest religion is qualified and can be restricted when it is justified as proportionate and for a legitimate aim, such as protecting the rights of others. This allows for an element of compromise and negotiation between different, sometimes competing interests at the enforcement level.[31] Similarly, religion and belief is protected at work by the provisions of EU Directive 2000/78, which protects against discrimination on grounds of religion or belief. Although direct discrimination cannot be justified, where, because of the nature of the occupation or the context in which the work is carried out, a religion or belief constitutes a genuine occupational requirement for the job in question and it is proportionate to impose that requirement, any resulting discrimination will be lawful.[32] Indirect discrimination can be justified too where there is a legitimate aim for the requirement and the means of achieving the aim are appropriate and necessary.[33] Again, negotiation occurs at the enforcement level in this context, through the court assessment of the proportionality of any interference with religious equality.

Thus, legal frameworks covering religion and work both involve balancing competing rights to try to achieve a proportionate response. This process might alternatively be termed 'negotiating', 'reaching compromise', 'seeking concordance' or finding 'equilibrium', but, in each case, the different factors are reviewed and, as illustrated above in *Muhammed v. Leprosy Mission*, a finely graded assessment can be made as to how to balance competing interests. In effect, negotiation between the interests of religious employers and those of staff members occurs at enforce-

30 Article 2 Protocol 1 ECHR Right to education: No person shall be denied the right to education. In the exercise of any functions that it assumes in relation to education and to teaching, the State shall respect the right of parents to ensure such education and teaching in conformity with their own religious and philosophical convictions.

31 Hunter-Henin, 'Negotiating with religion' p. 193.

32 Equality Directive 2000/78 Article 4.

33 Article 2(2)(b).

ment level and is effected via the application of a proportionality test to any religious requirement imposed on staff.

In contrast, negotiation between the religious employer and the employee in the context of faith schools occurs at the preliminary stage at which the rule has been formulated,[34] leaving no discretion to those enforcing the rules and thus no space for compromise at enforcement level. Elements of compromise can be seen at the preliminary rule formulation level. For example, under the SSFA, voluntary aided schools, free schools and designated academies can discriminate against all teaching staff, but other schools' freedom to discriminate is limited to a fifth of staff. There is no negotiation at the enforcement stage, however: the rules that have been decided upon are not subject to a proportionality assessment.

Moreover, while there has clearly been some compromise at the rule formulation stage, the overall situation seems to be, at best, a very messy compromise, as the reduced discrimination in voluntary controlled schools does not appear to have a clear theoretical justification. It seems instead to be an attempt to lessen the burden on staff by limiting the impact of the rule in some schools. It could be argued that greater religious freedom should be allowed to schools with a stronger religious ethos (leaving aside debates over whether such freedom should be allowed within the state school system as a whole), but different treatment by the SSFA does not depend on the practical religiosity of the school, but instead on finance and governance structures. A better compromise would be to allow some negotiation at the enforcement stage, by way of a proportionality test, as is allowed in religious discrimination cases in contexts other than education.

The negotiation of religion in relation to education has been settled in a way that is unfavourable to teaching staff, compared with that reached for staff of other religious ethos employers. In seeking to understand why this is the case, it is worth considering the various voices that have contributed to the debate. It is suggested that the perspectives of all parties have not been adequately included, with the result that the compromise reached is not one of equilibrium or concordance. Instead the balance has been tilted in favour of religious actors who have been accorded access to state-funded education, whether as recipients or providers, that meets their religious requirements. Had teachers' voices been taken into account more clearly, the balance might have been tilted more evenly.

Voices in the negotiation

As referred to above, Christian churches have long been involved in the provision of education, predating the delivery of education by the state. However, the Anglican Church, the biggest faith school provider and biggest sponsor of academies,[35] has,

34 See Hunter-Henin, 'Negotiating with religion', this volume.

35 The Church of England claims to be the biggest provider of academies under the old scheme where academies needed to find sponsors, www.churchofengland.org/education/national-society/academies-%281%29.aspx (accessed 29 May 2012).

in recent years, become more explicit in its aim to use education as an opportunity to reach to a greater number and wider range of individuals with the Christian message. The Church of England's 2001 policy document, *The Way Ahead*,[36] states that 30 years ago, 'the emphasis was on the church's mission of service to the community, through education',[37] whereas the new policy notes that schools can provide churches with an opportunity to reach out to parents through the children attending its schools.

Concerning the employment of staff, *The Way Ahead* actively aims to encourage Christians to enter the teaching profession and suggests that ways need to be found to offer 'enhanced opportunities for Christians seeking Qualified Teacher Status', by offering additional qualifications for new entrants to work in church schools as well as developing training for head teachers. More recently, in the 2012 *Church School of the Future Review*,[38] there is no mention of teachers' rights in terms of non-discrimination. Indeed the only recommendation relating to staff in this review is to continue work on training and recruiting Christian teachers. The voice of the Anglican Church in questions of faith schooling has thus been firmly in favour of promoting faith schools, with questions of equality for staff of other faiths or no faith not part of the debate.

In contrast, the voice of teachers has been weaker. Unions and NGOs such as Accord have campaigned against religious discrimination against teachers in faith schools. Accord has catalogued examples of discrimination against staff members in faith schools,[39] but this voice does not seem to be heard as strongly as the concerns of parents regarding admission. Stories of parents attending church to get a place at a church school are commonplace in the media; narratives relating to discrimination against teachers are comparatively rare.

One might expect that the main voices in any negotiation over the role of staff members' religion in faith schools would be those of the school, the relevant religious organisation and the staff. In the context of faith schooling, however, the government also plays a very significant role. The provision of faith schools is supported by all main political parties. In the 2001 Labour Government's Green Paper, the Department for Education and Skills (DFES)[40] extolled the good record of faith schools in delivering high-quality education, in achieving good academic results and popularity with parents. It states: 'We therefore wish to welcome more schools provided by the churches and other major faith groups . . . where there is

36 Church House Publishing, London, 2001.

37 *Ibidem*, para 3.15.

38 *The Church School of the Future Review*, March 2012, Church of England Archbishop's Council Education, https://churchofengland.org/media/1417976/the%20church%20school%20of%20the%20future%20review%20-%20march%20%202012.pdf (accessed 2 July 2015).

39 http://accordcoalition.org.uk/wp-content/uploads/2011/12/Personal-testimonies-2011-FINAL1.pdf (accessed 29 May 2012).

40 The Department for Education and Skills, replaced by the Department for Children, Schools and Families in 2007.

a clear local demand from parents and the community.'[41] This approach is carried forward in current government policy, with the introduction of a programme of free schools and academies, many of which are faith based.

Has 'negotiation with religion' reached a fair compromise for staff?

In attempting to negotiate a fair balance, there are two obvious interests to address: faith organisations and staff. On the part of faith groups, involvement in state education provides an immense opportunity for outreach and it is unsurprising that some are keen to exploit the opportunities available. Viewed from the perspective of members of the teaching profession, however, such a strategy may be more problematic as it may significantly curtail the freedom of teachers who do not share the faith of the majority of faith schools to develop their careers across the full range of state-funded schools.

The factor that seems to set education apart from other religious settings is the role of the state in negotiations. This seems to have tipped the balance firmly towards the interests of religious actors over those of teaching staff by providing a legal environment that is more favourable to church schools than strictly allowed in EU law, which requires that any religious requirements imposed by religious employers be for a legitimate aim and proportionate. An assessment of the reasons for the approach taken to religious education by the main political parties lies beyond the scope of this chapter, but it is undoubtedly the case that religious education retains cross-party support, with little political debate about the impact that this has on the religious freedom of staff.

What the case of teachers in faith schools shows is that negotiation between rights and interests can be an effective process for reaching a fair compromise, but only if the relevant parties have an appropriate part in the negotiation. In the context of religious schooling, this means a greater voice for teaching staff and, perhaps, a reduced voice for the state, which arguably should be a neutral broker between different interests. In practical terms, any rebalancing of the settlement between religious schools and their staff would involve ensuring that some negotiation at the enforcement stage be permitted. This would allow the consequences of any solution for the individual to be taken into account.[42] How this might work in the schools context is considered below.

How might the settlement be renegotiated?

There is a strong legal basis for arguing that the current settlement regarding legal protection for teachers with respect to their religious freedom at work requires renegotiation. The lack of a proportionality test in the SSFA raises the question

41 *Building on Success in Schools* (London: DFES, 2001) p. 48.
42 Hunter-Henin, 'Negotiating with religion', this volume, p. 193.

of whether its provisions are compatible with the requirements of the Employment Equality Directive 2000/78. The Directive provides a general exception to discrimination where there is a genuine occupational requirement, where it serves a legitimate aim and the discrimination is proportionate to that aim. There are broader exceptions where the employer is a religious organisation, to allow for the maintenance of a religious ethos, permitting employers to demand loyalty from staff to that ethos. While exceptions to the non-discrimination principle can be acceptable within the Directive, therefore, the provisions of the SSFA are so broad that they may well not comply with the requirement in article 4 that exceptions be legitimate and justified. The failure of the SSFA to include a proviso that any religious discrimination in schools must be proportionate may make the protection of the SSFA incompatible with that provided for in the Directive.

If the provisions of the SSFA that allow discrimination against teachers on grounds of religion and belief were to be made subject to a requirement of proportionality, this would not only meet the objection that the current provisions fail to correctly implement the Directive, but also allow for a balance to be struck between the competing interests at stake. The introduction of a proportionality test would permit an assessment to be made at enforcement level as to how an appropriate balance should be maintained between upholding the rights of faith schools to maintain their religious ethos and of teachers to pursue their careers free from religious discrimination. It would enable each case to be considered at a local level, rather than determining, in advance and at the rule formulation stage, that discrimination against the teacher is always acceptable.

In effect, negotiation at the enforcement stage involves a balancing approach, performed by the imposition of a proportionality test. This is a more individualised approach and so it enables more individualised negotiation. The operation of the proportionality approach in the context of religion and schools can be seen in two cases involving religious dress in schools, one on the part of staff, one on the part of a pupil. These cases may serve as an example of how proportionality could apply in the faith school context.

The first case, *Azmi v. Kirklees Metropolitan Borough Council*,[43] involved a Muslim teaching assistant who wanted to wear the *niqab*[44] when in the presence of male colleagues.[45] The school was not prepared to allow her to wear the *niqab* when assisting in class.[46] In her subsequent discrimination claim, the court accepted that there was prima facie indirect discrimination,[47] but that the indirect discrimination was justified as the restriction on wearing the *niqab* was proportionate given the need to uphold the interests of the children in having the best possible education,

43 *Azmi v. Kirklees Met. Borough Council* [2007] I.C.R. 1154.

44 A niqab is a face covering for women that veils the face and hair down to the shoulders, with a small opening for the eyes.

45 Azmi, at 1157.

46 *Azmi* at 1161.

47 Since the refusal to allow Azmi to wear the niqab put her at a particular disadvantage when compared with others.

as the face covering was said to limit essential non-verbal communication. In applying the proportionality test at the local level, the court noted[48] that the school had investigated the situation before reaching the conclusion that the restriction was necessary and it was not possible to accommodate her request without harming the interests of the children. The *Azmi* case illustrates that proportionality requires careful review of the facts and circumstances of the case on the ground, rather than the imposition of a rule negotiated above the local level. It is noteworthy that, in *Azmi*, the school – coincidentally a voluntary controlled Church of England school – was prepared for her to wear religious dress such as a headscarf in class and for her to wear the *niqab* in the school. She was only prohibited from wearing the niqab when assisting in class. Had the school sought to ban such religious symbols in all parts of the school there is every indication that the court would have found this to be disproportionate. It would certainly have required very clear justifications that were relevant to the precise case before the court.

A similarly detailed approach at local level can be seen in *R (on the application of Begum) v. Headteacher and Governors of Denbigh High School.*[49] The case involved a pupil's refusal to wear the agreed school uniform, requesting instead to wear a *jilbab*.[50] In deciding that the school's decision to enforce the school uniform was proportionate, the court again undertook a careful review of the circumstances of the case. For example, the school had worked hard to promote harmony between the different races, religions and cultures represented in the school and the uniform (which already accommodated common Islamic dress[51]) was viewed as necessary to combat conflict between pupils and the development of sub-groups identified by dress.[52] As with *Azmi*, the court recognised that the school had undertaken detailed discussion, including consultation with local religious leaders, in reaching its decision.[53]

Of course, when decisions are taken at local level, it will always be arguable that a different court could have reached a different conclusion.[54] However, the courts' use of fact-based decision-making at the enforcement stage in both *Azmi* and *Begum* allowed for a more contextual and sensitive decision and arguably a fair compromise to be reached.

If a similar proportionality-based assessment were to be undertaken in the context of discrimination against staff, the outcome would be quite different to that arrived at under the current legal settlement. A proportionality approach taken at enforcement level would entail considering the facts and circumstances of the

48 *Azmi* at 1172.

49 *R (on the application of Begum) v. Headteacher & Governors of Denbigh High Sch*ool, [2006] UKHL 15.

50 A loose fitting garment that hides the contours of the body, worn by some Muslim women.

51 The uniform allowed for a *salwar kameez*, a sleeveless smock-like dress with the loose trousers, to be worn.

52 *Begum* at [18].

53 *Begum* at [33].

54 See Hunter-Henin, 'Negotiating with religion', this volume, p. 193; and S. Mancini, 'The Power of Symbols and Symbols as Power: Secularism and Religion as Guarantors of Cultural Convergence', *Cardozo L. Rev* 30 (2009): 2629; 2654 for criticism of the *Begum* decision.

individual case. A number of factors might be relevant. For example, a court could consider whether there were other options available for a teacher to work or look for promotion elsewhere. Where there is only one religious school among several others in a particular location, such as a city, the practical effect of discrimination by an employer may differ from where a faith school is the only maintained school in a locality or where a large proportion of schools in an area are faith schools. The consideration of proportionality might also involve an assessment of an individual school's actual ethos, based on current practice, rather than basing the employment rights of teachers on the constitutional and governance arrangements of the school. It might also mean that, as in the *McNab* case, while a religious requirement on teachers in religious roles could be proportionate, a requirement imposed on all staff would not be.

Thus, such a proportionality approach might allow for a settlement to be negotiated that achieves more equilibrium between the competing interests at stake. It might also allow for a more radical renegotiation of the settlement for teachers in faith schools, as the state may not be afforded such a strong voice in the debate. The current position, where negotiation has occurred at the rule formulation stage, has given a significant voice to the state, such that a compromise has been reached between the church and faith groups at the expense of the employment rights of staff. Given that these schools are almost entirely publicly funded, such a settlement is arguably inappropriate. Allowing a proportionality approach implemented at enforcement level would allow for local voices and local conditions to be taken into account and a better balance to be struck.

Renegotiating religion

The current settlement for staff in faith schools in England looks set to remain, particularly while government continues to enjoy its current position in the negotiation room, with its policy of promoting the free school and academy programme, which involves increasing the number of faith schools. The European Commission recently investigated on a complaint against the UK government that the law governing religious discrimination against teachers in faith schools is in breach of European equality law.[55] The intervention of the European Commission as a new party to the negotiations might have might have meant the entry of a new voice as part of the negotiation, with the hope that a fairer compromise could be reached in future. However, the European Commission found that on a narrow

55 British Humanist Association News: 'European Commission to investigate whether 'faith' schools break European employment laws' https://humanism.org.uk/2012/07/24/news-1084/(accessed 30 July 13). See also answer by the Parliamentary Under-Secretary of State for Schools (Lord Nash) to a Parliamentary Question from Lord Laird, in which the Government refers to an invitation by the European Commission for it to submit observations on the compatibility of Section 60 of the School Standards and Framework Act 1998 and the European Union Council Directive 2000/78/EC. Hansard 3 Jun 2013: Column WA144, www.publications.parliament.uk/pa/ld201314/ldhansrd/text/130603w0002.htm (accessed 30 July 2013).

interpretation, limited to ensure the maintenance of the religious character of the school, the SSFA, is in line with article 4 of the Directive.[56] This suggests that the current settlement is set to continue for the foreseeable future.

The position of English faith schools serves as useful illustration of the relationship between the religious and the secular more generally. The current compromise reached between religions and the state in the context of faith schooling have emerged from a long history of negotiation between religion and secularity in both education and more generally. This discussion of the contemporary debate in England in the particular context of education demonstrates that this negotiation is ongoing. It has been suggested that the current settlement is disadvantageous for many and that this has occurred because the negotiation has taken place with too much weight given to the voice of the state at the preliminary rule formulation stage. A more appropriate settlement would be achieved if the negotiation between different interests could occur at a local enforcement level, with greater participation by a wider range of relevant voices.

References

Building on Success in Schools (London: DFES, 2001).

The Church School of the Future Review (Church of England Archbishop's Council Education, March 2012).

Harte, J.C.D. 'The Development of the Law of Employment and Education', in Hill, M. *Religious Liberty and Human Rights* (Cardiff: University of Wales Press, 2002), 159–94.

Mancini, S. 'The Power of Symbols and Symbols as Power: Secularism and Religion as Guarantors of Cultural Convergence', *Cardozo Law Review* 30 (2009) 26–9.

Petchey, P. 'Legal Issues for Faith Schools in England and Wales', *Ecclesiastical Law Journal* (2008) 174.

Rivers, J. *The Law of Organized Religions: Between Establishment and Secularism* (Oxford: Oxford University Press, 2010).

Vickers, L. 'Religion and Belief Discrimination and the Employment of Teachers in Faith Schools', *Religion and Human Rights* 4 (2009) 1–20.

Voas, D. and Watt, L. *The Church Growth Research Programme Report on Strands 1 and 2 Numerical Change in Church Attendance: National, Local and Individual Factors* (Essex: Institute for Social and Economic Research, 2014). www.churchgrowthresearch.org.uk/progress_findings_reports (accessed 7 May 2014).

The Way Ahead (London: Church House, 2001).

56 See https://humanism.org.uk/wp-content/uploads/EU-Pilot-3800-12-JUST.pdf (accessed 30 July 2013).

14 Regulating religious diversity in liberal societies

Maleiha Malik

Introduction

Negotiation is an illuminating lens through which to understand contemporary debates about religious diversity in liberal societies. There are risks in what Lee refers to in the introduction to this volume as 'triumphalist' negotiation by secularists 'around' religion that marginalises its significance as well as 'constructive engagement' with religious authorities that leave unequal distributions of power unchallenged. Nevertheless, as the contributions in this volume make clear, a focus on negotiation can widen analysis in productive ways.

Negotiating religion, then, provides a valuable contribution to our thinking about religious diversity in Western liberal democracies. Yet, in the context of law, negotiation may fail to capture the significance of human rights and constitutional law that is 'non-negotiable' despite the pressures to accommodate religious diversity. Regulation is an established robust inter-disciplinary concept that includes forms of negotiation. Regulation has some of the advantages of negotiation because it allows an analysis of religion across various disciplines, such as law, as well as the social sciences and humanities. Regulation may include formal and informal negotiation, but it can also include techniques – such as criminal law, constitutional law and non-negotiable human rights governance – that unilaterally impose a clear bright line standard on all citizens including the religious.

Definitions of what regulation is or is not remain controversial. Julia Black proposes a definition that is especially helpful in the context of religion because it focuses on the use of authority to influence behaviour. Black concludes that regulation can be understood as 'the intentional use of authority to affect behaviour of a different party according to set standards, involving instruments of information-gathering and behaviour modification'.[1]

A focus on regulation is useful in discussion of religious diversity because it maintains absolute standards where necessary, but it also challenges the common assumptions that state law is the only source for articulating collective goals and

1 Quoted in Robert Baldwin, Martin Cave and Martin Lodge, 'Introduction: Regulation – The Field and Developing Agenda', in Robert Baldwin, Martin Cave and Martin Lodge, eds *The Oxford Handbook of Regulation* (Oxford: Oxford University Press, 2010) at page 12.

permissible standards, thereby widening the analysis to include multinational commercial organisations or civil society that may be a source of positive and negative social control. This shift, in turn, encourages an enquiry into the extent to which the state has the power to control religious diversity where it is emerging in sites in the private, public or civil society spheres such as in religious tribunals. One technique for state regulation of religious diversity is the Public Sector Equality Duty (PSED) that was introduced by the Equality Act 2010 and that is a useful tool for negotiating conflicts, frictions and tensions resulting from religious diversity. A further advantage is that this approach allows us to think about how non-legal techniques such as negotiation or mediation may have a role in managing religious diversity in international relations, national security as well as social and economic policy.

The challenge of religious diversity

Religious diversity is a social fact in most European liberal democracies.While it is true that there has always been significant religious diversity, the present context is different in significant respects. The experience of immigration is not new, but the scale and intensity of the global movement of people in large numbers has become more intense. The increasing presence of non-Western communities expands the 'geographical reach' of religious and cultural practices that originate in the Middle East, Africa or South Asia. Judges and decision-makers in family law disputes, for example, have already started to accept that they will have to formulate legal and policy responses to a wide range of religious practices, often with very little knowledge or experience.[2]

There have been significant changes in the nature of the state's response to cultural and religious diversity that are a helpful comparison with contemporary concerns. During earlier historical periods, it was not problematic that state law and policy was openly hostile towards some minorities such as Jews. The reformations of the sixteenth century that shattered the unity of Western Christendom raised challenges about how the state, but also individuals, should relate to those who are of a different faith. The discourse of 'tolerance' and 'intolerance' in European thought that emerged at this time was focused on religious difference. Yet, as Ben Kaplan notes, this narrative of European tolerance is often a myth rather than reality.[3]

One aspect of the myth is the assumption of a continuous story of progress in which the past religious intolerance is replaced by the Enlightenment values of

2 *Office of the Head of International Family Justice for England and 2012 Annual Report, 1 January – 31 December 2012* (London; Judiciary of England and Wales, 2012). See, for example, the range of jurisdictions, religions and cultures from Pakistan and South Asia, Africa and the Middle East involved in family law cases because of globalisation, increasing movement of persons across borders, and the ever-rising number of family units which are truly international.

3 Benjamin J. Kaplan, *Divided by Faith: Religious Conflict and the Practice of Toleration in Early Modern Europe* (Cambridge, MA: Harvard University Press, 2007) at page 6.

freedom, reason and equality that bequeaths modern constitutionalism and human rights. It may also suggest that those communities or societies that have not followed this path from religion to Enlightenment are not as evolved as Europeans. These insights may also be useful to evaluate state policy to tackle religious extremism that have been have been conducted against a background of the increased securitisation of state policies towards British Muslims and those politicians who want to present themselves as the 'champions' of Enlightenment values of tolerance[4] and gender equality[5] and fighting the 'irrational' forces of religious extremism.[6]

As well dispelling myths about tolerance, which help to separate the uses from the abuses of tolerance in the modern context, Kaplan provides a useful framework for a more complex understanding of the history of religious tolerance that may have relevance in the present. Kaplan notes that tolerance was not just an issue for ruling elites but it was also a form of behaviour and a social practice that can be understood as a form of interaction between people of different faiths. As Kaplan notes, this process had a complex relationship with the ideal and official policies. Those who did the tolerating made powerful claims about the truth of their religion and the false deviant character of the claims of others. In early modern Europe, there were a few people who were at the extremes such as those with no animosity and those who were willing to kill for a religious dispute. Nevertheless, Kaplan concludes that the vast majority of people were bound to live in communities that were religiously mixed. Peaceful co-existence was often punctuated by conflict. There were, not surprisingly, an elaborate set of arrangements and accommodations for people of opposing faiths to live together peacefully, given how deeply religion was integrated into the social, cultural and political life of early modern communities.

Kaplan also points out that tolerance was not an acceptance of religious diversity as it is sometimes understood in its modern use but it was, rather, a more grudging move that was a practical acceptance of an unpleasant reality.[7] From this perspective, tolerance was more a necessity that was required by the social fact of living in mixed religious communities rather than a freely chosen personal virtue. Kaplan's analysis provides important insights for the contemporary analysis of the regulation of religious diversity that results from migration. Liberal constitutionalism and human rights analysis gives priority to freedom and choice. Yet, for many citizens the religious diversity that they confront in their daily lives and in their

4 Wendy Brown, *Regulating Aversion: Tolerance in the Age of Identity and Empire* (Princeton, NJ: Princeton University Press, 2006).

5 For a discussion of the way in which Enlightenment values can become a weapon with which to attack minorities see Anne Phillips, *Multiculturalism without Culture* (Princeton, NJ: Princeton University Press, 2007). Phillips notes the way in which 'principles of gender equality were being deployed as part of the demonization of minority cultural groups' (at page 2).

6 Brown, *Regulating Aversion: Tolerance in the Age of Identity and Empire.* See chapters 1–4.

7 Ibid. at page 8.

communities is no longer a matter of choice.[8] The language of freedom and choice fails to understand that, for some, religious diversity is an 'unpleasant' social fact of their reality and daily lives rather than an active choice. In the international context, it is not difficult to see how Kaplan's summary of the myth of tolerance encourages a focus on non-European societies as a unique site for religious intolerance that requires the export of 'our' European values to solve intractable problems of religious conflict in 'their' societies. The relationship between religious freedom as a domestic guarantee of tolerance for religious minorities and the international context is complex, [9] and it is becoming increasingly significant in the European context because following the example of the USA the European Union has recently followed linked its external foreign policy to the goal of promoting religious freedom in non-European societies.[10]

Regulating religious diversity in liberal democracies

Regulating religious diversity in liberal societies requires a framework that differentiates between contexts – such as international and domestic or public and private – but also explores the relationship between them. As a starting point, the promotion of 'religious freedom' as a foreign policy goal linked to wider international and geopolitical factors or the lobbying of missionary groups seeking new contexts for proselytising should be clearly distinguished from the individual human right to religion and belief that is entrenched in domestic, regional and international constitutional and human rights instruments.[11] Next, an individual right to freedom of religion and belief, in turn, should be distinguished from claims about 'equality' and non-discrimination on the grounds of religion and belief in employment, education, housing as well as the delivery of private goods and services

8 Judith Butler, 'Is Judaism Zionism?', in *In the Power of Religion in the Public Sphere*, ed. Eduardo Mendieta; Jonathan Vanantwepen (New York: Columbia University Press, 2011). See page 83 where Butler commenting on Arendt's analysis of Eichmann states:

> According to Arendt, Eichmann and his superiors might choose with whom to cohabit the earth and failed to realise that the hetereogeneity of the earth's population is an irreversible condition of social and political life. The accusation bespeaks a firm conviction that none of us should be in the position of making such a choice, that those with whom we cohabit the earth are given to us, prior to choice, and so prior to any social or political contracts we might enter through deliberate volition. In fact, if we seek to make a choice where there is no choice, we are trying to destroy the conditions of our social and poltiical life.

9 Saba Mahmood, 'Religious Freedom, Minority Rights and Geopolitics', *Comparative Studies in Society and History* 54, 2 (2012).

10 Pasquale Annicchino, 'Freedom of Religion or Belief in the Foreign Policy of the European Union, Much Ado About Nothing', in *Religion and Civil Society: The Changing Faces of Religion and Secularity*, eds R. Alvira and M.A. Glendon (2014).

11 Pasquale Annicchino, 'Is the European Union Going Deep on Democracy and Religious Freedom', in *Working Paper for European University Institute – Robert Schuman Centre for Advanced Studies (RSCAS)* (2014–15).

that is a requirement of EU and domestic discrimination law. Once these distinctions are in place, it is also important to explore overlaps. One example of an overlap was the UK's sharia law debate, in which the 'War on Terror' provided a crucial media frame for UK domestic controversy following Archbishop Rowan Williams' comments about sharia law.[12]

A focus on 'hard law' would cause us to miss the way in which a wider set of EU 'soft law' policy in areas such as immigration or security is having an impact on religious freedom.[13] Many issues that are important to how liberal societies interfere with religious diversity cannot be easily understood within a traditional doctrinal analysis of legislation or case law. For example, in the UK, some of the most controversial issues concerning religion have been about policies such as the Prevent strategy that is part of counter-terrorism work that are delivered through surveillance by security agencies and funding of local groups by the Home Office.[14] Policies such as Prevent are not strictly a legal interference with religious freedom but they have significant implications for religious freedom, especially freedom of speech and associational rights, of British Muslims.[15] Most recently, it has been alleged in the 'Trojan Horse' controversy that extremist Muslims had used 'entrist' tactics to introduce gender segregation in Birmingham schools[16]

'Regulation', then, is helpful because it encourages analysis of 'soft' and vertical forms of exercising power over religion. Nevertheless, despite this welcome widening of the focus for analysis, constitutional and human rights law remain crucial techniques for regulation. Regulation entails the idea that the state can consciously use techniques that introduce rules and establish systems of control to influence socially valuable behaviour such as religion, but which may have beneficial or adverse side effects. Constitutional and human rights law provide a powerful mechanism for both the exercise of power and influence by the state (constitutional law) but also as a form for the control of the power of the nation state (regional human rights document such as the European Convention on Human Rights). Constitutional and human rights law sets the most clear and powerful message for the standard that needs to be met both in terms of freedom of religion as a positive value but also in terms of how to manage the negative consequences of religion.

In the UK, recent high profile cases on freedom of religion demonstrate when religious diversity may be accommodated, compared with situations where constitutional and human rights as a standard setting technique cannot be

12 Moore, K., Mason, P. and Lewis, J. M. W. 'Images of Islam in the UK: The Representation of British Muslims in the National Print News Media 2000–2008', in *Working Paper*. Cardiff: Cardiff University, 2008, 5–10.

13 Ronan McCrea, *Religion and the Public Order of the European Union* (Oxford University Press, 2010).

14 'Prevent Strategy UK Cmnd, 8092', in *Presented to Parliament by the Secretary of State for the Home Department by Command of Her Majesty* (June 2011); ibid.

15 Arun Kundnani, *The End of Tolerance: Racism in 21st Century Britain* (London: Pluto Press, 2007).

16 For reports see: Richard Adams, 'Governors of New Academies and Free Schools Told to Abide By "British Values"', *Guardian*, 19 June 2014.

negotiated.[17] In *Eweida v British Airways* a Christian employee of British Airways claimed that the BA dress code requiring personal jewellery to be concealed discriminated against her as a Christian because it did not allow her to wear a cross that was visible to the public. Ms Eweida lost in the UK Court of Appeal but the European Court of Human Rights (Eur. Ct. H. R.) held in favour of Ms Eweida by finding that British Airways should and could have accommodated her request to wear her cross with her uniform. In *Ladele v London Borough of Islington* a Christian registrar of marriages argued that a requirement to conduct a same-sex civil ceremony was a breach of her right to freedom of religion under article 9 of the European Convention on Human Rights; and also that this was religious discrimination under the Employment Equality (Religion or Belief) Regulations 2003. Ms Ladele won in the first instance in the Industrial Tribunal. She lost in the Employment Appeals Tribunal, the Court of Appeal and the Eur. Ct. H. R.

One way of framing the issue is to recognise that some religious viewpoints towards women, gays and lesbians are not compatible with the legal and institutional arrangements within which liberal constitutionalism operates, which now include constitutional and human rights commitments to equality for gays and lesbians. We now treat equality for women, gays and lesbians as an important constitutional standard that requires special protection.[18] Once it is clear that Ms Ladele is asking for an exemption from these common values, it also becomes clear that a liberal state is justified in refusing to extend accommodation to this practice.

It is often argued that there should be 'accommodation' of the religious conscience of, in these cases, Ms Ladele by allowing her to claim an exemption based on religion and belief. However, if we recall that a crucial function of constitutional and human rights law in the regulation of religious diversity is to maintain standards, then 'accommodation' in this context remains problematic because the right to same-sex civil partnership and the right to equality on the grounds of sexual orientation are constitutional matters. Ms Ladele was claiming an exemption from a general constitutional standard that is communicated in constitutional, human rights and discrimination law. Even if the accommodation could be efficiently administered so that the gay couple received exactly the same service in practice, there would be a problem because the accommodation contradicts the 'expressive' message of equality for gays and lesbians. In this context, constitutional and human rights standards perform an expressive function of passing information between the citizen and the state. This line of reasoning underlies a recent decision of the Court of Appeal of Saskatchewan, Canada that considered legislative exemptions for marriage registrars who did not want to perform same-sex ceremonies.[19] Although an identical service would have been

17 *Case of Eweida and Others V the United Kingdom App Nos 48420/10, 59842/10, 51671/10 and 36516/10*, (decisions of 15 January 2013).

18 Raymond Plant, 'Religion in a Liberal State', in *Religion in a Liberal State*, eds Malcolm Evans Gavin D'Costa, Tariq Modood and Julian Rivers (Cambridge: Cambridge University Press, 2013), 9–15.

19 *Marriage Commissioners Appointed under the Marriage Act (Re)*, 2011 SKCA 3.

provided to same-sex couples, it was held that there would still be a detriment for same-sex couples and a breach of their constitutional right to equality because it would undermine the expressive value of equality guarantees for gays and lesbians because the negative effects would 'ripple' out beyond the individual case to the wider community.[20]

The expressive function of equality for gays and lesbians helps to explain the recent decisions of the European Court of Human Rights in relation to religious freedom in *Eweida* and *Ladele*. *Eweida* type accommodation of religious symbols, dress codes or religious holidays may require some balancing with other interests such as business efficiency or the need to maintain a uniform in the workplace or schools. However, reasonable accommodation of religion in *Eweida* does not have any impact on constitutional rights or another person or dilute the general standard of equal treatment of gays and lesbians. On this analysis, the decision in *Eweida* that allows her to wear a cross is correct because there is no evidence of coercion of others and because religious freedom can be secured without causing a significant harm to others, including harm to their dignity because of the expressive function of same-sex discrimination law.[21]

By way of contrast to *Eweida*, the decision of the Eur. Ct. H. R. did not grant Ms Ladele an accommodation from the requirement to perform a same-sex civil partnership. Ms Ladele was already working as a marriage registrar in Islington before the introduction of the Civil Partnership Act 2004 made this a difficult case to adjudicate. The decision in *Ladele* is correct law and politics. There should be no accommodation for the religious where the exemption is from a key constitutional or human right such as the right to equality for gays and that has now become a quasi-constitutional standard providing a normative standard to guide the regulation of religious diversity.[22] This is of particular importance in *Ladele* because she is a public service who is providing a service (marriage) that can only be provided by the state. In these circumstances, individuals cannot expect to directly influence public services so that they conform to their personal religious beliefs, especially where the accommodation requires that they are exempt from a core value such as equality for gays and lesbians.

In extremis, then, where there is a stand off that results in human rights litigation, as in *Ladele*, liberal values can be enforced through constitutional, human rights and discrimination law as absolute standards for all citizens irrespective of their religious belief without the possibility of negotiation. Yet, at the same time, there is a need to allow those who are religious to be able to participate fully in the workplace and in public life. There is therefore a need to design a system that

20 Ibid., para 94.

21 For a recent decision that relies on this expressive function see decision that a bakery's refusal to bake a cake with a same-sex marriage slogan was prohibited same-sex discrimination in the provision of goods and services, see *Gareth Lee v Ashers Baking Co.* [2015] NICty 2 (Northern Ireland County Court).

22 Robert Wintemute, 'Accommodating Religious Beliefs: Harm, Clothing or Symbols and Refusals to Serve Others', *Modern Law Review*, no. 77.

is able to regulate and balance this range of concerns, through a mixture of legal and non-legal techniques. Even in situations such as *Ladele* it may be possible to use 'softer' forms of regulation that encourage negotiation between the actors rather than an 'all or nothing' dispute. It may be possible to design better training and management in the workplace to prevent disputes (for example, between religious conscience and sexual orientation equality) from becoming acrimonious. In the UK, for example, one example of a non-legal form of regulation of conflicts between religion and same-sex equality that encourages a softer 'negotiation based' approach is the main statutory workplace arbitration service (ACAS), which has issued guidelines about how employers can reconcile their responsibilities to safeguard non-discrimination on the grounds of religion and belief as well as sexual orientation.[23]

One advantage of using these softer techniques of regulation is that they avoid the 'winner–loser' consequences of litigation. They also permit those who have religious objections to same-sex marriage as well as gays and lesbians (and others) to communicate, collaborate and work together. The workplace is a practical context in which very many employees have no choice but to co-operate together. Within this context, constitutional, human rights and discrimination law provide limits on conduct that breaches principles of equality for gays and lesbians but it is still important to maintain a general level of tolerance towards those who are religious so that they can express their religious belief. Of course, where speech becomes a course of conduct that constitutes harassment, it is regulated and prohibited. Moreover, the freedom to state one's beliefs is legitimately more limited in the workplace, where the interests of protecting employees may justify curtailing the free speech of religious people who do not believe in equality for women, gays or lesbians. There may also be good arguments to regulate the speech of religious individuals who represent the state while they hold public office. Their private religious beliefs may, in some contexts, also be a public expression that is not compatible with their public role because it undermines the wider public commitment to equality and non-discrimination for women, gays and lesbians. However, this need not necessarily exclude the whole of the viewpoint of those who object to same-sex partnerships. In such cases, the speech–conduct distinction becomes crucial. Those with strong religious beliefs about women, gays and lesbians can hold that view; they may even appropriately express that view; but they cannot act on that view in a way that constitutes discriminatory harassment (through their speech) or discriminatory acts (through their conduct). It may sometimes be necessary to be more robust in confirming that in this situation the religious have a right to freedom of speech and belief although this may be limited if they are holding a public office or undertaking an official act.

So, Ms Ladele can believe that same-sex marriage is wrong and within limits she can even express that viewpoint. However, she cannot act on those beliefs in

23 B. Savage, *Sexual Orientation and Religion or Belief Discrimination in the Workplace* (London: ACAS, 2007); ibid.

certain spheres that we consider important areas in which law safeguards equality for gays and lesbians. In this sense, constitutional, human rights and discrimination law provides the overall framework within which the daily practical interactions of all the employees, religious employees who oppose same-sex marriage as well as gays, lesbians and all those who support such unions, must take place.

As Kaplan notes in relation to the practices of toleration in the early modern period, these practical contexts cannot be understood as a choice but, rather, they are a necessity. In addition, the actual participants who have to share the workplace need to create a joint practice that can include not only protected groups such as gays and lesbians but also those who are religious. In many situations the willingness of employees with differing points of view to work together may be described as a practical self-interpreted modus vivendi rather than a genuine conversion to the values of the other. Setting limits on legal intervention so that law focuses on the most extreme forms of speech that constitute harassment rather than seeking to control all forms of expression of those who have a religious but illiberal point of view is important in this context because there is a compelling interest in allowing the workplace and other spheres to be contexts in which individuals can meet and enter into robust discussions with those with a different point of view. The workplace is one forum where those who are religious opposing same-sex equality can come into contact with a different viewpoint as well interact with gays and lesbians. As Andrew Koppelman argues, there is a joint interest in allowing sufficient dialogue between religious people and gays and lesbians so that both sides can understand, challenge and reconsider what seem to be entrenched viewpoints.[24]

As well as the workplace, public funded institutions such as hospitals and schools are another context in which the religious and non-religious can come together to develop shared social practices of tolerance. The Equality Act 2010 has already put into place a legal structure that can encourage dialogue, negotiation and joint practices of tolerance by extending the harmonised Public Sector Equality Duty (PSED) to religion and belief. The PSED promotes equality and non-discrimination in the provision of public services part of the Equality Act 2010 but the Coalition Government put it under review as part of its 'red tape challenge'. The independent review of the PSED reported and made recommendations for improvement, although there was disagreement about whether or not the PSED was operating as intended.[25]

The PSED was first designed and implemented in Northern Ireland to reconcile Protestant and Catholic communities as part of the peace efforts and a recent review confirms that although there is room for improvement it has made an important contribution to those goals.[26] In the UK, the PSED was first introduced

24 Andrew Koppelman, 'You Can't Hurry Love: Why Antidiscrimination Protections for Gay People Should Have Religious Exemptions', *Brooklyn Law Review*, no. 72 (2006).

25 GEO, *The Independent Steering Group's Report of the Public Sector Equality Duty (Psed) Review and Government Response*. (London: Government Equalities Office, 6 September 2013).

26 Equality Commission for Northern Ireland, *Keeping It Effective: Reviewing the Effectiveness of Section 75 of the Northern Ireland Act 1998 – Final Report November 2008* (Belfast: Equality Commission for Northern Ireland, November 2008).

by the Race Relations (Amendment) Act 2000 requiring public bodies to take proactive steps to achieve racial equality. Duties covering disability and gender were subsequently introduced in the Equality Act 2006. The PSED has now been extended in a harmonised way across all the equality grounds of race, gender and disability as well as religion and belief, sexual orientation and age.

The inclusion of religion and belief within the PSED structure could provide a unique opportunity to consult widely with religious as well as non-religious community based groups as part of the design of public policies to ensure that potential conflicts are minimised or resolved before they become entrenched. This is an example of the benefits of negotiation that have been developed in this volume, as well as a proactive promotion of equality that can prevent conflicts leading to costly litigation and tensions in community relations. Moreover, a harmonised PSED that extends not only to race and gender but also religion and belief, sexual orientation, disability and age has the potential to ensure that less powerful groups within religious or racial minorities – e.g. women, lesbian, gay, bisexual and transgender people, persons with disability as well as the young and elderly – are consulted as part of the process of public consultation prior to the design of public services. The PSED requires public authorities to gather baseline evidence on discrimination and equality across a wide range of their functions. It provides a legal and policy mechanism for negotiation, monitoring, consultation and training that has the potential to cover all discrimination grounds. This allows the development of public services that are more appropriate for their users, potentially taking into account any tensions and conflicts between groups before policy decisions are finalised.

The more inclusive public institutions that should result from a harmonised PSED have the potential to manage religious diversity within a framework that promotes equality, integration and community cohesion. The PSED can contribute to cohesion and help to minimise conflict by ensuring that the needs of minority religious groups are aligned with the needs of other religious and non-religious social groups in the community through a process of consultation, negotiation and compromise. The PSED provides a regulatory mechanism for setting out core liberal standards of equality as well as a mechanism for developing dialogue and consultation with all groups together; even among groups that have divergent beliefs and interests.

It has been argued that the PSED should not cover religion or belief in order to maintain secularism or because religion and belief are divisive categories.[27] This objection misunderstands the PSED that creates a duty to consult and design appropriate policies rather than a guarantee that the religious practice will necessarily be accommodated. Consultation with religious groups does not give them a veto; and nor is consultation in itself a breach of the principle of secularism. Consulting with religious or belief groups is not a breach of secularism because

27 Anthony Lester and Paola Uccellari. 'Extending the Equality Duty to Religion, Conscience and Belief: Proceed with Caution', *European Human Rights Law Review*, 567.

merely listening to the religious views does not mean that public authorities have to implement all of the demands of such groups. This is the crucial difference between the PSED's regulatory techniques and the grant of a blanket exemption.

It is also sometimes argued that there should be no PSED in relation to religion or belief because of a risk of harm to women.[28] In fact, in an optimal situation where the PSED is applied appropriately the exact opposite is true. A harmonised PSED that applies to religion and belief as well as gender can prevent harm to women in religious minorities. Tackling violence against minority women requires appropriately designed services that meet the needs of not only majorities but also women in religious communities – e.g. domestic violence support that targets Muslim or Hindu women. A harmonised PSED designed after full consultation with women from within minority communities will require public authorities to consider how gender intersects with religion or belief to ensure that vulnerable women are protected through appropriate service delivery. It also provides an opportunity for public authorities to promote the wider goals of equality and non-discrimination within religious minorities. This process of mainstreaming the needs of religious minorities including 'minorities within minorities' is a disincentive to them setting up unregulated community-based structures. The PSED's process of consultation, negotiation and compromise within local civil society ensures that majorities and minorities are involved in joint decision-making processes, bounded by liberal principles of equality and non-discrimination, if they want access to essential public services such as education and health. This provides one opportunity to develop contemporary 'shared practices' of tolerance, as Kaplan puts it in the context of religious communities in the early modern period, under conditions of increasing religious diversity in liberal societies.

Negotiation, consultation and compromise may also have an important role in the private sphere. Recent attention has focused on the use of private arbitration by women who are seeking a religious marriage or divorce that is sanctioned 'in the eyes of God'.[29] The debate about religious law and religious arbitration assumes a sharp dichotomy between criminalising these private forms of dispute resolution and allowing them permission. This polarisation prevents a more nuanced debate about what type of regulation is most appropriate to secure a convergence between the goals of religious freedom, gender equality and minority protection. A thoughtful balance between legal intervention to defend core values such as gender equality and an appropriately designed system of soft regulation could in some circumstances allow these goals to converge rather than conflict.[30]

Another striking example of non-legal regulation to manage religious diversity is provided by the successful use of mediation to challenge disability discrimination that resulted from Muslim taxi drivers and restaurant owners refusing access to the blind because they believed that Islam did not permit contact with guide dogs.

28 Ibid.

29 Maleiha Malik, 'Minorities and Law: Past and Present', *Current Legal Problems* 67, 1 (2014): 67–98.

30 Ibid.

Negotiations between the Disability Rights Commission and Muslim religious authorities led to the use of mediation rather than litigation. One outcome of this mediation was a restatement of Islamic norms that prohibited contact with dogs making it clear that Muslims could come into contact with guide dogs in order to provide services (such as taxis or restaurants) to the blind and partially sighted. This particular dialogue was so successful in permanently shifting Muslim norms towards guide dogs that some mosques have now allowed entry to guide dogs.[31] In this situation, the desired outcome of ensuring that the blind or partially sighted have equal access taxis and restaurants was achieved after voluntary mediation with a statutory agency between the Disability Rights Commission and Muslim religious leaders rather than through the enforcement of the criminal law in the magistrates' courts. The focus was not just on the unilateral imposition of a 'liberal solution' that promotes equality or a final outcome that taxi drivers allow access to guide dogs.[32] Instead, mediation focused on an inclusive dialogical process and voluntarism to ensure that there was willing compliance by the Muslim taxi drivers and restaurant owners. There was a permanent shift in wider Muslim attitudes towards guide dogs. In this situation, voluntary mediation led to a convergence between Muslim norms and equality legislation that did not require the use of state coercion against a minority. This type of regulatory technique accepts that it is possible to develop a rational enquiry from within an intellectual and religious tradition that may, therefore, be able to provide a solution for the management of religious diversity without importing liberal principles from external sources.[33]

There are important limits to dialogue, negotiation and compromise that can become blurred in the rush to embrace soft regulatory techniques. In the example of Muslims and guide dogs, however, this needs to be distinguished from the situation in *Ladele* where a marriage registrar was objecting to performing a same-sex civil partnership because of her private religious beliefs as a Christian. *Ladele* raised a different set of questions because she was a public official carrying out marriage registration that is a special public rather than a private act.[34]

While a pluralist liberal society would make some space for religious beliefs such as those of Ms Ladele to co-exist with the beliefs of others, there is an expectation that when Ms Ladele acts as a public official and undertakes an official act she will comply with the liberal principles that underpin the constitutional and human rights equality guarantees for gays and lesbians. Negotiation may be helpful in many situations but where, as in *Ladele*, the discriminator is a public official and the stakes are the constitutional and human rights of a protected group such as

31 *From Conflict to Cohesion: Competing Interests in Equality Law and Policy* (London: Equality and Diversity Forum, 2008).

32 Malik, 'Minorities and Law: Past and Present'.

33 Alasdair Macintyre, *Whose Justice? Which Rationality?* (Duckworth, London, 1988) at pages 1–10.

34 See Lord Neuberger's comments that Ms Ladele was a public employee performing a secular not a religious function, *Lillian Ladele* v *The London Borough of Islington* [2009] EWCA Civ 1357 at paragraph 52.

gays or lesbians then ideas of negotiation have to give way to harder forms of regulation that require the unilateral enforcement of an imposition of a liberal norm on those, such as marriage registrars, who exercise public power in a liberal democracy.

Conclusion

As Kaplan notes, myths about religious tolerance entrench the view that religion is a cause of conflict because of primitive irrationality that 'we' in the West should now reject. Kaplan also reminds us that in the past mixed religious communities developed social practices of tolerance to live together because of necessity rather than choice. Contemporary religious diversity is often not a choice and it will, sometimes, lead to friction between individuals and groups in liberal societies. Regulating religious diversity in liberal societies requires a wide range of responses that range from non-negotiable constitutional and human rights standards through to mediation, dialogue, consultation and negotiation. If managed within intelligently designed frameworks of law and social policy, tensions arising from religious diversity may even act as a catalyst towards dialogue and a stable form of integration. In some contexts, such as the necessity for two employees to co-operate in a workplace, the outcome may be a practical and self-interested modus vivendi. Techniques such as the ACAS guidance on managing religion and sexual orientation in the workplace can facilitate co-operation and compromise. Regulatory techniques such as the PSED introduce mechanisms for consultation and negotiation to achieve this goal in the public sector and also generate a deeper and more meaningful identification with national and local institutions, including the media and civil society, in a joint enterprise that creates social cohesion and sustains a coherent political community rather than a plethora of self-interested splinter groups.[35] In the private sphere, voluntarism and mediation can deliver remarkable results to ensure that religious diversity is managed in ways that comply with liberal norms without the use of state coercion. As the example of Muslim taxi drivers and guide dogs suggests, this approach allows a religious tradition and its adherents to develop internal solutions to a conflict between its norms and liberal standards.

Ben Kaplan's analysis of religious tolerance in the past suggests that points of difference or even conflict arising from religious diversity were sometimes opportunities for individuals and communities to establish 'rules of engagement and employ a variety of mechanisms, formal and informal, to regulate conflict and keep it within bounds'.[36] Approached in this way, the tensions, conflicts and compromises that are a consequence of contemporary religious diversity may also provide an opportunity to generate a more stable liberal equilibrium.

35 Maleiha Malik, 'Minorities and Human Rights', in T. Campbell, K. D. E. Ewing and A. Tomkins, A., eds *Sceptical Approaches to the Human Rights Act, 2000*, Oxford, Oxford University Press, 277–97.

36 Kaplan, *Divided by Faith: Religious Conflict and the Practice of Toleration in Early Modern Europe.* See discussions at pages 9 and 358.

References

Adams, Richard. 'Governors of New Academies and Free Schools Told to Abide By "British Values"', *Guardian*, 19 June 2014.

Annicchino, Pasquale. 'Freedom of Religion or Belief in the Foreign Policy of the European Union, Much Ado About Nothing', in *Religion and Civil Society: The Changing Faces of Religion and Secularity*, eds R. Alvira and M.A. Glendon, 2014, 13–15. http://papers.ssrn.com/sol3/papers.cfm?abstract_id=2207568 (accessed 24 March 2016).

——. 'Is the European Union Going Deep on Democracy and Religious Freedom', in *Working Paper for European University Institute – Robert Schuman Centre for Advanced Studies (RSCAS)*, 2014–15.

Baldwin, Robert, Cave, Martin and Lodge, Martin. 'Introduction: Regulation – The Field and Developing Agenda', in *The Oxford Handbook of Regulation*, eds Robert Baldwin, Martin Cave and Martin Lodge. Oxford: Oxford University Press, 2010, 12.

Brown, Wendy. *Regulating Aversion: Tolerance in the Age of Identity and Empire*. Princeton, NJ: Princeton University Press, 2006.

Butler, Judith. 'Is Judaism Zionism?', in *In the Power of Religion in the Public Sphere*, eds Eduardo Mendieta and Jonathan Vanantwepen. New York: Columbia University Press, 2011, 83.

Case of Eweida and Others V the United Kingdom App Nos 48420/10, 59842/10, 51671/10 and 36516/10 (decisions of 15 January 2013).

Equality Commission for Northern Ireland. *Keeping It Effective: Reviewing the Effectiveness of Section 75 of the Northern Ireland Act 1998 – Final Report November 2008*. Belfast: Equality Commission for Northern Ireland, November 2008.

GEO. *The Independent Steering Group's Report of the Public Sector Equality Duty (Psed) Review and Government Response*. London: Government Equalities Office, 6 September 2013.

Kaplan, Benjamin J. *Divided by Faith: Religious Conflict and the Practice of Toleration in Early Modern Europe*. Cambridge, MA: Harvard University Press, 2007.

Koppelman, Andrew. 'You Can't Hurry Love: Why Antidiscrimination Protections for Gay People Should Have Religious Exemptions', *Brooklyn Law Review* 72 (2006): 125–46.

Kundnani, Arun. *The End of Tolerance: Racism in 21st Century Britain*. London: Pluto Press, 2007.

Lester, Anthony and Paola Uccellari. 'Extending the Equality Duty to Religion, Conscience and Belief: Proceed with Caution', *European Human Rights Law Review*, 567.

Macintyre, Alasdair. *Whose Justice? Which Rationality?* London: Duckworth, 1988.

McCrea, Ronan. *Religion and the Public Order of the European Union*. Oxford University Press, 2010.

Mahmood, Saba. 'Religious Freedom, Minority Rights and Geopolitics', *Comparative Studies in Society and History* 54, 2 (2012): 418–46.

Malik, Maleiha. 'Minorities and Human Rights', in *Sceptical Approaches to the Human Rights Act, 2000*, eds T. Campbell, K.D.E. Ewing and A. Tomkins. Oxford: Oxford University Press, 2000, 277–97.

———. *From Conflict to Cohesion: Competing Interests in Equality Law and Policy*. London: Equality and Diversity Forum, 2008.

———. 'Minorities and Law: Past and Present', *Current Legal Problems* 67, 1 (2014): 67–98.

Moore, K., Mason, P. and Lewis, J.M.W. 'Images of Islam in the UK: The Representation of British Muslims in the National Print News Media 2000–2008', in *Working Paper*. Cardiff: Cardiff University, 2008, 5–10.

Morgan, Bronwen and Karen Yeung. *An Introduction to Law and Regulation: Text and Materials*. Cambridge University Press, 2007.

Office of the Head of International Family Justice for England and 2012 Annual Report, 1 January–31 December 2012. London: Judiciary of England and Wales, 2012. www.judiciary.gov.uk/wp-content/uploads/JCO/Documents/Reports/international_family_justice_2013.pdf (accessed 23 March 2016).

Phillips, Anne. *Multiculturalism without Culture*. Princeton, NJ: Princeton University Press, 2007.

Plant, Raymond. 'Religion in a Liberal State', in *Religion in a Liberal State*, eds Malcolm Evans Gavin D'Costa, Tariq Modood and Julian Rivers. Cambridge: Cambridge University Press, 2013, 9–15.

'Prevent Strategy UK Cmnd, 8092', in *Presented to Parliament by the Secretary of State for the Home Department by Command of Her Majesty*, June 2011.

Savage, B. *Sexual Orientation and Religion or Belief Discrimination in the Workplace*. London: ACAS, 2007.

Wintemute, Robert. 'Accommodating Religious Beliefs: Harm, Clothing or Symbols and Refusals to Serve Others', *Modern Law Review* 77: 2.

Index

For Product Safety Concerns and Information please contact our EU representative GPSR@taylorandfrancis.com Taylor & Francis Verlag GmbH, Kaufingerstraße 24, 80331 München, Germany

Batch number: 10725973

Printed by Printforce, the Netherlands